AMERICAN MILITARY HISTORY

★ ★ ★ ★ ★ ★ ★ ★ ★ ★ ★ ★

VOLUME 2: 1902-1996

AMERICAN
MILITARY
HISTORY

★ ★ ★ ★ ★ ★ ★ ★ ★ ★ ★ ★

VOLUME 2: 1902-1996

Edited by
Maurice Matloff

COMBINED BOOKS
Pennsylvania

PUBLISHER'S NOTE

Combined Books, Inc., is dedicated to publishing books of distinction in history and military history. We are proud of the quality of writing and the quantity of information found in our books. Our books are manufactured with style and durability and are printed on acid-free paper. We like to think of our books as soldiers: not infantry grunts, but well dressed and well equipped avant garde. Our logo reflects our commitment to the modern and yet historic art of bookmaking.

We call ourselves Combined Books because we view the publishing enterprise as a "combined" effort of authors, publishers and readers. And we promise to bridge the gap between us—a gap which is all too seldom closed in contemporary publishing.

We would like to hear from our readers and invite you to write to us at our offices in Pennsylvania with your reactions, queries, comments, even complaints. All of your correspondence will be answered directly by a member of the Editorial Board or by the author.

We encourage all of our readers to purchase our books from their local booksellers, and we hope that you let us know of booksellers in your area that might be interested in carrying our books. If you are unable to find a book in your area, please write us.

For information, address:
COMBINED BOOKS., INC.
151 East 10th Avenue
Conshohocken, PA 19428

This edition of *American Military History* includes Chapters 1-28 from the 1989 edition, several of which have been partially revised, plus a new chapter dealing with the period after 1975, two new appendices, and some additions to the Suggested Readings.

Library of Congress Cataloguing-in-Publication Data
American military history / edited by Maurice Matloff.
     p.   cm.
    Includes bibliographical references and index.
    Contents: v. 1. 1775-1902 -- v. 2. 1902-1996.
    ISBN 0-938289-72-1 (v. 1 : hc : alk. paper). -- ISBN 0-938289-70-5
(v. 2 : pb). -- ISBN 0-938289-73-X (v. 2 : hc : alk. paper). -- ISBN
0-938289-71-3 (v. 2. : pb)
    1. United States--History, Military.   I. Matloff, Maurice, 1915- .

E181.A44   1973
355'.00973--dc20
                                                  96-7108
                                                    CIP

Printed in the United States of America.

Contributors

BELL, WILLIAM GARDNER (Chapter 14), a graduate of the Cavalry School and a former editor of the *Cavalry Journal* and *Armor Magazine,* has written frequently on the frontier Army and the American West.

COAKLEY, ROBERT W. (Chapters 2, 3, 4, and 23), Ph.D. (Virginia), is coauthor of the two *Global Logistics and Strategy* volumes in the U.S. Army in World War II series and author of *The Role of Federal Military Forces in Domestic Disorders* in the Historical Studies series.

CONN, STETSON (Chapter 19), Ph.D. (Yale), was coauthor of *The Framework of Hemisphere Defense* and *Guarding the United States and Its Outposts,* both in the U.S. Army in World War II series.

COOLING, BENJAMIN F., III (Chapters 10 and 11), Ph.D. (Pennsylvania), is author of, among others, *Forts Henry and Donelson: The Key to the Confederate Heartland* and editor of *New American State Papers—Military Affairs.*

DEMMA, VINCENT H. (Chapter 28), M.A. (Wisconsin), is a CMH historian specializing in the study of the role of the Army in the Vietnam conflict.

HERMES, WALTER G. (Chapters 26 and 27), Ph.D. (Georgetown), is author of *Truce Tent and Fighting Front* in the U.S. Army in the Korean War series.

JONES, VINCENT C. (Chapters 15 and 16), Ph.D. (Wisconsin), is author of *Manhattan: The Army and the Atomic Bomb* in the U.S. Army in World War II series.

MACDONALD, CHARLES B. (Chapters 17, 18, and 22), B.A., Litt.D. (Presbyterian), is author of, among others, *Company Commander,* and of *Three Battles, The Siegfried Line Campaign,* and *The Last Offensive,* volumes in the U.S. Army in World War II series.

MACGREGOR, MORRIS J., JR. (Chapters 5 and 6), M.A. (Catholic), is author of *The Integration of the Armed Forces, 1940–1965* in the Defense Studies series and coauthor of *Soldier-Statesmen of the Constitution* and *Blacks in the United States Armed Forces.*

MATLOFF, MAURICE (Chapters 1, 20, and 21), Ph.D. (Harvard), is coauthor of *Strategic Planning for Coalition Warfare, 1941–1942* and author of *Strategic Planning for Coalition Warfare, 1943–1944* in the U.S. Army in World War II series.

MAYO, LIDA (Chapters 7 and 8), B.A. (Randolph-Macon), was author of *The Ordnance Department: On Beachhead and Battlefront* and coauthor of *The Ordnance Department: Procurement and Supply* and *The Corps of Engineers: The War Against Germany,* all in the U.S. Army in World War II series.

MOSSMAN, B.C. (Chapters 24 and 25), B.A. (Nebraska State), is author of *Ebb and Flow,* a volume in the U.S. Army in the Korean War series, and coauthor of *The Last Salute: Civil and Military Funerals, 1921–1969.*

ROMANUS, CHARLES F. (Chapters 9 and 12), M.A. (Illinois), was coauthor of the three volumes on the China-Burma-India Theater and of *The Quartermaster Corps: Operations in the War Against Germany,* all in the U.S. Army in World War II series.

SCHEIPS, PAUL J. (Chapter 13), Ph.D. (American), is coauthor of *Bayonets in the Streets* and author of *Hold the Fort* and numerous other works, principally on the frontier Army and the use of troops in domestic disturbances.

NOFI, ALBERT A. (Chapter 29), Ph.D. (CUNY), is author *The '98 Campaign, The Spanish American War,* and coauthor of *Dirty Little Secrets of World War II* and *Deceit.*

Contents

Maps

AMERICAN
MILITARY
HISTORY
★ ★ ★ ★ ★ ★ ★ ★ ★ ★ ★ ★
VOLUME 2: 1902-1996

CHAPTER 16

Transition and Change, 1902–1917

For the United States the opening years of the twentieth century were a time of transition and change. At home they marked the beginning of a peaceful revolution—often designated the "Progressive Era"—when political leaders such as Theodore Roosevelt undertook to solve the economic and social problems arising out of the rapid growth of large-scale industry in the late nineteenth century. Increasing public awareness of these problems as a result of the writings of the "Muckrakers" and social reformers provided popular support for efforts to solve them by legislative and administrative measures. In foreign affairs it was a period when the country had to begin adjusting its institutions and policies to the requirements of its new status as a world power. In spite of a tendency after the end of the War with Spain to follow traditional patterns and go back to essentially isolationist policies, the nation's new responsibility for overseas possessions, its expanding commercial interests abroad, and the continued unrest in the Caribbean made a reversion to insularity increasingly unfeasible.

The changing conditions at home and abroad inevitably affected the nation's military establishment. During the decade and a half between the War with Spain and American involvement in World War I, both the Army and the Navy would undergo important reforms in organization and direction. Although the United States did not become a participant in any major conflict during these years, both services were frequently called upon to assist with administration of the newly acquired overseas possessions. Both aided with protection of investments abroad threatened by native insurrections, revolutions, and other internal disturbances. And both contributed in other ways to upholding the vital interests of the nation in an era of greatly increased competition for commercial advantage and colonial empire.

Modernizing the Armed Forces

The intensification of international rivalries led most of the Great Powers to seek additional protection and advantage in diplomatic alliances and alignments. By the early years of the twentieth century the increasingly complex network of agreements had resulted in a new and precarious balance of power in world affairs. This balance was constantly in danger of being upset, particularly because of an unprecedented arms race, characterized by rapid enlargement of armies and navies and development of far more deadly weapons and tactics. While the United States remained aloof from "entangling alliances," it nevertheless continued to modernize and strengthen its own armed forces, giving primary attention to the Navy—the first line of defense.

The Navy's highly successful performance in the Spanish-American War increased the willingness of Congress and the American public to support its program of expansion and modernization. For at least a decade after the war Theodore Roosevelt, Senator Henry Cabot Lodge of Massachusetts, and other leaders who favored a "Big Navy" policy with the goal of an American fleet second only to that of Great Britain experienced little difficulty in securing the necessary legislation and obtaining the funds required for the Navy's expansion program.

For the Navy another most important result of the War with Spain was the decision to retain possessions in the Caribbean and the western Pacific. In the Caribbean the Navy acquired more bases for its operations such as that at Guantánamo Bay in Cuba. The value of these bases soon became apparent as the United States found itself intervening more frequently in the countries of that region to protect its expanding investments and trade. In the long run, however, acquisition of the Philippines and Guam was even more significant, for it committed the United States to defense of territory thousands of miles distant from the home base. American naval strength in the Pacific had to be increased immediately to insure maintenance of a secure line of communications for the land forces that had to be kept in the Philippines. One way to accomplish this increase, with an eye to economy of force, was to build a canal across the Isthmus of Panama, so that Navy ships could move more rapidly from the Atlantic to the Pacific as circumstances demanded. Another was to acquire more bases in the Pacific west of Hawaii, which was annexed in 1898. Japan's spectacular naval victories in the war with Russia and Roosevelt's dispatch of an American fleet on a round-the-world cruise lasting from December 1907 to February 1909 drew public attention to the problem. But most Americans failed to perceive the growing threat of Japan to United States possessions in the western Pacific, and the line of communications to the Philippines remained incomplete and highly vulnerable.

The Navy fared much better in its program to expand the fleet and incorporate the latest technological developments in ship design and weapons. The modernization program that had begun in the 1880's and had much to do with the Navy's effectiveness in the Spanish-American War continued in the early 1900's. Construction of new ships, stimulated by the war and Roosevelt's active support, continued at a rapid rate after 1898 until Taft's administration, and at a somewhat slower pace thereafter. By 1917 the United States had a Navy unmatched by any of the Great Powers except Great Britain and Germany.

The Army, aware of the serious deficiencies revealed in the War with Spain and of the rapid technological changes taking place in the methods of warfare, also undertook to modernize its weapons and equipment. Development of high-velocity, low-trajectory, clip-loading rifles capable of delivering a high rate of sustained fire had already made obsolete the Krag-Jörgensen rifle, adopted by the Army in 1892. In 1903 the Regular Army began equipping its units with the improved bolt-action, magazine-type Springfield rifle, which incorporated the latest changes in weapons technology. The campaigns of 1898 also had shown that the standard rod bayonet was too flimsy; starting in 1905, the Army replaced it by a one pound knife bayonet with a 16-inch blade. In 1906 addition of a greater propellant charge in ammunition for the Springfield provided even higher muzzle velocity and deeper penetration of the bullet. Combat at close quarters against the fierce charges of the Moros in the Philippines demonstrated the need for a hand arm less cumbersome and having greater impact than the .38-caliber revolver. The Army found the answer in the recently developed .45-caliber Colt automatic pistol, adopted in 1911.

Far more significant in revolutionizing the nature of twentieth century warfare than these improved hand weapons was the rapid-firing machine gun. The manually operated machine gun—the Gatling gun—which the Army had adopted in 1866, was employed successfully in the Indian wars and the Spanish-American War. American inventors, including Hiram Maxim, John Browning, and Isaac N. Lewis, the last an officer in the Army's coast artillery, took a leading part in developing automatic machine guns in the years between the Civil War and World War I. Weapons based upon their designs were adopted by many of the armies of the world. But not until fighting began in World War I was it generally realized what an important role the machine gun was to have in modern tactics. Thus in the years between 1898 and 1916, Congress appropriated only an average of $150,000 annually for procurement of machine guns, barely enough to provide four weapons for each Regular regiment and a few for the National Guard. Finally in 1916 Congress voted $12 million for machine gun procurement, but the War Department held up its expenditure until 1917 while a board tried to decide which type of weapon was best suited to the needs of the Army.

Development of American artillery and artillery ammunition continued
to lag behind that of western European armies. The Army did adopt in 1902 a
new basic field weapon, the 3-inch gun with an advanced recoil mechanism.
Also, to replace the black powder that had been the subject of such widespread
criticism in the War with Spain, both the Army and the Navy took steps to
increase the domestic output of smokeless powder. By 1903 production was
sufficient to supply most American artillery.

Experience gained in the Spanish-American War also brought some significant changes in the Army's coastal defense program. The hurriedly improvised measures taken during the war to protect Atlantic ports from possible
attack by the Spanish Fleet emphasized the need for modern seacoast defenses.
Under the strategical concepts in vogue, construction and manning of these
defenses were primarily an Army responsibility since in wartime the naval
fleet had to be kept intact, ready to seek out and destroy the enemy's fleet. On
the basis of recommendations by the Endicott Board, the Army already had
begun an ambitious coastal defense construction program in the early 1890's,
and in 1905 a new board headed by Secretary of War William Howard Taft
made important revisions in this program with the goal of incorporating the
latest techniques and devices. Added to the coastal defense arsenal were fixed,
floating, and mobile torpedoes and submarine mines. At the same time, the
Army's Ordnance Department tested 16-inch rifles for installation in the coastal
defense fortifications, in keeping with the trend toward larger and larger guns
to meet the challenge of naval weapons of ever-increasing size.

Of the many new inventions that came into widespread use in the early
twentieth century in response to the productive capacity of the new industrial
age, none was to have greater influence on military strategy, tactics, and organization than the internal combustion engine. It made possible the motor vehicle,
which, like the railroad in the previous century, brought a revolution in military
transportation, and the airplane and tank, both of which would figure importantly in World War I.

Reorganization of the Army: Establishment of the General Staff

After the Spanish-American War the Army also underwent important
organizational and administrative changes aimed in part at overcoming some
of the more glaring defects revealed during the war. Although the nation had
won the war with comparative ease, many Americans realized that the victory
was attributable more to the incompetence of the enemy than to any special
qualities displayed by the Army. In fact, as a postwar investigating commission

appointed by President McKinley and headed by Maj. Gen. Granville M. Dodge brought out, there was serious need for reform in the administration and direction of the Army's high command and for elimination of widespread inefficiency in the operations of the War Department.

No one appreciated the need for reform more than Elihu Root, a New York lawyer appointed Secretary of War in 1899 by McKinley. The President had selected Root primarily because he seemed well qualified to solve the legal problems that would arise in the Army's administration of recently acquired overseas possessions. But Root quickly realized that if the Army was to be capable of carrying out its new responsibilities as an important part of the defense establishment of a world power, it had to undergo fundamental changes in organization, administration, and training. Root, as a former corporation lawyer, tended to see the Army's problems as similar to those faced by business executives. "The men who have combined various corporations . . . in what we call trusts," he told Congress, "have reduced the cost of production and have increased their efficiency by doing the very same thing we propose you shall do now, and it does seem a pity that the Government of the United States should be the only great industrial establishment that cannot profit by the lessons which the world of industry and of commerce has learned to such good effect."

Beginning in 1899, Root outlined in a series of masterful reports his proposals for fundamental reform of Army institutions and concepts to achieve that "efficiency" of organization and function required of armies in the modern world. He based his proposals partly upon recommendations made by his military advisers (among the most trusted were Maj. Gen. Henry C. Corbin, The Adjutant General, and Lt. Col. William H. Carter) and partly upon the views expressed by officers who had studied and written about the problem in the post-Civil War years. Root arranged for publication of Col. Emory Upton's *The Military Policy of the United States* (1904), an unfinished manuscript which advocated a strong, expansible Regular Army as the keystone of an effective military establishment. Concluding that after all the true object of any army must be "to provide for war," Root took prompt steps to reshape the American Army into an instrument of national power capable of coping with the requirements of modern warfare. This objective could be attained, he hoped, by integrating the bureaus of the War Department, the scattered elements of the Regular Army, and the militia and volunteers.

Root perceived as the chief weakness in the organization of the Army the long-standing division of authority, dating back to the early nineteenth century, between the Commanding General of the Army and the Secretary of War. The

Commanding General exercised discipline and control over the troops in the field while the Secretary, through the military bureau chiefs, had responsibility for administration and fiscal matters. Root proposed to eliminate this division of authority between the Secretary of War and the Commanding General and to reduce the independence of the bureau chiefs. The solution, he suggested, was to replace the Commanding General of the Army with a Chief of Staff, who would be the responsible adviser and executive agent of the President through the Secretary of War. Under Root's proposal, formulation of broad American policies would continue under civilian control.

A lack of any long-range planning by the Army had been another obvious deficiency in the War with Spain, and Root proposed to overcome this by the creation of a new General Staff, a group of selected officers who would be free to devote full time to preparation of military plans. Planning in past national emergencies, he pointed out, nearly always had been inadequate because it had to be done hastily by officers already overburdened with other duties. Pending Congressional action on his proposals, Root in 1901 appointed an *ad hoc* War College Board to act as an embryonic General Staff. In early 1903, in spite of some die-hard opposition, Congress adopted the Secretary of War's recommendations for both a General Staff and a Chief of Staff, but rejected his request that certain of the bureaus be consolidated.

By this legislation Congress provided the essential framework for more efficient administration of the Army. Yet legislation could not change overnight the long-held traditions, habits, and views of most Army officers, or of some Congressmen and the American public. Secretary Root realized that effective operation of the new system would require an extended program of re-education. This need for re-education was one important reason for the establishment of the Army War College in November 1903. Its students, already experienced officers, would receive education in problems of the War Department and of high command in the field. As it turned out they actually devoted much of their time to war planning, becoming in effect the part of the General Staff which performed this function.

In the first years after its establishment the General Staff achieved relatively little in the way of genuine staff planning and policy making. While staff personnel did carry out such appropriate tasks as issuing in 1905 the first Field Service Regulations for government and organization of troops in the field, drawing up the plan for an expeditionary force sent to Cuba in 1906, and supervising the Army's expanding school system, far too much of their time was devoted to day-to-day routine administrative matters.

The General Staff did make some progress in overcoming its early weaknesses. Through experience, officers assigned to the staff gradually gained awareness of its real purpose and powers. In 1910 when Maj. Gen. Leonard Wood became Chief of Staff he reorganized the General Staff, eliminating many of its time-consuming procedures and directing more of its energies to planning. With the backing of Secretary of War Henry L. Stimson (1911–13), Wood dealt a decisive blow to that element in the Army itself that opposed the General Staff. In a notable controversy, he and Stimson forced the retirement in 1912 of the leader of this opposition, Maj. Gen. Fred C. Ainsworth, The Adjutant General.

The temporary closing of most Army schools during the Spanish-American War and the need to co-ordinate the Army's educational system with the Root proposals for creating a War College and General Staff had provided an opportunity for a general reorganization of the whole system, with the over-all objective of raising the standards of professional training of officers. In 1901 the War Department directed that the schools of instruction for officers thereafter should be the Military Academy at West Point; a school at each post of elementary instruction in theory and practice; the five service schools—the Artillery School, Engineer School of Application, School of Submarine Defense (mines and torpedoes), School of Application for Cavalry and Field Artillery, and Army Medical School; a General Staff and Service College at Leavenworth; and a War College. The purpose of the school at Leavenworth henceforth was to train officers in the employment of combined arms and prepare them for staff and command positions in large units. To meet the requirements for specialized training as a result of new developments in weapons and equipment, the Army expanded its service school system, adding the Signal School in 1905, the Field Artillery School in 1911, and the School of Musketry in 1913.

Creation of the General Staff unquestionably was the most important organizational reform in the Army during this period, but there were also a number of other changes in the branches and special staff designed to keep the Army abreast of new ideas and requirements. The Medical Department, for example, established Medical, Hospital, Army Nurse, Dental, and Medical Reserve Corps. In 1907 Congress approved of division of the artillery into the Coast Artillery Corps and the Field Artillery, and in 1912 it enacted legislation consolidating the Subsistence and Pay Departments with the Quartermaster to create the Quartermaster Corps, a reform earlier recommended by Secretary Root. The act of 1912 also established an enlisted Quartermaster service corps, marking the beginning of the practice of using service troops instead of civilians and combat soldier details.

In the new field of military aviation, the Army failed to keep pace with early twentieth century developments. Contributing to this delay were the reluctance of Congress to appropriate funds and resistance within the military bureaucracy to diversion of already limited resources to a method of warfare as yet unproved. The Army did not entirely neglect the new field—it had used balloons for observation in both the Civil and Spanish-American Wars and, beginning in 1898, the War Department subsidized for several years Samuel P. Langley's experiments with power-propelled, heavier-than-air flying machines. In 1908, after some hesitation, the War Department made funds available to the Aeronautical Division of the Signal Corps (established a year earlier) for the purchase and testing of Wilbur and Orville Wright's airplane. Although the Army accepted this airplane in 1909, another two years passed before Congress appropriated a relatively modest sum—$125,000—for aeronautical purposes. Between 1908 and 1913, it is estimated that the United States spent only $430,000 on military and naval aviation, whereas in the same period France and Germany each expended $22 million, Russia, $12 million, and Belgium, $2 million. Not until 1914 did Congress authorize establishment of a full-fledged Aviation Section in the Signal Corps. The few military airplanes available for service on the Mexican border in 1916 soon broke down, and the United States entered World War I far behind the other belligerents in aviation equipment, organization, and doctrine.

Reorganization of the Army: The Regular Army and the Militia

In the years after the Spanish-American War nearly a third of the Regular Army troops, on the average, served overseas. Most were in the Philippines suppressing the insurrection and when that conflict officially ended in mid-1902, stamping out scattered resistance and organizing and training a native force known as the Philippine Scouts. Other Regulars were garrisoned in Alaska, Hawaii, China, and elsewhere. To carry out its responsibilities abroad and to maintain an adequate defense at home, the Regular Army from 1902 to 1911 had an average of about 75,000 officers and men, far below the 100,000 that Congress had authorized in 1902 to fill thirty infantry and fifteen cavalry regiments, supported by a corps of artillery. To make up for this deficiency in size of the Regular forces and at the same time to remedy some of the defects revealed in the mobilization for the War with Spain, the planners in the War Department recommended a reorganization of the volunteer forces.

Secretary Root took the lead in presenting to Congress in 1901 a program for reform of the National Guard. In response to his recommendations, Congress in 1903 passed the Dick bill, which thoroughly revised the obsolete Militia Act of 1792. It separated the militia into two classes—the Organized Militia, to be known as the National Guard, and the Reserve Militia—and provided that, over a five-year period, the Guard's organization and equipment be patterned after that of the Regular Army. To help accomplish these changes in the Guard, the Dick bill made available federal funds; prescribed drill at least twice a month, supplemented with short annual training periods; permitted detailing of Regular officers to Guard units; and directed holding of joint maneuvers each year. Failure of the new measure, however, to modify significantly the long-standing provisions that severely restricted federal power to call up Guard units and control Guard personnel limited its effectiveness. Subsequent legislation in 1908 and 1914 reduced these restrictions to some extent, giving the President the right to prescribe the length of federal service and, with the advice and consent of the Senate, to appoint all officers of the Guard while the Guard was in federal service.

Although the largest permanent unit of the Regular Army in peacetime continued to be the regiment, experience in the Spanish-American War, observation of new developments abroad, and lessons learned in annual maneuvers all testified to the need for larger, more self-sufficient units, composed of the combined arms. Beginning in 1905, the *Field Service Regulations* laid down a blueprint for the organization of divisions in wartime, and in 1910 the General Staff drew up a plan for three permanent infantry divisions to be composed of designated Regular Army and National Guard regiments. Because of trouble along the Mexican border in the spring of 1911, the plan was not carried out. Instead, the Army organized a provisional maneuver division, ordering its component units, consisting of three brigades comprised of nearly 13,000 officers and men, to concentrate at San Antonio, Texas. The division's presence there, it was hoped, would end the border disturbances.

The effort proved only how unready the Army was to mobilize quickly for any kind of national emergency. Assembly of the division required several months. The War Department had to collect Regular Army troops from widely scattered points in the continental United States and denude every post, depot, and arsenal to scrape up the necessary equipment. Even so, when the maneuver division finally completed its concentration in August 1911, it was far from fully operational, since none of its regiments were up to strength or adequately armed and equipped. Fortunately, the efficiency of the division was not put to any battle test, and within a short time it was broken up and its component units were returned to their home stations. Because those members of Congress who had Army installations in their own districts insisted on retaining them, the War Department was prevented from relocating units so that there would be a greater concentration of troops in a few places. The only immediate result of the Army's attempt to gain experience in the handling of large units was an effort to organize on paper the scattered posts of the Army so that their garrisons, which averaged 700 troops each, could join one of three divisions. But these abortive attempts to mobilize larger units were not entirely without value. In 1913 when the Army again had to strengthen the forces along the Mexican border, a division assembled in Texas in less than a week, ready for movement to any point where it might be needed.

Caribbean Problems and Projects

The close of the War with Spain brought no satisfactory solution for the Cuban problem. As a result of years of misrule and fighting, conditions on the island when the war ended were deplorable. Under provisions of the Teller amendment, the United States was pledged to turn over the rule of Cuba to its people. American forces, however, stayed on to assist the Cubans in achieving at least a modicum of economic and political stability. The first step was to set up a provisional government, headed in the beginning by Maj. Gen. John R. Brooke and later by General Wood. This government promptly undertook a program of rehabilitation and reform. An outstanding achievement was eliminating yellow fever, which had decimated Army troops during the war. Researches and experiments carried out by the Army Medical Department culminated in the discovery that the dread disease is transmitted by a specific type of mosquito.

When order had been restored in Cuba, a constituent assembly met. Under the chairmanship of General Wood, it drew up an organic law for the island patterned after the American Constitution. At the insistence of the United States, this law included several clauses known as the Platt amendment, which also appeared in the subsequent treaty concluded in 1903 by the two countries. The amendment limited the amount of debt Cuba could contract, granted the United States naval bases at Guantánamo and Bahia Honda, and gave the United States the right to intervene to preserve "Cuban independence" and maintain a government "adequate to the protection of life, property and individual liberty." In 1902, after a general election and the inauguration of the republic's first president, the Americans ended their occupation. But events soon demonstrated that the period of tutelage in self-government had been too short. In late 1906, when the Cuban Government proved unable to cope with a new rebellion, the United States intervened to maintain law and order. On the advice of Secretary of War Taft, President Roosevelt dispatched more than 5,000 troops to Havana, the so-called Army of Cuban Pacification, which remained in Cuba until early 1909. Again in 1912 and 1917, the United States found it necessary to intervene, but each time withdrew its occupying forces as soon as order was restored. Not until 1934 did the United States, consistent with its new Good Neighbor Policy, give up the right of intervention embodied in the Platt amendment.

Emergence of the United States as a world power with a primary concern for developments in the Caribbean Sea increased the long-time American interest in an isthmian canal. Discovery of gold in California in 1848 and the rapid growth of the west coast states had underlined the importance of developing a shorter sea route from Atlantic ports to the Pacific. The strategic need for a canal was dramatized for the American people during the Spanish-American War by the sixty-six-day voyage of the battleship *Oregon* from Puget Sound around Cape Horn to Santiago, where it joined the American Fleet barely in time to participate in the destruction of Cervera's ships.

A few months after the end of the War with Spain, McKinley told Congress that a canal under American control was "now more than ever indispensable." By the Hay-Pauncefote Treaty of 1901, the United States secured abrogation of the terms of the Clayton-Bulwer Treaty of 1850 that required the United States to share equally with Great Britain in construction and operation of any future isthmian canal. Finally, in 1903, the long-standing question of where the canal should be built—Nicaragua or Panama—was resolved in favor of Panama. An uprising in Panama against the government of Colombia provided President Roosevelt with an opportunity to send American naval units to support the rebels, assuring establishment of an independent republic. The new republic readily agreed to permit the United States to acquire control of a ten-mile strip across the isthmus, to purchase the property formerly belonging to the French syndicate that had attempted to construct a canal in the 1880's, and to build, maintain, and operate an interoceanic canal. Congress promptly appropriated the necessary funds for work to begin and the Isthmian Canal Commission set about investigating the problem of who should construct the canal.

When the commission advised the President that overseeing the construction of so vast a project was beyond the capabilities of any private concern, Roosevelt decided to turn the job over to the Army. He reorganized the commission, assigning to it new members—the majority were Army officers— and in 1907 appointed Col. George W. Goethals as its chairman and chief engineer. In this capacity, Goethals, a graduate of the Military Academy who had served in the Corps of Engineers since 1882, had virtually sole responsibility for administration of the canal project. Displaying great **organizational** ability, he overcame **many** serious difficulties, including **problems** of engineering, employee grievances, housing, and sanitation, to complete the canal by 1914. Goethals owed a part of his success to the support he received from the Army's Medical Department. Under the leadership of Col. William C. Gorgas, who earlier had played an important role in administering the sanitation program in Cuba, the Army carried through measures to control malaria and virtually wipe out yellow fever, ultimately converting the Canal Zone into a healthy and attractive place to live and work.

The completed Panama Canal stood as a magnificent engineering achievement and an outstanding example of the Army's fulfillment of a peacetime mission; but its opening and operation under American administration were also highly significant from the point of view of military strategy. For the Navy, the Canal achieved economy of force by eliminating the necessity for maintaining large fleets in both the Atlantic and Pacific. For the Army, it created a new strategic point in the continental defense system that had to be strongly protected by the most modern fortifications manned by a large and well-trained garrison.

The Army on the Mexican Border

Early in the twentieth century, the Army found itself frequently involved in hemispheric problems, not only with the countries of the Caribbean region, but also with the United States' southern neighbor, Mexico. That nation, after a long era of relative political stability, entered a period of revolutionary turmoil. Beginning in 1911, internal conflicts in the northern part of the country led to recurrent incidents along the Mexican border, posing a serious threat to peace. President William Howard Taft first ordered strengthening of the border patrols and then, in the summer of 1911, concentration of the maneuver division at San Antonio. After a period of quiet, General Victoriano Huerta in 1913 deposed and replaced President Francisco Madero. The assassination of Madero shortly thereafter led to full-scale civil war between Huerta's forces and those of General Venustiano Carranza, leader of the so-called Constitutionalists, and Emiliano Zapata, chief of the radicals. Woodrow Wilson, who had succeeded Taft as President, disapproved of the manner in which Huerta had come to power. In a significant shift from traditional American policy, the President decided not to recognize Huerta on the grounds that his assumption of power did not meet the test of "constitutional legitimacy." At the same time, Wilson imposed an arms embargo on both sides in the civil war. But in early 1914, when Huerta's forces halted the Constitutionalists, Wilson endeavored to help Carranza by lifting the embargo.

Resentment over Wilson's action contributed to the arrest in February of American sailors by followers of Huerta in the port of Tampico. Although they were soon released with an expression of regret from Huerta, Rear Adm. Henry T. Mayo, commanding the American Fleet in the area, demanded a public apology. Huerta refused. Feeling that intervention was unavoidable and seeing an opportunity to deprive Huerta of important ports, President Wilson supported Admiral Mayo and proposed to occupy Tampico, seize Veracruz, and blockade both ports. When a German steamer carrying a cargo of ammunition arrived unexpectedly at Veracruz in late April, the United States put ashore a contingent of marines and sailors to occupy the port and prevent unloading of the ship. Naval gunfire checked a Mexican counterattack and by the end of the month an American force of nearly 8,000—about half marines and half Army troops—under command of Maj. Gen. Frederick Funston occupied the city. For a time war with Mexico seemed inevitable, but both Wilson and Huerta accepted mediation and the Mexican leader agreed to resign. Carranza had barely had time to assume office when his erstwhile ally, Francisco "Pancho" Villa, rebelled and proceeded to gain control over most of northern Mexico.

Despite the precariousness of Carranza's hold on Mexico, President Wilson decided to recognize his government. It was now the turn of Villa to show resentment. He instigated a series of border incidents which culminated in a surprise attack by 500 to 1,000 of his men against Columbus, New Mexico, on March 9, 1916. Villa's troops killed a substantial number of American soldiers and civilians and destroyed considerable property before units of the 13th Cavalry drove them off. The following day, President Wilson ordered Brig. Gen. John J. Pershing into Mexico to assist the Mexican Government in capturing Villa.

On March 15 the advance elements of this punitive expedition entered Mexico in "hot pursuit." For the next several months, Pershing's troops chased Villa through unfriendly territory for hundreds of miles, never quite catching up with him but managing to disperse most of his followers. Although Carranza's troops also failed to capture Villa, Carranza soon showed that he had no desire to have the United States do the job for him. He protested the continued presence of American troops in Mexico and insisted upon their withdrawal. Carranza's unfriendly attitude, plus orders from the War Department forbidding attacks on Mexicans who were not followers of Villa, made it difficult for Pershing to deal effectively with other hostile Mexicans who blocked his path

GENERAL PERSHING AND HIS TROOPS *during the pursuit of Villa.*

without running the risk of precipitating war. Some clashes with Mexican Government troops actually occurred. The most important took place in June at Carrizal where scores were killed or wounded. This action once again created a critical situation and led President Wilson to call 75,000 National Guardsmen into federal service to help police the border.

Aware that the majority of Americans favored a peaceful solution, Wilson persuaded Carranza to resume diplomatic negotiations. The two leaders agreed in late July to submit the disputes arising out of the punitive expedition to a joint commission for settlement. Some time later the commission ruled that the American unit commander in the Carrizal affair was at fault. Although the commission broke up in January 1917 without reaching agreement on a plan for evacuating Pershing's troops, relations between the United States and Germany had reached so critical a stage that Wilson had no alternative but to order withdrawal of the punitive expedition.

Pershing failed to capture Villa, but the activities of the American troops in Mexico and along the border were not entirely wasted effort. Dispersal of Villa's band put an end to serious border incidents. More important, from a military point of view, was the intensive training in the field received by both Regular Army and National Guard troops who served on the border and in Mexico. Too, the partial mobilization drew further attention to the still unsolved problem of developing a satisfactory system for maintaining in peacetime the nucleus of those trained forces that would be required to supplement the Regular Army in national emergencies. Fortunately, many defects in the military establishment, especially in the National Guard, came to light in time to be corrected before the Army plunged into the war already under way in Europe.

CHAPTER 17

World War I: The First Three Years

As the armed camp that Europe had become by the summer of 1914 approached the point of explosion, the United States was markedly unprepared for any role that a European holocaust might create for the New World. Nor was there any widespread agitation to alter that situation, for despite the nation's increased involvement in world affairs, most Americans looked to the tactic of the ostrich to keep them out of the trouble. Americans, President Woodrow Wilson would admonish once war came, should remain "impartial in thought as well as in action."

Although the Navy, the nation's first line of defense, was the world's third largest, the Army was woefully inadequate for coping with anything much more complex than domestic disturbances or border defense. In striking contrast to 1.5 million trained men available in France and more than 2 million in Germany, the U.S. Army was short even the 100,000-man strength that Congress had authorized in 1902. Within the Army high command the contest of authority between the General Staff and the powerful bureau chiefs still went on, for all Elihu Root's reforms, and argument persisted over Emory Upton's rejection of the militia system in favor of the concept of an expansible army.

How War Came in Europe

The event that set off war in Europe came in late June at Sarajevo where a fanatical Serbian nationalist assassinated the heir to the Austro-Hungarian throne. In other times and under different conditions, this act might not have been enough to catapult the world into the most widespread and costly conflict man had yet known, one that eventually would put under arms sixty-five million men from thirty countries representing every continent, and one that would involve sea battles around the globe and major land campaigns not only in Europe but in parts of Africa and Asia Minor.

Yet as matters stood that summer of 1914, Europe was a tinderbox awaiting a spark. The situation was, in the words of President Wilson's personal adviser, Col. Edward M. House, "militarism run stark mad."

European nationalism had much to do with it. In Germany, a newly united nation forged from a loose-knit confederation of quarreling states no longer had the strong guiding hand of its able creator, Chancellor Otto von Bismarck, but instead had the chauvinistic direction of Wilhelm II, the kaiser. In Italy, also only recently united, vacillation and indecision reigned. In Russia, center of bellicose pan-Slavism, an autocratic czar already was feeling the pressure of people's revolt. In the Balkans, various minorities, particularly the Serbs, were challenging the patchwork amalgamation that was the Austro-Hungarian empire.

At the same time the industrial revolution, with its attendant commercial expansion, had prompted Germany to seek entry into the colonial system that long had been the province of France and Britain. As the Germans built the navy that was essential to their ambition, Britain's age-old supremacy of the seas was challenged. Germany's rise also threatened France on the ground, already tangibly demonstrated in the war of 1870–71, which produced in the French a lasting bitterness and such a burning desire to regain the lost provinces of Alsace and Lorraine that many saw a war of irredentism as inevitable.

The Germans continued to expand their military machine in keeping with their ever-growing aspirations, and as the French followed suit, an arms race of frightening proportions ensued. Meanwhile, the nations banded together in alliances designed to offset one another. There was at first the Triple Alliance composed of Germany, Austria, and Italy. On the other side, the Entente Cordiale between Britain and France gradually merged with the Dual Alliance of France and Russia to become the Triple Entente. With the defection of Italy, Germany and Austria became the Central Powers, which Bulgaria and Turkey eventually joined. The Triple Entente became, with the addition of Italy, the nucleus of the Allied Powers.

Despite some halfhearted efforts to localize the dispute over the assassinated prince, the fact that Russia backed Serbia and the kaiser promised Austria full support meant that the only real question was the date when the war was to begin. The answer to that came on July 28 when Austria declared war on Serbia. In view of the entangling alliances and the bulging arsenals, entry of all the major powers into the conflict was all but preordained.

The Early Campaigns

The bellicosity of Germany toward both Russia and France dictated for the Germans a two-front war. To meet this contingency, the German General Staff had laid its plans to defeat France swiftly before the Russians with their ponderous masses could fully mobilize, then to shift forces rapidly to the east and destroy the Russians at will.

The maneuver designed to defeat the French was the handiwork of Germany's gifted former Chief of Staff, Count Alfred von Schlieffen, who lent his name to the plan. Deducing that the French would attack in Alsace and Lorraine, Schlieffen proposed to trap them in a massive single envelopment, a great scythelike movement through the Low Countries and into northern France, thence west and south of Paris. Schlieffen was prepared to give ground on his left wing in Alsace-Lorraine to insure keeping the French armies occupied until a powerful right wing—the tip of the scythe—could complete the envelopment. So basic to the plan was the power of the right wing that the old man reputedly stressed it in his dying words. (*Map 38*)

Schlieffen's successor, Helmuth von Moltke, failed to heed this proviso. Moltke eliminated the invasion of the Netherlands, thus confining the German right wing to a narrow fortified corridor on either side of the Belgian city of Liège. Wary of the theory of giving ground in Alsace-Lorraine, he shifted troops from the right to strengthen the defense on the left. Similarly worried about the strength of the German forces assigned to contain the Russians, Moltke withdrew four and a half corps from the right wing to move to the east.

These vagaries almost did in the Schlieffen plan, yet such surprise did the maneuver achieve that by late August French and British were in full retreat, the threat to Paris so real that the French Government abandoned the city. At that point Moltke again wavered, for word came that the Russians had mobilized far faster than expected and had begun to attack. Under pressure from the kaiser, Moltke again violated Schlieffen's dictum, pulling out two more corps from his right wing. In an effort to compensate for this diminution by reducing the depth of the envelopment, he ordered the tip of the scythe to pass east rather than west of Paris.

The two corps that Moltke withdrew had no effect in the east, since they arrived only after the Germans already had repelled the Russians in the battles of Tannenberg and the Masurian Lakes. Had Moltke retained them, they might not have been enough to carry the Schlieffen plan through to victory; but since their departure was what had prompted Moltke to alter the scope of the envelopment, their presence would have sharply changed the nature of what followed, the "Miracle of the Marne."

Paris spared, the French Commander in Chief, General Joseph Joffre, rallied the retreating French and British armies along the Marne east of the city, while in Paris the city's commander assembled the garrison—some of them transported in sputtering Parisian taxis—and hurled them against the German flank. That

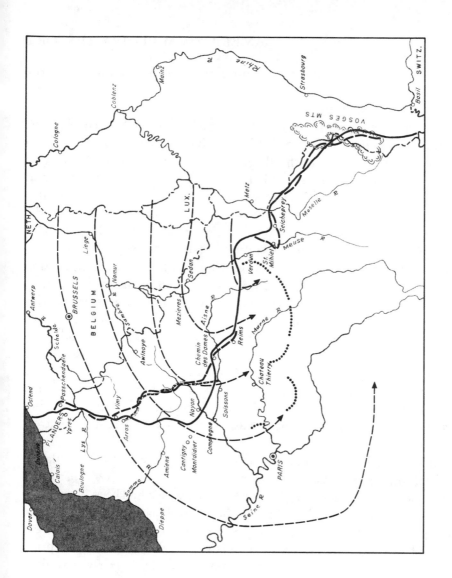

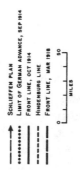

WESTERN FRONT

Sep 1914 – Mar 1918

●●●●●●► SCHLIEFFEN PLAN

━━━━ LIMIT OF GERMAN ADVANCE, SEP 1914

●●●●●●●● FRONT LINE, OCT 1914

━ ━ ━ HINDENBURG LINE

━━━━ FRONT LINE, MAR 1918

```
0        50
|————————|
   MILES
```

MAP 38

action afforded time for main British and French forces to turn, halt the Germans at the Marne River east of Paris, and drive them back to the Aisne River, forty miles to the north.

As stalemate developed along the Aisne, each side tried to envelop the northern flank of the other in successive battles that by October had extended the opposing lines all the way to the Belgian coast. The year would end with the Germans in control of most of Belgium and of the rich mining and industrial provinces of northern France, while the Allies, to their good fortune, managed to hold on to most of the Channel ports, which were vital if the British were to supply their troops on the Continent and if the Germans were to be denied critical bases for operations against the Royal Navy.

Hurting from unexpectedly brutal losses and stunned at the indecision of the first four months of warfare, Allied and German armies alike went to ground. The landscape from Switzerland to the sea soon was scarred with opposing systems of zigzag, timber-revetted trenches, fronted by tangles of barbed wire sometimes more than 150 feet deep and featured here and there by covered dugouts providing shelter for troops and horses and by observation posts in log bunkers or concrete turrets. Out beyond the trenches and the barbed wire was a muddy desert called no man's land where artillery fire had eliminated habitation and vegetation alike, where men in nighttime listening posts strained to hear what the enemy was about, and where rival patrols clashed.

It would eventually be apparent to both sides that they had miscalculated, that the newly developed machine gun and improved indirect fire artillery had bolstered not the offense but the defense, and that which had been presaged—but ignored—in the U.S. Civil War and in the Russo-Japanese War had come to be. The spade had become the *sine qua non* of the battlefield, lessening the applicability of such principles of war as maneuver, economy of force, surprise, and making critical the principle of mass. Masses of men—nearly 2 million Germans, 3 million Allied troops; masses of artillery—barrages lasted days and even weeks before an offensive; and masses of casualties—British and French in 1915 lost 1.5 million men killed, wounded, and missing. Yet through it all the opposing lines stood much as they had at the start. For more than two years they would vary less than ten miles in either direction.

To meet the high cost of the long, deadly struggle, the opposing powers turned more than ever before in history to the concept of the nation in arms. Even Britain, for so many years operating on the theory of a powerful navy and only a small though highly professional army, resorted to conscription and sent massive new armies to the Continent. To appease the appetite of the vast armies for munitions, equipment, and supplies, the nations harnessed their mines, factories, and railroads to war production, levied high income taxes, froze wages and prices, rationed food and other commodities.

On the battlefield, commanders persisted in a vain hope that somehow the stalemate might be ended and breakthrough and exploitation achieved. Although the Germans spent much of their effort in 1915 in a futile campaign for quick victory against the Russians, it was they who first came close to a breakthrough on the Western Front. They did so in April with a greenish mist of chlorine gas released from thousands of canisters against a French colonial division on the British sector of the front. The colonials broke, but the Germans were unprepared to exploit the advantage. The first use of poison gas thus was a strategic blunder wasting total surprise for nothing more than local gains.

The British similarly blundered the next year when they also introduced a new weapon prematurely. This was the tank, an ungainly, ponderous offspring of a marriage of armor with the caterpillar tractor; it owed its name to British attempts to deceive the Germans that the vehicle was a water storage device. In the first commitment in September 1916, 34 tanks helped British infantry advance a painful mile and a half. There would be other attacks in later months involving tanks in strengths close to 500, but the critical element of surprise already had passed. Tanks later would prove sufficient to achieve the penetration everybody sought, but they were too slow and too subject to mechanical failure to fill the old role of horse cavalry as the tool of exploitation.

For all the lack of decision, both poison gas and the tank soon were established weapons, although the Germans were slow to accept the tank. Another weapon, meanwhile, found full acceptance on both sides: the airplane, frail forerunner of modern tactical and strategic bombers. Used at first primarily for reconnaissance, then as a counterreconnaissance weapon to fight the enemy's planes, and finally as an offensive weapon to attack ground troops, before the war ended aircraft engaged in strategic missions against railroads, factories, and cities, presaging the mass destruction that was to follow in another great war.

A fourth new weapon was the submarine, which the Germans employed with a ruthless skill that would bring them close to victory but would in the end provoke the instrument of their downfall. When the Germans first opened submarine warfare early in 1915, only 27 U-boats, as the submarines were called, were ready for action. Even this number quickly achieved impressive results, soon sinking more than 150,000 tons of Allied shipping each month. U-boat crews could not always correctly identify vessels which they attacked, and many neutral ships were sunk. The first American vessel to be involved was the merchant ship *Gulflight*, struck by a torpedo on the first day of May, but the event with sharpest impact on public opinion followed a week later when a submarine off the coast of Ireland sank the British liner *Lusitania*, with the loss of 1,198 lives, including 128 Americans.

The Impact of the War on the United States

The sinking of the *Lusitania* shocked an American public that, while unable to follow the President's dictum on impartiality of thought, had nevertheless displayed up to this point little desire to become directly involved in Europe's bloodbath. Although most Americans had from the first resented the submarine campaign, Britain too was violating the freedom of the seas with a blockade not only of Germany but of neutral European nations as well. This had raised the question of whether the acts of both sides were not equally reprehensible; but the heavy loss of life in the sinking of the *Lusitania* invoked fresh ire against the Germans. Membership in patriotic organizations flourished, and voices advocating preparedness found new listeners.

Among the voices were those of Elihu Root, ex-President Theodore Roosevelt, and former Secretary of War Henry L. Stimson. Another was that of General Wood, whose term as the Army's Chief of Staff had expired just over a year after President Wilson and his peace-oriented administration had come to office. Following a practice he had introduced while Chief of Staff of conducting summer camps where college students paying their own way could receive military training, Wood lent his support to a similar four-week camp for business and professional men at Plattsburg Barracks, New York. Known as the "Plattsburg idea," its success justified opening other camps, assuring a relatively small but influential cadre possessing basic military skills and imbued with enthusiasm for preparedness.

Yet these were voices of a heavily industrialized and articulate east. Few like them were to be heard from the rural south, the west, or a strongly isolationist midwest, where heavy settlements of German-Americans (called by some, derisively, "hyphenated Americans") detected in the talk of preparedness a heavy leaning toward the nation's historic Anglo-Saxon ties. There was in the country, too, a strong tide of outright pacifism, which possessed an eloquent spokesman in Wilson's Secretary of State, William Jennings Bryan.

How deep were Bryan's convictions became apparent in the government's reaction to the sinking of the *Lusitania*. Although Bryan agreed with the President's first diplomatic protest over the sinking, he dissented when the President, dissatisfied with the German reply and determined to insist on the right of neutrals to engage in commerce on the high seas, insisted on a second and stronger note. The Secretary resigned.

Although sinkings by submarine continued through the summer of 1915, Wilson's persistent protest at last produced an apparent diplomatic victory when in September the Germans promised that passenger liners would be sunk only after warning and with proper safeguards for passengers' lives. Decelerating their campaign, the Germans actually acted less in response to American protests than to a realization that they lacked enough submarines to achieve victory by that means.

American commerce with Europe meanwhile continued, particularly in munitions, but because of the British blockade almost all was with the Allied nations. The British intercepted ships carrying foodstuffs to Germany and held them until their cargoes rotted. Just after mid-1915 they put even cotton on a long list of contraband and blacklisted any U.S. firm suspected of trading with the Central Powers. These were deliberate and painful affronts, but so profitable was the munitions trade that only the southern states, hurt by the loss of markets for cotton, raised loud protest. In October 1915 President Wilson repealed a ban earlier imposed on loans to belligerents, thereby further stimulating trade with the Allies.

While Americans as a whole remained opposed to entering the war, their sympathy for the Allied cause grew. A combination of Allied propaganda and German ineptitude was largely responsible. The propagandists were careful to insure that nobody forgot the German violation of Belgian neutrality, the ordeal of "Little Belgium." Stories of babies mutilated and women violated by German soldiers were rampant. The French executed nine women as spies during the war, but it was the death of a British nurse, Edith Cavell, at the hands of the Germans that the world heard about and remembered. Clumsy German efforts at propaganda in the United States backfired when two military attachés were discovered financing espionage and sabotage. The Germans did their cause no further good when one of their submarines in October 1916 surfaced in Newport Harbor, sent an officer ashore to deliver a letter for the German ambassador, then submerged and sank nine Allied ships close off the New England coast.

Continuing to champion neutrality and seeking—however unsuccessfully—to persuade the belligerents to establish international rules of submarine warfare, President Wilson was personally becoming more aware of the necessity for military preparedness. Near the end of a nationwide speaking tour in February 1916, he not only called for creation of "the greatest navy in the world" but, also urged widespread military training for civilians, lest some day the nation be faced with "putting raw levies of inexperienced men onto the modern field of battle." Still upholding the cause of freedom of the seas, he refused to go along with congressmen who sought to forbid Americans to travel on armed merchant ships.

Wilson nevertheless continued to demonstrate a fervent hope for neutrality. A submarine attack in March on the French steamer *Sussex* with Americans aboard convinced the President's adviser, Colonel House, and his new Secretary of State, Robert Lansing, that the nation should sever diplomatic relations with Germany, a course that a fiery speech of self-justification by the German chancellor in the Reichstag and a cynical reply to an American note of protest did nothing to discourage. Wilson instead went only so far as to dispatch what amounted to an ultimatum, demanding that the Germans cease the submarine war against passenger and merchant vessels or face severance of relations with the United States.

While questioning the American failure to deal as sternly with the British blockade and rejecting the charge of unrestricted submarine warfare, Germany again agreed to conform to American demands for prior warning and for protecting the lives of passengers. Wilson, in turn, saw that unless something could be done about the British blockade the German vow probably would be short-lived. When a protest to the British availed nothing, the President offered the services of the United States to negotiate a peace. That brought little positive response from either side.

The National Defense Act of 1916

Some of the President's growing sympathy for the cause of preparedness could be traced to increasing concern on the part of members of his administration, most notably the Secretary of War, Lindley M. Garrison. As an annex to the Secretary's annual report in September 1915, Garrison had submitted a study prepared by the General Staff entitled, "A Proper Military Policy for the United States." Like proposals for reform advanced earlier by Stimson and Wood, the new study turned away from the Uptonian idea of an expansible Regular Army, which Root had favored, to the more traditional American concept of a citizen army as the keystone of an adequate defense force. Garrison proposed more than doubling the Regular Army, increasing federal support for the National Guard, and creating a new 400,000-man volunteer force to be called the Continental Army, a trained reserve under federal control as opposed to the state control of the Guard.

Although Wilson refused to accept more than a small increase in the Regular Army, he approved the concept of a Continental Army. Garrison's proposal drew support, too, in the Senate, but not enough to overcome adamant opposition in the House of Representatives from strong supporters of the National Guard. Influential congressmen countered with a bill requiring increased federal responsibility for the Guard, acceptance of federal standards, and agreement by the Guard to respond to a Presidential call to service. Under pressure from these congressmen, Wilson switched his support to the Congressional plan. This, among other issues, prompted Garrison to resign.

There the matter might have bogged down had not Pancho Villa shot up Columbus, New Mexico. Facing pressing requirements for the National Guard on the Mexican border, the two halls of Congress at last compromised, incorporating the concept of the citizen army as the foundation of the American military establishment but not in the form of a Continental Army. They sought instead to make the National Guard the nucleus of the citizen force.

Passed in May and signed into law the next month, the bill was known as the National Defense Act of 1916. It provided for an army in no way comparable to those of the European combatants and produced cries of outrage from those still subscribing to the Uptonian doctrine. It also contained a severe restriction inserted by opponents of a strong General Staff, sharply limiting the number of officers who could be detailed to serve on the staff at the same time in or near Washington. The bill represented nevertheless the most comprehensive military legislation yet enacted by the U.S. Congress.

The National Defense Act of 1916 authorized an increase in the peacetime strength of the Regular Army over a period of five years to 175,000 men and a wartime strength of close to 300,000. Bolstered by federal funds and federal-stipulated organization and standards of training, the National Guard was to be increased more than fourfold to a strength of over 400,000 and obligated to respond to the call of the President. The act also established both an Officers' and an Enlisted Reserve Corps and a Volunteer Army to be raised only in time of war. Additional officers were to be trained in colleges and universities under a Reserve Officers' Training Corps program.

Going beyond the heretofore recognized province of military legislation, the National Defense Act of 1916 also granted power to the President to place orders for defense materials and to force industry to comply. The act further directed the Secretary of War to conduct a survey of all arms and munitions industries. A few months later the Congress demonstrated even greater interest in the industrial aspects of defense by creating a civilian Council of National Defense made up of leaders of industry and labor, supported by an advisory commission composed of the secretaries of the principal government departments, and charged with the mission of studying economic mobilization. The administration furthered the preparedness program by creating a U.S. Shipping Board to regulate sea transport while developing a naval auxiliary fleet and a merchant marine.

The War in 1916

As Wilson, through the fall of 1916, waged a campaign for re-election on a peace platform, the war on the Western Front remained a stalemate despite two of history's greatest and bloodiest battles. In a switch of main effort from Eastern to Western Front, Moltke's successor as Chief of the General Staff, Erich von Falkenhayn, chose the fortress town of Verdun, which he deemed of immense moral and psychological significance to France, for massive attack in a campaign designed to bleed France white. There followed the Battle of the Somme in which the British with French support attacked in quest of breakthrough and victory. Neither achieved much more than to run up the casualty total: 460,000 French at Verdun, 300,000 German; 614,000 Allied troops on the Somme, 650,000 German.

The appalling carnage of these battles brought the relief of Falkenhayn, replaced by the heroes of the Eastern Front, Paul von Hindenburg as Chief of the General Staff, and Erich Ludendorff as First Quartermaster General, his deputy, although it was Ludendorff rather than the aging Hindenburg who dominated in this command arrangement. It also wrote the end to the field career of the French Commander in Chief, Field Marshal Joffre. In England, a government fell.

On the Eastern Front, the Russians had rallied after giving up Poland to the Germans and struck back with a major offensive against the Austrians that carried almost to the passes leading through the Carpathian Mountains. It was the greatest Russian victory of the war, but it cost a million men and left the poorly armed, poorly equipped Russian soldier ready to embrace revolution.

That year, too, Italians and Austrians ground each other down along the Isonzo in northeastern Italy, while an adventure in peripheral warfare, launched the preceding year at the instigation of Winston Churchill, First Lord of the Admiralty, ended indecisively in evacuation of the Gallipoli peninsula. Indecisive too was the war's greatest sea battle, when a cornered German surface fleet ventured out of the Baltic to meet the British Fleet in the Battle of Jutland, then withdrew to the corner for the rest of the war, but only after inflicting more losses than it received.

During the last three months of 1916, the German submarine campaign again mounted in intensity. Each month the British lost 176,000 tons of shipping. Counting Allied and neutral shipping, the losses averaged 192,000 tons a month, a shocking increase over the previous year that reflected a continuing growth of the U-boat fleet.

An End to Neutrality

As a new year of war opened, German leaders decided that they had lost so many men at Verdun and on the Somme that they would have to assume the defensive on the Western Front; their only hope of quick victory lay with the submarines, of which they now had close to 200. By operating an unrestricted campaign against all shipping, whatever the nationality, in waters off the British Isles and France, the Germans believed they could defeat the Allies within six months. While they recognized the strong risk of bringing the United States into the war by this tactic, they believed they could starve the Allies into submission before the Americans could raise, train, and deploy an Army.

The German ambassador in Washington continued to encourage Wilson to pursue his campaign for peace even as the Germans made their U-boats ready. On January 31, 1917, Germany informed the U.S. Government and other neutrals that beginning the next day U-boats would sink all vessels, neutral and Allied alike, without warning.

While the world waited to learn the American reaction, President Wilson searched for some alternative to war. Three days later, still groping desperately for a path to peace, he went before the Congress, not to ask a declaration of war, but to announce a break in diplomatic relations. This step, Wilson hoped, would be enough to turn the Germans from their new course.

Wilson could not know it at the time but an intelligence intercept already had placed in British hands a German telegram that, when released, would remove any doubt as to German intentions toward the United States. This message was sent in January from the German Foreign Secretary, Arthur Zimmermann, to the German ambassador to Mexico, proposing that in the event of war with the United States, Germany and Mexico conclude an alliance, with the adherence of Japan. In exchange for Mexico's taking up arms against the United States, Germany would provide generous financial assistance. Victory achieved, Mexico was to regain her lost territory of Texas, New Mexico, and Arizona.

Cognizant of the impact the message was bound to have on the United States, the British were nevertheless slow to release it; they had to devise a method to assure the Americans of its authenticity while concealing from the Germans that they had broken the German diplomatic code. On February 23, just over a month after intercepting the telegram, the British turned over a copy to the American ambassador in London.

When President Wilson received the news, he was angered but still unprepared to accept it as cause for war. In releasing the message to the press, he had in mind not inciting the nation to war but instead moving Congress to pass a bill authorizing the arming of American merchant ships, most of which were standing idle in American ports because of the submarine menace. As with the break in diplomatic relations, this, the President hoped, would so impress the Germans that they would abandon their unrestricted submarine campaign.

Although Congress and most of the nation were shocked by revelation of the Zimmermann message, their hopes for neutrality shattered, pacifists and pro-Germans countered with a roar of disbelief that the message was authentic. Zimmermann himself silenced them when in Berlin he admitted having sent the telegram.

In the next few weeks, four more American ships fell victim to German U-boats. Fifteen Americans died. At last convinced that the step was inevitable, the President went before Congress late on April 2 to ask for a declaration of war. Four days later, on April 6, 1917, the United States declared war on Germany.

A Year of Crisis in Europe

The United States entered the war even as Allied fortunes were approaching their nadir.

In Russia in March a spontaneous revolution had erupted, prompting the czar to abdicate and initiating a struggle for power between moderate Socialists and hard-core revolutionaries, the Bolsheviks. The moderates won, formed a provisional government, and vowed to continue the war, a development that made going to war more palatable to many Americans, since the overthrow of the old dynastic-imperial system gave logic to a Wilsonian phrase that this was a war "to make the world safe for democracy."

The reign of the moderates was destined to be brief, partly because the Germans contrived to foment trouble by permitting an exiled revolutionary leader, Nikolai Lenin, to pass from Switzerland through Germany in a special train to Russia. There Lenin joined with other leaders, including Leon Trotsky, in an open campaign to upset the moderate government. As forces of the

Central Powers launched a counteroffensive in July close behind a short-lived Russian offensive, Russian units, riven by revolutionary cells, collapsed, with soldiers deserting by the tens of thousands. The way was prepared for the Bolsheviks to seize power in the October Revolution. The new government under Lenin and Trotsky sued for peace.

On the Western Front the year's operations began with great expectations on the Allied side as a new French commander, General Robert Nivelle, prepared a grandiose, end-the-war offensive. With support from a converging British attack from the north, Nivelle planned to send four French armies to cut in behind a great bulge in the line between Soissons and Arras. Unfortunately, Nivelle was too open with his preparations. The Germans moved first, pulling back from the bulge to a previously prepared position which the Allies would name the Hindenburg Line. In the process they laid waste to the land behind them, and in occupying a shorter line gained 13 divisions for their reserve. In exchange for the usual minor gains, the British incurred 84,000 casualties, the French 187,000.

The worst was still to come. Mutiny broke out in one French regiment and spread swiftly through 54 divisions. The government relieved Nivelle, putting in his place to restore the Army's morale and discipline Henri Philippe Pétain, who had emerged as the hero of the earlier battle for Verdun.

With the French temporarily *hors de combat,* the British took up the struggle with a giant offensive in Flanders. First came a limited objective attack to straighten a minor bulge in the line known as the Messines Ridge. Working like moles, the British dug five miles of underground tunnels, laid a million pounds of explosives, then literally blew up the Messines Ridge. With some 20,000 Germans killed or wounded in one blow, the British took the ridge; but when they launched their main offensive a few miles to the north, breakthrough was as elusive as ever. In a battle that persisted into late fall—Passchendaele, they called it, after a ridge that was the first objective—British casualties totaled 245,000, German half that number.

More disastrous still were the results of an Austrian offensive launched with German assistance in Italy in the fall. In what became known as the Battle of Caporetto, the Italians in one blow lost 305,000 men; 275,000 of them surrendered as the Army fell back a hundred miles in panic. British and French divisions had to be rushed to Italy to keep the Italians in the war.

A combination of all these crises prompted the Allied governments to strive seriously for the first time to create some form of unified command. Yet for all the peril, no government was yet prepared to yield its troops to foreign command. The Allies created a Supreme War Council with both political and military representation from all the Allied nations, a step toward an over-all command, but only a step.

Despite the seriousness of the crises on land, the most portentous of all as the United States entered the war was the crisis at sea. In February 1917 alone, German U-boats had sunk 781,000 tons of Allied and neutral shipping, and the British were predicting a loss in April of almost 900,000 tons. At this rate, the British reckoned, the Germans soon would force them out of the war; by October 1917, the end would be in sight.

The United States Prepares for War

Although far from ready for war, the U.S. Navy fortunately was in a position to take immediate steps to aid the Allies. An emissary from Washington, Rear Adm. William S. Sims, helped to convince the British Admiralty to employ a new tactic to counter the rampaging submarines, a system of convoys whereby destroyers and other warships escorted groups of merchant vessels across the Atlantic. By early May, 6 U.S. destroyers had begun to participate in this system, and before the summer was out the number would grow to 37, while 5 U.S. battleships were operating in European waters.

The convoy system did not defeat the submarine, but it was effective enough to break the crisis. During the last half of 1917 total ship sinkings declined steadily; in December less than 400,000 tons of shipping was lost. In the meantime, the United States had joined Britain in a massive shipbuilding program.

The U.S. Army was in no position to make its weight felt immediately. Counting that part of the National Guard federalized for duty on the Mexican border, the Army numbered only 210,000 men with an additional 97,000 Guardsmen still in state service. Not a single unit of divisional size existed and so hobbled by the restriction written into the National Defense Act was the General Staff that only 19 officers were on duty in the headquarters in Washington. Although the experience in Mexico had given the little Army some seasoning, the main result of that involvement had been to point up shortages in equipment and other deficiencies. Except for 890,000 Springfield rifles, the Army's arsenal was nearly bare.

Given the state of the Army and the fact that the United States went to war over the limited issue of unrestricted submarine warfare, the nation conceivably might have confined its contribution to the war at sea, but such a concept received neither general nor official support. Starting with the President's war message to Cóngress, the intent was to send ground troops to Europe and to do all possible to defeat the German empire and end the war.

Congress, the President, the government moved swiftly in that direction. The House of Representatives authorized a $7 billion bond issue; to build up and manage the merchant marine, the President created the Emergency Fleet Corporation; the Treasury Department opened a drive to float a $2 billion Liberty Loan. The Army General Staff, meanwhile, quickly decided that to bolster Allied morale a division should be shipped as promptly as possible to France as tangible evidence that the United States intended to fight.

Forming a division required collecting as a nucleus four infantry regiments from the Mexican border, building them up to strength with men from other regiments and with recruits, and calling Reserve officers to fill out the staffs. By mid-June the 1st Infantry Division had begun to embark amid dockside confusion not unlike that in the Spanish-American War. Not only did the men lack many of their weapons but a large number had never even heard of some of them. Yet the pertinent fact was that a division was on the way to provide a much-needed boost for the war-weary Allied nations. On the Fourth of July, a battalion of the 16th Infantry marched through Paris to French cheers of near delirium, but it would be months before the 1st Division would be sufficiently trained to participate in the war even on a quiet sector of the front.

To command the American Expeditionary Forces, President Wilson chose the man with command experience in Mexico, John J. Pershing, even though Pershing was junior to five other major generals in the Army. Within three weeks of the appointment, Pershing was on his way to France to survey the situation and furnish the War Department with an estimate of the forces that would have to be provided. He was present for the 16th Infantry's parade on the Fourth of July and participated in a ceremony at the tomb of General Lafayette, where a Quartermaster colonel—not Pershing, as many would long believe—uttered the words, "Lafayette, we are here."

As Pershing was preparing to sail for Europe, Congress in mid-May passed a Selective Service Act based on a plan developed by the War Department after careful study of conscription in the Civil War. It was a model act, one that eliminated such inequities as substitutes, purchased exemptions, and bounties, and assured that conscripts would serve for the duration of the emergency. To spare the Army any opprobrium connected with administering the draft, this was made the responsibility of local civilian boards. Although these local boards were empowered to grant selective exemptions based on essential occupations and family obligations, all males between the ages of 21 and 30 had to register. These ages later were extended from 18 to 45.

The Selective Service Act also established the broad outlines of the Army's structure. There were to be three increments: (1) the Regular Army, to be raised immediately to the full wartime strength of 286,000 authorized in the National Defense Act of 1916; (2) the National Guard, also to be expanded immediately to the authorized strength of approximately 450,000; and (3) a National Army (the National Defense Act had called it a Volunteer Army), to be created in two increments of 500,000 men each at such time as the President should determine.

Much of the identity of these three segments eventually would be lost as recruits and draftees alike were absorbed in all units, so that in mid-1918 the War Department would change the designation of all land forces to one "United States Army." The original segment to which regiments, brigades, and divisions belonged nevertheless continued to be apparent from numerical designations. For the Regular Army, for example, divisions were numbered up to 25, while numbers 26 through 75 were reserved for the National Guard and higher numbers for divisions of the National Army.

Just how large an army the United States was to raise depended in large measure on the situation in Europe and on General Pershing's recommendations from his vantage point there. Soon after Pershing's arrival in France, he called for approximately a million men to be sent to France before the end of 1918. This was the smallest number, Pershing noted, that would afford an independent fighting force, a full field army of 20 divisions and necessary supporting troops. This number, Pershing warned, probably would constitute only a start.

The War Department in turn translated Pershing's recommendation into a plan to send instead by the end of 1918 30 divisions with supporting services, a total of 1,372,000 men; but so disastrous were the developments in Europe in succeeding months—the Nivelle offensive, Passchendaele, Caporetto, the Russian Revolution—that Pershing felt impelled to revise his estimate. In June 1918, he would ask for 3,000,000 men with 66 divisions to be in France by May 1919. This figure he quickly raised to an estimate of 80 divisions by April 1919, followed shortly by a request for 100·divisions by July of the same year.

Although the War Department questioned whether 100 divisions could be sent to France by the summer of 1919 and even whether that many would be necessary to win the war, detailed study produced a promise to raise 98 divisions and to have 80 of them in France by the summer of 1919. This meant, in turn, an increase in the original program of 30 divisions by the end of 1918, raising the goal to 52 divisions.

Part of the War Department's concern was based on the size of the U.S. division—28,000 men—almost double that of Allied and German divisions, which meant in numbers of men that 100 U.S. divisions were the equivalent of almost 200 Allied divisions. This size was a result of one of Pershing's early recommendations, which, along with advice of military missions sent from France and Britain, prompted radical changes in organization of the U.S. infantry division.

The need, as Pershing saw it, was for a division large enough to provide immense striking and staying power, one larger in size than most army corps of the Civil War. As determined by the War Department, the division was to be organized in 2 infantry brigades of 2 regiments each, a field artillery brigade with 1 heavy and 2 light regiments, a regiment of combat engineers, 3 machine gun battalions, plus signal, medical, and other supporting troops.

As the war proceeded, the Army actually would reach a peak strength of 3,685,458. This included 62 divisions, 43 of which were sent overseas. On this basis, when the war came to an end, the Army was running close to the projected goal of 52 divisions to be in France by the end of 1918.

How fast the Army could expand at the start depended in large measure on the availability of housing and of arms, equipment, and supplies. New Regular regiments and small units were organized immediately, using existing housing facilities, while the new National Guard formations were called in two increments and housed in tent camps, mainly in warmer southern states. Although over nine million men registered for the draft in June, the first would be called to fill the divisions of the National Army only in September after a priority building program could provide the first of the vast new cantonments that would be required. A special Cantonment Division of the Quartermaster Corps worked with a civilian Committee on Emergency Construction to provide these facilities.

In the matter of arms, munitions, and equipment, the demands were so urgent and so tremendous, not only for the Army but also for the Navy and the Allies, that as the authors of the National Defense Act of 1916 had anticipated, and as the European powers early had discovered, industry too had to be mobilized. For this task, the Council of National Defense as created by the National Defense Act provided a central planning office and control. The council early established a Munitions Standards Board, composed of industrialists to determine standards for munitions manufacturers, which grew by stages into a War Industries Board with broad powers to co-ordinate all purchasing

GRAND REVIEW, CAMP DEVENS, MASSACHUSETTS

by agencies of the Army and Navy, to establish production priorities, to create new plans and convert existing plants to priority uses, and to co-ordinate the activities of various civilian war agencies.

Despite these efforts, the demand for arms was so immense and immediate and the time required for contracts to be let and industry to retool so lengthy that the Army for a long time would have to train with obsolete and even wooden guns and in the end would have to depend heavily on Allied manufacture. The one weapon providing no particular problem was the rifle. To add to already existing stocks, the Army's own arsenals increased production of Springfields, while plants that had been filling Allied orders modified the British Lee-Enfield rifle to take U.S. ammunition for use by U.S. troops. All American units reaching France during the first year had to be equipped with Allied machine guns and automatic rifles, but new and excellent Browning machine guns and automatic rifles began coming off U.S. production lines in volume by mid-1918. Of some 2,250 artillery pieces used by American forces in France, only a hundred were of U.S. manufacture. Similarly an embryonic U.S. Tank Corps used French tanks, and in some instances British and French tank battalions supported U.S. troops. The Air Section that expanded rapidly to 11,425 flying officers, of whom 5,000 reached France, also had to depend primarily on planes provided by the Allies. The United States did produce a good 12-cylinder Liberty airplane engine, and a few U.S. planes saw service in latter weeks of the war.

The record of U.S. industry was somewhat better in terms of the soldier's personal needs, including his food. The Army worked closely with a War Food Administration to avoid the food scandals of earlier wars. Inductions had to be slowed briefly until sufficient uniforms could be accumulated, and shortages in some items persisted, but as a result less of industry's failures than of a cumbersome Quartermaster contracting system, which was eventually corrected. The Army in any case made extensive purchases abroad but mainly in bulky items to relieve the burden on transatlantic shipping—horses, coal, lumber for overseas camps, and a few textile items like blankets.

Providing officers for the new divisions was another factor affecting the speed of the Army's expansion, for at the start the Army had only 9,000 officers against an immediate requirement of 200,000. Although the General Staff at first contemplated scattering the officers and noncommissioned officers of the Regular Army to form cadres for the National Army, in keeping with Uptonian doctrine, it early became apparent that the small number of Regulars would be submerged and lost in the sea of conscripts. This was one of the factors influencing the General Staff's decision to form a division of Regulars for early shipment to France.

Eschewing the obvious though questionable expedient of appointing officers directly from civilian life, the Army provided direct commissions only for specialists like doctors and those uniquely qualified by civilian experience for the technical services. As a start, the Army conducted sixteen Officers' Training Camps for civilians and reservists on the order of the old "Plattsburg idea"; but in the main the Army drew its officers from the ranks of qualified enlisted men in the Regular Army, from the Reserve Officers' Training Corps and a Student Army Training Corps in colleges and universities, and in the largest numbers of all from Officers' Training Camps in division cantonments and later eight consolidated Officers' Training Schools. Officer candidates were admitted to these schools only after careful screening and then were given three months of intensive training. The 60 percent who made the grade were commissioned in the new National Army. Called in some circles "90-day wonders," these officers nevertheless provided the Army with a leadership far surpassing that of the average new officer in any previous war.

How much training time the soldier needed before going overseas was long a matter of conjecture, but the War Department finally settled on four months' training in the United States. This was so rudimentary, particularly since the units with which the individual soldier went to war were similarly

1st Lt. Edward V. Rickenbacker, First American Ace, *with his Spad plane, France, 1918.*

inexperienced, that General Pershing set up a thorough training course for all divisions once they arrived in France. Conducted with British and French assistance, Pershing's program was so lengthy as to provoke impatience on the part of the Allies and criticism on the part of many American officers.

Getting the troops to their training centers, then to ports of embarkation, and finally across the Atlantic was such a mammoth undertaking and had to be executed on such an emergency basis that confusion and mismanagement could hardly have been unexpected. To co-ordinate rail transportation, the government established a Railway War Board, which later became the Railroad Administration, but so congested did the railroads become that the government eventually seized and ran them through the Railroad Administration. The Shipping Board that had been created close on adoption of the National Defense Act of 1916 had had more time for preparation, but shipping nevertheless remained a critical item and ports often were glutted with supplies. The government cut imports drastically to conserve shipping, established a mass construction program of standardized cargo vessels, and seized interned German vessels and a few others of foreign registry; but British vessels still had to handle much of the traffic.

Changes in the Army High Command

As expansion and overseas deployment proceeded, the unprecedented and in some cases overwhelming demands of the situation had an inevitable impact on many of the Army's historic institutions. The most marked and at the same time of the most import for the future was on the organization of the General Staff and the authority of the Chief of Staff.

The office of the Chief of Staff had yet to find an assertive incumbent until early in March 1918, when the War Department brought back from France Pershing's artillery commander, Maj. Gen. Peyton C. March. In recalling March, the Secretary of War, Newton D. Baker, had reorganization of the General Staff specifically in mind, for a recent Senate investigation of quartermaster, supply, and transportation problems had focused attention on deficiencies that the early months of expansion had revealed.

In the Overman Act, passed by the Congress in May 1918, which granted the President broad authority to reorganize executive agencies during the war emergency, March obtained the tool needed to establish at long last General Staff authority over the heretofore powerful bureau chiefs. Given the additional authority of the rank of full general, March decreed that these chiefs were subordinate to the General Staff and were to report to the Secretary of War only through the Chief of Staff.

Drastically reorganizing the General Staff, March created four main divisions: Operations; Military Intelligence; Purchase, Storage, and Traffic; and War Plans. The titles fairly well explained the functions, except that Operations and War Plans shared the functions of the former War College Division and that Purchase, Storage, and Traffic provided the Army for the first time a central control over logistics. Under this reorganization, the total military and civilian strength of the General Staff increased to just over a thousand.

Lest there remain any room for misinterpreting the role of the Chief of Staff, March, with Secretary Baker's support, issued general orders spelling out the authority in specific terms. The order read, in part:

The Chief of Staff by law (Act of May 12, 1917) takes rank and precedence over all officers of the Army, and by virtue of that position and by authority of and in the name of the Secretary of War he issues such orders as will insure that the policies of the War Department are harmoniously executed by the several corps, bureaus, and other agencies of the Military Establishment and that the Army program is carried out speedily and efficiently.

That, in theory, completed at last the reform of the General Staff that Elihu Root had started, but in practice, an obstacle remained in the person of the field commander in France, General Pershing, who had been promoted to four-star rank ahead of March. Pershing had gone to France with an almost total authority to do the job as he saw it, and, despite technical subordination to March, Pershing resisted any effort by the Chief of Staff to assert authority over his command. The Secretary of War on a number of occasions had to act as arbiter between the two and, in matters related to the American Expeditionary Forces, usually acceded to Pershing's will rather than March's.

The final evolvement of the Chief of Staff as the incontestably supreme military chief of the Army would have to await Pershing's return and his assumption of the job himself, yet Peyton C. March stood, along with Root, as a primary architect of the position.

CHAPTER 18

World War I: The U.S. Army Overseas

Included in the orders General Pershing received from the Secretary of War before he left for France was a stipulation "to cooperate with the forces of the other countries . . . but in so doing the underlying idea must be kept in view that the forces of the United States are a separate and distinct component of the combined forces, the identity of which must be preserved." This was a requirement that influenced many of Pershing's early decisions in regard to the American Expeditionary Forces and was to be for long months a recurring source of contention between Pershing and Allied commanders who were nearing the end of their manpower resources.

Training and Organizing U.S. Troops

For assembling American troops, Pershing chose the region southeast of Paris. Since the British were committed to that part of the front north of Paris and since the French had achieved their greatest concentration in protection of the capital, they had tied up the Channel ports and the railroads north and northeast of Paris. By locating southeast of the city, U.S. forces would be close to the Lorraine portion of the front, a likely spot for committing an independent American force. The French had few troops there and important objectives lay within reasonable striking distance—coal and iron mines and railroads vital to the Germans. This part of the front could be served by the ports of southern and southwestern France and by rail lines less committed to French and British requirements. Pershing set up his headquarters near the source of the Marne in Chaumont.

To Pershing, the training not only of the hastily assembled 1st Division but also of the others that followed before the end of 1917 (the 2d—half Regular Army, half Marine; 26th—New England National Guard; and 42d—called the "Rainbow Division" because it was a composite of Guardsmen from many states) was seriously inadequate. Many of the men in these divisions were recruits, replacements for those pulled out to help train newly forming units.

Pershing devised an intensive training schedule for the 1st Division and planned to follow a similar program for the other three with the idea of withholding all four from active sectors until all were ready, whereupon, late in 1918, they might be committed as the nucleus of an independent American force. Reinforced by other units arriving in 1918, Pershing in 1919 could open an offensive aimed at victory.

For training in trench warfare, Pershing gratefully accepted the help of experienced Allied officers. He also followed the Allied system of setting up special training centers and schools to teach subjects such as gas warfare, demolitions, and the use of the hand grenade and the mortar. Yet in the belief that the French and British had become too imbued with trench warfare to the exclusion of the open maneuvers that eventually would be necessary to achieve victory, he insisted on additional training in offensive tactics, including detailed work in rifle marksmanship and use of the bayonet.

Not until late October 1917 did Pershing submit the 1st Division to trial experience in the line. One battalion at a time from each regiment spent ten days with a French division. The first U.S. Army casualties of the war resulted from this deployment when early in November the Germans staged a trench raid against the same battalion that had paraded in Paris. With a loss of 3 of their own men, the Germans killed 3 Americans and captured 11.

The cycle in the trenches completed, Pershing submitted the 1st Division to further training to correct the deficiencies observed at the front. Only in mid-January of 1918, six months after its arrival in France, was the division ready in Pershing's view to move as a unit into a quiet sector of the trenches.

General Pershing had in the meantime been setting up the staff and logistical organization for managing the growing American force. Reflecting a strong similarity to the French system, his General Staff ultimately included a chief of staff, a deputy chief, and five assistant chiefs supervising five sections: G–1 (Personnel), G–2 (Intelligence), G–3 (Operations), G–4 (Supply), and G–5 (Training). Staffs for divisions and later for corps and armies followed a similar organization, while to fill the new staff positions Pershing set up a General Staff College with a 3-month course.

To provide logistical support, Pershing created a Line of Communications under a single commander responsible directly to him. It was organized into base sections, each with one or more ports, an intermediate section for storage and classification of supplies, and an advanced section for distribution to the zone of operations. After American units entered combat, depots in the advanced section made up supplies for each division in trains which moved to division railheads, whence the divisions moved the supplies to the front in wagons and trucks. The designation Line of Communications was later changed to Services of Supply under command of Pershing's original chief of staff, Maj. Gen. James G. Harbord.

Pressure From French and British

Carrying out the comprehensive training program required all the determination at Pershing's disposal, for once the first exultation accompanying the arrival of American troops in France had predictably passed, practical French and British commanders saw that it would be a long time before independent American units could assume any appreciable portion of the combat burden. They began to insist almost immediately that American soldiers be fed into Allied divisions as replacements.

The Allies felt their request was logical. They had the experienced commanders and units, the necessary artillery, aviation, and tank support, but they lacked men. The American situation was the reverse. Their way, they argued, the power of the American soldier could be quickly brought to bear and hasten the victory. Yet this was reckoning without a sense of national pride that existed among both the soldiers themselves and the American people.

Pershing refused.

Although the Allied governments tried to bypass Pershing by going directly to Washington, they found the Secretary of War and the President firmly behind their field commander. When General Tasker H. Bliss, who had served briefly as the U.S. Army Chief of Staff, was sent as the American representative to the Supreme War Council, Allied governments tried this channel to break Pershing's adamant resolve; but although Bliss was inclined to be more conciliatory than Pershing, he yielded nothing on the principle of a separate American force.

The issue arose again early in 1918 when the British offered to provide the shipping to transport 150 battalions of infantry, which would be used to fill out British divisions that because of the manpower shortage had been reduced from 12 battalions of infantry to 9. After four or five months, according to the British plan, Pershing might withdraw the battalions to form them into American divisions.

This too Pershing refused, but well aware that a lack of ships was slowing the American build-up, he suggested that the British transport divisions instead. Because the same shipping that could move 150 infantry battalions could accommodate only about 3 divisions, which would mean only 36 infantry battalions, the British declined, but eventually they agreed to transport 6 divisions without equipment on the condition that Pershing outfit and train them in the British zone. Ten divisions would eventually arrive under this program.

The matter of a separate American force stood for the moment with Pershing still in unqualified control, yet in view of Allied persistence and of pending developments at the front the question was bound to arise again and again.

The German Offensive, March 1918

As the year 1918 opened, two more U.S. divisions were destined for early arrival in France, but if Pershing kept to his training schedule the American presence was a long way from assertion on the battlefield. The original excitement among the French and British over America's entry into the war had given way to renewed pessimism, for the Allied position appeared less favorable than at any time since the opening battle of the Marne. To the weary French and British, President Wilson's January proclamation of a 14-point peace proposal, however statesmanlike, appeared too idealistic.

So perturbed by the shocking losses of Passchendaele was the British Prime Minister, Lloyd George, that he withheld replacements to assure that his field commander, Sir Douglas Haig, would have to remain on the defensive. Nor could a French Army not yet fully recovered from the mutinies be expected to swing to the attack. The Allies appeared to have no alternative for 1918 but to hold on grimly until enough American troops arrived to assure the numerical superiority essential to victory.

Aside from the calamities of the Nivelle offensive, Passchendaele, and Caporetto, the Allies faced the prospect of sharply increased German numbers made available by the Russian defection. The number of German divisions shifted from east to west would have been even greater had the new Bolshevik government not reneged on its decision to get out of the war and had the Germans not blundered in response. The Bolsheviks had come to Brest-Litovsk in December 1917 to talk only of a peace that would restore Russia's prewar boundaries and impose no indemnities, a concept that strained German credulity. What came of the first encounter at Brest-Litovsk was neither peace nor war but a bizarre new confrontation between Germany and Russia that still tied down eighty German divisions.

Russia, said the Bolsheviks, would not make peace; neither would its forces continue the war even if the Germans still fought. In response, the German armies in the east began in February 1918 to march deeper into Russia. They marched on even after the Bolsheviks at last agreed to real peace, only to become involved eventually in guerrilla warfare against their rear. Throughout the spring and summer of 1918 a million Germans that might have been decisive on the Western Front remained embroiled in Russia.

Within Germany, by the start of 1918, the duo of Hindenburg and Ludendorff had gradually accumulated almost dictatorial powers, with Ludendorff dominating more than ever. They decided that they had to strike early in 1918 in a final grand effort to achieve victory in the west before American manpower could be brought to bear. Germany, possibly more than France and Britain, was hurting gravely from the long war: on the home front, starvation was becoming a stark reality, and the previous summer there had been Marxist-inspired mutinies in the German Navy. The replacements going to German divisions were old men and boys.

By recalling divisions from Italy and some from the east, Ludendorff managed to assemble over 3,500,000 men on the Western Front, including 192 divisions. He planned to attack in early spring with 62 divisions along the Somme against the British, whose armies had little space for recoil before they would find themselves with their backs on the Channel. Having split the British and French, he then would turn to defeat the French. (*Map 39*)

For success Ludendorff counted on numerical superiority (4 to 1), surprise, and the first mass application of new tactics developed originally in the east by Lt. Gen. Oscar von Hutier. The so-called "Hutier tactics" involved a relatively short (several hours) but intensive artillery preparation, heavy on gas and smoke, followed by a rolling barrage creeping ahead of the infantry at a predetermined rate. Organized in small battle groups built around a light machine gun, the infantry infiltrated to cut off strongpoints rather than assault them, leaving that task to others who came behind. The enemy's forward positions ruptured, the infantry advanced swiftly to overrun the enemy artillery and break into the clear. In both these phases, light artillery was attached to assault battalions, a tactical use of horse-drawn field pieces heretofore considered suicidal in trench warfare.

The new tactics put a premium on courage, stamina, initiative, and co-ordination, qualities which, for lack of time, the Germans could instill in only about two dozen specially selected divisions. These were pulled from the line, filled out with men from other divisions, and put through an intensive training program.

Despite elaborate efforts to achieve surprise, a new confidence radiating from Berlin and intelligence gathered from prisoners at the front made it clear to the Allies that the Germans were readying a major offensive. The British even determined the general strength, place, and finally the date of the attack, and they had a strong indication of the tactics the Germans would employ. But Haig, short of reserves, could do little in advance to prepare to counter the blow,

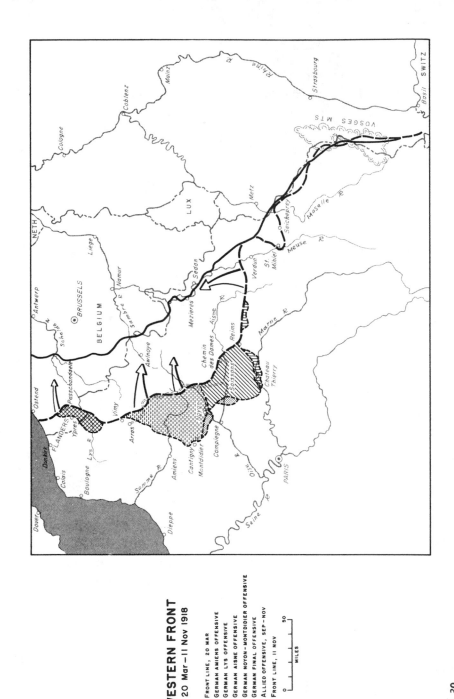

WESTERN FRONT
20 Mar – 11 Nov 1918

FRONT LINE, 20 MAR
GERMAN AMIENS OFFENSIVE
GERMAN LYS OFFENSIVE
GERMAN AISNE OFFENSIVE
GERMAN NOYON – MONTDIDIER OFFENSIVE
GERMAN FINAL OFFENSIVE
ALLIED OFFENSIVE, SEP – NOV
FRONT LINE, 11 NOV

0   50
MILES

MAP 39

while the French High Command refused to believe that if Ludendorff intended a decisive offensive he would strike the British rather than the French.

The big blow came on March 21 in a fog with the main effort against the British right wing. When night fell, the Germans had achieved a penetration along a 50-mile front and were pointing toward Amiens, a communications hub on the Somme that in German hands would effectively split the French and British armies. The only question remaining was, did Ludendorff have the means to exploit his success.

If Ludendorff's success or failure depended on early commitment of Allied reserves, he had little cause for concern. Despite a mutual pledge by Haig and Pétain to go to each other's aid in event of crisis, so imbued was Pétain with the belief that the Germans were bound to strike a harder blow against the French that he was slow to send help. Although he gradually dispatched six divisions to the south flank of the penetration, these acted less to stem the German tide than to screen against any German turn toward Paris.

Ludendorff nevertheless was running into trouble. To broaden the penetration at the northern shoulder, he threw in 20 more divisions; but these were untrained in the Hutier tactics and failed to pierce a solid British defense. The long-fought-over terrain along the Somme slowed the advance of the main effort, and a hastily created British defensive force composed mainly of rear-echelon service troops occupied old trenches east of Amiens to halt the advance on that critical city. The German divisions in the lead were becoming exhausted, and supplies failed to get forward.

By the end of March, Ludendorff's offensive had bogged down. He had achieved a brilliant tactical victory—an advance of forty miles in eight days, 70,000 prisoners, 200,000 other Allied casualties; but strategically the result was empty. He had failed either to destroy the British armies or to separate them from the French, and he had taken as many casualties as he had inflicted, most of them in the highly trained shock divisions, losses he could not replace.

Unity of Command

A combination of the crisis and of Pétain's dilatory response to Haig's pleas for help also harmed German chances of ultimate victory. Although Haig himself had vitiated an earlier attempt to create a 30-division reserve for the Supreme War Council by pleading inability to spare his quota, he was so shaken by the crisis on the Somme that he volunteered to subordinate British troops around Amiens to a Frenchman, General (later Marshal of France) Ferdinand Foch. As an instructor in prewar years at the École de Guerre, Foch had established a reputation as a military theorist and earlier in the war had successfully co-ordinated British, French, and Belgian operations in Flanders. Out of this agreement to subordinate all troops around the Amiens salient to Foch grew a broader understanding to subordinate, first, all British and French troops on the Western Front, then, later, all Allied forces.

The Allies at last had a unified command, even though they qualified it with weakening provisos: one that Foch had only "strategic direction" while "tactical control" remained with national commanders, another that each national commander could appeal a decision of the supreme commander to his home government. These qualifications, in theory, sharply diminished Foch's authority; but through military acumen, determination, and force of personality, Foch would make the arrangement work.

The Lys Offensive, April 1918

Ludendorff, meanwhile, clung to a belief that with another blow he could shatter the British armies. This time he chose a point a few miles north of the Amiens salient along the Lys River in Flanders, close by the scene of the bloody British offensive known as Passchendaele. Now he had 35 divisions.

Following an intensive bombardment, mainly with gas shells, eight German divisions attacked early on April 9 along the south bank of the Lys and quickly took advantage of the collapse of a Portuguese division to plunge five miles past the last of the trenches into open country. The next day other divisions attacking along the north bank of the Lys also achieved a penetration.

By the fourth day of the attack, the British were in serious danger. Putting the new unified command to a test, Field Marshal Haig called on Foch for help, but having long observed the tenacity of the British soldier on defense, Foch was convinced Haig could hold without involving reserves that could be better saved for a counteroffensive once the Germans had exhausted their resources. Although Haig fumed, Foch would agree to send only a few divisions.

Haig at that point issued what became known as his "backs to the wall" order: "There is no other course open to us but to fight it out. . . . With our backs to the wall and believing in the justice of our cause, each one of us must fight on to the end."

As the British soldier responded nobly, hungry German troops often slowed their attack to forage for food. In the end, Ludendorff had no choice but to call off the offensive. As April drew to a close, he held another vulnerable salient that included the Passchendaele Ridge but little else of tactical importance, this at a cost to the British of 305,000 casualties of all types but to the Germans even more, 350,000.

The first major action involving an American division had developed in the meantime far from the flaming Somme and Lys on a quiet sector in Lorraine, not far from the town of St. Mihiel. Here the 26th Division on April 20 came under a heavy bombardment, followed by a German attack in regimental strength aimed at seizing the village of Seicheprey. Boxing in the defenders with artillery barrages, the Germans took the village, only to lose it in the afternoon to a U.S. counterattack. The Germans held on to a nearby wood through the day, but American riflemen, cut off and scattered early in the fighting, regrouped to regain their positions the next day. The Germans left behind 160 dead, but they took 136 prisoners and inflicted 634 casualties.

During these weeks, General Pershing came under renewed pressure from the British and French to make up losses in Allied divisions with individual American replacements. While Pershing at the height of the crisis on the Somme had offered to place U.S. troops at Foch's disposal, he had been thinking only of the existing crisis while remaining faithful in the long run to the concept of an autonomous American army. Long and sometimes tempestuous were the arguments, voluminous the cables between Allied capitals, but in the end Pershing would go only so far as to agree that infantry and engineers of the divisions being transported in British shipping might be brought to France ahead of their artillery. Allied commanders, including Foch, finally endorsed the principle of forming as soon as possible an independent American force.

The Aisne Offensive, May 1918

As these arguments proceeded, the front was for a few weeks relatively quiet. It was a quiet before a storm, for Ludendorff was determined to persist in his struggle in Flanders to pin the British armies against the Channel.

To draw off Allied reserves from Flanders, Ludendorff decided on a diversionary attack against the Chemin des Dames, an elongated, commanding ridgeline northeast of Paris covering Soissons. Although this was the sector where Pétain had feared attack in March, with no attack forthcoming he had progressively thinned the defense. So imbued with the natural strength of the position was the local commander that he had neglected to erect a defense in depth, concentrating his men instead on the forward slope of the Chemin des Dames. In the face of heavy bombardment combined with the Hutier tactics, he was inviting disaster.

It was not long in coming. Although forewarned by an American intelligence analysis that an attack was in the offing, the French refused to heed the signs until the day before the attack was to begin. All the French troops could do in the time remaining was to stand warily at their posts while Foch belatedly began moving reserves.

With 17 divisions forward and 13 in follow-up reserve, the Germans attacked early on May 27 behind a barrage by close to 5,000 guns. German infantry plunged quickly over and beyond the Chemin des Dames, jumping the Aisne and Vesle Rivers, and gaining up to 20 miles in the first 24 hours.

Although this was to have been but a diversionary attack, Ludendorff was too elated by the breakthrough, too tempted by the open road to Paris to bring it to a halt. Three days later, on the last day of May, his troops would reach the Marne at Château-Thierry, less than fifty miles from the French capital, almost as close as Moltke had come in 1914.

Under pressure of this new crisis, General Pershing again went to Foch, this time to offer 5 American divisions to be used along the Marne as Foch deemed necessary. By the night of May 31, the machine gun battalion of the 3d Division, moved up swiftly in trucks, was in position to help French troops hold the bridge site over the Marne at Château-Thierry, and the rest of the division was on the way to help hold the river line. The next day the 2d Division (which included a Marine brigade) took up defensive positions north of the Marne and west of Château-Thierry astride the main highway to Paris.

Despair gripped not only the French stragglers falling back from the front but also the Allied High Command. What they could not know was that again Ludendorff was overextended, that he could strike in earnest for Paris only after broadening the wings of his narrow salient and bringing up supplies and reserves.

For two days Ludendorff's advance troops beat vainly against a hastily dug American line. At last they desisted, but the infantrymen and marines of the 2d Division would give them no rest. Beginning on June 6, the 2d Division attacked in costly but intrepid strikes against Belleau Wood and the villages of Bouresches and Vaux. Although this fighting would continue for three weeks, it was apparent from the first that the sudden, dramatic introduction of a new force had brought Ludendorff's thrust to a halt. For the Americans it was a costly debut—9,777 casualties, including 1,811 dead—but the moral effect on both sides was great.

The moral effect was all the more pronounced because of another action that antedated the 2d Division's achievement, the first offensive by an American division in the war. It began as a preliminary to a planned French counterattack against the Amiens salient, a counterattack that because of Ludendorff's break-through to the Marne failed to come off. It was an attack by the 1st Division against the village of Cantigny on commanding ground near the tip of the salient.

Supported by American and French artillery and by French tanks, one regiment took the village in a swift maneuver early on May 28, then held on grimly as counterattack followed counterattack into the next day. The Americans lost 1,607 men, including 199 killed, but in the process they achieved a victory presaging greater events to follow.

The German Offensive, June 1918

Conscious of this new force entering the battle, conscious too of the necessity to maintain the initiative if ever the British armies were to be broken, Ludendorff wanted to pull back from the highly vulnerable Marne salient, but the effect on German morale would have been too adverse. Denied use of these troops for renewing the offensive against the British in Flanders, he decided on still another diversionary attack. By taking ground that might serve as a buffer for a railroad passing through Soissons, Ludendorff would improve supply into the Marne salient and at the same time pose a new threat to Paris that would, he hoped, pull Allied reserves from Flanders.

Ludendorff on June 9 sent one army westward from Soissons, another southward from the south flank of the Amiens salient between the towns of Noyon and Montdidier. As the two thrusts joined, they would merge the Amiens and Marne salients into one big, less vulnerable bulge in the line and release divisions to move to Flanders.

Yet this time there was no surprise and this time the French were ready with a defense in depth. They held the Germans to a tortuous advance of nine miles, then stopped them with counterattacks. By the fifth day, the attack had run its course.

A Growing American Force

As a temporary lull settled over the front, General Pershing on July 4 announced that a million Americans had arrived in France. Nine divisions had had some combat experience, mainly in quiet sectors; 2 others were completing their training; and 8 more had recently arrived. The total was 19, each one double the size of an Allied or German division.

In June Pershing had created three corps headquarters. The I Corps under Maj. Gen. Hunter Liggett first took responsibility for a sector near Château-

Thierry, while the II Corps under Maj. Gen. George W. Read controlled the 27th and 30th Divisions that were destined to fight through the rest of the war with the British. The III Corps under Maj. Gen. Robert L. Bullard had yet to enter the line.

With 250,000 U.S. troops arriving every month, the effect of the American presence on Allied troops and the French population was stimulating, electric. Winston Churchill saw it this way:

> The impression made upon the hard-pressed French by this seemingly inexhaustible flood of gleaming youth in its first maturity of health and vigour was prodigious. None were under twenty, and few over thirty. As crammed in their lorries they clattered along the roads, singing the songs of a new world at the tops of their voices, burning to reach the bloody field, the French Headquarters were thrilled with the impulse of new life. . . . Half trained, half organized, with only their courage, their numbers and their magnificent youth behind their weapons, they were to buy their experience at a bitter price. But this they were quite ready to do.

For all the influx of new strength, no one yet saw any quick ending of the war, any indication that the Germans might have only one more offensive left in them.

The Last German Offensive, July 1918

The meager gains of Ludendorff's diversionary attack in June having failed either to secure the railroad at Soissons or to draw Allied reserves from Flanders, Ludendorff planned yet another diversionary attack before returning to the offensive in Flanders. A month in preparation, the new offensive began on July 15, one army driving southeast from the Marne salient, another attacking south from positions east of the city of Reims, a total of 52 divisions. Meeting on the Marine, the two armies were to cut a sizable segment from the Allied line and in the process solve the supply problem in the Marne salient by taking the railroads at Reims.

Ludendorff called this the *Friedensturm*—Peace Offensive. That was a mistake, for should failure occur in an offensive associated with such a grandiose aim, the German soldier would be in no condition to recover from the despair that was bound to follow. The slackening of discipline among troops too long denied all but the barest necessities had first emerged in the Lys offensive, but it had become even more apparent during the drive to the Marne as many men deserted the battle to loot wine cellars in the champagne country around Soissons. Weak from malnutrition, the soldiers were peculiarly susceptible to an influenza epidemic that swept the trenches in June and was to keep recurring into November. On the eve of each new offensive, hundreds were deserting to the enemy.

A wave of desertions combined with information gleaned from aerial photographs, observation posts, and patrols told the French what was coming, when, and where. East of Reims, the French commander, whose troops included the 42d U.S. Division, elected to pull the bulk of his men from the forward trenches, leaving only outposts in what was known as a "sacrifice line." While the vacated positions absorbed the German artillery bombardment, the French laid down a counterbarrage. As German troops battered by shellfire neared the "sacrifice line," French and American troops fell back to an intermediate position. After repeating the delaying tactics, French and Americans again withdrew, this time to a main line of resistance. At this third line they held. By noon of the first day the issue was no longer in doubt.

Anxious to deny any German foothold across the Marne, the French opposite the other prong of the German attack had opted against these tactics. Here German gains were greater—up to four miles beyond the Marne at some points—and a French division, occupying a re-entrant formed by a bend in the river, folded, leaving four attached American companies of the 28th Division in a desperate plight. Most of these men were killed or captured. Yet the 3d Division on the French left held, its 38th Infantry, beset on three sides, executing such a steadfast defense that the regiment earned a nickname, "Rock of the Marne."

By noon of the second day, Ludendorff recognized that this prong of his attack also had been blunted. He called off the offensive.

Allied Counteroffensive

Even as the Germans were preparing what turned out to be their last offensive, General Foch had been assembling Allied divisions to launch a counteroffensive directed at first toward a limited objective—cutting the highway leading from Soissons to Château-Thierry, the main supply route of German troops in the Marne salient—but with the certainty that, if successful, the attack would be extended to erase the entire salient. In the forefront of the attack were two U.S. divisions—the 1st and 2d—operating under a French corps command.

A heavy rain fell as the troops moved to their jump-off positions the night of July 17, providential, as it turned out, since it helped conceal Allied preparations. After only a short but intensive artillery preparation early on the 18th, Allied infantry moved to the attack from near Soissons in the north to Château-Thierry in the south. In the corps with U.S. divisions, 350 French tanks early

MEN OF THE 26TH DIVISION NEAR CHÂTEAU-THIERRY, *July 1918.*

took the lead. When night fell, the two armies had advanced in some places up to five miles.

Although these two U.S. divisions were soon relieved by French and British units, the drive continued and expanded to the east, bringing in the 3d, 4th, 26th, and 28th Divisions and eventually the 32d, 42d, and 77th Divisions, and headquarters of the I and III Corps. The Germans began abandoning their Marne salient, though deliberately and in good order, retiring to successive defensive positions all the way to the Vesle River with the Chemin des Dames at their backs.

A Separate American Army

As the Allied drive came to a halt at the end of the first week of August, new hope of victory stirred in the ranks. The drive had carried no more than 20 miles, but the results were infinitely more important than the amount of territory regained. The counteroffensive had eliminated the threat to Paris, spoiled Ludendorff's cherished ambition of striking a deathblow in Flanders, and so dimmed German chances of victory that even Ludendorff could no longer hope for more than a stalemate. Furthermore, the initiative had passed to the Allies, whose fresh force had proven beyond doubt (though at a cost of 50,000 casualties) its ability on the offensive. In the bid to win before the Americans could intervene in force, Ludendorff had failed.

As this counteroffensive (sometimes called, in conjunction with the last German offensive, the Second Battle of the Marne) neared an end, General Pershing pressed his case for an independent American army and a separate

AMERICAN MILITARY POLICE PATROLLING A ROAD *near Château-Thierry.*

sector of the front. Foch was sympathetic, for a separate American force fitted in with plans he was formulating to eliminate three other German-held salients on the front. British and French together were to reduce the Amiens salient, then the British would erase the Lys salient while the Americans eliminated another salient in Lorraine that had stood for four years and took its name from a town at the tip, St. Mihiel.

With Pershing himself as commander, headquarters of the First Army officially opened on August 10. The new command encompassed the I and III Corps and 19 U.S. divisions.

As demonstrated earlier in making American units available to Allied armies, Pershing for all his adamant resolve to create an independent American force never objected to allowing some U.S. divisions to fight under Allied command; he objected instead to the use of American troops as individual replacements or in small increments to fill out depleted Allied units. Even as he formed the First Army he left the II Corps and its two divisions with the British, while he allowed several other divisions to serve under French command.

The one division whose employment violated Pershing's principle was the 93d, which had only infantry regiments without trains or artillery. This was a Negro division, one of only two organized and sent to France during the war, although thousands of other Negroes served overseas in the Services of Supply. The 93d's regiments were assigned to the French, reorganized according to French tables, and used as integral parts of French divisions. The other Negro division, the 92d, served in the First Army.

The Somme Offensive

As Pershing was forming the First Army, French and British armies under Haig launched converging attacks from the northwest and southwest against the Amiens salient. They achieved as much surprise as had the Germans against the Chemin des Dames. Using 300 tanks in the lead, ten British divisions, including Australians and Canadians, scored a swift breakthrough, brushing aside German units in rout, gaining seven miles in the first few hours, and making of August 8, in Ludendorff's words, a "black day" for the German Army.

Yet the slow, ponderous tanks could not long sustain such a pace, and horse cavalry was of no use when the enemy stiffened. Coming against a strong German stand in old trenches dating from 1915, Haig paused, shifted the emphasis of his attack farther north, then in a methodical campaign gradually pushed the Germans back. By the end of August the Germans were retiring into the positions whence they had begun their big March offensive, the Hindenburg Line. The Amiens salient, like that on the Marne, was a thing of the past. Meanwhile, other British units helped by the U.S. II Corps with the 27th and 30th Divisions had almost finished erasing the Lys salient.

On the German side, the events of 8 August had cast a pall over the High Command. "We have nearly reached the limit of our power to resist," said Hindenburg. "The war must be ended." When Ludendorff agreed, Wilhelm II instructed his Foreign Secretary to find a way out of the war, but the underlying idea was to retain as much as possible of the territory that the German armies had conquered. Under such a condition, there was little real hope for peace.

The St. Mihiel Offensive

As the British drive progressed, General Pershing and his staff shifted divisions to Lorraine. Their goal was to push beyond the St. Mihiel salient to seize Metz or at least to cut the highway running from Metz all the way to Antwerp, the enemy's main line of lateral communications. When Foch saw the plan, he was so enthusiastic that he increased the French participation from 4 to 10 divisions.

Foch's endorsement of the American plan preceded the British success in pushing the Germans into the Hindenburg Line. Planning an early attack along the Somme to break that line, Marshal Haig suggested to Foch that instead of attacking toward Metz the Americans should be employed from

FRENCH TANKS RETURNING FROM THE FRONT

positions west of Verdun to attack northward toward Mézières along the French-Belgian frontier northeast of Reims. Such an attack would serve not only to cut the enemy's railroad but also to converge with the British attack.

Seeing in Haig's proposal a possibility of victory before the year was out, Foch endorsed the idea. Presenting it to General Pershing, he directed that once the St. Mihiel salient was eliminated the American objective should be changed from Metz to Mézières. In the drive on Mézières, Foch was to employ two armies, one wholly American under Pershing, the other Franco-American under French command.

Foch's proposal for a Franco-American army under French command appeared to Pershing as a threat to the long-sought independent American force which he had so recently achieved. He insisted that, while the American army "will fight wherever you may decide, it will not fight except as an independent American army." Foch declined to press the issue.

Reducing the scope of the attack on the St. Mihiel salient to nine U.S. and five French divisions, Pershing and his staff began to prepare two offensives to be mounted within 23 days in areas 40 miles apart. That was something no single army had yet attempted on the Western Front.

The Germans, fortunately, were to make the task easier. Conscious of the vulnerability of the St. Mihiel salient and of a major Allied offensive in the making, they began to pull out of the salient two days before Pershing planned to attack.

Under Pershing's plan, a French corps was to press the tip of the salient while the V Corps under Maj. Gen. George H. Cameron, in its first combat action, hit the west flank. Meanwhile General Liggett's I Corps and the IV Corps under Maj. Gen. Joseph T. Dickman, also new in the line, was to attack the south flank, the two American thrusts to meet in the center of the salient at the town of Vigneulles. French and British provided the bulk of the artillery support— 3,000 guns—while the only tanks available were 267 light French Renaults. Although the French furnished many of the tank crews, others were Americans of the 304th Tank Brigade, commanded by Lt. Col. George S. Patton, Jr. An Allied air force controlled by an exponent of air power, Col. William Mitchell, consisted of almost 1,500 planes (600 piloted by Americans), the largest concentration of aircraft yet assembled.

Following a four-hour artillery bombardment, the tank-infantry advance began before daylight on September 12. Most of the tanks fell victim early to mechanical failure or mud, but they were hardly needed. Resistance was from the first surprisingly moderate, particularly on the southern flank where the Germans had already thinned their forward troops as a step in the general withdrawal. By nightfall of the first day a gap of only ten miles separated the two converging American forces.

When Pershing learned that roads leading out of the salient were filled with withdrawing Germans, he urged continued attack through the night to block all escape routes. A regiment of the 26th Division pushed swiftly from the west to enter Vigneulles two hours after midnight, there to be joined soon after dawn by a regiment of the 1st Division.

This first victory of the war by an American army netted 15,000 prisoners at a cost of only 7,000 casualties. It was so easy that some have referred to it as the action in which the Americans relieved the Germans, but the observation fails to take into account that the Germans had begun to pull back because they dreaded what was coming.

The Meuse-Argonne Offensive

Even as Pershing had been preparing and launching this first big American attack, Foch's original plan had been growing by bounds. No longer was the offensive to be confined to a British strike along the Somme and an American drive on Mézières. The new plan also included a Belgian-British-French attack along the Lys and French attacks in between British and Americans. It was to be a grand assault all along the front—said Foch: "Tout le monde à la bataille!". The aim was to cut the enemy's rail line at Mézières and Aulnoye, the latter in front of the British, and thereby force the Germans to retire inside their frontier before winter set in. For the offensive Foch had 220 divisions—160 in line, 60 in reserve. They included 42 of the big American divisions, although some of these had only recently arrived and Pershing would be forced to cannibalize others to obtain replacements. Ten American divisions would still serve with British and French armies.

Assisted by the French Fourth Army on the left, the American attack was to begin first, on September 26. It posed a tremendous logistical effort involving rapid transfer of some 800,000 men, 200,000 French moving out of the new American sector west of Verdun, and 600,000 Americans moving in. That it was completed in secrecy and in time for the jump-off was attributable in large measure to the planning of a young officer on Pershing's staff, Col. George C. Marshall. Again the British and French furnished most of the artillery and tanks (190 French lights) and some of the 800 aircraft supporting the attack.

The terrain over which the advance was to pass was studded with natural and man-made obstacles. From high ground east of the Meuse River, which formed the right boundary for the attack, and from densely wooded high ground of the Argonne Forest in the left of the attack zone, German eyes could look down on much of the battlefield; and in the center, between the forest and the river, the Germans held a hogback ridge replete with fortified spurs and stone-walled villages. The Germans had established three lines with trenches, barbed wire, deep dugouts, and concrete fighting posts, while a fourth was under construction farther back. Particularly formidable were strongpoints at Montfaucon, Cunel, and Barricourt.

In a sector approximately twenty miles wide, Pershing massed three corps, each to employ two divisions forward, one in reserve. With a superiority in men of 8 to 1, he hoped to make the ten miles through the first three German positions in one sustained drive.

The infantry began to advance before daylight after a 3-hour artillery bombardment. Achieving surprise, they caught the Germans with only four divisions in the line. General Bullard's III Corps on the right pushed five miles through both the first and second German positions, but General Cameron's V Corps in the center ground to a halt before the bristling defenses of Mont-faucon, and General Liggett's I Corps on the left could advance little more than a mile through the thick, almost trackless Argonne Forest.

During the next few days, the troops plodded slowly forward, at last carrying Montfaucon and putting the V Corps through the second German line, but progress amid the trees and dank ravines of the Argonne Forest still was slow. Flanking fire from east of the Meuse and from uncleared portions of the Argonne harried units on the right and in the center. Most of the supporting tanks succumbed to the usual troubles of mud and mechanical failure. Congestion and muddy roads hampered resupply. Most serious of all was the inexperience of the troops, for having used his experienced divisions in the St. Mihiel salient Pershing had had to withhold them from the first assault. Units got lost, message traffic broke down, some commanders failed.

Any hope that an advance by the French Fourth Army on the left might unhinge the Germans in front of the U.S. troops went for naught, for the French were making no more rapid gains. As September came to an end, Pershing had no choice but to pause to reorganize.

Elsewhere on the Western Front, progress was, with one exception, not much more encouraging. The Belgian-French-British effort on the Lys bogged down in rain and mud, as had every offensive in that region, while the French in the center of the Allied line were not to begin their attack until British and Americans on their flanks had driven deep enough to threaten the Germans opposite them with entrapment. Only the British along the Somme provided any indication of decisive success, scoring a deep penetration of the Hindenburg Line with the help of the 27th and 30th Divisions of the U.S. II Corps. The penetration was soon expanded to create a gap all the way through the fortifications, but the effort left British troops temporarily spent.

Despite the disappointing progress of the grand offensive from an Allied viewpoint, it was enough to start a collapse within the German High Command. On September 28, Ludendorff mused at such length on the miseries besetting him that he worked himself into a rage, foamed at the mouth, and fell to the floor. That evening he called on Hindenburg. The situation, the two agreed, was infinitely worse than in August when they had first urged the kaiser to seek peace, advice that had produced no results. They had no alternative now but to agree to surrender all conquered territory in the west and try to negotiate a peace on the basis of President Wilson's Fourteen Points.

On October 4 the German chancellor cabled Wilson asking for an armistice. Without informing the Allied governments, Wilson answered with a request for clarification. The German chancellor replied on October 12 that the Germans agreed to all Fourteen Points; but by this time word of the peace feeler had reached the French and British, who for their part were in no mood to accept Wilson's unilateral actions. Furthermore, Ludendorff himself had recovered from his convulsive fit, had seen that the Allied offensive had imposed no rout, and had come to believe the Germans could get terms that would allow them to withdraw behind their own frontier, reorganize their armies, and resist any peace proposals they deemed unacceptable.

Yet events were taking place that were destined to tie Ludendorff's hands and harden Wilson's resolve. Not the least of these were continued fierce German resistance and the revelation, in those areas where the Germans were forced to retire, of wanton destruction and a barbaric disregard for human life more flagrant than those excesses of 1917 when they had left behind a wasteland in retiring into the Hindenburg Line.

On the Meuse-Argonne front, Pershing's First Army renewed its offensive on October 4 after inserting experienced divisions into the line, but during the brief pause in operations Ludendorff had brought in reinforcements. The fight to clear the rest of the Argonne Forest and pierce the third German line progressed no more swiftly than before.

In the Argonne a "lost battalion" of the 77th Division was surrounded for five days before other troops could break through to free 194 survivors out of an original 600. In the Argonne, too, an American patrol took about 75 Germans by surprise and was herding them toward the rear when German machine gunners opened fire, killing and wounding 9 out of 17 in the patrol. When a German lieutenant led a charge aimed at the survivors, Pfc. Alvin C. York, a Tennessee sharpshooter, cut down 15 Germans one by one until at last surviving members of this group too surrendered. When a count could be taken, it revealed that York had captured 132 of the enemy.

To dispense with the troublesome German flanking fire from heights on the other side of the Meuse, General Pershing broadened his attack to include the east bank. To control that phase, Pershing created the Second Army under General Bullard. Relinquishing command of the First Army to General Liggett, Pershing himself moved up to the level of army group.

Despite the added strength on the east bank, the fight continued slow and costly, for Ludendorff looked on the offensive as such a threat to the vital railroad through Mézières that he eventually committed 27 of his reserve divisions to this sector. Some help developed on the left when on October 5 the U.S. 2d Division, attacking with the French, captured high ground known as Blanc Mont, prompting a slow German withdrawal before the Fourth Army back to the Aisne River. On the 10th, the I Corps finally cleared the last of the Argonne Forest, but bitter fighting continued through the rest of the month for the fortified hills between the forest and the Meuse. Not until the last day of October was the third German position broken all along the line.

The British in the meantime had renewed their offensive, driving forward inexorably as the Germans fell back grudgingly from one prepared position to another. It was in this section that much of the evidence of German destruction and barbarity was found.

At the same time, continuing activities of the U-boats also helped to crystallize Allied resolve. On the 10th, a submarine torpedoed a passenger steamer off the coast of Ireland with a loss of 300 lives. A few days later another U-boat sank an Irish mail boat taking the lives of 520 passengers, mostly women and children.

Affected by the public outcry over these incidents, President Wilson made clear in his reply to the second German note that the Allied military leaders would set the terms of the armistice, that there was no other way to deal with a government that persisted in illegal and inhumane acts. The note concluded that if the United States had to deal "with the military masters and the monarchial autocrats of Germany now, or if it is likely to have to deal with them later in regard to the international obligations of the German Empire, it must demand, not peace negotiations but surrender."

Confidence restored, Ludendorff called on his government to reject the terms; but the government was by this time listening to the voices of a disillusioned people, the noise of riots in the streets, and to the threat of Marxist revolution. On October 27 the kaiser dismissed Ludendorff, who repaired in disguise to Sweden, and events strode swiftly toward a climax. The German naval commander tried to take the High Seas Fleet to sea in a last bid for glory, but the crews mutinied and brought the ships back into port with revolutionary flags flying. Revolutionary councils formed among the soldiers in the trenches. Bulgaria in late September had already dropped out of the war; Turkey followed on October 30; Austria-Hungary on November 3. On November 6 Ludendorff's successor, General Wilhelm Groener, urged the government to conclude an armistice within three days or face chaos.

All along the front, meanwhile, the Allied armies had renewed their offensives in what became a general advance. In the far north two U.S. divisions—the 37th and 91st—fought with the Belgian-French-British force under the Belgian king. Haig's British troops entered their objective of Aulnoye on November 5, while the French armies maintained steady pressure against the German center.

Beginning on the first of November, the U.S. First Army renewed the attack with the V Corps in the center driving six miles the first day to take heights just south of the fourth German line near Barricourt. This feat assured success of the whole operation, for it prompted German withdrawal behind the Meuse. On November 5 the III Corps forced a crossing of the Meuse, and three days later American troops held high ground overlooking the city of Sedan, a few miles east of Mézières, and brought the lateral railroad under artillery fire. There the advance stopped as Marshal Foch shifted the American boundary eastward to allow the French the honor of retaking Sedan, scene of a disastrous French defeat in 1870.

The Meuse-Argonne was the greatest battle yet fought by the U.S. Army. Almost 1,250,000 American troops had participated during the course of the offensive. Casualties were high—120,000 of all types—but the results impressive. Until the last, this battle had worried German commanders most; unlike other sectors of the front, here they had little space short of a vital objective that they could afford to trade for time.

The German Surrender

Under pressure of continuing Allied attack and of public agitation at home, the Germans early on November 8 sent delegates to a railroad siding in the Compiègne Forest west of Soissons to discuss armistice terms. The next day the kaiser abdicated, fleeing to the Netherlands in exile, and the Germans proclaimed a republic.

Under terms of the armistice, the Germans were to withdraw from all occupied territory, including Alsace and Lorraine; retire all armies to the east bank of the Rhine; provide the Allies with bridgeheads beyond the Rhine; and relinquish specific amounts of military equipment that would preclude their continuing the war.

The fighting ended at the eleventh hour of the eleventh day of the eleventh month, 1918.

Men died right up to the last, but finally, after more than four grim years, it was over. Of the men of all nations in uniform, more than 8,500,000 died, and total casualties exceeded 37,500,000, a price that would forever invite criticism of the way commanders on both sides fought the war. American casualties alone totaled 320,710.

So ended the first adventure of the United States in departing from its traditional policy of noninvolvement in European affairs. That the nation could make such a decisive contribution in so short a time hardly could have been conceived in advance.

That there would be mistakes, blunders, shortcomings under such a rapid expansion and commitment was perhaps inevitable. Until mid-1918, for example, when separate replacement training camps were at last established, units both in the United States and overseas had to be broken up to provide replacements. This practice was damaging to morale and damaging too in that it sent many poorly trained men into the lines. So close did the American supply system in France come to breaking down that in the summer of 1918, under threat of intervention from Washington, Pershing had to exert special efforts to rescue it. Pershing himself was overburdened with command responsibilities—theater, line of communications, and tactical. The dependence on the Allies for air, artillery, and tank support, however inevitable in such a rapid deployment, did nothing for efficiency on the battlefield. On the home front some Americans vented their hostility on other Americans for no more valid reason than their ancestry.

Yet countless other things were done effectively. The nation handled conscription with minimum friction and without disruption of the economy. The Army expanded with almost incredible speed while still maintaining efficiency. The Navy performed invaluable service in defeating the submarine and, with British help, in getting the Army safely overseas. Although the war ended before American industry could demonstrate its full wartime potential, the record, with some exceptions, was impressive nevertheless.

Most important of all, the nation and its Army had provided a force that reached embattled Europe in time to rejuvenate flagging Allied fortunes and provide sufficient advantage to assure victory for the Allied side.

CHAPTER 19

Between World Wars

Soon after the armistice of November 1918 the War Department urged the Congress to authorize the establishment of a permanent Regular Army of nearly 600,000 and a three-month universal training system that would permit a quick expansion of this force to meet the requirements of a new major war. The Congress and American public opinion rejected these proposals. It was hard to believe that the defeat of Germany and the exhaustion of the other European powers did not guarantee that there would be no major war on land for years to come. Although the possibility of war with Japan was recognized, American leaders assumed that such a war, if it came, would be primarily naval in character. Indeed, the fundamental factor in the military policy of the United States during the next two decades was reliance on the United States Navy as the first line of national defense.

Another basic factor that determined the character of the Army between world wars was the decision of the United States not to join the League of Nations and therefore to reject participation in an active and co-operative world security system to maintain peace. The American people soon showed themselves unwilling to support an Army in being any larger than required to defend the continental United States and its overseas territories and possessions, to keep alive a knowledge of the military arts, and to train inexpensive and voluntary civilian components. Since the Army had huge stocks of matériel left over from its belated production for World War I, the principal concern of the War Department until the 1930's was manpower to fulfill these peacetime missions.

Demobilization

Planning for demobilization had begun less than a month before the armistice, since few in the United States had expected the war to end so quickly. When the fighting in Europe stopped, almost all officers and men in the Army became eligible for discharge. The War Department had to decide how to muster out these men as rapidly and equitably as possible without unduly disrupting the national economy, while at the same time maintaining an effective force for occupation and other postwar duties. It decided in favor of the traditional method of demobilization by units as the one best calculated to achieve these ends. Units in the United States were moved to thirty demobilization centers located throughout the country, so that men after processing could be discharged near their homes. Units overseas were brought back just as rapidly as shipping space could be found for them, processed through debarkation centers operated by the Transportation Service, and then sent to the demobilization centers for discharge. In practice the unit system was supplemented by a great many individual discharges and by the release of certain occupational groups, notably railroad workers and anthracite coal miners.

In the first full month of demobilization the Army released about 650,000 officers and men, and within nine months it demobilized nearly 3,250,000 without seriously disturbing the American economy. A demobilization of war industry and disposal of surplus matériel paralleled the release of men, but the War Department kept a large reserve of weapons for peacetime or new emergency use. Despite the lack of much advance planning demobilization worked reasonably well. The Army was concerned at the outset because it had no authority to enlist men to replace those discharged. A law of February 28, 1919, permitted enlistments in the Regular Army for either one or three years; and by the end of the year the active Army, reduced to a strength of about 19,000 officers and 205,000 enlisted men, was again a Regular volunteer force.

Immediate Duties

At home during 1919 and 1920 Army forces continued the guard on the border of Mexico required by revolutionary disturbances in that country. Because of the lack of National Guard forces (not yet reorganized) the active Army until the summer of 1921 also had to supply troops on numerous occasions to help suppress domestic disorders, chiefly arising out of labor disputes and race conflicts in a restless postwar America.

Abroad, a newly activated United States Third Army moved into Germany on December 1, 1918, to occupy a segment of territory between Luxembourg and the Rhine River around Coblenz. As many as nine divisions participated in the German occupation during the spring of 1919. Similarly, an Army regiment sent to Italy before the end of hostilities participated for four months in the occupation of Austria. In Germany, American troops had no unusual difficulties with the populace, and soon after the peace conference ended in May 1919 the occupation forces were rapidly reduced. They numbered about 15,000 at the beginning of 1920. After rejecting the Treaty of Versailles the United States remained technically at war with Germany until the summer of 1921, when a separate peace was signed. Thereafter, the occupying force was gradually withdrawn, and the last thousand troops left for home on January 24, 1923.

Revolutionary turmoil in Soviet Russia induced President Wilson in August 1918 to direct Army participation in expeditions of United States and Allied forces that penetrated the Murmansk-Archangel region of European Russia and into Siberia via Vladivostock. The north Russian force, containing about 5,000 American troops under British command, suffered heavy casualties while guarding war supplies and communication lines before being withdrawn in June 1919. The Siberian force of about 10,000 under Maj. Gen. William S. Graves had many trying experiences in attempting to rescue Czech troops and in curbing Japanese expansionist tendencies between August 1918 and April 1920. Together these two forces incurred about as many combat casualties as the Army expeditionary force of similar size had sustained in Cuba in 1898. After the withdrawals from Germany and **Russia,** the only Army forces stationed on foreign soil until 1941 were the garrison of about 1,000 maintained at Tientsin, China, from 1912 until 1938, and a force of similar strength dispatched from the Philippines to Shanghai for five months' duty in 1932. The Marine Corps rather than the Army provided the other small foreign garrisons and expeditionary forces required after World War I, particularly in the Caribbean area.

Reorganization Under the National Defense Act of 1920

After many months of careful consideration, Congress passed a sweeping amendment of the National Defense Act of 1916. The new National Defense Act of June 4, 1920, which governed the organization and regulation of the Army until 1950, has been widely acknowledged to be one of the most constructive pieces of military legislation ever adopted in the United States. It rejected the theory of an expansible Regular Army urged by Army leaders since the days of John C. Calhoun. Instead, it established the Army of the United States as an organization of three components, the professional Regular Army, the civilian National Guard, and the civilian Organized Reserves (Officers' and Enlisted Reserve Corps). Each component was to be so regulated in peacetime that it could contribute its appropriate share of troops in a war emergency. In effect the act acknowledged the actual practice of the United States throughout its history of maintaining a standing peacetime force too small to be expanded to meet the needs of a great war, and therefore necessarily of depending on a new Army of civilian soldiers for large mobilizations. In contrast to earlier practice, the training of civilian components now became a major peacetime task of the Regular Army, and principally for this reason the Army was authorized a maximum officer strength of 17,726—more than three times the actual officer strength of the Regular Army before World War I. At least half of the new permanent officers were to be chosen from among non-Regulars who had served during the war. The act also provided that officer promotions, except for doctors and chaplains, were henceforth to be made from a single list, a step that equalized opportunity for advancement throughout most of the Army. The Regular Army was authorized a maximum enlisted strength of 280,000, but the actual enlisted as well as officer strength would depend on the amount of money voted in annual appropriations.

The new defense act also authorized the Army to continue all of its arm and service branches established before 1917, and to add three new branches, the Air Service, the Chemical Warfare Service, and a Finance Department, the first two reflecting new combat techniques demonstrated in the late war. The Tank Corps of World War I, representing another new technique, was absorbed by the Infantry. The act specifically charged the War Department with mobilization planning and preparation for the event of war. It assigned the military aspects of this responsibility to the Chief of Staff and the General Staff and the planning and supervision of industrial procurement to the Assistant Secretary of War.

World War I experience both in Washington and in France had greatly strengthened the position and authority of the General Staff. When General Pershing became Chief of Staff in 1921 he reorganized the War Department General Staff on the model of his wartime General Headquarters staff in France, to include five divisions: G-1 dealing with personnel, G-2 with intelligence, G-3 with training and operations, G-4 with supply, and a new War Plans Division that dealt with strategic planning and related preparations for the event of war. It was the War Plans Division that helped to draft "color" plans for the event of war with individual nations (as ORANGE, for war with Japan), and it was also planned that the staff of the War Plans Division would provide the nucleus for any new wartime General Headquarters established to direct operations. The General Staff divisions assisted the Chief of Staff in his supervision of the military branches of the War Department and of the field forces. The principal organizational change thereafter in the 1920's came in 1926 with the establishment of the Air Corps as an equal combat arm and with provision for its enlargement and modernization.

The field forces in the continental United States were put under the command and administration of nine corps areas approximately equal in population, and those overseas in Panama, Hawaii, and the Philippines under departments with similar authority. The division rather than the regiment became the basic Army unit, especially in mobilization planning, and each corps area was allocated 6 infantry divisions—1 Regular Army, 2 National Guard, and 3 Reserve. In addition, a cavalry division patrolled the Mexican border, and in Pacific outposts Army mobile units were organized as separate Hawaiian and Philippine Divisions. The defense act had contemplated a higher organization of divisions into corps and armies, but no such tactical organizations existed in fact for many years.

Education for and within the Army between world wars received far greater attention than ever before. This situation reflected the emphasis in the National Defense Act on preparedness in peacetime as well as the increasing complexity of modern war. The United States Military Academy and the Reserve Officers' Training Corps program furnished most of the basic schooling for new officers. Thirty-one special service schools provided branch training. These branch schools trained officers and enlisted men of the civilian components besides those of the Regular Army, and furnished training through extension courses as well as on location. Three general service schools provided the capstone of the Army educational system. The oldest, located at Fort Leavenworth, Kansas, and known after 1928 as the Command and General Staff School, provided officers with the requisite training for divisional command and General Staff positions. In Washington the Army War College and, after 1924, the Army Industrial College trained senior officers of demonstrated ability for the most responsible command and staff positions. In establishing the Industrial College the Army recognized the high importance of logistical training for the conduct of modern warfare.

Regular Army Strength and Support

When the National Defense Act was adopted in June 1920, the Regular Army numbered about 200,000—about two-thirds the maximum strength authorized in the act. In January 1921 Congress directed a reduction in enlisted strength to 175,000, and in June 1921 to 150,000, as soon as possible. A year later Congress limited the active Army to 12,000 commissioned officers and 125,000 enlisted men, not including the 7,000 or so in the Philippine Scouts, and Regular Army strength was stabilized at about this level until 1936. Appropriations for the military expenses of the War Department also became stabilized during this same period, amounting to about $300 million a year. This was about half of what a full implementation of the National Defense Act had been estimated to cost. The United States during these years spent rather less on its

Army than on its Navy, in line with the national policy of depending on the Navy as the first line of defense. War Department officials, especially in the early 1920's, repeatedly expressed alarm over the failure of Congress to appropriate enough money to carry out the terms of the National Defense Act. They believed that it was essential for minimum defense needs to have a Regular Army with an enlisted strength of 150,000 or (after the Air Corps Act of 1926) of 165,000. As Chief of Staff Douglas MacArthur pointed out in 1933, the United States ranked seventeenth among the nations in active Army strength; but foreign observers rated its newly equipped Army Air Corps second or third in actual power.

In equipment the Air Corps offered a marked contrast to the rest of the Army. For almost two decades ground units had to get along as best they could with weapons left over from World War I. The Army was well aware that these old weapons were becoming increasingly obsolete, and that new ones were needed. For example, General MacArthur in 1933 described the Army's tanks (except for a dozen experimental models) as completely useless for employment against any modern unit on the battlefield. Although handicapped by very small appropriations for research and development, Army arsenals and laboratories worked continuously during the 1920's and 1930's to devise new items of equipment and to improve old ones. Service boards, links between branch schools and headquarters, tested pilot models and determined the doctrine for their employment so that it could be incorporated in training manuals. But not much new equipment was forthcoming for ground units in the field until Army appropriations began to rise in 1936.

For a number of years only about one-fourth of the officers and one-half of the enlisted men of the Regular Army were available for assignment to tactical units in the continental United States. Many units existed only on paper; almost all had only skeletonized strength. Instead of nine infantry divisions, there were actually three. In May 1927 one of these divisions, a cavalry brigade, and 200 planes participated in a combined arms maneuver in Texas, but for the most part Regular units had to train as battalions or companies. The continued dispersion of skeletonized divisions, brigades, and regiments among a large number of posts, many of them relics of the Indian wars, was a serious hindrance to the training of Regulars, although helpful in training the civilian components. Efforts to abandon small posts continued to meet with stubborn opposition from local interests and their elected representatives in Congress. In the infantry, for example, in 1932 the 24 regiments available in the United States for field service were spread among 45 posts, with a battalion or less at 34. Most of the organic transportation of these units was of World War I vintage, and the Army did not have the money to concentrate them for training by other means. Nor were there large posts in which they could be housed. The best training of larger units occurred overseas in the fairly sizable garrisons maintained by the Army in Hawaii, the Philippines, and Panama. In the early 1930's the great depression had the immediate effect of cuts in appropriations and pay that further reduced the readiness of Army units for military service.

Civilian Components

One of the major purposes of the National Defense Act had been to promote the integration of the Regular Army and the civilian components by establishing uniformity in training and professional standards. While in practice this purpose fell considerably short of full realization, nevertheless the new Army system saw an unprecedented amount of civilian military training. This training brought the Regular out of his traditional isolation from the civilian community, and it acquainted large numbers of civilians with the problems and views of the professional soldier. All together, the civilian components and the groups in training that contributed to their ranks had an average strength of about 400,000 between the wars. The end result of the civilian training program was to be an orderly and effective mobilization of National Guard and Reserve elements into the active Army in 1940 and 1941.

The absorption of the National Guard into the Army during World War I had left the states without any Guard units after the armistice. The act of 1920 contemplated a National Guard of 436,000, but its actual peacetime strength became stabilized at about 180,000. This force relieved the Regular Army of any duty in curbing domestic disturbances within the states from 1921 until 1941, and stood ready for immediate induction into the active Army whenever necessary. The War Department, in addition to supplying Regular officers for instruction and large quantities of surplus World War I matériel for equipment, applied about one-tenth of its military budget to the support of the Guard in the years between wars. Guardsmen engaged in 48 armory drills and 15 days of field training each year. Though not comparable to active Army units in readiness for war, the increasingly federalized Guard was better trained in 1939 than it had been when mobilized for Mexican border duty in 1916. Numerically, the National Guard was the largest component of the Army of the United States between 1922 and 1939.

In addition to the Guard, the civilian community had of course a very large number of trained officers and enlisted men after World War I, which assured the nation of a natural reservoir of manpower for the Army for a decade or more after the war. Only a very few of these men joined the Enlisted Reserve Corps, but large numbers of officers maintained their commissions in the Officers' Reserve Corps through five-year periods during which they received further training through school and extension courses and in brief tours of active duty. The composition of the Officers' Reserve Corps, which numbered about 100,000 between the wars, gradually changed as its ranks were refilled by men newly commissioned after training in the Reserve Officers' Training Corps (ROTC) or the Citizens' Military Training Camp (CMTC) programs.

The ROTC program began long before the passage of the National Defense Act, in military colleges of which the first was Norwich University, established in 1819, in state land-grant schools set up under the Morrill Act of 1862, and in a number of private colleges and universities. For several decades before World War I the Army detailed annually up to 100 Regular officers as instructors, and supplied equipment, for college military training; but until the defense acts of 1916 and 1920 the program was only loosely associated with the Army's own needs. The new dependence on the civilian components for Army expansion, and the establishment of the Officers' Reserve Corps as a vehicle to retain college men in the Army of the United States after graduation, gave impetus to a greatly enlarged and better regulated ROTC program after 1920. By 1928 there were ROTC units in 325 schools, about 225 of them being senior units enrolling 85,000 students in colleges and universities. Regular Army officers detailed as professors of military science instructed these units, and about 6,000 men graduating from them were commissioned each year in the Officers' Reserve Corps. This inexpensive program paid rich dividends when the nation again mobilized to meet the threat of war in 1940 and 1941.

The Army's CMTC program, a very modest alternative to the system of universal military training proposed in 1919, provided about 30,000 young volunteers with four weeks of military training in summer camps each year. Those who completed four years of CMTC training became eligible for Reserve commissions, the CMTC thus providing another (though much smaller) source for the rolls of the Officers' Reserve Corps and the National Guard.

Domestic Employment

The most notable domestic use of Regular troops in twenty years of peace happened in the nation's capital in the summer of 1932. Some thousands of "Bonus Marchers" remained in Washington after the adjournment of Congress dashed their hopes for immediate payment of a bonus for military service in

World War I. On July 28, when marshals and police tried to evict one group encamped near the Capitol, a riot with some bloodshed occurred. Thereupon President Herbert C. Hoover called upon the Army to intervene. A force of about 600—cavalrymen and infantrymen with a few tanks—advanced to the scene under the leadership of Chief of Staff MacArthur in person, two other generals, and, among junior officers, two whose names would in due course become much more familiar, Majors Dwight D. Eisenhower and George S. Patton, Jr. The troops cleaned up the situation near the Capitol without firing a shot, and then proceeded with equal efficiency to clear out all of the marchers from the District of Columbia. From a military point of view the Army had performed an unpleasant task in exemplary fashion, and with only a few minor injuries to participants; but the use of military force against civilians, most of them veterans, tarnished the Army's public image and helped to defeat the administration in the forthcoming election.

Aside from the bonus incident, the most conspicuous employment of the Army within the United States during these years of peace was in a variety of nonmilitary tasks that only the Army had the resources and the organization to tackle quickly. In floods and blizzards and hurricanes it was the Army that was first on the spot with cots, blankets, and food. In another direction, Army Engineers expanded their work on rivers and harbors for the improvement of navigation and flood control. For four months in 1934 the Air Corps, on orders from President Franklin D. Roosevelt, took over the carrying of air mail for the Post Office Department with somewhat tragic consequences, since the corps was wholly unprepared for such an undertaking.

The most important and immediately disruptive nonmilitary duty began in 1933, after Congress passed an act that put large numbers of jobless young men into reforestation and other reclamation work. President Roosevelt directed the Army to mobilize these men and thereafter to run their camps without in any way making the Civilian Conservation Corps (CCC) program a military project in disguise. Within seven weeks the Army mobilized 310,000 men into 1,315 camps, a mobilization more rapid and orderly than any in the Army's history. For more than a year the War Department had to keep about 3,000 Regular officers and many noncommissioned officers assigned to this task, and in order to do so the Army had to strip tactical units of their leadership. Unit training was brought to a standstill, and the readiness of units for immediate military employment was almost destroyed. In the second half of 1934 the War Department called a large number of Reserve officers to active duty to replace the Regulars, and, by August 1935, 9,300 Reserve officers (not counted in active Army strength) were serving with the CCC. A good many of them continued in this service until 1941, but the Army never wanted to insert military training into the program, in part because the CCC camps were so small and so isolated. Despite its initial and serious interference with normal Army operations, in the long run the CCC program had a beneficial effect on military preparedness. It furnished many thousands of Reserve officers with valuable training, and it gave nonmilitary but disciplined training to many hundreds of thousands of young men who were to become soldiers and sailors in World War II.

National and Military Policy

For fifteen years, from 1921 to 1936, the American people, their representatives in Congress, and their Presidents thought that the United States could and should avoid future wars with other major powers, except possibly Japan. They believed the nation could achieve this goal by maintaining a minimum of defensive military strength, avoiding entangling commitments with Old World nations, and yet using American good offices to promote international peace and the limitation of armaments. The United States took the initiative in 1921 in calling a conference in Washington to consider the limitation of armaments. The resulting naval treaty of 1922 temporarily checked a race for naval supremacy. It froze capital ship strengths of the United States, Great Britain, and Japan in a 5–5–3 ratio for a number of years. This ratio and restrictions on new naval base construction assured that neither the United States nor Japan could operate offensively in the Pacific as long as treaty provisions were respected. In effect these provisions also meant that it would be impossible for the United States to defend the Philippines against a Japanese attack. On the other hand, a general agreement among the western nations and Japan to maintain the *status quo* in the Pacific and in China offered fair assurance against a Japanese war of aggression, but only as long as the western powers did not themselves become embroiled in the European-Atlantic area.

In 1928 the United States and France joined in drafting the Pact of Paris, which renounced war as an instrument of national policy. Thereafter, the United States announced to the world that, if other powers did likewise, it would limit its armed forces to those necessary to maintain internal order and defend national territory against aggression and invasion. In 1931 the chief of the Army's War Plans Division advised the Chief of Staff that the defense of frontiers was precisely the cardinal task for which the Army had been organized, equipped, and trained. There was no real conflict between national policy and the Army's conception of its mission during the 1920's and early 1930's. But in the Army's opinion the government and the American public, in their antipathy to war, failed to support even minimum needs for national defense.

Across the oceans, the clouds of war began to form again in 1931 when the Japanese seized Manchuria and then defied the diplomatic efforts of the League of Nations and the United States to pry them loose. In 1933 Japan quit the League and a year later announced that it would no longer be bound by the naval limitation treaties after they expired in 1936. In Europe, Adolf Hitler came to power in Germany in 1933, and by 1936 Nazi Germany had denounced the Treaty of Versailles, embarked on rearmament, and occupied the demilitarized Rhineland. Hitler's partner in dictatorship, Italy's Benito Mussolini, began his career of aggression by attacking Ethiopia in 1935. A revolution in Spain in 1936 not only produced a third dictatorship but also an extended war that became a proving ground for World War II. The neutrality acts passed by the Congress between 1935 and 1937 were a direct response to these European developments, and the United States tried to mend its international position in other ways by opening diplomatic relations with Soviet Russia in 1933, by promising eventual independence to the Philippines in 1934, and by liquidating its protectorates in the Caribbean area and pursuing the policy of the Good Neighbor toward Latin America generally.

No quick changes in American military policy followed. But beginning in 1935 the armed forces received substantially larger appropriations that permitted them to improve their readiness for action. Army improvements during the next three years reflected not only the increasingly critical international situation but also the careful planning of the War Department during General Douglas MacArthur's tour as Chief of Staff from 1930 to 1935. His recommendations led to a reorganization of the combat forces and a modest increase in their size, and were accompanied by more realistic planning for using the manpower and industrial might of the United States for war, if that should become necessary.

The Army Strengthened

The central objective of the Chief of Staff's recommendations had been to establish a small hard-hitting force ready for emergency use. In line with this objective the Army wanted to mechanize and motorize its Regular combat units as soon as it could, and to fill their ranks so that they could be trained effectively. The Army also needed new organizations to control training of the larger ground and air units and teams of combined arms in peacetime and to command them if war came. For these purposes the War Department between 1932 and 1935 created four army headquarters and a General Headquarters Air Force in the continental United States under command of the Chief of Staff. Under these headquarters, beginning in the summer of 1935, Regular and National Guard divisions and other units trained together each year in summer maneuvers and other exercises, including joint exercises with the Navy. In the same year Congress authorized the Regular Army to increase its enlisted strength to the long-sought goal of 165,000. This increase was accompanied during the following years by substantially greater expenditures for equipment and housing, so that by 1938 the Regular Army was considerably stronger and far readier for action than it had been in the early 1930's. But in the meantime the strength and power of foreign armies had been increasing even more rapidly.

In the slow rebuilding of the 1930's, the Army concentrated on equipping and training its combat units for mobile warfare rather than for the static warfare that had characterized operations on the Western Front in World War I. Through research it managed to acquire some new weapons that promised increased firepower and mobility as soon as equipment could be produced in quantity. In 1936 the Army adopted the Garand semiautomatic rifle to replace the 1903 Springfield, and during the 1930's it perfected the mobile 105-mm. howitzer that became the principal divisional artillery piece of World War II and developed light and medium tanks that were much faster than the lumbering models of World War I. In units, horse power gave way to motor power as rapidly as new vehicles could be acquired. To increase the maneuverability of its principal ground unit, the division, the Army decided after field tests to triangularize the infantry division by reducing the number of its infantry regiments from four to three, and to make it more mobile by using motor transportation only. The planned wartime strength of the new division was to be little more than half the size of its World War I counterpart.

Modern war is so complex and modern armies are so demanding in equipment that industrial mobilization for war must precede the large-scale employment of manpower by at least two years if a war is to be fought effectively. The Army's Industrial Mobilization Plan of 1930 established the basic principles for harnessing the nation's economic strength to war needs, and revisions of this plan to 1939 improved the pattern. Manpower planning culminated in the Protective Mobilization Plan of 1937. Under this plan the first step was to be the induction of the National Guard, to provide with the Regular Army an Initial Protective Force of about 400,000. The Navy and this defensive force would then protect the nation while the Army engaged in an orderly expansion to planned strengths of one, two, and four million, as necessary. Along with manpower planning there evolved for the first time prior to actual war a definite training plan, which included the location, size, and scheduling for replacement training centers, unit training centers, and schools, detailed unit and individual training programs, and the production of a variety of training manuals. While these plans were to help guide the mobilization that began in the summer of 1940, they had their faults. As it turned out the planners set their sights too low. They assumed a maximum mobilization of World War I dimension, whereas World War II was to call forth more than twice as many men and proportionately an even greater industrial effort for the Army. The plans also assumed until 1939 that mobilization for war would come more or less suddenly, instead of relatively slowly during many months of nominal peace.

The Beginnings of World War II

The German annexation of Austria in March 1938 followed by the Czech crisis in September of the same year awakened the United States and the other democratic nations to the imminence of another great world conflict. The new conflict had already begun in the Far East when Japan had invaded China in 1937. After Germany seized Czechoslovakia in March 1939, war in Europe became inevitable, since Hitler had no intention of stopping with that move and Great Britain and France for their part decided that they must fight rather than yield anything more to Hitler. In August Germany made a deal with the Soviet Union, which provided for a partition of Poland and a Soviet free hand in Finland and the northern Baltic states. Then on September 1, 1939, Germany invaded Poland. When France and Great Britain responded by declaring war on Germany, they embarked on a course that could not lead to victory without aid from the United States. Yet an overwhelming majority of the American people wanted to stay out of the new war if they could, and this sentiment necessarily governed the initial responses of the United States Government and of its armed forces to the perilous international situation.

President Roosevelt and his advisers, being fully aware of the danger, had launched the nation on a limited preparedness campaign at the beginning of 1939. By then the technological improvement of the airplane had introduced a new factor into the military calculations of the United States. The moment was approaching when it would be feasible for a hostile Old World power to

establish air bases in the Western Hemisphere from which the Panama Canal—
then the key to American naval defense—or the continental United States
itself might be attacked. Such a development would destroy the oceanic security
that the American nation had so long enjoyed. The primary emphasis in 1939
was therefore on increasing the striking power of the Army Air Corps. At
the same time Army and Navy officers collaborated in drafting the RAINBOW
plans that superseded existing color plans and thereafter helped to guide the
development and conduct of the American armed forces toward the war. A
month after the European war began the President, in formally approving the
RAINBOW 1 plan, changed the avowed national military policy from one of
guarding the United States and its possessions only to one of hemisphere
defense, and the policy of hemisphere defense was to be the focus of Army
plans and actions until the end of 1940.

Immediately after the European war started the President proclaimed a
limited national emergency and authorized increases in Regular Army and
National Guard enlisted strengths to 227,000 and 235,000, respectively. He also
proclaimed American neutrality in the war, but at his urging Congress presently
gave indirect support to the western democracies by ending the prohibition on
munitions sales to nations at war embodied in the Neutrality Act of 1937.
British and French orders for munitions in turn helped to prepare American
industry for the large-scale war production that was to come. When the quick
destruction of Poland was followed by a lull in the war, the tempo of America's
own defense preparations slackened. The Army concentrated on making its
Regular force ready for emergency action by providing it with full and modern
equipment as quickly as possible, and in April 1940 by engaging 70,000 troops
in the first genuine corps and army training maneuvers in American military
history. How adequate the Army was depended on the survival of France and
Great Britain. The successful German seizure of Denmark and Norway in
April 1940 followed by the quick defeat of the Low Countries and France and
the grave threat to Great Britain forced the United States in June to adopt a
new and greatly enlarged program for defense, for it then looked as if the
nation might eventually have to face the aggressors of the Old World almost
alone.

The Prewar Mobilization

Under the leadership of Chief of Staff General George C. Marshall and,
after July, of Secretary of War Henry L. Stimson, the Army embarked in the
summer of 1940 on a large expansion designed to protect the United States and
the rest of the Western Hemisphere against any hostile forces that might be

unleashed from the Old World. Army expansion was matched by a naval program designed to give the United States a two-ocean Navy strong enough to deal simultaneously with the Japanese in the Pacific and the naval strength that Germany and its new war partner, Italy, might acquire in the Atlantic if they defeated Great Britain. Both expansion programs had the overwhelming support of the American people, who though still strongly opposed to entering the war were now convinced that the danger to the United States was very real. Congressional appropriations between May and October 1940 reflected this conviction. The Army received more than $8 billion for its needs during the succeeding year—a sum greater than

GENERAL MARSHALL

what had been granted for the support of its military activities during the preceding twenty years. The munitions program approved for the Army on June 30, 1940, called for procurement by October 1941 of all items needed to equip and maintain a 1,200,000-man force, including a greatly enlarged and modernized Army Air Corps, and by September the War Department was planning to create an Army of a million and a half as soon as possible.

To fill the ranks of this new Army, Congress on August 27 approved induction of the National Guard into federal service and the calling up of the Organized Reserves. Then it approved the first peacetime draft of untrained civilian manpower in the nation's history, in the Selective Service and Training Act of September 14, 1940. Units of the National Guard, and selectees and the Reserve officers to train them, entered service as rapidly as the Army could construct camps to house them. During the last six months of 1940 the active Army more than doubled in strength, and by mid-1941 it achieved its planned strength of one and a half million officers and men.

A new organization, General Headquarters, took charge of training the Army in July 1940. In the same month the Army established a separate Armored Force, and subsequently Antiaircraft and Tank Destroyer Commands, which, with the Infantry, Field Artillery, Coast Artillery, and Cavalry, broadened the front of ground combat arms to seven. The existing branch schools and a new Armored Force School concentrated during 1940 and 1941 on improving the fitness of National Guard and Reserve officers for active duty, and in early 1941 the War Department established officer candidate schools to train men selected from the ranks for junior leadership positions. In October 1940 the four armies assumed command of ground units in the continental United States, and thereafter trained them under the supervision of General Headquarters. The corps area commands became administrative and service organizations. Major overseas garrisons were strengthened, and the Army established new commands to supervise the garrisoning of Puerto Rico and Alaska where there had been almost no Regular Army troops for many years. In June 1941 the War Department established the Army Air Forces to train and administer air units in the United States. In July it began the transformation of General Headquarters into an operational post for General Marshall as Commanding General of the Field Forces. By the autumn of 1941 the Army had 27 infantry, 5 armored, and 2 cavalry divisions, 35 air groups, and a host of supporting units in training in the continental United States. But most of these units were still unready for action, in part because the United States had shared so much of its old and new military equipment with the nations that were actively fighting the Axis triumvirate of Germany, Italy, and Japan.

Toward War

On the eve of France's defeat in June 1940 President Roosevelt had directed the transfer or diversion of large stocks of Army World War I weapons, and of ammunition and aircraft, to both France and Great Britain, and after France fell these munitions helped to replace Britain's losses in the evacuation of its expeditionary force from Dunkerque. More aid to Britain was forthcoming in September when the United States agreed to exchange fifty over-age destroyers for offshore Atlantic bases, and the President announced that henceforth production of heavy bombers would be shared equally with the British. An open collaboration with Canada from August 1940 onward led to a strong support of the Canadian war effort, Canada having followed Great Britain into war in September 1939. The foreign aid program culminated in the Lend-Lease Act of March 1941, which swept away the pretense of American neutrality by openly avowing the intention of the United States to become an "arsenal of democracy" against aggression. Prewar foreign aid was nonetheless a measure of self defense; its fundamental purpose was to help contain the military might of the Axis powers until the United States could complete its own protective mobilization.

Thus by early 1941 the focus of American policy had shifted from hemisphere defense to a limited participation in the war. Indeed by then it appeared to Army and Navy leaders and to President Roosevelt that the United States might be drawn into full participation in the not too distant future. Assuming the probability of simultaneous operations in the Pacific and Atlantic, they agreed that Germany was the greater menace and that if the United States did enter the war it ought to concentrate on the defeat of Germany first. This principle was accepted in staff conversations between American and British military representatives in Washington ending on March 29, 1941.

After these conversations the Army and Navy adjusted the most comprehensive of the prewar planning concepts, RAINBOW 5, to accord with American military preparations and actions during the remaining months of 1941 before the Japanese attack. During these months the trend was steadily toward American participation in the war against Germany. In April the President authorized an active naval patrol of the western half of the Atlantic Ocean. In May the United States decided to accept responsibility for the development and operation of military air routes across the North Atlantic via Greenland and across the South Atlantic via Brazil. During May it also appeared to the President and his military advisers that a German drive through Spain and Portugal to northwestern Africa and its adjacent islands might be imminent. This prospect together with German naval activity in the North Atlantic led the President to proclaim an unlimited national emergency, and to direct the Army and Navy to prepare an expeditionary force to be sent to the Azores as a step toward blocking a German advance toward the South Atlantic. Then, in early June, the President learned that Hitler was preparing to attack the Soviet Union, a move that would divert German military power away from the Atlantic, at least for the time being.

The Germans invaded the Soviet Union on June 22, and three days later Army troops landed in Greenland to protect it against German attack and to build air bases for the air ferry route across the North Atlantic. Earlier in June the President had also decided that Americans should relieve British troops guarding Iceland, and the initial contingent of American forces reached there in early July, to be followed by a sizable Army expeditionary force in September. In August the President and British Prime Minister Winston Churchill met in Newfoundland and drafted the Atlantic Charter, which defined the general terms of a just peace for the world. By October the United States Navy was fully engaged in convoy-escort duties in the western reaches of the North Atlantic, and Navy ships, with some assistance from Army aircraft, were joining with British and Canadian forces in warring against German submarines. In November Congress voted to repeal prohibitions against the arming of American merchant vessels and their entry into combat zones, and the stage was set, as Prime Minister Churchill noted on November 9, for "constant fighting in the Atlantic between German and American ships."

Apparently all of the overt American moves in 1941 toward involvement in the war against Germany had solid backing in American public opinion, with only an increasingly small though vociferous minority criticizing the President for the nation's departures from neutrality. But the American people were still not prepared for an open declaration of war.

As the United States moved toward war in the Atlantic area, American policy toward Japan also stiffened. Although the United States wanted to avoid a two-front war, it was not ready to do so by surrendering vital areas or interests to the Japanese as the price of peace. When in late July 1941 the Japanese moved large forces into what became South Vietnam, the United States responded by freezing Japanese assets and cutting off oil shipments to Japan. At the same time the War Department recalled General MacArthur to active duty to command both United States and Philippine Army forces in the Far East and it also decided to send Army reinforcements to the Philippines, including heavy bombers intended to dissuade the Japanese from making any more southward moves. For their part the Japanese, while continuing to negotiate with the United States, tentatively decided in September to embark on a war of conquest in Southeast Asia and the Indies as soon as possible, and to try to immobilize American naval opposition by an opening air strike against the great American naval base of Pearl Harbor in Hawaii. When intensive last-minute negotiations in November failed to produce any accommodation, the Japanese made their decision for war irrevocable.

The Japanese attack of December 7, 1941 on Pearl Harbor and the Philippines at once ended the division of American opinion toward participation in the war, and America went to war with a unanimity of popular support that was unprecedented in the military history of the United States. This was also the first time in its history that the United States had entered a war with a large Army in being and an industrial system partially retooled for war. The Army numbered 1,643,477, and it was ready to defend the Western Hemisphere against invasion. But it was not ready to take part in large-scale operations across the oceans. Many months would pass before the United States could launch even limited offensives.

CHAPTER 20

World War II: The Defensive Phase

About one o'clock in Washington on the afternoon of December 7, 1941, the first news of the Japanese attack on Pearl Harbor, Hawaii, reached the War Department. The news came as a shock, even as the attack itself had come. It caught by surprise not only the American people at large, who learned of the attack a short while later, but also their leaders, including the very officers who had earlier been so much concerned over the possibility of just such an attack. One explanation is that these officers and their political superiors were momentarily expecting the Japanese to use all their forces against weakly held British and Dutch positions in the Far East (and probably, but not certainly, against the Philippines). But without warning in the early morning of December 7, powerful carrier-borne air forces had smashed the U.S. Pacific Fleet at anchor in Pearl Harbor. The same day (December 8 in the Philippines), about noon, Formosa-based bombers caught the bulk of the U.S. Far East Air Force lined up on Clark and Iba fields not far from Manila in central Luzon and virtually destroyed it. For the second time within a quarter-century, Americans found themselves fully involved in a war they had not sought—this time in the first truly global conflict.

The Outbreak of War: Action and Reaction

The attack on Pearl Harbor was one of the most brilliant tactical feats of the war. From 6 carriers which had advanced undetected to a position 200 miles north of Oahu, some 350 aircraft came in through the morning mist, achieving complete tactical surprise. They bombed and strafed the neatly aligned Army planes on Hickam and Wheeler Fields, as well as Navy and Marine Corps aircraft, and they carefully singled out as targets major units of the Navy's battle force at anchor in the harbor. Fortunately, the fleet's 3 carriers were away at the time, and the attackers failed to hit the oil tanks and naval repair shops on shore. But the blow was devastating enough. About 170 aircraft were destroyed and 102 damaged, all 8 battleships were sunk or badly damaged, besides many other vessels, and total casualties came to about 3,400, including 2,402 service men and civilians killed. Japanese losses were about 49 aircraft and 5 midget submarines. In an astonishing achievement, the enemy managed to apply in one shattering operation a combination of the principles of surprise, objective, mass, security, and maneuver. In its larger strategic context, the Pearl Harbor attack also exemplifies the principles of the offensive and economy of force. The joint Congressional committee investigating the attack called it the "greatest military and naval disaster in our Nation's history."

These two attacks—on Pearl Harbor and on the Philippines—effectively crippled American striking power in the Pacific. The Philippines and other American possessions in the western Pacific were isolated, their loss a foregone conclusion. The Hawaiian Islands and Alaska lay open to invasion; the Panama Canal and the cities, factories, and shipyards of the west coast were vulnerable to raids from the sea and air. Months would pass before the United States could regain a capacity for even the most limited kind of offensive action against its oriental enemy. As Japanese forces moved swiftly southward against the Philippines, Malaya, and the Netherlands Indies, Japan's Axis partners, Germany and Italy, promptly declared war on the United States, thus ending the uncertainty as to whether the United States would become a full-fledged belligerent in the European war. For the first time in its history, the United States was embarked upon an all-out, two-front war.

Meanwhile Britain was battling to maintain its hold on the eastern Mediterranean region which lay athwart the historic lifeline to possessions and Commonwealth associates in the Far East. Late in 1940 small British forces based in Egypt gained important successes against Italian armies in Libya, and the Greeks in the winter of 1940–41 resoundingly defeated an invading Italian army and chased it back into Albania. But German armies quickly came to the aid of their Italian ally. In April 1941 the famous panzer divisions, supported by overwhelming air power, swept through the Balkans, crushing the Yugoslav and Greek armies, and a British expeditionary force hastily dispatched to aid the latter. The following month German airborne forces descended on the island of Crete and swamped British and Greek defenders in a spectacular, though costly, attack. In Libya a powerful German-Italian army under General Erwin Rommel drove the British back across the Egyptian border, isolating a large garrison in Tobruk and threatening the Nile Delta. Against these disasters Britain could count only the final expulsion of the Italians from the Red Sea area and of the Vichy French from Syria, the suppression of pro-German uprisings in Iraq, and the achievement of a precarious naval ascendancy in the eastern and western portions of the Mediterranean. During the remainder of

1941 the British gradually built up strength in eastern Libya, and late in the year they succeeded in relieving Tobruk and pushing Rommel back to his original starting point at El Agheila.

Since mid-1940 the military fortunes of the anti-Axis powers had declined as the European war expanded. Germany had crushed all its continental European opponents in the west, and then attempted to destroy Britain's air forces as a prelude to an invasion across the English Channel. In the air battles over Britain in August and September 1940 the Royal Air Force won a brilliant victory. But during the following winter and spring the waning threat of invasion had been replaced by the equally deadly and more persistent menace of economic strangulation. German aircraft pulverized Britain's ports and inland cities, while U-boats, surface raiders, and mines decimated shipping. By 1941 the imports on which the United Kingdom depended for existence had dwindled to less than two-thirds of their prewar volume, and the British people faced the prospect of ultimate starvation.

In June 1941, however, the storm center of the war had moved elsewhere. Only slightly delayed by the conquest of the Balkans, Hitler on June 22, 1941, hurled German might against the Soviet Union, the only remaining power on the European continent capable of challenging his dominance. By early December, when the onset of winter and stiffening Soviet resistance finally brought the advance to a halt, the German armies had driven to the suburbs of Moscow, inflicted huge losses on the Red Army, and occupied a vast expanse of European Russia embracing its most densely populated and industrialized regions. This, as it turned out, was the high tide of German success in World War II; Hitler, like Napoleon, was to meet disaster on the wind-swept plains of Russia. But in December 1941 few were willing to predict this outcome. British and United States leaders assembling in Washington at the end of that month to make plans for dealing with the crisis had to reckon with the probability that in the year to come, unless the Western Allies could somehow force Germany to divert substantial forces from the eastern front, the German steamroller would complete the destruction of the Soviet armies. Hitler would then be able, with the resources and enslaved peoples of all Europe at his feet, to throw his full power against the West.

American military leaders had already given thought to this grim prospect, and to the implications it held for America's role in the war. In the Victory Program, drawn up by the Army and Navy at the President's behest during the summer of 1941, the leaders of the two services had set forth in some detail the strategy and the means they considered necessary to win ultimate victory if, as they expected, Soviet Russia succumbed to the Axis onslaught. The strategy was the one laid down in the RAINBOW 5 war plan—wear Germany down by bombing, blockade, subversion, and limited offensives, while mobilizing the strength needed to invade the European continent and to defeat Germany on its own ground. Japan meanwhile would be contained by air and sea power, local defense forces, China's inexhaustible manpower, and the Soviet Union's Siberian divisions. With Germany out of the running, Japan's defeat or collapse would soon follow. As for the means, the United States would have to provide them in large part, for the British were already weary and their resources limited. The United States would serve not merely, to use the President's catchy phrase, as the "arsenal of democracy," supplying weapons to arm its allies, but also as the main source of the armies without which wars, above all this war, could not be won. Army leaders envisaged the eventual mobilization of 215 divisions, 61 of them armored, and 239 combat air groups, requiring a grand total, with supporting forces, of 8.8 million men. Five million of these would be hurled against the European Axis. It was emphasized that victory over the Axis Powers would require a maximum military effort and full mobilization of America's immense industrial resources.

Yet the Victory Program was merely an expression of professional military views, not a statement of national military policy. That policy, on the eve of Pearl Harbor, was still ostensibly hemisphere defense. The pace of rearmament and mobilization, in the summer and fall of 1941, was actually slowing down. Signs pointed to a policy of making the American contribution to the defeat of the Axis, as columnist Walter Lippmann put it, one "basically of Navy, Air, and manufacturing," something a great deal less than the all-out effort envisaged in the Victory Program. Public and Congressional sentiment, moreover, still clung to the hope that an immediate showdown with the Axis Powers could be avoided and that the country would not be forced into full belligerent participation in the war, as evidenced by a near defeat of the bill to extend Selective Service, continuation of a prohibition against sending selectees outside the Western Hemisphere, and apathetic public response to submarine attacks on American destroyers in September and October.

The Japanese attack on Pearl Harbor and the Philippines changed the picture. A wave of patriotic indignation over Japanese duplicity and brutality swept the country. Isolationism virtually evaporated as a public issue, and all parties closed ranks in support of the war effort. Indeed, in retrospect, despite the immediate tactical success the Japanese achieved at Pearl Harbor, that attack proved to be a great blunder for them, politically and strategically. The President, early in January, dramatized the magnitude of the effort now demanded by proclaiming a new set of production goals—60,000 airplanes in

1942 and 125,000 in 1943; 45,000 tanks in 1942 and 75,000 in 1943; 20,000 anti-aircraft guns in 1942 and 35,000 in 1943; half a million machine guns in 1942 and as many more in 1943; and 8 million deadweight tons of merchant shipping in 1942 and 10 million in 1943. Vanished were the two illusions that America could serve only as an arsenal of democracy, contributing weapons without the men to wield them, or, conversely, that the nation could rely solely on its own fighting forces, leaving other anti-Axis nations to shift for themselves. "We must not only provide munitions for our own fighting forces," Roosevelt advised Secretary of War Henry L. Stimson, "but vast quantities to be used against the enemy in every appropriate theater of war." A new Victory Program boosted the Army's ultimate mobilization goal to 10 million men, and the War Department planned to have 71 divisions and 115 combat air groups organized by the end of 1942, with a total of 3.6 million men under arms. As an Army planner had predicted back in the spring of 1941, the United States now seemed destined to become "the final reserve of the democracies both in manpower and munitions."

Late in December 1941 President Roosevelt and Prime Minister Churchill met with their advisers in Washington (the ARCADIA Conference) to establish the bases of coalition strategy and concert immediate measures to meet the military crisis. They faced an agonizing dilemma. Prompt steps had to be taken to stem the spreading tide of Japanese conquest. On the other hand, it seemed likely that the coming year might see the collapse of Soviet resistance and of the British position in the Middle East. In this difficult situation the Allied leaders made a far-reaching decision that shaped the whole course of the war. Reaffirming the principle laid down in Anglo-American staff conversations in Washington ten months earlier, they agreed that the first and main effort must go into defeating Germany, the more formidable enemy. Japan's turn would come later. Defeating Germany would involve a prolonged process of "closing and tightening the ring" about Fortress Europe. Operations in 1942 would have to be defensive and preparatory, though limited offensives might be undertaken if the opportunity offered. Not until 1943 at the earliest could the Allies contemplate a return to the European continent "across the Mediterranean, from Turkey into the Balkans, or by landings in Western Europe."

Another important action taken at the ARCADIA Conference was the establishment of the Combined Chiefs of Staff (CCS). This was a committee consisting of the professional military chiefs of both countries, responsible to the President and Prime Minister for planning and directing the grand strategy of the coalition. Its American members were the Army Chief of Staff, General Marshall; the Chief of Naval Operations, Admiral Harold R. Stark (replaced

early in 1942 by Admiral Ernest J. King); and the Chief (later Commanding
General) of the Army Air Forces, Lt. Gen. Henry H. Arnold. In July 1942 a
fourth member was added, the President's personal Chief of Staff, Admiral
William D. Leahy. Since the CCS normally sat in Washington, the British
Chiefs of Staff, making up its British component, attended in person only at
important conferences with the heads of state. In the intervals they were represented in Washington by the four senior members of the permanent British
Joint Staff Mission, headed until late in 1944 by Field Marshal Sir John Dill,
the former Chief of the British Imperial General Staff. Under the CCS a system
of primarily military subordinate committees grew up, specifically designated
to handle such matters as strategic and logistical planning, transportation, and
communications.

By February 1942 the Joint Chiefs of Staff (JCS), consisting of the U.S.
members of the CCS, had emerged as the highest authority in the U.S. military
hierarchy (though never formally chartered as such), and responsible directly
to the President. Like the CCS, the JCS in time developed a machinery of
planning and working committees, the most important of which were the Joint
Staff Planners, the Joint Strategic Survey Committee, and the Joint Logistics
Committee. No executive machinery was created at either the CCS or JCS level.
The CCS ordinarily named either the British Chiefs or the U.S. Joint Chiefs
to act as its executive agent, and these, in turn, employed the established
machinery of the service departments.

In the spring of 1942 Britain and the United States agreed on a worldwide
division of strategic responsibility. The U.S. Joint Chiefs of Staff were to be
primarily responsible for the war in the Pacific, and the British Chiefs for the
Middle East-Indian Ocean region, while the European-Mediterranean-Atlantic
area would be a combined responsibility of both staffs. China was designated
a separate theater commanded by its chief of state, Chiang Kai-shek, though
within the United States' sphere of responsibility. In the Pacific, the Joint Chiefs
established two main theaters, the Southwest Pacific Area (SWPA) and the
Pacific Ocean Areas (POA), the former under General MacArthur, the latter
under Admiral Chester W. Nimitz. POA was further subdivided into North,
Central, and South Pacific areas, the first two directly controlled by Nimitz,
the third by his deputy, Admiral William F. Halsey, Jr. (*See Map 42.*) Later in
1942, the U.S. air and service troops operating in China, India, and northern
Burma were organized as U.S. Army Forces, China-Burma-India, under Lt.
Gen. Joseph W. Stilwell. On various other far-flung lines of communications
U.S. Army forces, mostly air and service troops during 1942, were organized
under similar theater commands. In June Maj. Gen. Dwight D. Eisenhower

arrived in England to take command of the newly established European Theater of Operations, and after the landings in North Africa late in the year a new U.S. theater was organized in that region.

The British and the Americans had decided at the ARCADIA Conference that Allied forces in each overseas theater would operate, as far as possible, under a single commander, and this principle was subsequently applied in most theaters. Within theaters subordinate unified commands were created, in some cases for Allied ground, naval, or air forces, and most frequently for task forces formed to carry out a specific operation or campaign. The authority of Allied theater commanders over national forces was always restricted with respect to areas and missions, and, as a last resort, senior national commanders in each theater could appeal to their own governments against specific orders or policies of the theater commander. In practice, this right of appeal was rarely invoked.

In essence, unified command at the Allied level gave the commander control of certain specific forces for operational purposes, rather than jurisdiction over a given geographical area. Administration of national forces and the allocation of resources were usually handled through separate national channels. In certain cases, inter-Allied boards or committees, responsible to the Allied theater commander, controlled the common use of critical resources (such as petroleum products) or facilities (such as railways and shipping) within a theater. Administration of U.S. forces overseas also generally followed separate Army and Navy channels, except in the Pacific where, from 1943 on, supply, transportation, and certain other services were jointly administered to a limited degree.

Even before Pearl Harbor, Army leaders had realized that the peacetime organization of the War Department General Staff, dating back to 1921, was an inadequate instrument for directing a major war effort. Originally a small co-ordinating and planning body, the General Staff, and especially its War Plans and Supply Divisions, rapidly expanded during the emergency period into a large operating organization, increasingly immersed in the details of supervision to the detriment of its planning and policy-making functions. The Chief of Staff, to whom some sixty-one officers and agencies had direct access, carried an especially heavy burden.

Three additional features of the organization demanded remedy. One was the continued subordination of the Army Air Forces to General Staff supervision, which conflicted with the Air Forces' drive for autonomy. Another was the anomalous position of General Headquarters (GHQ), whose role as command post for the field forces and responsibilities in the fields of training and logistics clashed with the authority of the General Staff at many points. Finally, the division of supply responsibilities between the Supply Division (G–4) and the Office of the Under Secretary of War—with requirements and distribution assigned to the former and procurement to the latter—was breaking down under the pressure of mobilization.

Spurred by the Pearl Harbor disaster, which seemed to accentuate the need for better staff co-ordination in Washington, General Marshall on March 9, 1942, put into effect a sweeping reorganization of the War Department. Under the new plan, which underwent little change during the war years, the General Staff, except for the War Plans and Intelligence Divisions, was drastically whittled down and limited in function to broad planning and policy guidance. An expanded War Plans Division, soon renamed Operations Division (OPD), became General Marshall's command post and, in effect, a superior general staff for the direction of overseas operations. The Army Air Forces, though in some respects on a lower level of administrative authority than before, had virtually complete control of the development of its special weapon—the airplane. Administering its own personnel and training, it organized and supported the combat air forces to be employed in theaters of operations and came also to exercise considerable influence over both strategic and operational planning.

In the reorganization of March 9 two new commands were created, the Army Ground Forces (AGF) and the Services of Supply, later renamed the Army Service Forces (ASF). The former, headed by Lt. Gen. Lesley J. McNair, took over the training mission of GHQ, now abolished, and absorbed the ground combat arms. To the ASF, commanded by Lt. Gen. Brehon B. Somervell, were subordinated the supply (renamed technical) and administrative services, the nine corps areas, and most of the Army posts and installations throughout the United States, including the ports of embarkation through which troops and supplies flowed to the forces overseas. In supply matters, Somervell now reported to two masters, the Chief of Staff for requirements and distribution and the Under Secretary of War, Mr. Robert P. Patterson, for procurement. His subordination to the latter was, in reality, only nominal since most of Patterson's organization was transferred bodily to Somervell's headquarters. Except for equipment peculiar to the Army Air Forces, the ASF thus became the Army's central agency for supply in the United States. It drew up the Army's "shopping list" of requirements, the Army Supply Program; through the seven technical services (Quartermaster, Ordnance, Signal, Chemical, Engineer, Medical, and Transportation) it procured most of the Army's supplies and equipment; it distributed these materials to the Army at home and abroad, as well as to

Allies under lend-lease; it operated the Army's fleet of transports; and it trained specialists and service units to perform various specialized jobs. General Somervell himself became General Marshall's principal logistical adviser.

All this looked to the future. In the first few weeks after Pearl Harbor, while the Navy was salvaging what it could from the wreckage at Pearl Harbor and striving to combat German submarines in the western Atlantic, the War Department made desperate efforts to bolster the defenses of Hawaii, the Philippines, the Panama Canal, Alaska, and the U.S. west coast. By the end of December, the danger of an attack on the Hawaii-Alaska-Panama triangle seemed to have waned, and the emphasis shifted to measures to stave off further disasters in the Far East. The British and Americans decided at ARCADIA that the Allies would attempt to hold the Japanese north and east of the line of the Malay Peninsula and the Netherlands Indies and to re-establish communications with the Philippines to the north. To co-ordinate operations in this vast theater, the Allied leaders created the ABDA (American-British-Dutch-Australian) Command, including the Netherlands Indies, Malaya, Burma, and the Philippines. British Lt. Gen. Sir Archibald P. Wavell was placed in over-all command. Through India from the west and Australia from the east, the Allies hoped in a short time to build up a shield of air power stout enough to blunt the Japanese threat.

For a time it seemed as though nothing could stop the Japanese juggernaut. In less than three weeks after Pearl Harbor, the isolated American outposts of Wake and Guam fell to the invaders, the British garrison of Hong Kong was overwhelmed, and powerful land, sea, and air forces were converging on Malaya and the Netherlands Indies. Picked, jungle-trained troops drove down the Malay Peninsula toward the great fortress of Singapore, infiltrating and outflanking successsive British positions. Two of the most formidable warships in the British Navy, the battleship *Prince of Wales* and the battle cruiser *Repulse*, were sunk by Japanese torpedo planes off the east coast of Malaya, a loss that destroyed the Allies' last hope of effectively opposing Japan's naval power in the Far East. Attacked from the land side, Singapore and its British force of over 80,000 troops surrendered on February 15, 1942. Meanwhile the Japanese had invaded the Netherlands Indies from the north, west, and east. In a series of actions during January and February, the weak Dutch and Australian naval forces, joined by the U.S. Asiatic Fleet withdrawing from the Philippines, were destroyed piecemeal, only four American destroyers escaping south to Australia. On March 9 the last Allied ground and air forces in the Netherlands Indies, almost 100,000 men (mostly Indonesian troops) surrendered to the invaders. In Burma, the day before, the British had been forced under heavy bombing to evacuate Rangoon and retreat northward. Before the end of April the Japanese had completed the ocupation of Burma, driving the British westward into India and the bulk of U.S. Lt. Gen. Joseph W. Stilwell's Chinese forces back into China; General Stilwell and the remnants of other Chinese units retreated to India. In the process the Japanese had won possession of a huge section of the Burma Road, the only viable route between China and India. Henceforth and until late in the war communication between China and its allies was to be limited to an air ferry from India over the "hump" of the Himalayan Mountains. During the late spring strong Japanese naval forces reached the coastal cities of India and even attacked Britain's naval base on Ceylon.

By May 1942 the Japanese had thus gained control of Burma, Malaya, Thailand, French Indochina, and the Malay Archipelago, while farther to the east they had won strong lodgments on the islands of New Guinea and New Britain and in the Solomons, flanking the approaches to Australia and New Zealand from the United States. This immense empire had been won at remarkably little cost through an effective combination of superior air and sea power and only a handful of well-trained ground divisions. The Japanese had seized and held the initiative while keeping their opponents off balance. They had concentrated their strength for the capture of key objectives such as airfields and road junctions and for the destruction of major enemy forces while diverting only minimum forces on secondary missions, thus giving an impression of overwhelming numerical strength. They had frequently gained the advantage of surprise and had baffled their enemies by their speed and skill in maneuver. The whole whirlwind campaign, in short, had provided Japan's enemies with a capsule course of instruction in the principles of war.

Fall of the Philippines

Only in the Philippines, almost on Japan's southern doorstep, was the timetable of conquest delayed. When the Japanese struck, the defending forces in the islands numbered more than 130,000, including the Philippine Army which, though mobilized to a strength of ten divisions, was ill trained and ill equipped. Of the U.S. Army contingent of 31,000, more than a third consisted of the Philippine Scouts, most of whom were part of the Regular Army Philippine Division, the core of the mobile defense forces. The Far East Air Force, before the Japanese attack, had a total of 277 aircraft of all types, mostly obsolescent but including 35 new heavy bombers. Admiral Thomas C. Hart's Asiatic Fleet, based on the Philippines, consisted of 3 cruisers, 13 old destroyers,

6 gunboats, 6 motor torpedo boats, 32 patrol bombers, and 29 submarines. A regiment of marines, withdrawn from Shanghai, also joined the defending forces late in November 1941. Before the end of December, however, American air and naval power in the Philippines had virtually ceased to exist. The handful of bombers surviving the early attacks had been evacuated to Australia, and the bulk of the Asiatic Fleet, its base facilities in ruins, had withdrawn southward to help in the defense of the Netherlands Indies.

The main Japanese invasion of the Philippines, following preliminary landings, began on December 22, 1941. While numerically inferior to the defenders, the invading force of two divisions with supporting units was well trained and equipped and enjoyed complete mastery of the air and on the sea. The attack centered on Luzon, the northernmost and largest island of the archipelago, where all but a small fraction of the defending forces were concentrated. The main landings were made on the beaches of Lingayen Gulf, in the northwest, and Lamon Bay in the southeast. General MacArthur's plan was to meet and destroy the invaders on the beaches, but his troops were unable to prevent the enemy from gaining secure lodgments. On December 23 MacArthur ordered a general withdrawal into the mountainous Bataan Peninsula, across Manila Bay from the capital city. Manila itself was occupied by the Japanese without resistance. The retreat into Bataan was a complex operation, involving converging movements over difficult terrain into a cramped assembly area from which only two roads led into the peninsula itself. Under constant enemy attack, the maneuver was executed with consummate skill and at considerable cost to the attackers. Yet American and Filipino losses were heavy, and the unavoidable abandonment of large stocks of supplies foredoomed the defenders of Bataan to ultimate defeat in the siege that followed. An ominous portent was the cutting of food rations by half on the last day of the retreat.

By January 7, 1942, General MacArthur's forces held well-prepared positions across the upper part of the Bataan Peninsula. Their presence there, and on Corregidor and its satellite island fortresses guarding the entrance to Manila Bay, denied the enemy the use of the bay throughout the siege. In the first major enemy offensive, launched early in January, the "battling bastards of Bataan" at first gave ground but thereafter handled the Japanese so roughly that attacks ceased altogether from mid-February until April, while the enemy reorganized and heavily reinforced. The defenders were, however, too weak to seize the initiative themselves.

General MacArthur, meanwhile, was ordered by the President to leave his post and go to Australia in order to take command of Allied operations against the Japanese in the Southwest Pacific. In mid-March he and a small party made

GENERAL WAINWRIGHT BROADCASTING TO AMERICAN FORCES

their way through the Japanese lines by motor torpedo boat to Mindanao, and from there were flown to Australia. Command of the forces in the Philippines devolved upon Lt. Gen. Jonathan M. Wainwright.

By April the troops on Bataan were subsisting on about fifteen ounces of food daily, less than a quarter of the peacetime ration. Their diet, consisting mostly of rice supplemented by carabao, mule, monkey, or lizard meat, was gravely deficient in vitamins and provided less than 1,000 calories a day, barely enough to sustain life. Weakened by hunger and poor diet, thousands succumbed to malaria, dengue, scurvy, beriberi, and amoebic dysentery, made impossible to control by the shortage of medical supplies, especially quinine. Desperate efforts were made to send food, medicine, ammunition, and other supplies through the Japanese blockade to the beleaguered forces. But during the early weeks, before the enemy cordon had tightened, it proved impossible, despite promises of lavish pay and bonuses, to muster the necessary ships and crews. Even so, sizable stocks were accumulated in the southern islands, but only about 1,000 tons of rations ever reached Manila Bay. Shipments in converted destroyers from the United States were too late and too few, and only insignificant quantities could be brought in by submarine and aircraft.

At the beginning of April the Japanese, behind a pulverizing artillery barrage, attacked again. The American lines crumpled, and in a few days the defending forces virtually disintegrated. On April 9 Maj. Gen. Edward P. King, Jr., commanding the forces on Bataan, surrendered. For almost another month the garrison on Corregidor and the other islands, swelled by refugees from Bataan, held out under air bombardment and almost continuous plunging fire from heavy artillery massed on adjacent shores and heights—one of the most intense artillery bombardments, for so small a target, of the entire war. On the night of May 5, after a final terrific 5-day barrage, Japanese assault troops won a foothold on Corregidor, and the following night, when it became apparent that further resistance was useless, General Wainwright surrendered unconditionally. Under his orders, which the Japanese forced him to broadcast, other American commanders in the Philippines capitulated one by one. By early June, except for scattered guerrilla detachments in the hills, all organized resistance in the islands had ceased.

Deploying American Military Strength

After more than a year and a half of rearming, the United States in December 1941 was still in no position to carry the war to its enemies. On December 7 the Army numbered some 1,644,000 men (including about 120,000 officers), organized into 4 armies, 37 divisions (30 infantry, 5 armored, 2 cavalry), and over 40 combat air groups. Three of the divisions were overseas (2 in Hawaii, 1 in the Philippines), with other garrison forces totaling less than 200,000. By spreading equipment and ammunition thin, the War Department might have put a substantial force into the field to repel an attack on the continental United States; 17 of the divisions at home were rated as technically ready for combat. But these divisions lacked the supporting units and the training necessary to weld them into corps and armies. More serious still, they were inadequately equipped with many weapons that recent operations in Europe had shown to be indispensable—for example, tank and antitank guns, antiaircraft artillery, radios, and radar—and some of these shortages were aggravated by lack of auxiliary equipment like fire control mechanisms.

Above all, ammunition of all kinds was so scarce that the War Department was unwilling to commit more than one division and a single antiaircraft regiment for service in any theater where combat operations seemed imminent. Only one division-size task force, in fact, was sent to the far Pacific before April 1942. Against air attacks, too, the country's defenses were meager. Along the Pacific coast the Army had only 45 modern fighter planes ready to fly, and only twelve

3-inch antiaircraft guns to defend the whole Los Angeles area. On the east coast there were only 54 Army fighter planes ready for action. While the coastal air forces, primarily training commands, could be reinforced by aircraft from the interior of the country, the total number of modern fighter aircraft available was less than 1,000. Fortunately, there was no real threat of an invasion in force, and the rapidly expanding output of munitions from American factories promised to remedy one of these weaknesses within a few months. Furthermore, temporary diversions of lend-lease equipment, especially aircraft, helped to bolster the overall defense posture within the first few weeks after Pearl Harbor. The Army hoped by April to have as many as thirteen divisions equipped and supplied with ammunition for combat.

To deploy these forces overseas was another matter. Although the U.S. merchant marine ranked second only to Great Britain's and the country possessed an immense shipbuilding capacity, the process of chartering, assembling, and preparing shipping for the movement of troops and military cargo took time. Time was also needed to schedule and organize convoys, and, owing to the desperate shortage of escort vessels, troop movements had to be widely spaced. Convoying and evasive routing, in themselves, greatly reduced the effective capacity of shipping. Moreover, vast distances separated U.S. ports from the areas threatened by Japan, and to these areas went the bulk of the forces deployed overseas during the months immediately following Pearl Harbor. Through March 1942, as a result, the outflow of troops to overseas bases averaged only about 50,000 per month, as compared with upwards of 250,000 during 1944, when shipping was fully mobilized and plentiful and the sea lanes were secure.

There seemed a real danger early in 1942, however, that German U-boats might succeed in reducing transatlantic deployment to a trickle—not so much by attacking troop transports, most of which could outrun their attackers, as by sinking the slow cargo ships on which the forces overseas depended for support. Soon after Germany's declaration of war, the U-boats struck at the virtually unprotected shipping lanes in the western Atlantic, and subsequently extended their attacks to the Gulf of Mexico and Caribbean areas and the mouth of the St. Lawrence. During the spring of 1942 tankers and freighters were torpedoed in plain view of vacationers on east coast beaches, and coastal cities dimmed or extinguished their lights in order that ships might not provide silhouetted targets for the U-boats. The Navy lacked the means to cope with the peril. In late December 1941 it had only twenty assorted surface vessels and about a hundred aircraft to protect the whole North Atlantic coastal frontier. During the winter and spring these were supplemented by another hundred

Army planes of longer range, several armed British trawlers, and as many improvised craft as could be pressed into service.

But the toll of ship sinkings increased. In March 788,000 deadweight tons of Allied and neutral dry cargo shipping were lost, in June 936,000 tons. Tanker losses reached an all-time peak of 375,000 tons in March, leading to complete suspension of coastal tanker movements and to gasoline rationing in the seaboard states. During the first six months of 1942 losses of Allied shipping were almost as heavy as during the whole of 1941 and exceeded new construction by almost 2.8 million deadweight tons. Although the United States was able by May to balance its own current losses by building new ships, Britain and other Allied countries continued until the following August to lose more than they could build, and another year passed before new construction offset cumulative losses.

Slowly and with many setbacks a system of countermeasures was developed. Convoying of coastal shipping, with ships sailing only by day, began in the spring of 1942. North-South traffic between U.S. and Caribbean and South American ports was also convoyed, on schedules interlocked with those of the transatlantic convoys. The latter, during 1942, were protected in the western half of the Atlantic by the U.S. and Canadian Navies, in the eastern half by the British. Troops were transported across the Atlantic either without escort in large, speedy liners like the *Queen Elizabeth* and the *Queen Mary*—which between them carried almost a quarter of all U.S. troops sent to Europe—or in heavily escorted convoys. Throughout the war, not a single loaded troop transport was sunk on the United Kingdom run. The slow merchant ships were convoyed in large groups according to speed.

But with responsibility for U.S. antisubmarine operations divided between the Navy and Army Air Forces, effective co-operation was hampered by sharp disagreement over organization and methods, and available resources throughout 1942 were inadequate. The U-boats, meanwhile, were operating with deadly effect and in growing numbers. Late in the year they began to hunt in packs, resupplied at sea by large cargo submarines ("milch cows"). The Allied convoys to Murmansk and other northern Soviet ports suffered especially heavy losses on their long passage around the top of the Scandinavian peninsula. In November shipping losses from all causes soared above 1.1 million deadweight tons— the peak, as it turned out, for the entire war, but few at the time dared so to predict.

In the Pacific, fortunately, the principal barriers to deployment of U.S. forces were distance and lack of prepared bases, not enemy submarines. Japan's fleet of undersea craft made little effort to prey on the Allied sea lanes and probably, over the vast reaches of the Pacific, could not have inflicted serious damage in any case. The chief goal of American deployment to the Pacific during most of 1942, following the initial reinforcement of Hawaii and the Panama Canal, was to build up a base in Australia and secure the chain of islands leading to it. Australia was a vast, thinly populated, and, except in its southeastern portion, largely undeveloped island continent, 7,000 miles and almost a month's sail from the U.S. west coast. It had provided a haven for some 4,000 American troops who, on December 7, had been at sea, bound for the Philippines, and in January a task force of division size (Poppy Force) was hastily assembled and dispatched to New Caledonia to guard its eastern approaches. During the first few weeks the main effort of the small American forces went into sending relief supplies to the Philippines and aircraft and troops to Java to stem the Japanese invasion. Beginning in March, as the futility of these efforts became evident, and coincident with the arrival of General MacArthur to assume command of all Allied forces in the Southwest Pacific, the construction of base facilities and the build-up of balanced air and ground forces got under way in earnest.

This build-up had as its first object the defense of Australia itself, for at the end of January the Japanese had occupied Rabaul on New Britain Island, thus posing an immediate threat to Port Moresby, the weakly held Australian base in southeastern New Guinea. In February President Roosevelt pledged American help in countering this threat, and in March and April two infantry divisions (the 41st and 32d) left the United States for the Southwest Pacific. At the same time, construction of air and refueling bases was being rushed to completion in the South Pacific islands that formed steppingstones along the ocean routes to Australia and New Zealand. After the western anchor of this chain, New Caledonia, was secured by the Poppy Force, Army and Marine garrisons and reinforcements were sent to various other islands along the line, culminating with the arrival of the 37th Division in the Fiji Islands in June.

These moves came none too soon for, during the spring, the Japanese, after occupying Rabaul, pushed into the southern Solomons, within easy striking distance of the American bases on Espíritu Santo and New Caledonia. They also occupied the northeastern coast of New Guinea, just across the narrow Papuan peninsula from Port Moresby, which the Americans and Australians were developing into a major advanced base in preparation for an eventual offensive northward. The stage was thus set for a major test of strength in the Pacific—American forces spread thinly along an immense arc from Hawaii to Australia, with outposts far to the north in Alaska; the Japanese securely in possession of the vast areas north and west of the arc and, with the advantage of interior lines, prepared to strike in force at any point. The first test came in May, when the Japanese made an attempt from the sea to take Port Moresby. This was successfully countered in the great carrier battle of the Coral Sea. Thereupon the Japanese struck eastward, hoping to destroy the U.S. Pacific Fleet and to seize Midway—a bid for naval supremacy in the Pacific. A diversionary attack on Dutch Harbor, the most forward U.S. base in Alaska, caused considerable damage, and the Japanese were able to occupy the islands of Kiska and Attu in the foggy Aleutian chain. But the main Japanese forces, far to the south, were crushingly defeated, with especially heavy losses in carriers and aircraft. The Battle of Midway in June 1942 was one of the truly decisive engagements of the war. By seriously weakening Japan's mobile striking forces, Midway left the Japanese virtually helpless to prevent the consolidation of American positions and the eventual development of over-whelming military supremacy throughout the Pacific. Only two months later, in fact, American forces took the first step on the long "road back" by landing on Guadalcanal in the **southern** Solomons.

Although the RAINBOW 5 plan was put into effect immediately after Pearl Harbor, the desperate situation in the Pacific and Far East and the shortage of shipping and escorts ruled out most of the scheduled Atlantic, Caribbean, and South American deployments. In January reinforcements were sent to Iceland and a token force to Northern Ireland, and by June two full divisions (the 34th Infantry and the 1st Armored) had reached Ireland, while the remainder of the 5th Infantry had arrived in Iceland, completing the relief of the U.S. Marine brigade and most of the British garrison. No more divisions sailed eastward until August. Meanwhile, garrisons in the Atlantic and Caribbean were being built up to war strength. But plans to occupy the Azores, Canaries, and Cape Verdes, and to capture Dakar on the west African coast went by the board, primarily for lack of shipping. Also abandoned after lengthy discussion was a project (GYMNAST) proposed by Prime Minister Churchill at the ARCADIA Conference for an Anglo-American occupation of French North Africa.

Thus, despite the reaffirmation of the "Germany first" strategy at ARCADIA, the great bulk of American forces sent overseas during the first half of 1942 went to the theaters of war against Japan. Of the eight Army divisions that left the country before August, five went to the Pacific. Including two more already in Hawaii, and a Marine division at sea, bound for New Zealand (eventually for the landings on Guadalcanal in August), eight divisions were deployed against Japan in July 1942. Of the approximately 520,000 Army troops in overseas bases, 60 percent were in the Pacific (including Alaska) and the newly established China-Burma-India theater; the remainder were almost all in Caribbean and western Atlantic garrisons. Of 2,200 Army aircraft overseas, about ,300 were in the Pacific (including Alaska) and Far East, 900 in the western Atlantic and Latin America. Not until August did the U.S. Army Air Forces in the British Isles attain sufficient strength to fly a single independent bombing mission over northern France.

Planning for a Cross-Channel Invasion

The Army's leaders and planners, schooled in a tradition that emphasized the principles of mass and offensive, had been fretting over the scale of deployment to the Pacific since early in the year. Late in January Brig. Gen. Dwight D. Eisenhower, then a War Department staff officer whom General Marshall had assigned to handle the crisis in the Pacific, noted, "We've got to go to Europe and fight—and we've got to quit wasting resources all over the world." In the joint committees Army planners urged that as soon as the situation could be stabilized in the Southwest Pacific, U.S. forces should begin to concentrate in the British Isles for an offensive against Germany. Secretary Stimson and others were pressing the same views on the President. In the middle of March the Joint Chiefs of Staff approved this course of action, and in April, at the President's order, General Marshall and Harry Hopkins, the President's personal representative, went to London to seek British approval.

Logistical considerations heavily favored both the general strategy of concentration against Germany and the specific plan of invading northwestern Europe from a base in the British Isles. Because the target area was close to the main sources of British and American power, two to three times as many forces could be hurled against northwestern Europe, with a given amount of shipping, as could be supported in operations against Japan. Britain itself was a highly industrialized country, fully mobilized after two and a half years of war, and well shielded by air and naval power—a ready-made base for a land invasion and air attacks on Germany's vitals. While invasion forces were assembling, moreover, they would serve to garrison the British Isles. Finally, an attack across the English Channel would use the only short water crossing to the Continent from a base already available and would thrust directly at the heart of Fortress Europe by the main historic invasion routes.

Even so, the plan was a desperate gamble. If northwestern Europe offered the Allies a position of strength, the Germans, too, would be strong there, close to their own heartland, served by the superb rail and road net of western and central Europe, shielded by submarines based along the entire length of Europe's Atlantic front. The limited range of fighter aircraft based in southern England narrowly restricted the choice of landing areas. Much hinged on the USSR, where for the present the bulk of Germany's land forces were pinned down. If the Soviet Union collapsed, an invasion from the west would be a suicidal venture. The invasion must therefore be launched before the Soviet armies were crushed and, moreover, in sufficient strength to draw substantial German forces away from the Eastern Front in order to avert that very catastrophe.

On the face of it, these two requirements seemed to cancel each other. For Allied planners had little hope that the Russians could stand up under another summer's onslaught, and it was obvious, in view of the scarcity of shipping, that any attack the Western Allies could mount by the coming summer or early fall would be hardly more than a pinprick. The best solution General Marshall's planners could offer to this dilemma was to set the invasion for the spring of 1943 (ROUNDUP), in the hope that until then, through air bombardment of Germany and a continued flow of matériel to the Soviet Union, the Allies could help the Soviet armies to stave off defeat. If these measures should fail, and Soviet resistance seemed about to collapse, then, with whatever forces were on hand, the Allies would have to invade the Continent in 1942 (SLEDGEHAMMER)— and no later than September, before bad weather closed down over the Channel. The same course would be followed in the unlikely event that Germany itself showed signs of serious weakness in 1942.

In London, Mr. Hopkins and General Marshall found the British delighted that the United States was ready to commit itself to a major offensive against Germany in 1943. The British readily agreed that preparations should begin immediately for an invasion the following spring, and they undertook to provide more than half the shipping needed to move about a million American troops and immense quantities of matériel to the United Kingdom. They warned, however, that their first concern at present was to maintain their position in the Middle East, where, late in January, Rommel's revitalized Africa Korps had inflicted a serious reverse on the Eighth Army. Both sides were now feverishly building up for a new offensive. The British also expressed deep misgivings over the proposed emergency cross-Channel operation in the fall. Nevertheless, the British approved the American plan, essentially the War Department's plan, "in principle"—a phrase that was to give much trouble in the coalition war. The immediate relief felt by General Marshall's staff in Washington was reflected by General Eisenhower, then Chief, Operations Division, War Department General Staff, who noted: ". . . at long last, and after months of struggle . . . we are all definitely committed to one concept of fighting! If we can agree on major purposes and objectives, our efforts will begin to fall in line and we won't just be thrashing around in the dark."

But on the American side, too, there were strong reservations. Admiral King did not contest in principle the "Germany first" strategy. But he was determined not to allow preparations for the cross-Channel invasion to jeopardize "vital needs" in the Pacific, by which, as he candidly stated early in May, he meant the ability of U.S. forces "to hold what we have against any attack that the Japanese are capable of launching." Only the President's peremptory order on May 6 that the invasion build-up in Britain must not be slowed down (it had, indeed, scarcely begun) prevented a large-scale diversion of forces and shipping to the Pacific to counter the Japanese offensive that culminated in the great naval battles of the Coral Sea and Midway. The President himself made it clear, on the other hand, that aid to the Soviet Union would have to continue on a mounting scale, whatever the cost to BOLERO (the American build-up in the United Kingdom) in matériel and shipping. And even Army leaders were unwilling to assign shipping for the movement until the scheduled build-up of garrisons in the Western Hemisphere and various other overseas stations had been completed, which, it was estimated, would not be until August at the earliest. Until then British shipping would have to carry the main burden.

Not until June 1942, therefore, did the first shipload of American troops under the new plan set sail for England in the great British luxury liner, *Queen Elizabeth*. Almost simultaneously a new crisis erupted in the Middle East. At the end of May, after a four-month lull, Rommel seized the initiative and swept around the southern flank of the British Eighth Army, which held strong positions in eastern Libya from El Gazala on the coast south to Bir Hacheim. After two weeks of hard fighting, in which the British seemed to be holding their own, Rommel succeeded in taking Bir Hacheim, the southern anchor of the British line. During the next few days British armor, committed piecemeal in an effort to cover a withdrawal to the northeast, was virtually wiped out by skillfully concealed German 88-mm. guns. The Eighth Army once again retreated across the Egyptian frontier, and on June 21 Tobruk, which the British had expected, as in 1941, to hold out behind Axis lines, was captured with its garrison and large stores of trucks, gasoline, and other supplies.

News of this disaster reached Prime Minister Churchill in Washington, where he had gone early in the month to tell the President that the British were unwilling to go through with an emergency cross-Channel landing late in 1942. General Marshall immediately offered to send an armored division to help the hard-pressed British in Egypt, but it was decided, for the present, to limit American aid to emergency shipments of tanks, artillery, and the ground components of three combat air groups. This move required the diversion for many weeks of a substantial amount of U.K. shipping from the North Atlantic on the long voyage around the Cape of Good Hope. But the heaviest impact on the invasion build-up in the United Kingdom resulted from the diversion of British shipping to the Middle East and the retention there of shipping the British had earmarked for the build-up. For the time being, British participation in the BOLERO program virtually ceased.

By the end of August, with only seven months to go before the invasion was to be launched, only about 170,000 American troops were in or on their way to the British Isles, and the shipment of equipment and supplies, particularly for the development of cantonments, airfields, and base facilities, was hopelessly behind schedule. There seemed little likelihood that enough shipping would be available to complete the movement across the Atlantic of a million troops, with the ten to fifteen million tons of cargo that must accompany them, by April 1943 as scheduled. And even if the shipping could have been found, Britain's ports and inland transportation system would have been swamped before the influx reached its peak. Thus, by the late summer of 1942, a spring 1943 ROUNDUP appeared to be a logistical impossibility.

Torch Replaces Sledgehammer-Roundup

By this time, in fact, American military leaders had become discouraged about a cross-Channel invasion in spring of 1943, though not primarily because of the lag in the build-up program. In June the British had decided that SLEDGE-HAMMER, for which they had never had any enthusiasm, could not be undertaken except in a situation which offered good prospects of success—that is, if the Germans should seem about to collapse. At the moment, with the German summer offensive just starting to roll toward the Caucasus and the lower Don, such a situation did not appear to be an imminent possibility. The British decision was influenced in part by the alarming lag in deliveries of American landing craft, of which less than two-thirds of the promised quota for the operation was expected to materialize. The British also argued that the confusion and losses attendant upon executing SLEDGEHAMMER—and the cost of supporting the beachhead once it was established—were likely to disrupt preparations for the main invasion the following spring. Since SLEDGEHAMMER, if carried out, would have to be, in the main, a British undertaking, the British veto was decisive. The operation was canceled.

As a substitute, the British proposed a less risky venture—landings in French North Africa—which they were confident could be accomplished in stride, without harm to ROUNDUP. To Stimson, Marshall, King, and Arnold this proposal was anathema. Failure would be a costly, perhaps fatal rebuff to Allied prestige.

Success might be even more dangerous, the Americans feared, for it might lead the Allies step by step into a protracted series of operations around the southern periphery of Europe, operations that could not be decisive and would only postpone the final test of strength with Germany. At the very least, an invasion of North Africa would, the Americans were convinced, rule out a spring 1943 invasion of the Continent. The Army planners preferred the safer alternative of simply reinforcing the British in Egypt.

The British proposal was, nevertheless, politically shrewd, for it was no secret that President Roosevelt had long ago expressed a predilection for this very undertaking. He was determined, besides, that American ground forces go into action somewhere in the European area before the end of 1942. Already half persuaded, he hardly needed Churchill's enthusiastic rhetoric to win him over to the new project. When General Marshall and his colleagues in the Joints Chiefs of Staff suggested, as an alternative, that the United States should immediately go on the defensive in Europe and turn all-out against Japan, Roosevelt brusquely rejected the idea.

In mid-July, Hopkins, Marshall, and King went to London under orders from the President to reach agreement with the British on some operation in 1942. After a vain effort to persuade the British to reconsider an invasion of the Continent in 1942, the Americans reluctantly agreed on July 24 to the North Africa operation, now christened TORCH, to be launched before the end of October. The President, overruling Marshall's suggestion that final decision be postponed until mid-September in order to permit a reappraisal of the Soviet situation, cabled Hopkins that he was "delighted" and that the orders were now "full speed ahead." Into the final agreement, however, Marshall and King wrote their own conviction that the decision on TORCH "in all probability" rulled out invasion of the Continent in 1943 and meant, further, that the Allies had accepted "a defensive, encircling line of action" in the European-Mediterranean war.

End of the Defensive Stage

With the decision for TORCH, the first stage in the search for a strategic plan against Germany came to an end. In retrospect, 1941–42 had been a period of defensive strategy, and a strategy of scarcity. The British and American approaches to war had had their first conflict, and the British had won the first round. That British notions of strategy had tended to prevail was not surprising. British forces had been mobilized earlier and were in the theaters in far greater numbers than American forces. The United States was still mobilizing its manpower and resources. It had taken the better part of the year after Pearl

Harbor for U.S. forces to have an appreciable effect in the theaters. Strategic planning in 1942 had been largely opportunistic, hand to mouth, and limited by critical shortages in shipping and munitions. Troops had been parceled out piecemeal to meet immediate threats and crises. Despite the "Germany first" decision, the total U.S. Army forces deployed in the war against Japan by the end of the year actually exceeded the total U.S. Army forces deployed in the war against Germany. The one scheme to put Allied planning on an orderly, long-range basis and to achieve the concepts of mass and concentration in which General Marshall and his staff had put their faith had failed. By the close of the critical first year after Pearl Harbor, an effective formula for halting the dissipation of forces and matériel in what it regarded as secondary ventures still eluded the Army high command.

CHAPTER 21

Grand Strategy and the Washington High Command

In 1943 the debate within the Grand Alliance over strategy against the Axis Powers entered a new stage. The midwar period—roughly to the establishment of a foothold in Normandy in the summer of 1944—was the period of increasing plenty. The power to call the turn on strategy and to choose the time and place to do battle passed to the Allies. U.S. troops and supplies flowed out in ever-increasing numbers and quantity, and the full impact of American mobilization and production was felt not only in the theaters but also in Allied councils. But the transition to the strategic initiative introduced many new and complex problems for the high command in Washington. Active and passive fronts were now established all over the world. The Torch decision had thrown all Allied planning into a state of uncertainty. For General Marshall and the Army planners in the Washington command post the basic strategic question was how to limit operations in subsidiary theaters and carry the war decisively to the Axis Powers. They had to start over and seek new and firmer long-range bases upon which to plan for victory in the multifront coalition war.

Strategic Planning for Offensive Warfare: Midwar

The decision for Torch opened a great debate on European strategy between the Americans and the British that endured down to the summer of 1944. The issues that emerged were disputed in and out of the big international conferences of midwar from Casablanca in January 1943 to Second Quebec in September 1944. In that debate Churchill eloquently urged ever onward in the Mediterranean—Sicily, landing in Italy, Rome, the Pisa-Rimini line; then "north and northeast." President Roosevelt, himself fascinated by the possibilities in the Mediterranean, to a considerable extent seconded these moves, despite the reluctance of the American Chiefs. Pleading his case skillfully, the British leader stressed the need to continue the momentum, the immediate advantages, the "great prizes" to be picked up in the Mediterranean, the need to continue the softening-up process, while the Allies awaited a favorable opportunity to invade the Continent across the English Channel. The fact that sizable Allied forces were present in the Mediterranean and that there was an immediate chance to weaken the enemy in that area were telling arguments.

At the same time the Americans—with General Marshall as the foremost military spokesman—gradually made progress toward limiting the Mediterranean advance, toward directing it to the west rather than to the east, toward linking it directly with a definite major cross-Channel operation, and thereby winning their way **back** to the idea of waging a war of mass and concentration on the Continent. Part of their task was to secure agreement with President Roosevelt, part with the British, and eventually the Russians. The series of decisions reached at the 1943 conferences—Casablanca in January, Washington (TRIDENT) in May, First Quebec (QUADRANT) in August, and Cairo-Tehran (SEXTANT-EUREKA) in November and December—reflect the compromises of the Americans and the British between opportunism and long-range commitments, between a war of attrition and a war of mass and concentration.

Each of these conferences marked a milestone in coalition strategy and in the maturation of American strategic planning. At Casablanca General Marshall made a last vigorous but vain stand for a cross-Channel operation in 1943. The conferees did approve a round-the-clock combined bomber offensive against Germany that both the Americans and the British viewed as a prerequisite to a future cross-Channel operation. But no real long-range plan for the defeat of the Axis Powers emerged. Casablanca merely recognized that the Anglo-Americans would retain the initiative in the Mediterranean, and defined the short-range objective in terms of a prospective operation against Sicily.

Unlike the small, disunited American delegation, the well-prepared British operated as a cohesive team and presented a united front. President Roosevelt, still attracted to the Mediterranean, had not yet made the notion of a big cross-Channel attack his own. A striking illustration of the want of understanding between the White House and the military staffs came in connection with the unconditional surrender formula to which he and Churchill publicly committed themselves at Casablanca. The President had simply informed the JCS of his intention to support that concept as the basic Allied aim in the war at a meeting at the White House shortly before the conference. But no study of the meaning of this formula for the conduct of the war was made by either the Army or the Joint Staff before or during the conference—nor did the President encourage his military advisers to do so.

To the American military staff it appeared at the time that the long experience of the British in international negotiations had carried the day. Keenly
disappointed, Brig. Gen. Albert C. Wedemeyer, General Marshall's principal
adviser at Casablanca, wrote: ". . . we lost our shirts and . . . are now committed to a subterranean umbilicus operation in midsummer. . . . we came,
we listened, and we were conquered."

General Wedemeyer admired the way the British had presented their case:
"They swarmed down upon us like locusts with a plentiful supply of planners
and various other assistants with prepared plans. . . . As an American I wish
that we might be more glib and better organized to cope with these super
negotiators. From a worm's eye viewpoint it was apparent that we were confronted by generations and generations of experience in committee work and in
rationalizing points of view. They had us on the defensive practically all the
time."

The American military staff took the lessons of Casablanca to heart. If they
did not become more glib, they at least organized themselves better. To meet
the British on more equal terms, they overhauled their joint planning system and
resolved to reach closer understandings with the President in advance of future
meetings. As a by-product of the debate and negotiation over grand strategy in
midwar, the planning techniques and methods of the Americans became more
nearly like those of their British ally, even if their strategic ideas still differed.
They became more skilled in the art of military diplomacy, of quid pro quo, or
what might be termed the "tactics" of strategic planning. At the same time
their strategic thinking became more sophisticated. The Casablanca Conference
represented the last fling for the "either-or" school of thought in the American
military staff. Henceforth, they began to think not in terms of this *or* that
operation, but in terms of this *and* that—or what one planner fittingly called
"permutations and combinations." The outstanding strategic questions for them
were no longer to be phrased in terms of either a Mediterranean or a cross-
Channel operation, but in terms of defining the precise relations between
them—and the Combined Bomber Offensive.

In the debate, the American Joint Chiefs of Staff countered British demands
for more emphasis upon the Mediterranean, particularly the eastern Mediterranean, by supporting further development of Pacific offensives. Holding open
the "Pacific alternative" carried with it the threat of non cross-Channel operation
at all—which the British did not wish. The war in the Pacific thereby offered
the United States staff a significant lever for keeping the Mediterranean issue
under control. At the same time General Marshall recognized that the Mediterranean offensive could not be stopped completely with North Africa or Sicily

and that definite advantages would accrue from knocking out Italy, opening up the Mediterranean further for Allied shipping, and widening the air offensive against Germany.

Beginning with the compromise agreements at TRIDENT in the spring of 1943, the American representatives could point to definite steps toward fixing European strategy in terms of a major cross-Channel undertaking for 1944. At that conference they assented to a plan for eliminating Italy from the war, which the British urged as the "great prize" after Sicily. But the forces, the Americans insisted, were to be limited so far as possible to those already in the Mediterranean. At the same time, they won British agreement to the transfer of 4 American and 3 British divisions from the Mediterranean to the United Kingdom. Both sides agreed to continue the Combined Bomber Offensive from the United Kingdom in four phases to be completed by April 1944 and leading up to an invasion across the Channel. Most encouraging was the President's unequivocal announcement in favor of a cross-Channel undertaking for the spring of 1944. The British agreed that planning should start for mounting such an operation with target date, May 1944, on the basis of 29 divisions built up in the United Kingdom (Operation ROUNDHAMMER, later called OVERLORD). The bare outlines of a new pattern of European strategy began to take shape.

That pattern took clearer shape at QUADRANT. There the American Chiefs urged a firm commitment to OVERLORD, the plan developed by a British-American planning staff in London. The British agreed but refused to give it the "overriding priority" over all operations in the Mediterranean area that the Americans desired. Plans were to proceed for eliminating Italy from the war, establishing bases as far north as Rome, seizing Sardinia and Corsica, and landing in southern France. Forces for these operations would be limited to those allotted at TRIDENT. With a definite limitation on the Mediterranean offensive, authorization for a definite allocation of forces for the approved cross-Channel operation, and for an extended Combined Bomber Offensive in support of it, the strategic pattern against Germany was taking on more final form.

After QUADRANT came new danger signals for the Washington high command. The British were making overtures for active operations in the Aegean, which the Americans interpreted, wrongly or rightly, as a prelude to a move on the Balkans and a consequent threat to the cross-Channel strategy. At the Moscow Conference in October 1943 came other warning signs from another and more unexpected source. At that meeting of the foreign ministers, a prelude to the full-dress conference at Tehran to follow, the representatives of the Anglo-American staffs met for the first time with the Russian staff. In a surprise

TEHRAN CONFERENCE

maneuver, the Russians, who from the beginning had been pleading for the second front in Europe, intimated that they might be willing to accept an active campaign in Italy as the second front.

With these portents in mind, the uneasy American Joint Chiefs of Staff accompanied the President on board the USS *Iowa* en route to the Cairo Conference in November 1943. During the rehearsals on that voyage for the meetings ahead the President afforded his military advisers a rare glimpse into his reflections on the political problems that were bound up with the war and its outcome. His concern lest the United States be drawn into a permanent or lengthy occupation of Europe came out sharply in the discussion with the JCS on the zones of occupation in postwar Germany. As he told the JCS, "We should not get roped into accepting any European sphere of influence." Nor did he wish the United States to become involved in a prolonged task of reconstituting France, Italy, and the Balkans. "France," he declared, "is a British baby." Significantly, the President added, "There would definitely be a race for Berlin. We may have to put the United States Divisions into Berlin as soon as possible." With a pencil he quickly sketched on a simple map of Europe the zonal boundaries he envisaged, putting Berlin and Leipzig in a big American zone in northern Germany—one of the most unusual records of the entire war and later brought back to Washington by Army officers in the American delegation.

Tehran proved to be the decisive conference in European strategy. There, for the first time in the war, President Roosevelt, Prime Minister Churchill, and their staffs met with Marshal Stalin, the Soviet leader, and his staff. Churchill made eloquent appeals for operations in Italy, the Aegean, and the east Mediterranean, even at the expense of a delay in OVERLORD. For reasons of its own, the USSR put its weight behind the American concept of strategy. Confident of its capabilities, demonstrated in its great comeback since the critical days of Stalingrad, the Soviet Union asserted its full power as an equal member of the Allied coalition. Stalin came out vigorously in **favor** of OVERLORD and limiting further operations in the Mediterranean to **one** directly assisting OVERLORD, an invasion of southern France. In turn, the Russians promised to launch an all-out offensive on their front to accompany the Allied moves. Stalin's strong stand put the capstone on Western strategy against Germany. The Anglo-American Chiefs agreed to launch OVERLORD during May 1944 in conjunction with a southern France operation, and to consider these the supreme operations for that year.

The final blueprint for Allied victory in Europe had taken shape. Germany was to be crushed between the jaws of a gigantic vise applied from the west and the east. How much reliance President Roosevelt had come to place in General Marshall was reflected in his decision not to release Marshall for the command of the cross-Channel attack. As he told General Marshall, "I . . . could not sleep at night with you out of the country." President Roosevelt gave the nod to General Eisenhower, who had built a solid reputation as the successful leader of coalition forces in the Mediterranean. Preparations for the big cross-Channel attack began in earnest.

The last lingering issue in the long drawn-out debate was not settled until the summer of 1944. In the months following Tehran, the southern France operation came perilously close to being abandoned in favor of the British desire for further exploitation in Italy and possibly even across the Julian Alps into the Hungarian plain. Complicating the picture was a shortage of landing craft to carry off both OVERLORD and the southern France attack simultaneously. But General Marshall and the Washington military authorities, backed by President Roosevelt, remained adamant on the southern attack. The British and the Americans did not reach final agreement on a southern France operation until August—two months after the OVERLORD landings—just a few days before the operation was actually launched, when Churchill reluctantly yielded. This concluding phase of the debate represented the last gasp of the peripheral strategy with a new and sharper political twist. Churchill was now warily watching the changing European scene with one eye on the retreating Germans, and the other on the advancing Russians.

A number of misconceptions grew up in the postwar period about this Anglo-American debate over strategy. What was at stake in the midwar debate was not whether there should be a cross-Channel operation. Rather the question was: Should that operation be a full-bodied drive with a definite target date that the Americans desired, or a final blow to an enemy critically weakened in a war of opportunity that the British desired? It is a mistake to assume that the British did not from the first want a cross-Channel operation. The difference lay essentially in the precise timing of that attack and in the extent and direction of preparatory operations. Once agreed on the major blow, the British stoutly held out for a strong initial assault that would insure success in the operation. It is also a mistake to assume that the Americans remained opposed to all Mediterranean operations. Indeed, much of their effort in 1943–44 was spent in reconciling those operations with a prospective cross-Channel operation.

What about the question of a Balkan alternative that has aroused so much controversy? Would it not have been wiser to have invaded the continent through the Balkans and thereby forestall Soviet domination? The fact must be emphasized that this is a postwar debate. The Balkan invasion was never proposed by any responsible leader in Allied strategy councils as an alternative to OVERLORD; nor did any Allied debate or combined planning take place in those terms. After the war Churchill steadfastly denied that he wanted a Balkan invasion. The British contended that the Americans had been frightened by the specter rather than by the substance of their proposals. And indeed the American staff had been frightened by the implications of Churchillian proposals for raids, assistance to native populations, throwing in a few armored divisions, and the like—for the eastern Mediterranean and Balkan regions. For the American staff Mediterranean operations had offered a striking demonstration of how great the costs of a war of attrition could be. The so-called "soft underbelly" of Italy, to which the Prime Minister had glowingly referred, turned out to be a hard-shelled back demanding more and more increments of American and Allied men and means. The mere thought of being sucked step by step, by design or by circumstance, into a similar undertaking in the Balkans, an area of poor terrain and communications—even if it were an unrealistic fear on the part of the American staff—was enough to send shivers up the spines of American planners. Certainly, neither the President nor the American staff wanted to get involved in the thorny politics of the Balkan area, and both were determined to stay out. The Balkan question was never argued out in frank military or political terms by the Allies during World War II.

Frustrated by the loss of what he regarded as glittering opportunities in the Mediterranean, Churchill struck out after the war at the American wartime "logical, large-scale mass-production thinking." But as Gordon Harrison, the author of *Cross-Channel Attack,* put it: "To accuse Americans of mass-production thinking is only to accuse them of having a mass-production economy and of recognizing the military advantage of such an economy. The Americans were power-minded." From the beginning they thought in terms of taking on the main German armies and beating them. Back of the American staff's fear of a policy of attritional and peripheral warfare against Germany in midwar lay their continued anxiety over its ultimate costs in men, resources, and time. This anxiety was increased by their concern with getting on with the war against Japan. Basic in their thinking was a growing realization of the ultimate limits of American manpower and a growing anxiety about the effects of a long-continued period of maximum mobilization on the home front. All of these factors combined to confirm their faith in the doctrine of military concentration.

As it turned out, the final strategy against Germany was a compromise of American and British views—of British peripheral strategy and the American principle of concentration. To the extent that the cross-Channel operation was delayed a year later than the Americans wished in order to take advantage of Mediterranean opportunities and to continue the softening up process, the British prevailed. Perhaps still haunted by the ghosts of Passchendaele and Dunkerque, the British were particularly sensitive to the requisite conditions for OVERLORD—for example, how many enemy troops could be expected to oppose it. But, as the Americans had hoped from the beginning, the cross-Channel attack turned out to be a conclusive operation with a fixed target date; it was given the highest priority and the maximum force to drive directly at the heart of German power.

Thus, by the summer of 1944 the final blueprinting of the Allied strategy for defeating Germany was completed. Despite the compromises with opportunism, American staff notions of fighting a concentrated, decisive war had been clearly written into the final pattern. Those notions had been reinforced by the addition, from Casablanca onward, of the unconditional surrender aim. The peripheral trend had been brought under control, and General Marshall had managed to conserve American military power for the big cross-Channel blow. The Americans had learned to deal with the British on more nearly equal terms. The military chiefs had drawn closer to the President and the U.S. side was able to present a united front vis-à-vis the British.

During the Anglo-American debate of midwar, significant changes had taken place in the alignment of power within the Grand Alliance. These shifts had implications as important for war strategy as for future relations among the wartime partners. By the close of 1943 the mighty American industrial and military machine was in high gear. The growing flow of American military strength and supplies to the European theater assured the acceptance of the American strategic concept. The Soviet Union, steadily gathering strength and confidence in 1943, made its weight felt at a critical point in the strategic debate. Britain had virtually completed its mobilization by the end of 1943, and stresses and strains had begun to appear in its economy. Compared to the Soviet Union and the United States, Britain was becoming relatively weaker. In midwar the Americans drew up with and threatened to pass the British in deployed strength in the European theater. Within the coalition Britain's military power and notions of fighting the war were being overtaken. Tehran, which fixed the final European strategy, marked a subtle but important change in the foundations of the Alliance. For the strategists of the Pentagon and of the Kremlin the doctrine of concentration had provided a common bond.

Completing the Strategic Patterns

From the standpoint of the Washington high command, the main story of military strategy in World War II, except for the important and still unanswered question of how to defeat Japan, came to an end in the summer of 1944. The last stage—culminating in the surrender of Germany and of Japan—was the period of the payoff, of the unfolding of strategy in the field. In this final phase, the problems of winning the war began to run up against the problems of winning the peace.

Once the Allied forces became firmly lodged on the European continent and took up the pursuit of the German forces, the war became for General Marshall and his staff essentially a matter of tactics and logistics—the Supreme Allied Commander, General Eisenhower, assuming the responsibility for making decisions as military circumstances in the field dictated. But to Churchill, disturbed by the swift Soviet advance into Poland and the Balkans, the war seemed more than ever a contest for great political stakes. In the last year of the European conflict therefore, the two approaches often became a question of military tactics versus political considerations.

By the summer of 1944 the shape of things to come was already apparent. Once on the Continent, General Eisenhower was given more and more responsibility for political decisions, or fell heir to them by default. Lacking political guidance and direction from Washington, the commander in the field made decisions on the basis of military considerations. He fell back on the U.S. staff notions of defeating the enemy and ending the war quickly and decisively with the fewest casualties. This trend became even more marked in 1945 in the commander's decision to stop at the Elbe and not attempt to take Berlin or Prague ahead of the Russians.

As usual, General Marshall and the U.S. staff backed the decisions of the commander in the field. Typical of Marshall's approach were two statements he made in April 1945—one in response to a British proposal to capture Berlin, the other concerning the liberation of Prague. With reference to Berlin, Marshall joined with his colleagues in the JCS in emphasizing to the British Chiefs of Staff "that the destruction of the German armed forces is more important than any political or psychological advantages which might be derived from possible capture of the German capital ahead of the Russians. . . . Only Eisenhower is in a position to make a decision concerning his battle and the best way to exploit successes to the full." With respect to Prague, Marshall wrote to Eisenhower "Personally and aside from all logistic, tactical or strategic implications, I would be loath to hazard American lives for purely political purposes." Such views of the Army Chief of Staff took on added significance, for during Roosevelt's final and his successor's early days in office the burden of dealing with important issues fell heavily on the senior military advisers in the Washington high command. Marshall's stand on these issues was entirely consistent with earlier Army strategic planning. Whatever the ultimate political outcome, from the standpoint of a decisive military conclusion of the war against Germany it made little difference whether the forces of the United States or those of the Soviet Union took Berlin and Prague. At the same time, in purely military dealings with the Russians in the closing months of the European conflict, and as Soviet and American troops drew closer, the American staff began to stiffen its stand and a firmer note crept into its negotiations for co-ordination of Allied efforts. Early in 1945 Marshall advised Eisenhower to forget diplomatic niceties in dealing with the Russians and urged him to adopt a direct approach "in simple Main Street Abilene style."

Churchill's inability to reverse the course of the last year of the war underscored the changed relationships between U.S. and British national military weight and the shifting bases of the Grand Alliance. With British manpower already mobilized to the hilt, after the middle of 1944 British production became increasingly unbalanced, and the British fought the remainder of the war with a contracting economy. The Americans did not hit the peak of their military manpower mobilization until May 1945—the month Germany surrendered. Reaching their war production peak at the end of 1943, they were able to sustain it at high levels to the end of the war. The greater capacity of the American economy and population to support a sustained, large-scale Allied offensive effort showed up clearly in the last year of the European war. Once entrenched on the Continent, American divisions began to outnumber the British more and more. Through the huge stockpiles of American production already built up and through his control of the growing U.S. military manpower on the Continent, General Eisenhower was able to put the imprint of U.S. staff thinking on how to win the war. Whatever his political predilections, Churchill had to yield. As the war against Germany lengthened beyond the hoped-for end in 1944, British influence in high Allied councils went into further decline. The last year of the war saw the United States and the Soviet Union emerging as the two strongest military powers in Europe, the one as intent on leaving Europe soon as the other was on pushing its strategic frontiers westward. On the Western side the struggle was to be concluded the way the American military chiefs had wished to wage it from the beginning—as a conventional war of concentration.

Meanwhile, as the war with Germany was drawing to a close, the strategy for defeating Japan had gradually been taking shape. Despite the Germany-first principle, the so-called secondary war simply would not stand still. From the beginning, in the defensive as well as in the offensive stage, the Pacific exerted a strong pull on American forces and resources. Nor would American public opinion tolerate a strictly defensive, limited war against Japan until Germany was beaten. Though final plans had to await the defeat of Germany, the pace of advance in the Pacific became so fast that it almost caught up with the European conflict. In the Pacific, as in the Mediterranean, American strategists learned that forces in being had a way of creating their own strategy.

While European war strategy was fashioned on the international level, the war against Japan from the beginning was almost exclusively an American affair, and its strategy essentially an interservice concern. The American plans and decisions in the Pacific war were presented to the international conferences, where they usually received Allied approval with little debate. Disputes and arguments were on the service level for the most part, with General Marshall and Admiral King working out compromises between themselves. In the process General Marshall often acted as mediator between the Navy and General MacArthur.

MEDIUM TANKS ON AN AMERICAN ASSEMBLY LINE

The traditional naval concern with the Pacific and the necessarily heavy reliance in the theater upon shipping, especially assault shipping, put the main burden of developing offensive strategy upon the Navy. But Navy plans for a central Pacific offensive had to be reconciled with General MacArthur's concept of approaching Japan via the New Guinea–Philippines axis. Thus a twofold approach—"a one-two punch"—replaced the original single axis strategy. This double axis advance produced a strategy of opportunity similar to that urged by the British for the war in Europe and took the Allies to the threshold of Japan by the time the European war ended. The critical question of whether Japan could be defeated by bombardment and blockade alone, or whether an invasion would be necessary, was long debated. In Washington during the late spring of 1945 the Army's argument that plans and preparations should be made for an invasion was accepted as the safe course to follow.

The rapid pace of the Pacific advance outran the American plans for the China-Burma-India Theater, and that theater declined in strategic importance in the war against Japan. Disillusioned by the inability of China to play an active role in the final defeat of Japan, American military leaders sought to substitute the USSR. To save American lives in a Pacific OVERLORD, those leaders in general became eager to have the USSR enter the war against Japan and pin down Japanese forces on the Asiatic mainland. Before final plans for a Pacific OVERLORD could be put into effect, however, the Japanese surrendered. The dramatic dropping of atomic bombs on August 6 and 9 on Hiroshima

and Nagasaki, respectively, came as a complete surprise to the American public
and to the Army strategic planners, with the exception of a handful of top
officers in the Washington command post who were in on the secret. In a sense
the supersession of strategic plans by a revolutionary development of weapons
was a fitting climax to a war that had throughout shown a strong tendency
to go its own way.

The last year of the war witnessed, along with the finishing touches on
grand strategy, the change-over from the predominantly military to the politico-
military phase. As victory loomed, stresses and strains within the coalition
became more apparent. With the Second Quebec Conference in September
1944 agreement among the Allies on military plans and war strategy became
less urgent than need to arrive at acceptable politico-military terms on which
the winning powers could continue to collaborate. That need became even more
marked at Yalta in February 1945 and at the Potsdam Conference in July 1945.
To handle these new challenges after building up a staff mechanism geared
to the predominantly military business of fighting a global and coalition war
necessitated considerable adjustment of Army staff processes and planning. In
midwar Army planning had been geared to achieve the decisive blow on the
Continent that had been a cardinal element in the planners' strategic faith.
Scarcely were the Western Allies ensconced on the Continent, however, when
the challenges of victory and peace were upon the Army planners. They entered
the last year of the war with the coalition disintegrating, the President failing
in health, and a well-organized politico-military machine lacking. Besides
the frictions generating on the foreign fronts, the Army still had to cope with
the immense problem of what to do with the beaten foe—with terms of surrender, occupation, and postwar bases. The military fell heir—by default—
to problems no longer easily divided into military and political.

Expansion and Distribution of the Wartime Army

To the Washington high command strategic plans were one vital ingredient
in the formula for victory. Manpower was another. Indeed, at stake in the
midwar debate was the fresh and flexible military power of the United States.
That power was also General Marshall's trump card in negotiations with the
coalition partners. To put a brake on diversionary deployments to secondary
theaters and ventures and to conserve American military manpower for the
big cross-Channel blow became the major preoccupation of the Chief of Staff
and his advisers in midwar. Behind their concern for effective presentation
of the American strategic case at the midwar international conferences lay

the growing uneasiness of General Marshall and his staff over the American manpower problem. To continue what appeared to them to be essentially a policy of drift in Allied strategy raised grave issues about mobilizing and deploying U.S. forces. To support a war of attrition and peripheral action, in place of concentrated effort, raised serious problems about the size and kind of Army the United States should and could maintain.

To establish a proper manpower balance for the United States in wartime was as difficult as it was important. In light of the 15 to 16 million men estimated to be physically fit for active military service, on the surface it seemed hard to understand why there should be any U.S. manpower problem at all. The problem as well as the answer stemmed basically from the fact that the Allies had from the beginning accepted the proposition that the single greatest tangible asset the United States brought to the coalition in World War II was the productive capacity of its industry. From the very beginning, U.S. manpower calculations had to be closely correlated with the needs of war industry.

The Army had therefore to compete for manpower not only with the needs of the other services but also with the claims of industry. By 1943 the "arsenal of democracy" was just beginning to hit its full productive stride. To cut too deeply into the industrial manpower of the country in order to furnish men for the Army and Navy might interfere seriously with arming U.S. and Allied troops. Furthermore, the United States was fighting a global conflict. To service its lines of communications extending around the world required large numbers of men, and great numbers of troops were constantly in transit to and from the theaters. To carry the fight across the oceans demanded a powerful Navy and a large merchant fleet, which also had to be given a high priority for manpower. Each industry as well as each theater commander was continually calling for more men. The problem for the Army was not only how much it should receive for its share of the manpower pool but also how it should divide that share most effectively to meet the diverse demands made upon it.

By 1943 the realization among the Army staff was growing that the U.S. manpower barrel did have a bottom. Even before the end of 1942 it was becoming visible. Also evident was the fact that, while the United States would remain the major "arsenal of democracy," it could no longer be regarded as a limitless source of munitions. The pool of unemployed that had cushioned the shock of mobilization for three years had been almost exhausted. Industrial expansion had slowed down, labor had become tight in many areas, and in November 1942 the President had placed a ceiling of 8.2 million officers and men upon the Army's expansion during 1943, intimating at the same time that this limit would probably hold for the duration of the war. General Marshall and his colleagues in the JCS were still determined that the United States make a major contribution in fighting forces to the defeat of the Axis Powers. But postponement of the invasion of northwestern Europe, together with the indicated limitations on American manpower and resources, made it necessary to reconsider the nature of that contribution. To match strategy, manpower, and production for the offensive phase of the war became a basic task of the Washington high command in the remainder of the war.

Supply programs for 1943 reflected prospective changes in the American role in the war. Cuts fell most heavily on the ground munitions program, which was reduced by more than one-fifth, and on lend-lease to nations other than the Soviet Union. Some reductions were also made in naval ship construction, but the program for building escort vessels was left intact and the merchant shipbuilding program was actually enlarged. The emphasis was on producing first of all the tools needed to defeat the U-boats and secure the sea lanes for the deployment of American forces overseas, and at the same time to insure that ample shipping would be available for this purpose. Soviet armies had to be assured a continuous flow of munitions to enable them to stave off the Germans. Meanwhile, airpower had to be built up and brought to bear as rapidly as possible, while the slower mobilization and deployment of ground forces was under way—heavy bombers to batter the German homeland, carrier-borne aircraft to restore mobility and striking power to the forces in the Pacific. The ground army, finally, had to be shaped to operate, at least during the coming year and a half, in relatively small packages at the end of long lines of communications in a great variety of terrain. Its units had to be compact, versatile, and easily transportable, but also mobile and able to hit hard. Every ton of shipping, as General McNair declared, had to deliver the maximum of fighting power.

The changing requirements and circumstances of coalition warfare in the offensive phase greatly affected plans and programs for expanding the U.S. Army—in total growth and internal distribution of strength as well as in overseas deployment. Manpower squeezes, together with strategic, logistical, and operational considerations, helped to change the shape as well as the size of the Army. By the end of 1942 the U.S. Army had grown to a strength of 5.4 million officers and men. Although this was still well under the ceiling of 8.2 million set by the President in November, the mobilization of ground combat elements was already nearing completion. Seventy-three divisions were then in being, and no more than 100 were expected to be activated. In June 1943 the goal was reduced to 90 divisions, with an overall strength ceiling of 7.7 million—far under the heavily mechanized force of 215 divisions which the framers of the Victory

Program in 1941 had considered none too large to take on the German Army Actually the U.S. Army in 1945 reached a peak strength of 8.3 million and 89 divisions. The last division was activated in August 1943.

The strength of ground combat units in the Army increased hardly at all after 1942, even though 16 divisions and some 350 separate artillery and engineer battalions were added after that date. These additional units had to be formed by means of redistribution and economies within existing personnel allotments in the same categories. Since the Army as a whole increased by almost 3 million men after 1942, its ground combat elements, even including replacements, declined from over half of the Army's total strength at the beginning of 1942 to about a third in the spring of 1945. It was no mean achievement merely to maintain the Army's combat units at full strength during the heavy fighting of 1944 and 1945. Neither the Germans nor the Japanese were able to do as much.

Mindful of the untrained divisions sent overseas in World War I, General Marshall from the first set as his goal thorough and realistic training of large units in the United States, culminating in large-scale maneuvers by corps and armies. Since all divisions had been activated by August 1943 and the mass deployment of the Army overseas did not begin until late in that year, most divisions were thoroughly trained. The major threat to an orderly training program came in 1944 when many trained divisions had to be skeletonized in order to meet the demand for trained replacements. Equipment shortages were a serious obstacle to effective training in early 1943, as in 1942, as was also the shortage of trained commissioned and noncommissioned officers to provide cadres.

In 1943 the Army's ground combat forces continued to undergo the drastic reorganization and streamlining begun in 1942. Troop basis cuts reduced the planned number of armored divisions from 20 to 16, eliminated all motorized divisions, and cut back tank destroyer and antiaircraft units. The armored corps disappeared. Armored and infantry divisions were reduced in personnel and equipment. Tanks taken from armored divisions were organized into separate tank battalions, to be attached to divisions as needed, and motor transport was pooled under corps or army headquarters for greater flexibility.

The division remained the basic fighting team of arms and services combined in proportions designed for continuous offensive action under normal battle conditions. Its triangular organization was retained. The infantry division contained 3 regiments, and included, besides 4 artillery battalions (3 armed with 105-mm. howitzers, 1 with 155-mm. howitzers), a reconnaisance troop (scout cars and light tanks), and engineer, ordnance, signal, quartermaster, medical, and military police units. Each regiment could readily be teamed with an artillery battalion. Reinforced with other elements of the division, or with elements assigned by corps or army headquarters, it formed the regimental combat team. The total strength of the infantry division was reduced from its prewar strength of 15,245 to 14,253.

The armored division, as organized in 1942, had consisted of 2 tank regiments and 1 armored infantry regiment, plus 3 battalions of armored artillery and an armored reconnaissance battalion. This arrangement was calculated to produce 2 combat commands, with varying proportions of tanks and infantry in division reserve. The armored division also included supporting elements corresponding to those in the infantry divisions but motorized to increase mobility. In the armored division as reorganized in 1943, battalions replaced regiments. The new model contained 3 medium tank battalions, 3 armored infantry battalions, and 3 armored artillery battalions. These, with supporting elements, could be combined readily into 3 combat commands (A, B, and Reserve). The total strength of the armored division was reduced from 14,620 to 10,937. Two armored divisions remained "heavy" divisions, with the old organization, until the end of the war.

The only other special type of division of real importance retained in 1943 was the airborne division. Including parachute and gliderborne regiments, it was designed as a miniature infantry division, with lighter, more easily transportable artillery and the minimum of vehicles and service elements needed to keep it fighting after an airdrop until it could be reinforced. Its strength was only 8,500 until early 1945 when it was raised to 12,979. By the beginning of 1945 other experimental and special-type divisions—mountain, motorized, light, jungle, and cavalry—had either disappeared or largely lost their special characteristics.

Underlying all this change were the basic aims of making ground forces mobile, flexible, and easily transportable, by increasing the proportion of standardized and interchangeable units in less rigid tactical combinations. Nor did this streamlining involve any sacrifice of effective power. Army leaders were convinced, and experience on the whole proved, that these units could not only move faster and farther, but could also strike even harder than the units they replaced.

Premobilization planning had contemplated that Negro Americans would be included in the ranks of a wartime Army proportionately to their number in the whole population and proportionately, also, in each of the arms and services. Neither goal was achieved, but the number of Negro troops in the Army reached a peak strength of over 700,000 and more than 500,000 of them served overseas. Contemporary attitudes and practices in American society kept

Negroes in segregated units throughout the war, although the Army gradually eliminated many of the obvious types of discrimination that almost inevitably flowed from their segregation. The bulk of Negro soldiers overseas were in supply and construction units; but many others who served in the two Negro divisions, in separate combat support battalions, and in a fighter group, directly engaged the enemy on the ground and in the air.

In 1944 the manpower shortage became nation-wide. The Army, under the double pressure of accelerated deployment schedules and heavy demands for infantry replacements for battle casualties in the two-front full-scale war, was driven to stringent measures. The Army Specialized Training Program, which had absorbed 150,000 soldiers in college study, was dissolved, and the aviation cadet training program was drastically curtailed. To release soldiers for battle, the Army drew heavily on limited service personnel and women for noncombat duties. The induction of female volunteers had begun in mid-1942 and in the following year, for the first time in the Army's history, women had been given a full legal military status as the Women's Army Corps (WAC). Growing in strength, the WAC reached a peak of 100,000 by the spring of 1945.

As the Army moved overseas, many posts were consolidated or closed, releasing large numbers of overhead personnel. Margins of overstrength and basic privates in tactical units were eliminated or reduced. Coast artillery units were converted to heavy artillery, hundreds of antiaircraft units were dissolved, and nondivisional infantry regiments became a source of infantry replacements. To meet the threat of the German counteroffensive in the Ardennes in December 1944, the handful of divisions remaining in the United States, most of them earmarked for the Pacific, were rushed to Europe, and the United States was left without a strategic reserve. In May 1945 the overall ground army numbered 68 infantry, 16 armored, and 5 airborne divisions.

The extent to which the Army depended on its air arm to confer striking power and mobility is suggested by the enormous growth of the Army Air Forces—from about 400,000 men at the beginning of 1942 to a peak of over 2.4 million early in 1944. At the end of the war in Europe it had 243 organized groups in being, and a numerical strength of 2.3 million men. More than 1.5 million of the worldwide AAF strength in March 1945 consisted of service troops, troops in training, and overhead.

After 1942 the growth of the ground army also was very largely in services and administrative elements. By March 1945 these comprised 2.1 million (not counting hospital patients and casuals en route) of the ground army's 5.9 million personnel. This growth reflected both the global character of the war, with its long lines of communications, and the immense numbers of noncombatant specialists needed to operate and service the equipment of a modern mechanized army. They were a manifestation, too, of the American people's insistence on providing the American citizen soldier with something like his accustomed standard of living. Less tangible and more difficult to control was the demand for large administrative and co-ordinating staffs, a demand that was self-generating since administrators themselves had to be administered and co-ordinators co-ordinated. One of the most conspicuous phenomena of global war was the big headquarters. In the European theater in 1944 "over-head" personnel, largely in higher headquarters, numbered some 114,000 men. On the eve of V–E Day, with overseas deployment for the two-front war complete, almost 1.3 million of the 2.8 million men who remained in the United States were in War Department, AGF, ASF, and AAF overhead agencies to operate the Zone of Interior establishment.

The demand for noncombatant personnel was swelled by the assignment to the Army of various administrative tasks. One was the administration of military lend-lease. Another was the development of the atomic bomb, the supersecret, $2 billion Manhattan Project assigned to the Corps of Engineers. Two of the Army's overseas commands—the China-Burma-India Theater and the Persian Gulf Command—had missions that were largely logistical in character. From the first the Pacific theaters generated the heaviest demands for service troops, to build, operate, and service the manifold facilities needed by a modern army in regions where these were virtually nonexistent. To a lesser degree these needs were also present in the Mediterranean, and operations against the Germans everywhere involved the task of repairing the ruin wrought by the enemy. Big construction projects like the Alcan Highway (from western Canada to Alaska) and the Ledo Road in Burma added to the burden. To carry out the Army's vast procurement program—to compute requirements, negotiate contracts, and expedite production—called for a multitude of highly trained administrators, mostly civilian businessmen whom the Army put into uniform.

Thus, for every three fighting men in the ground army, there were two technicians and administrators somewhere behind, engaged in functions other than killing the enemy. Behind the fighting front, too, stretched the "pipeline," filled with what General McNair once called "the invisible horde of people going here and there but seemingly never arriving." In March 1945 casuals en route or in process of assignment numbered 300,000. Far more numerous were the replacements, who at this time totaled 800,000 in the ground army; AAF replacements numbered 300,000. Almost no provision had been made for replacements in the early troop basis. The necessity of providing spaces for them, as well as for larger numbers of service and AAF troops, in the Army's total allotment of manpower went far to account for the difference between the 215 divisions in the original Victory Program and the 89 actually organized.

Replacements kept the effective strength of the Army from declining. The number of soldiers in hospitals in World War II seldom fell below 200,000, and at the beginning of 1945 reached a peak of almost 500,000. Throughout the war, the Army suffered a total of 936,000 battle casualties, including 235,000 dead; to the latter must be added 83,400 nonbattle deaths. The Army's dead represented about 3 percent of the 10,420,000 men who served in its ranks during World War II.

Despite the acknowledged primacy of the European war, only gradually did the flow of American troops overseas take the direction desired by the Army planners. Not until OVERLORD was given top priority at the Tehran Conference at the end of 1943 could the double war finally begin to assume the focus and flow into the channels planned by the War Department in the early stages of the coalition war. During 1943 the Army sent overseas close to 1.5 million men, including 13 divisions. Over two-thirds of these totals, including more than 1 million troops and 9 divisions, were deployed against Germany. In these terms the balance was finally being redressed in favor of the war against Germany. The cumulative totals at the end of 1943 showed 1.4 million men, including 17 divisions, deployed against Germany, as opposed to 913,000 troops, including 13 divisions, lined up against Japan—a sharp contrast to the picture at the end of 1942, when in manpower and number of divisions the war against Japan had maintained an edge over the war in Europe.

On the other hand, the failure of the Allies to agree on a specific plan for the cross-Channel attack until Tehran permitted deployment in the war against Japan to develop at a much quicker pace than the planners had expected. It was not until October 1943 that the divisions in Europe exceeded those in the Pacific. And when the effort expended by the Navy and Marine Corps, especially in the Pacific, is added to Army deployment overseas, a different picture emerges. Actually, after two years of war, the balance of U.S. forces— and resources—between the European and Japanese arenas was fairly even. Indeed, of the total of 3.7 million men—Army, Navy, and Marines—overseas during 1943, slightly more than half were arrayed against Japan. By the close of that year the growing costs of fighting a multifront war on an opportunistic basis and the difficulty of keeping a secondary war secondary in the absence of a firm long-range plan for the primary war had been driven home to the Army planners.

By the end of the midwar period—in September 1944—General Marshall and his staff could survey the state of Army deployment with considerable satisfaction. Channeling U.S. military power to the United Kingdom for a concentrated attack against Germany had been a long struggle. More divisions were sent overseas in the first nine months of 1944—the bulk of them going to the European theater—than had been shipped overseas during the previous two years. To support OVERLORD and its follow-up operations, the Army funneled forces into the European theater and later into continental Europe in ever-increasing numbers during the first three quarters of 1944. Slightly over 2 million men, including 34 divisions and 103 air groups, were in the European theater at the end of September 1944—over 45 percent of the total number of troops overseas in all Theaters. By then, the overall breakdown of Army troops overseas gave the war against Germany a 2 to 1 advantage over the Japanese conflict, and this was matched by the Army divisional distribution. Forty divisions were located in Europe and the Mediterranean, with 4 more en route, against 21 in the Pacific. In the air, the preponderance lay even more heavily in favor of Europe. With the bulk of the Army's combat strength overseas deployed against the Reich, and with most of the divisions that were in the United States slated to go to the European theater, General Marshall and his planners could consider their original concept well on the way to accomplishment. Although there were still over 3.5 million men left in the continental United States at the end of September, there were only 24 combat divisions remaining. The Army planners had hoped to maintain some of the divisions as a strategic reserve to cope with emergencies.

When the crisis caused by the Ardennes breakthrough of December 1944 denuded the United States of all the remaining divisions, the possibility of having raised too few divisions caused War Department leaders from Stimson on down some anxious moments. Fortunately this was the last unpleasant surprise; another such crisis would have found the divisional cupboard bare. Indeed, the decision for 90 divisions—the Army's "cutting edge"—was one of the greatest gambles taken by the Washington high command in World War II.

Thus, in the long run, Marshall and his staff were not only able to reverse the trend toward the Pacific that had lasted well into 1943 but had gone to the other extreme during 1944. Because of unexpected developments in the European war, not one division was sent to the Pacific after August 1944, and planning deployment totals for the Pacific for 1944 were never attained. European deployment, on the other hand, mounted steadily and substantially exceeded the planners' estimates. At the end of April 1945, when the Army reached its peak strength of 5.4 million overseas, over 3 million were in the European theater and 1.2 million in the Pacific. Regardless of the type of war fought in World

War II—concentration and invasion in Europe, or blockade, bombardment, and island hopping in the Pacific—each required a tremendous outlay of American military strength and resources.

Balancing Means and Ends

Throughout the conflict the matching of means with ends, of logistics with strategy, continued to be a complex process, for World War II was the greatest coalition effort and the first really global war in which the United States had been involved. The wherewithal had to be produced and delivered to a multitude of allies and so far-flung fronts over long sea lines of communications and all somehow harnessed to some kind of strategic design to defeat the enemies. As the war progressed, the Army strategic planners learned to appreciate more and more the limits of logistics in the multifront war. From the standpoint of the Americans, the basic strategic decisions they supported from the beginning— the Germany-first decision and the primacy of the cross-Channel attack—were in large measure justified by logistics. Each would capitalize on the advantages of concentrating forces and material resources on a single major line of communications and link the major arsenal represented by the United States with the strategically located logistical base offered by Great Britain. The realities of logistics had in part defeated their original BOLERO strategy, and forces and resources in being in other theaters had generated their own offensive strategy.

In the midwar era, while Allied plans remained unsettled, the competing claims of the Pacific and Mediterranean for a strategy of opportunism, the continuing needs of other far-flung fronts, added to the accumulated "fixed charges"—for example, aid to China, Britain, and the Soviet Union, and the rearming of the French—took a heavy toll of American resources. The full-blown war economy was matched by the full-blown war on the global scale. In and out of the international conferences of midwar in the era of relative plenty, the adjustment of means and ends went on and logistics remained a limiting, if not always the final determining, factor in the strategic debate. The scope, timing, landing places, and even the choice of specific operations were to a large extent influenced by the availability of the wherewithal, by the quantities that could be produced and delivered to the fighting fronts.

To logisticians in World War II, the balance among supplies and equipment, trained troops, and the shipping to transport them—the only means then feasible for mass movement overseas—was of continuing concern. In planning for that balance the factor of lead time was particularly important. For example, for the invasion of Normandy in June 1944 planning for the production of material had to start two years in advance, the buildup in England at least a year in advance, and the actual planning of detailed logistical support six months before the landings. Usually the shorter the lead time for logistical preparations, the narrower the range of strategic choices tended to be.

To the end the Army was, of course, one cog in the mighty American war machine, and it had to compete for resources with its sister services and with allies. The home front, too, had to be supported. While the war cut deeply into the life of the American people, it was fought with a "guns and butter" policy without any real sacrifice in the American standard of living. The Army was not anxious to cut into that standard of living. Nor did it have final say over the allocation and employment of key resources. To balance the allocation of forces, supplies, and shipping among the many fronts and nations, within the frame-work of the close partnership with the British, required a degree of central logistical control and direction at both combined and national level unknown in earlier wars. A complex network of Anglo-American and national civilian and military agencies for logistical planning emerged. In the melding of resources and plans that went on in and out of the international conferences, planners took their cue from the basic decisions of the CCS—in this sense, the top logistical as well as strategic planning organization.

An imposing structure of federal agencies and committees grew up in Washington to control the nation's economic mobilization. Its keystone was the influential War Production Board (WPB) that controlled the allocation and use of raw materials, machine tools, and facilities, with powers similar to those of the War Industries Board in World War I. In the military sphere the War Department, like the Navy Department, had a large degree of autonomy in controlling requirements planning, production, and distribution of material for its forces. The actual procurement—that is, purchasing and contracting of munitions and other war materials—was carried out directly by the Army's technical services and the Navy's bureaus. Within the Joint Chiefs of Staff orga-nization many logistical problems at issue between the services were settled by negotiation. The War Shipping Administration (WSA) operated and allocated the critical United States merchant shipping. Close co-operation between WSA and the British Ministry of War Transport resulted in the pooling of the two merchant fleets, comprising the bulk of the world's mercantile tonnage. Other civilian agencies dealt with such critical commodities as food, petroleum products, and rubber. In the spring of 1943 most of the mobilization agencies were subordinated to a new co-ordinating unit, the Office of War Mobilization headed by former Justice James F. Byrnes.

Theoretically U.S. munitions production along with that of the British empire was placed in a "common pool" and distributed according to strategic need. Allocations were made by two Munitions Assignments Boards, each representing both countries and responsible to the CCS. One board, sitting in Washington, allocated U.S. production, while a second in London allocated British production. Using the principles of lend-lease and reciprocal aid, these two boards made allocations to other Western Allied countries as well as to the United States and Britain. Supplies for the Soviet Union were governed by separate diplomatic protocols, and the boards seldom attempted to alter their provisions in making assignments. The common pool theory, however, proved somewhat too idealistic for complete application. It really applied from the start almost entirely to American production, for the British had little surplus to distribute. Their contributions to the American effort, though substantial, normally took the form of services and soft goods rather than military hardware. In these circumstances, the Americans almost inevitably came to question the application of the common pool theory and to make assignments on the premise that each partner had first call on its own resources. British participation in the allocation of American production became only nominal in the later war years.

However imperfect the application of the common pool concept, lend-lease, with its counterpart, reciprocal aid, proved an admirable instrument of coalition warfare. Lend-lease did what President Roosevelt had initially intended it should. It removed the dollar sign from Allied supply transactions and gave the Allies an unprecedented flexibility in distributing materials without generating complicated financial transactions or postwar problems such as the war debts of World War I had created. Under the Lend-Lease Act of March 1941, the War Department turned over to Allied countries approximately $25 billion worth of war materials. About 58 percent went to Britain, 23 percent to Russia, 8 percent to France, 7 percent to China, and the remainder to other countries. Included in these supplies were some 37,000 light and medium tanks, nearly 800,000 trucks, and 3,400 locomotives. The Army Service Forces was the Army's operating agency for administering this program, and from 1942 on military lend-lease requirements were included with U.S. Army requirements in the Army supply program. This American largess was distributed almost exclusively under the principle of achieving complete military victory in the war, not of contributing to the postwar political purposes of any ally.

Even with American production in high gear during 1943–45, critical shortages or bottlenecks developed to hamper operations at various stages. In early 1943, as in 1942, the most stringent limiting factor was ocean shipping to transport troops and supplies overseas. Indeed, in the spring of 1943, when

LST Discharging Cargo Over a Ponton Causeway, *Gela, Sicily.*

President Roosevelt decided to divert scarce shipping to support the faltering British economy, he had to overrule the JCS, deeply concerned over American military requirements—one of the few occasions in the war he did so. After mid-1943, amid the changing requirements of the war in full bloom, the logistical bottlenecks tended to be specialized rather than general. From late 1943 until June 1944 the most serious critical shortage became the supply of assault shipping to land troops and supplies in amphibious operations. In the case of landing craft, the shortage was most severe in one specific category, the Landing Ship Tank (LST). In April 1944 Winston Churchill became exasperated enough to wonder whether history would ever understand why "the plans of two great empires like Britain and the United States should be so much hamstrung and limited" by an "absurd shortage of the L.S.T.'s." In the last stage, after troops were ashore and fighting on the European continent, the principal bottleneck shifted to port and inland clearance capacity in both that area and in the Pacific.

The basic problem of allocating resources between the war against Germany and the war against Japan remained almost to the end. Although the basic decision of "Germany first" held throughout the conflict, one of the most persistent questions concerned the proportion in which available resources should be divided between the two wars. This question reflected some divergence of political, military, geographical, and psychological factors in the Anglo-

American strategy of the war. For Britain, the war against Japan tended to be a side show, and its leaders tended to emphasize the effort in Europe and the Mediterranean at the expense of the Pacific. The United States more than met its commitments in Europe but insisted from the beginning on a margin of safety in the war against Japan, for which it early had been given major responsibility. Furthermore, the pull to the Pacific in midwar that the U.S. Navy and General MacArthur, both now on the offensive, particularly welcomed became for the Washington high command a lever against overcommitment in the Mediterranean. At the midwar conferences the Anglo-American debate focused on the division of resources among the theaters where the two nations combined their efforts—the Mediterranean, northwest Europe, and Southeast Asia. For the Pacific, American military leaders simply presented their decisions, logistical as well as strategic, to the conferences for the stamp of approval. In effect, American military leaders in midwar went far toward asserting unilateral control over the division of American resources between the two wars.

In the final analysis, the multifront nature of the war developed as a product of changing circumstances rather than of a predetermined grand design. Coalition strategy evolved as a result of a complex, continuing process—a constant struggle to adjust ends and means, to reconcile diverse pressures, pulls, and shifting conditions in the global war, and to effect compromises among nations with diverse national interests. That strategy, frequently dictated by necessity, often emerged from events rather than determined them.

The Washington high command was to end the war as it began it—without a fully developed theory on how to match strategic plans, manpower, and resources for a coalition, global war. But throughout its search for the formula for victory it had consistently pursued its goal of winning the war decisively, of complete military victory, without concern for postwar political aims. Whatever general political objectives the President had, he was committed to no strategic doctrine except complete victory. The political and military spheres of American national policy continued their customary separate ways.

Institutionally, World War II became for American strategists and logisticians an organization war, a war of big planning staffs in the capitals and the theater headquarters. Strategy and logistics became big business—established industries in the huge American wartime military establishment. World War II contributed significantly to the education of American Army planners in these arts. General Marshall, for example, once succinctly observed that his military experience in World War I had been based on roads, rivers, and railroads; in World War II he had to learn all over again and to acquire "an education based on oceans."

Throughout Americans evinced their national habit in war—a penchant for quick, direct, and total solutions. The strategic principles they stressed were entirely in harmony with their own traditions and capacities. They proved particularly adept in adapting their mass-production economy to war purposes and in applying power on a massive scale. How far they had come in the quarter century since World War I was evidenced by a comparison of their strategic experience in the two coalition world wars of the twentieth century. In World War I the United States, a junior partner, conformed to the strategy set by the Allies; in World War II the United States came to hold its own in allied war councils and played an influential role in molding Allied strategy, virtually dictating the strategy of the Pacfic war. In meeting the problems of global coalition warfare, in the greatest conflict in which the United States had been involved, American strategists and logisticians came of age.

The multifront war of mass, technology, and mobility that taxed the strategists and logisticians in Washington also challenged the overseas commands and the tacticians in the field. As the war had progressed, the role of the theater commands in strategy, logistics, and tactics had become increasingly significant. It is appropriate, therefore, at this point to turn from Washington high command to the Army overseas and to trace the actual course of operations in the double war.

CHAPTER 22

World War II: The War Against Germany and Italy

With the invasion of North Africa (Operation TORCH), the U.S. Army in late 1942 began a ground offensive against the European Axis that was to be sustained almost without pause until Italy collapsed and Germany was finally defeated. More than a million Americans were to fight in lands bordering the Mediterranean Sea and close to four million on the European continent, exclusive of Italy, in the largest commitment to battle ever made by the U.S. Army. Alongside these Americans were to march British, Canadian, French, and other Allied troops in history's greatest demonstration of coalition warfare, while on another front massed Soviet armies were to contribute enormously to the victory.

The North African Campaign, November 1942–May 1943

Although the decision to launch Operation TORCH had been made largely because the Allies could not mount a more direct attack against the European Axis early in the war, there were specific and attractive objectives—to gain French-controlled Morocco, Algeria, and Tunisia as a base for enlisting the French empire in the war, to assist the British in the Libyan Desert in destroying Axis forces in North Africa, to open the Mediterranean to Allied shipping, and to provide a steppingstone for subsequent operations.

The Germans and their Italian allies controlled a narrow but strategic strip of the North African littoral between Tunisia and Egypt with impassable desert bounding the strip on the south. (*Map 40*) Numbering some 100,000 men under a battle-tested German leader, Field Marshal Rommel, the German-Italian army in Libya posed a constant threat to Egypt and the Near East as well as to French North Africa and, since the Axis also controlled the northern shores of the Mediterranean, served to deny the Mediterranean to Allied shipping. Only a few convoys seeking to supply British forces on the island of Malta ever ventured into the Mediterranean, and these took heavy losses.

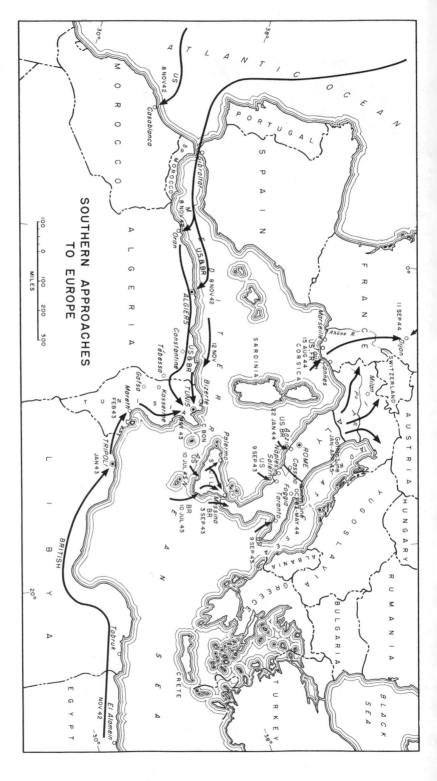

MAP 40

SOUTHERN APPROACHES
TO EUROPE

MILES
100   0   100   200   300

ATLANTIC OCEAN

MOROCCO

US
8 NOV 42
Casablanca

SP. MOROCCO
Gibraltar
8 NOV 42
Oran
US & BR

PORTUGAL

SPAIN

ALGERIA

ALGIERS
US & BR
8 NOV 42
12 NOV

FRANCE
11 SEP 44
Dijon
SWITZERLAND
Rhône R.
Marseille
US, FR
15 AUG 44
Cannes
CORSICA

AUSTRIA

HUNGARY

Constantine

Tébessa

Bizerte
TUNIS
US & BR
BON
7 MAY 43

SARDINIA

Milan
Po
Gothic Line
JAN-APR 45
ROME
Cassino
Gustav Line
Anzio
22 JAN 44
Naples
9 SEP 43
Salerno
US
Foggia
Taranto
BR
9 SEP 43

YUGOSLAVIA

RUMANIA

Gafsa
Kasserine
Mareth
FEB 43
TRIPOLI
JAN 43

Palermo
US
10 JUL 43
Messina
BR
3 SEP 43
BR
10 JUL 43

TYRRHENIAN SEA

ALBANIA

BULGARIA

BLACK SEA

BRITISH

LIBYA

Tobruk

IONIAN SEA

GREECE

TURKEY

EGYPT

El Alamein
NOV 42

CRETE

MEDITERRANEAN SEA

Moving against French Africa posed for the Allies special problems rooted in the nature of the armistice that had followed French defeat in 1940. Under terms of that armistice, the Germans had left the French empire nominally intact, along with much of the southern half of Metropolitan France, yet in return the French Government was pledged to drop out of the war. Although an underground resistance movement had already begun in France and an Allied-equipped force called the Free French was assembling in the British Isles, that part of the regular French Army and Navy left intact by the armistice was sworn to the service of the Vichy government. This pledge had led already to the anomaly of Frenchman fighting Frenchman and of the British incurring French enmity by destroying part of the fleet of their former ally.

If bloodshed was to be averted in the Allied invasion, French sympathies had to be enlisted in advance, but to reveal the plan was to risk French rejection of it and German occupation of French Africa. Although clandestine negotiations were conducted with a few trusted French leaders, these produced no guarantee that French forces would not resist.

Partly because of this intricate situation, the Allies designated an American, General Eisenhower, to command the invasion in order to capitalize on absence of rancor between French and Americans by giving the invasion an American rather than a British complexion. American troops were to make up the bulk of the assault force, and the Royal Navy was to keep its contribution as inconspicuous as possible.

The operation was to begin in western Egypt, where the British Commander in Chief, Middle East, General Sir Harold R. L. G. Alexander, was to attack with the veteran British Eighth Army under Lt. Gen. Bernard L. Montgomery against Field Marshal Rommel's German-Italian army. Coming ashore in French Africa, General Eisenhower's combined U.S.-British force was to launch a converging attack against Rommel's rear.

In selecting beaches for the invasion, U.S. planners insisted upon a landing on the Atlantic coast of Morocco lest the Germans seal the Strait of Gibraltar and cut off support to forces put ashore on the Mediterranean coast. Because both troops and shipping were limited, a landing on the Atlantic coast restricted the number and size of landings possible inside the Mediterranean. Although a landing as far east as Tunisia was desirable because of vast overland distances (from the Atlantic coast to Tunis is more than a thousand miles), proximity of Axis aircraft on Sicily and Sardinia made that too perilous.

Making the decision on the side of security, the Allies planned simultaneous landings at three points—in Morocco near the Atlantic port of Casablanca and in Algeria near the ports of Oran and Algiers. Once the success of these landings was assured, a convoy was to put ashore small contingents of British troops to seize ports in eastern Algeria while a ground column headed for Tunisia in a race to get there before the Germans could move in.

Given the assignment to invade North Africa only at the end of July 1942, the U.S. Army faced enormous difficulties in meeting a target date in November of the same year. Troops had had little training in amphibious warfare, landing craft were few and obsolete, and much equipment was inferior to that of the Axis forces. So few U.S. troops were available in England that troops for the landing near Casablanca had to be shipped direct from the United States, one of history's longest sea voyages preceding an amphibious assault.

After soundly defeating an Axis attack, Montgomery's Eighth Army on October 23 auspiciously opened an offensive at El 'Alamein, there to score a victory that was to be a turning point in British fortunes. A little over two weeks later, before daylight on November 8, the U.S. Navy put U.S. Army forces ashore near Casablanca, while the Royal Navy landed other U.S. troops and contingents of British troops near Oran and Algiers. The entire invasion force consisted of over 400 warships, 1,000 planes, and some 107,000 men, including a battalion of paratroopers jumping in the U.S. Army's first airborne attack.

Although the invasion achieved strategic surprise, the French in every case but one fought back at the beaches. Dissidence among various French factions limited the effectiveness of some of the opposition, but any resistance at all raised the specter of delay that might enable the Germans to beat the Allies into Tunisia. Three days passed before the French agreed to cease fire and take up arms on the Allied side.

French support at last assured, the Royal Navy put British troops ashore close to the Tunisian border while an Allied column began the long overland trek. The British troops were too few to do more than secure two small Algerian ports, the ground column too late. Over the narrow body of water between Sicily and North Africa the Germans poured planes, men, and tanks. Except for barren mountains in the interior, Tunisia was for the moment out of Allied reach.

The Tunisia Campaign

Recoiling from the defeat at El 'Alamein, Rommel's German-Italian army in January 1943 occupied old French fortifications near the southern border of Tunisia, the Mareth Line, there to face Montgomery's Eighth Army, while more than 100,000 enemy troops under General Juergen von Arnim faced westward against General Eisenhower's Allied force. Although the Italian high command in Italy exercised loose control, the Axis nations failed to establish a unified command over these two forces.

The Allied plan to defeat Rommel by converging attacks having been foiled, General Eisenhower had no choice but to dig in to defend in the Tunisian mountains until he could accumulate enough strength to attack in conjunction with a renewed strike by Montgomery against the Mareth Line. Before this could be accomplished, Rommel on February 14 sent strong armored forces through the passes in central Tunisia against the U.S. II Corps, commanded by Maj. Gen. Lloyd R. Fredendall. Rommel planned to push through the Kasserine Pass, then turn northwestward by way of an Allied supply base at Tébessa to reach the coast and trap the Allied units.

In a series of sharp armored actions, Rommel quickly penetrated thinly held American positions and broke through the Kasserine Pass. Although success appeared within his grasp, lack of unified command interfered. Planning an attack of his own, General von Arnim refused to release an armored division needed to continue Rommel's thrust. Concerned that Rommel lacked the strength for a deep envelopment by way of Tébessa, the Italian high command directed a turn northward, a much shallower envelopment.

The turn played into Allied hands, for the British already had established a blocking position astride the only road leading northward. At the height of a clash between Rommel's tanks and the British, four battalions of American artillery arrived after a forced march from Oran. On February 22 these guns and a small band of British tanks brought the Germans to a halt. Warned by intelligence reports that the British Eighth Army was about to attack the Mareth Line, Rommel hurriedly pulled back to his starting point.

The Axis offensive defeated, the U.S. II Corps, commanded now by Maj. Gen. George S. Patton, Jr., launched a diversionary attack on March 17 toward the rear of the Mareth Line, while Montgomery's Eighth Army a few days later struck the line in force. By the end of the first week of April, the two forces had joined.

With all their forces now linked under the tactical command of General Alexander, the Allies opened a broad offensive that within a month captured the ports of Bizerte and Tunis and compressed all Axis troops into a small bridgehead covering the Cape Bon peninsula at the northeastern tip of Tunisia. The last of some 275,000 Germans and Italians surrendered on May 10.

Although the original Allied strategy had been upset by the delay imposed by French resistance and the swift German build-up in Tunisia, Allied troops achieved victory in six months, which in view of their limited numbers and long lines of communications, was impressive. A few days later the first unopposed British convoy since 1940 reached beleaguered Malta.

American troops in their first test against German arms had made many mistakes. Training, equipment, and leadership had failed in many instances to meet the requirements of the battlefield, but the lessons were clear and pointed to nothing that time might not correct. More imporant was the experience gained, both in battle and in logistical support. Important too was the fact that the Allied campaign had brought a French army back into the war. Most important of all, the Allies at last had gained the initiative.

The Sicily Campaign, July–August 1943

Where the Allies were to go after North Africa had already been decided in January 1943 at the Casablanca Conference. As with the decision to invade North Africa, the next step—invading Sicily (Operation HUSKY)—followed from recognition that the Allies still were unready for a direct thrust across the English Channel. Utilizing troops already available in North Africa, they could make the Mediterranean safer for Allied shipping by occupying Sicily, perhaps going on after that to invade Italy and knock the junior Axis partner out of the war.

As planning proceeded for the new operation, General Eisenhower (promoted now to four-star rank) remained as supreme commander, while General Alexander, heading the 15th Army Group, served as ground commander. Alexander controlled Montgomery's Eighth Army and a newly created Seventh U.S. Army under Patton (now a lieutenant general).

How to invade the Vermont-size, three-cornered island posed a special problem. The goal was Messina, the gateway to the narrow body of water between Sicily and Italy, the enemy's escape route to the Italian mainland. Yet the Strait of Messina was so narrow and well fortified that Allied commanders believed the only solution was to land elsewhere and march on Messina by way of shallow coastal shelves on either side of towering Mount Etna.

Applying the principle of mass, Alexander directed that all landings be made in the southeastern corner of the island, British on the east coast, Americans on the southwest. Behind British beaches a brigade of glider troops was to capture a critical bridge, while a regiment of U.S. paratroopers took high ground behind American beaches. After seizing minor ports and close-in airfields, Patton's Seventh Army was to block to the northwest against Axis reserves while Montgomery mounted a main effort up the east coast.

Because Sicily was an obvious objective after North Africa, complete strategic surprise was hardly possible, but bad weather helped the Allies achieve tactical surprise. As a huge armada bearing some 160,000 men steamed across the Mediterranean, a mistral—a form of unpredictable gale common to the Mediterranean—sprang up, so churning the sea that General Eisenhower was for a time tempted to order delay. While the heavy surf swamped some landing craft and made all landings difficult, it put the beach defenders off their guard. Before daylight on July 10, both British and Americans were ashore in sizable numbers.

As presaged in North Africa, poor performance by Italian units left to German reserves the task of repelling the invasion. Although preattack bombardment by Allied planes and confusion caused by a scattered jump of U.S. paratroopers delayed German reaction, a panzer division mounted a sharp counterattack against American beaches before the first day was out. It came dangerously close to pushing some American units into the sea before naval gunfire and a few U.S. tanks and artillery pieces that had got ashore drove off the German tanks.

To speed reinforcement, the Allies on two successive nights flew in American and British paratroopers. In both instances, antiaircraft gunners on ships standing offshore and others on land mistook the planes for enemy aircraft and opened fire. Losses were so severe that for a time some Allied commanders questioned the wisdom of employing this new method of warfare.

The Germans meanwhile formed a solid block in front of the British along the east coast, prompting General Patton to urge expanding the role of his Seventh Army. First cutting the island in two with a drive by the II Corps, commanded now by Maj. Gen. Omar N. Bradley, Patton sent a provisional corps pushing rapidly through faltering Italian opposition to the port of Palermo and the northwestern tip of the island. This accomplished within fourteen days after coming ashore, Patton turned to aid the British by attacking toward Messina along a narrow northern coastal shelf.

As both Allied armies in early August readied a final assault to gain Messina, the Germans began to withdraw to the mainland. Despite Allied command of sea and air, they managed to evacuate all their forces, some 40,000 troops. When on August 17, thirty days after the invasion, U.S. patrols pushed into Messina, the Germans had incurred some 10,000 casualties, the Italians probably as many as 100,000, mostly prisoners of war. Allied losses were 22,000.

The American force that fought in Sicily was far more sophisticated than that which had gone into battle in North Africa. New landing craft, some capable of bearing tanks, had made getting ashore much quicker and surer, and new amphibious trucks called DUKW's eased the problem of supply over the beaches. Gone was the Grant tank with its side-mounted gun, lacking wide traverse; in its place was the Sherman with 360-degree power-operated traverse for a turret-mounted 75-mm. piece. Commanders were alert to avoid a mistake often made in North Africa of parceling out divisions in small increments, and the men were sure of their weapons and their own ability. Some problems of co-ordination with tactical air remained, but these soon would be worked out.

The Surrender of Italy

Even as the Allies had been preparing to invade Sicily, the Italian people and their government had become increasingly disenchanted with the war. Under the impact of the loss of North Africa, the invasion of Sicily, and a first bombing of Rome, the Italian king forced Mussolini to resign as head of the government.

Anxious to find a way out of the war, a new Italian government made contact with the Allies through diplomatic channels, leading to direct talks with General Eisenhower's representatives. The Italians, it soon developed, were in a quandary—they wanted to pull out of the war, yet they were virtual prisoners of German forces in Italy that Hitler, sensing Italian defection, strongly reinforced. Although plans were drawn for airborne landings to secure Rome coincident with announcement of Italian surrender, these were canceled in the face of Italian vacillation and inability to guarantee strong assistance in fighting the Germans. The Italian government nevertheless agreed to surrender, a fact General Eisenhower announced on the eve of the principal Allied landing on the mainland.

The Italian Campaign, September 1943–May 1945

Since the Allied governments had decided to pursue after Sicily whatever course offered the best chance of knocking Italy from the war, invading the mainland logically followed. This plan also presented an opportunity to tie down German forces and prevent their employment either on the Russian front or against the eventual Allied attack across the English Channel. Occupying Italy also would provide airfields close to Germany and the Balkans.

How far up the peninsula of Italy the Allies were to land depended almost entirely on the range of fighter aircraft based on Sicily, for all Allied aircraft carriers were committed to the war in the Pacific. Another consideration was a desire to control the Strait of Messina to shorten sea supply lines.

On September 3 a British force under Montgomery crossed the Strait of Messina and landed on the toe of the Italian boot against surprisingly moderate opposition. Following Eisenhower's announcement of Italian surrender, a British fleet steamed brazenly into the harbor of Taranto in the arch of the Italian boot to put a British division ashore on the docks, while the Fifth U.S. Army under Lt. Gen. Mark W. Clark staged an assault landing on beaches near Salerno, twenty-five miles southeast of Naples.

Reacting in strength against the Salerno invasion, the Germans two days after the landing mounted a vigorous counterattack that threatened to split the beachhead and force abandonment of part of it. For four days, the issue was in doubt. Quick reinforcement of the ground troops (including a regiment of paratroopers jumping into the beachhead), gallant fighting, liberal air support, and unstinting naval gunfire at last repulsed the German attack. On September 15 the Germans began to withdraw, and the next day patrols of the British Eighth Army arrived from the south to link the two Allied forces. Two weeks later American troops took Naples, thereby gaining an excellent port, while the British seized valuable airfields around Foggia on the other side of the peninsula.

Although the Germans seriously considered abandoning southern Italy to pull back to a line in the Northern Apennines, the local commander, Field Marshal Albert Kesselring, insisted that he could hold for a considerable time on successive lines south of Rome. This proved to be an accurate assessment. The Allied advance was destined to proceed slowly, partly because of the difficulty of offensive warfare in rugged mountainous terrain and partly because the Allies limited their commitment to the campaign, not only in troops but also in shipping and the landing craft that were necessary if the enemy's strong defensive positions were to be broken by other than frontal attack.

Because the build-up for a cross-Channel attack—the main effort against Germany—was beginning in earnest, the Allies could spare few additional troops or shipping to pursue the war in Italy. Through the fall and winter of 1943–44, the armies would have to do the job in Italy with what was at hand, a total of eighteen Allied divisions.

A renewed offensive in October 1943 broke a strong German delaying position at the Volturno River, twenty miles north of Naples, and carried as far as a so-called Winter Line, an imposing position anchored on towering peaks around the town of Cassino. Casting about for a way to break this line, General Eisenhower obtained permission to retain temporarily from the build-up in Britain enough shipping and landing craft to make an amphibious end run. General Clark was to use a corps of his Fifth U.S. Army to land on beaches near Anzio, some thirty miles south of Rome and sixty miles behind the Winter

Line. By threatening or cutting German lines of communications to the Winter Line, the troops at Anzio were to facilitate Allied advance through the line and up the valley of the Liri River, the most obvious route to Rome.

Provided support by a French corps equipped with American arms, General Clark pulled out the U.S. VI Corps under Maj. Gen. John P. Lucas to make the envelopment. While the VI Corps—which included a British division—sailed toward Anzio, the Fifth Army launched a massive attack aimed at gaining access to the Liri valley. Although the VI Corps landed unopposed at Anzio on January 22, 1944, the attack on the Winter Line gained little.

Rushing reserves to Anzio, Field Marshal Kesselring quickly erected a firm perimeter about the Allied beachhead and successfully resisted every attempt at breakout. On February 16 Kesselring launched a determined attack to eliminate the beachhead that only a magnificent defense by U.S. and British infantry supported by artillery, tanks, planes, and naval gunfire at last thwarted.

Through the rest of the winter and early spring, the Fifth and Eighth Armies regrouped and built their combined strength to twenty-five divisions, mainly with the addition of French and British Commonwealth troops. General Eisenhower, meanwhile, had relinquished command in the Mediterranean early in January to go to Britain in preparation for the coming invasion of France. He was succeeded by a Britisher, Field Marshal Sir Henry M. Wilson.

On May 11 the Fifth and Eighth Armies launched a new carefully synchronized attack to break the Winter Line. Passing through almost trackless mountains, French troops under General Clark's command scored a penetration that unhinged the German position. As the Germans began to fall back toward Rome, the VI Corps attacked from the Anzio beachhead but failed to make sufficient progress to cut the enemy's routes of withdrawal. On June 4, 1944, U.S. troops entered Rome.

With D-day in Normandy only two days off, the focus of the Allied war against Germany shifted to France, and with the shift came a gradual diminution of Allied strength in Italy. Allied forces nevertheless continued to pursue the principle of the offensive. Reaching a new German position in the Northern Apennines, the Gothic Line, they started in August a three-month campaign that achieved penetrations, but they were unable to break out of the mountains. This period also saw a change in command as General Clark became commander of the Allied army group and Lt. Gen. Lucian K. Truscott assumed command of the Fifth Army.

In the spring of 1945 the Fifth and Eighth Armies penetrated a final German defensive line to enter the fertile plains of the Po River valley. On May 2, the Germans in Italy surrendered, the first formal capitulation of the war.

A German Trench on the Gothic Line, *overlooking a circling road.*

Less generally acclaimed than other phases of World War II, the campaign in Italy nevertheless had a vital part in the overall conduct of the war. At the crucial time of the Normandy landings, Allied troops in Italy were tying down twenty-six German divisions that well might have upset the balance in France. As a result of this campaign, the Allies obtained airfields useful for strategic bombardment of Germany and the Balkans, and conquest of the peninsula further guaranteed the safety of Allied shipping in the Mediterranean.

Cross-Channel Attack

Even as the Allied ground campaign was proceeding on the shores of the Mediterranean, three other campaigns were under way from the British Isles—the campaign of the U.S. Navy and the Royal Navy to defeat the German submarine, a U.S.-British strategic bombing offensive against Germany, and a third, intricately tied in with the other two, a logistical marathon to assemble the men and tools necessary for a direct assault against the foe.

Most critical of all was the antisubmarine campaign, for without success in that, the two others could progress only feebly at best. The turning point in that campaign came in April 1943, when the full effect of all the various devices used against the U-boat began to be apparent. Despite German intro-duction of an acoustical torpedo that homed on the noise of an escort's propellers, and later of the *schnorkel*, a steel tube extending above water by means of which the U-boat could charge its batteries without surfacing, Allied shipping losses continued to decline. In the last two years of the war the submarines would sink only one-seventh of the shipping they did in the earlier years.

In the second campaign, the combined bomber offensive that U.S. and British chiefs at Casablanca had directed, the demands of the war in the Pacific and the Mediterranean slowed American participation. Not until the summer of 1943 were sufficient U.S. bombers available in Britain to make a substantial contribution, and not until February 1944 were U.S. airmen at last able to match the big thousand-plane raids of the British.

While the Royal Air Force struck by night, bombers of the U.S. Army Air Forces hit by day, both directing much of their attention to the German aircraft industry in an effort to cripple the German air arm before the invasion. Although the raids imposed delays on German production, the most telling effect was the loss of German fighter aircraft and trained pilots rising to oppose the Allied bombers. As time for the invasion approached, the German air arm had ceased to represent a real threat to Allied ground operations, and Allied bombers could shift their attention to transportation facilities in France in an effort to restrict the enemy's ability to move reserves against the invasion.

The logistical build-up in the British Isles, meanwhile, had been progressing at an ever-increasing pace, easily the most tremendous single logistical under-taking of all time. The program entailed transporting some 1,600,000 men across the submarine-infested Atlantic before D-day and providing for their shelter, hospitalization, supply, training, and general welfare. Mountains of weapons and equipment, ranging from locomotives and big bombers to dental fillings, also had to be shipped.

Planning for the invasion had begun long before as the British, standing alone, looked to the day when they might return to the Continent. Detailed planning began in 1943 when the Combined Chiefs of Staff appointed a Britisher, Lt. Gen. Frederick E. Morgan, as chief of staff to a supreme com-mander yet to be named. Under Morgan's direction, British and American officers drew up plans for several contingencies, one of which, Operation OVERLORD, anticipated a large-scale assault against a still powerful German Army. This plan served as the basis for a final plan developed early in 1944 after General Eisenhower, designated as the supreme commander, arrived in Britain and established his command, Supreme Headquarters, Allied Expeditionary Force, or SHAEF.

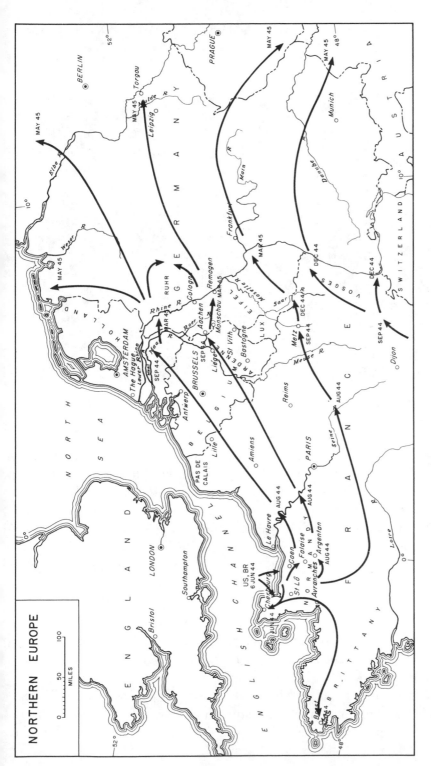

NORTHERN EUROPE

MILES

0   50   100

MAP 41

GENERAL EISENHOWER TALKING TO PARATROOPERS *before their drop behind the Normandy beaches.*

The over-all ground commander for the invasion was the former head of the British Eighth Army, General Montgomery, who also commanded the 21 Army Group, the controlling headquarters for the two Allied armies scheduled to make the invasion. The British Second Army under Lt. Gen. Sir Miles C. Dempsey was to assault on the left; the First U.S. Army under Bradley (promoted now to lieutenant general) on the right.

A requirement that the invasion beaches had to be within easy range of fighter aircraft based in Britain and close to at least one major port sharply limited the choice. The state of German defenses imposed further limitations, leaving only one logical site, the base of the Cotentin peninsula in Normandy, southeast of Cherbourg. (*Map 41*) To facilitate supply until Cherbourg or some other port could be opened, two artificial harbors were to be towed from Britain and emplaced off the invasion beaches.

Despite a weather forecast of high winds and a rough sea, General Eisenhower made a fateful decision to go ahead with the invasion on June 6. During the night over 5,000 ships moved to assigned positions, and at two o'clock, the

U.S. Troops Moving Ashore at Omaha Beach on D-Day

morning of the 6th, the operation for which the world had long and anxiously waited opened. One British and two U.S. airborne divisions (the 82d and 101st) dropped behind the beaches to secure routes of egress for the seaborne forces. Following preliminary aerial and naval bombardment, the first waves of infantry and tanks began to touch down at 6:30, just after sunrise. A heavy surf made the landings difficult but, as in Sicily, put the defenders off their guard.

The assault went well on British beaches, where one Canadian and two British divisions landed, and also at Utah, westernmost of the U.S. beaches, where the 4th Division came ashore. The story was different at Omaha Beach; there an elite German division occupying high bluffs laced with pillboxes put the landings in jeopardy. Allied intelligence had detected the presence of the enemy division too late to alter the landing plan. Only through improvisation and personal courage were the men of two regiments of the 1st Division and one of the 29th at last able to work their way up the bluffs and move slowly inland. Some 50,000 U.S. troops nevertheless made their way ashore on the two beaches before the day was out. American casualties were approximately 6,500, British and Canadian, 4,000—in both cases lighter than expected.

The German command was slow to react to the invasion, having been misled not only by the weather but also by an Allied deception plan which continued to lead the Germans to believe that this was only a diversionary assault, that the main landings were to come later on the Pas de Calais. Only in one instance, against the British who were solidly ashore, did the Germans mount a sizable counterattack on D-day.

Build-up and Breakout

While Allied aircraft and French resistance fighters impeded the movement of German reserves, the Allies quickly built up their strength and linked the beachheads. U.S. troops then moved against Cherbourg, taking the port, after bitter fighting, three weeks following the invasion. Other Allied forces had in the meantime been deepening the beachhead between Caen and the road center of St. Lô, so that by the end of June the most forward positions were twenty miles from the sea, and the Germans still had been able to mount no major counterattack.

Commanded by Field Marshal Gerd von Rundstedt, the Germans nevertheless defended tenaciously in terrain ideally suited to the defense. This was hedgerow country, where through the centuries French farmers had erected high banks of earth around every small field to fence livestock and protect crops from coastal winds. These banks were thick with the roots of shrubs and trees, and in many places sunken roads screened by a canopy of tree branches ran between two hedgerows. Tunneling into the hedgerows and using the sunken roads for lines of communication, the Germans turned each field into a small fortress.

For all the slow advance and lack of ports (a gale on June 19 demolished one of the artificial harbors and damaged the other), the Allied build-up was swift. By the end of June close to a million men had come ashore, along with some 586,000 tons of supplies and 177,000 vehicles. General Bradley's First Army included four corps with 2 armored and 11 infantry divisions. British strength was about the same.

Seeking to end the battle of the hedgerows, the British attempted to break into more open country near Caen, only to be thwarted by concentrations of German armor. General Bradley then tried a breakout on the right near St. Lô. Behind an intensive aerial bombardment that utilized both tactical aircraft and heavy bombers, the First Army attacked on July 25. By the second day American troops had opened a big breach in German positions, whereupon armored divisions drove rapidly southward twenty-five miles to Avranches at the base of the Cotentin peninsula. While the First Army turned southeastward, the

Third U.S. Army under General Patton entered the line to swing through Avranches into Brittany in quest of ports.

The arrival of the Third Army signaled a major change in command. General Bradley moved up to command the 12th Army Group, composed of the First and Third Armies, while his former deputy, Lt. Gen. Courtney H. Hodges, assumed command of the First Army. Montgomery's 21 Army Group consisted of the British Second Army and a newcomer to the front, the First Canadian Army under Lt. Gen. Henry D. G. Crerar. General Montgomery continued to function as overall ground commander, an arrangement that was to prevail for another five weeks until General Eisenhower moved his headquarters to the Continent and assumed direct command of the armies in the field.

In terms of the preinvasion plan, General Eisenhower intended establishing a solid lodgment area in France extending as far east as the Seine River to provide room for air and supply bases. Having built up strength in this area, he planned then to advance into Germany on a broad front. Under Montgomery's 21 Army Group, he would concentrate his greatest resources north of the Ardennes region of Belgium along the most direct route to the Ruhr industrial region, Germany's largest complex of mines and industry. Bradley's 12th Army Group, meanwhile, was to make a subsidiary thrust south of the Ardennes to seize the Saar industrial region along the Franco-German frontier. A third force invading southern France in August was to provide protection on Bradley's right.

The First Army's breakout from the hedgerows changed that plan, for it opened the German armies in France to crushing defeat. When the Germans counterattacked toward Avranches to try to cut off leading columns of the First and Third Armies, other men of the First Army held firm, setting up an opportunity for exploiting the principle of maneuver to the fullest. While the First Canadian Army attacked toward Falaise, General Bradley directed mobile columns of both the First and Third Armies on a wide encircling maneuver in the direction of Argentan, not far from Falaise. This caught the enemy's counterattacking force in a giant pocket. Although a 15-mile gap between Falaise and Argentan was closed only after many of the Germans escaped, more than 60,000 were killed or captured in the pocket. Great masses of German guns, tanks, and equipment fell into Allied hands.

While the First Army finished the business at Argentan, Patton's Third Army dashed off again toward the Seine River, with two objects: eliminating the Seine as a likely new line of German defense and making a second, wider envelopment to trap those German troops that had escaped from the first pocket. Both Patton accomplished. In the two pockets the enemy lost large segments of two field armies.

Invasion of Southern France

Even as General Eisenhower's armies were scoring a great victory in Normandy, the Allies on August 15 staged another invasion, this one in southern France (Operation DRAGOON) to provide a supplementary line of communications through the French Mediterranean ports and to prevent the Germans in the south from moving against the main Allied armies in the north. Lack of landing craft had precluded launching this invasion at the same time as OVERLORD.

Under control of the Seventh U.S. Army, commanded now by Lt. Gen. Alexander M. Patch, three U.S. divisions, plus an airborne task force and French commandos, began landing just after dawn. Defending Germans were spread too thin to provide much more than token resistance, and by the end of the first day the Seventh Army had 86,000 men and 12,000 vehicles ashore. The next day French troops staged a second landing and moved swiftly to seize the ports of Toulon and Marseille.

Faced with entrapment by the spectacular Allied advances in the north, the Germans in southern France began on August 17 to withdraw. U.S. and French columns followed closely and on September 11 established contact with Patton's Third Army. Under the 6th Army Group, commanded by Lt. Gen. Jacob L. Devers, the Seventh Army and French forces organized as the 1st French Army passed to General Eisenhower's command.

Pursuit to the Frontier

As Allied columns were breaking loose all over France, men and women of the French resistance movement began to battle the Germans in the streets of the capital. Although General Eisenhower had intended to bypass Paris, hoping to avoid heavy fighting in the city and to postpone the necessity of feeding the civilian population, he felt impelled to send help lest the uprising be defeated. On August 25 a column including U.S. and French troops entered the city.

With surviving German forces falling back in defeat toward the German frontier, General Eisenhower abandoned the original plan of holding at the Seine while he opened the Brittany ports and established a sound logistical base. Determined to take advantage of the enemy's defeat, he reinforced Montgomery's 21 Army Group by sending the First U.S. Army close alongside the British, thus providing enough strength in the northern thrust to assure quick capture of ports along the English Channel, particularly the great Belgian port of Antwerp. Because the front was fast moving away from Brittany, the Channel ports were essential.

Ports posed a special problem, for with the stormy weather of fall and winter approaching, the Allies could not much longer depend upon supply over the invasion beaches, and Cherbourg had only a limited capacity. Even though Brittany now was far behind the advancing front, General Eisenhower still felt a need for the port of Brest. He put those troops of the Third Army that had driven into the peninsula under a new headquarters, the Ninth U.S. Army commanded by Lt. Gen. William H. Simpson, and set them to the task. When Brest fell two weeks later, the port was a shambles. The port problem nevertheless appeared to be solved when on September 4 British troops took Antwerp, its wharves and docks intact; but the success proved to be illusory. Antwerp is on an estuary sixty miles from the sea, and German troops clung to the banks, denying access to Allied shipping.

The port situation was symptomatic of multitudinous problems that had begun to beset the entire Allied logistical apparatus (organized much like Pershing's Services of Supply, but called the Communications Zone). The armies were going so far and so fast that the supply services were unable to keep pace. Although enough supplies were available in Normandy, the problem was to get them to forward positions that sometimes were more than 500 miles beyond the depots. Despite extraordinary measures such as establishing a one-way truck route called the Red Ball Express, supplies of such essential commodities as gasoline and ammunition began to run short. This was the penalty the Allied armies would have to pay for the decision to make no pause at the Seine.

The logistical crisis sparked a difference over strategy between General Eisenhower and General Montgomery. In view of the logistical difficulties, Montgomery insisted that General Patton's Third Army should halt in order that all transportation resources might be concentrated behind his troops and the First Army. This allocation, he believed, would enable him to make a quick strike deep into Germany and impel German surrender.

Acting on the advice of logistical experts on his staff, General Eisenhower refused. Such a drive could succeed, his staff advised, only if all Allied armies had closed up to the Rhine River and if Antwerp were open to Allied shipping. The only choice, General Eisenhower believed, was to keep pushing all along the line while supplies held out, ideally to go so far as to gain bridgeheads over the Rhine.

There were obstacles other than supply standing in the way of that goal. Some were natural, like the Moselle and Meuse Rivers, the Vosges Mountains in Alsace, the wooded hills of the Ardennes, and a dense Huertgen Forest facing the First Army near Aachen. Others were man made, old French forts around Metz and the French Maginot Line in northeastern France, as well as dense fortifications all along the German border—the Siegfried Line, or, as the Germans called it, the West Wall. By mid-September the First Army had penetrated the West Wall at several points but lacked the means to exploit the breaks.

Although General Eisenhower assigned first priority to clearing the seaward approaches to Antwerp, he sanctioned a Montgomery proposal to use Allied airborne troops in a last bold stroke to capitalize on German disorganization before logistics should force a halt. While the British Second Army launched an attack called Operation GARDEN, airborne troops of a recently organized First Allied Airborne Army (Lt. Gen. Lewis H. Brereton) were to land in Operation MARKET astride three major water obstacles in the Netherlands—the Maas, Waal, and Lower Rhine Rivers. Crossing these rivers on bridges to be secured by the airborne troops, the Second Army was to drive all the way to the IJssel Meer (Zuider Zee), cutting off Germans farther west and putting the British in a position to outflank the West Wall and drive into Germany along a relatively open north German plain.

Employing one British and two U.S. airborne divisions, the airborne attack began on September 17. On the first day alone approximately 20,000 paratroopers and glider troops landed in the largest airborne attack of the war. Although the drops were spectacularly successful and achieved complete surprise, the chance presence of two panzer divisions near the drop zones enabled the Germans to react swiftly. Resistance to the ground attack also was greater than expected, delaying quick link-up with the airheads. The combined operation gained a salient some fifty miles deep into German-held territory but fell short of the ambitious objectives, including a bridgehead across the Lower Rhine.

At this point, Montgomery (promoted now to field marshal) concentrated on opening Antwerp to Allied shipping, but so determined was German resistance and so difficult the conditions of mud and flood in the low-lying countryside that it was well into November before the job was finished. The first Allied ship dropped anchor in Antwerp only on November 28.

As a result of a cutback in offensive operations and extraordinary efforts of the supply services, the logistical situation had been gradually improving. In early November resources were sufficient to enable the U.S. armies to launch a big offensive aimed at reaching the Rhine; but, despite the largest air attack in direct support of ground troops to be made during the war (Operation QUEEN), it turned out to be a slow, arduous fight through the natural and artificial obstacles along the frontier. Heavy rain and severe cold added to the difficulties. By mid-December the First and Ninth Armies had reached the Roer River east of Aachen, twenty-three miles inside Germany, and the Third Army had come up to the West Wall along the Saar River northeast of Metz, but only the Seventh Army and the 1st French Army in Alsace had touched any part of the Rhine.

Having taken advantage of the pause imposed by Allied logistical problems to create new divisions and rush replacements to the front, the Germans in the west had made a remarkable recovery from the debacle in France. Just how remarkable was soon to be forcefully demonstrated in what had heretofore been a quiet sector held by the First Army's right wing.

The Ardennes Counteroffensive

As early as the preceding August, Adolf Hitler had been contemplating a counteroffensive to regain the initiative in the west and compel the Allies to settle for a negotiated peace. Over the protests of his generals, who thought the plan too ambitious, he ordered an attack by twenty-five divisions, carefully conserved and secretly assembled, to hit thinly manned U.S. positions in the Ardennes region of Belgium and Luxembourg, cross the Meuse River, and push on northwestward to Antwerp. In taking Antwerp, Hitler expected to cut off the British 21 Army Group and the First and Ninth U.S. Armies.

Under cover of inclement winter weather, Hitler concentrated his forces in the forests of the Eifel region, opposite the Ardennes. Before daylight on December 16, the Germans attacked along a 60-mile front, taking the VIII Corps and the south wing of the V Corps by surprise. In most places, German gains were rapid, for the American divisions were either inexperienced or seriously depleted from earlier fighting, and all were stretched thin.

The Germans nevertheless encountered difficulties from the first. Cut off and surrounded, small U.S. units continued to fight. At the northern shoulder of the penetration, divisions of the V Corps refused to budge from the vicinity of Monschau, thereby denying critical roads to the enemy and limiting the width of the penetration. At St. Vith American troops held out for six days to block a vital road center. To Bastogne to the southwest, where an armored detachment served as a blocking force, General Eisenhower rushed an airborne division which never relinquished that communications center even though

FIRST ARMY MEN SETTING UP A 57-MM. ANTITANK GUN

surrounded. Here Brig. Gen. Anthony C. McAuliffe delivered a terse one-word reply to a German demand for surrender: "Nuts!"

Denied important roads and hampered by air attacks as the weather cleared, the Germans fell a few miles short of even their first objective, the Meuse River. The result after more than a month of hard fighting that cost the Americans 75,000 casualties and the Germans close to 100,000 was nothing but a big bulge in the lines, from which the battle drew its popular name.

Faced with a shortage of infantry replacements during the enemy's counter-offensive General Eisenhower offered Negro soldiers in service units an opportunity to volunteer for duty with the infantry. More than 4,500 responded, many taking reductions in grade in order to meet specified requirements. The 6th Army Group formed these men into provisional companies, while the 12th Army Group employed them as an additional platoon in existing rifle companies. The excellent record established by these volunteers, particularly those serving as platoons, presaged major postwar changes in the traditional approach to employing Negro troops.

Although the counteroffensive had given the Allied command some anxious moments, the gallant stands by isolated units had provided time for the First and Ninth Armies to shift troops against the northern flank of the penetration and for the Third Army to hit the penetration from the south and drive through to beleaguered Bastogne. A rapid shift and change in direction of attack by the Third Army was one of the more noteworthy instances during the war of successful employment of the principle of maneuver.

By the end of January 1945, U.S. units had retaken all lost ground and had thwarted a lesser German attack against the 6th Army Group in Alsace. The Germans having expended irreplaceable reserves, the end of the war in Europe was in sight.

The Russian Campaigns

Much of the hope for an early end to the war rested with tremendous successes of the Soviet armies in the east. Having stopped the invading Germans at the gates of Moscow in late 1941 and at Stalingrad in late 1942, the Russians had made great offensive strides westward in both 1943 and 1944. Only a few days after D-day in Normandy the Red Army had launched a massive offensive which by mid-September had reached East Prussia and the gates of the Polish capital of Warsaw. In January 1945, as U.S. troops eliminated the bulge in the Ardennes, the Red Army started a new drive that was to carry to the Oder River, only forty miles from Berlin.

Far greater masses of troops were employed in the east than in the west over vast distances and a much wider front. The Germans had to maintain more than two million combat troops on the Eastern Front as compared with less than a million on the Western Front. Yet the Soviet contribution was less disproportionate than would appear at first glance, for the war in the east was a one-front ground war, whereas the Allies in the west were fighting on two ground fronts and conducting major campaigns in the air and at sea, as well as making a large commitment in the war against Japan. At the same time, the United States was contributing enormously to the war in Russia through lend-lease—almost $11 billion in materials, including over 400,000 jeeps and trucks, 12,000 armored vehicles (including 7,000 tanks, enough to equip some 20-odd U.S. armored divisions), 14,000 aircraft, and 1.75 million tons of food.

The Final Offensive

Soon after the opening of the Soviet January offensive, the Western Allies began a new drive to reach and cross the Rhine, the last barrier to the industrial heart of Germany. Exhausted by the overambitious effort in the Ardennes and forced to shift divisions to oppose the Russians, the Germans had little chance of holding west of the Rhine. Although Field Marshal von Rundstedt wanted to conserve his remaining strength for a defense of the river, Hitler would authorize no withdrawal. Making a strong stand at the Roer River and at places where the West Wall remained intact, the Germans imposed some delay but paid dearly in the process, losing 250,000 troops that could have been used to better advantage on the Rhine.

Falling back behind the river, the Germans had made careful plans to destroy all bridges, but something went amiss at the Ludendorff railroad bridge in the First Army's sector at Remagen. On March 7 a task force of the 9th Armored Division found the bridge damaged but passable. Displaying initiative and courage, a company of infantry dashed across. Higher commanders acted promptly to reinforce the foothold.

To the south, a division of the Third Army on March 22 made a surprise crossing of the Rhine in assault boats. Beginning late the next day the 21 Army Group and the Ninth U.S. Army staged a full-dress crossing of the lower reaches of the river, complete with an airborne attack rivaling in its dimensions Operation MARKET. The Third Army then made two more assault crossings, and during the last few days of March both the Seventh Army and the 1st French Army of the 6th Army Group crossed farther upstream. Having expended most of their resources west of the river, the Germans were powerless to defeat any Allied crossing attempt.

As the month of April opened, Allied armies fanned out from the Rhine all along the line with massive columns of armor and motorized infantry. Encircling the Ruhr, the First and Ninth Armies took 325,000 prisoners, totally destroying an entire German army group. Although the Germans managed to rally determined resistance at isolated points, a cohesive defensive line ceased to exist.

Since the Russians were within forty miles of Berlin and apparently would reach the German capital first, General Eisenhower put the main weight of the continuing drive behind U.S. armies moving through central Germany to eliminate a remaining pocket of German industry and to link with the Russians. The 21 Army Group meanwhile sealed off the Netherlands and headed toward the base of the Jutland peninsula, while the 6th Army Group turned southeastward to obviate any effort by the Nazis to make a last-ditch stand in the Alps of southern Germany and Austria.

By mid-April Allied armies in the north and center were building up along the Elbe and Mulde Rivers, an agreed line of contact with the Red Army approaching from the east. First contact came on April 25 near the town of Torgau, followed by wholesale German surrenders all along the front and in Italy.

With Berlin in Soviet hands, Hitler a suicide, and almost every corner of Germany overrun, emissaries of the German Government surrendered on May 7 at General Eisenhower's headquarters in Reims, France. The next day, May 8, was V–E Day, the official date of the end of the war in Europe.

The Situation on V–E Day

As V–E Day came, Allied forces in Western Europe consisted of 4½ million men, including 9 armies (5 of them American—one of which, the Fifteenth, saw action only at the last), 23 corps, 91 divisions (61 of them American), 6 tactical air commands (4 American), and 2 strategic air forces (1 American). The Allies had 28,000 combat aircraft, of which 14,845 were American, and they had brought into Western Europe more than 970,000 vehicles and 18 million tons of supplies. At the same time they were achieving final victory in Italy with 18 divisions (7 of them American).

The German armed forces and the nation were prostrate, beaten to a degree never before seen in modern times. Hardly any organized units of the German Army remained except in Norway, Czechslovakia, and the Balkans, and these would soon capitulate. What remained of the air arm was too demoralized even for a final suicidal effort, and the residue of the German Navy lay helpless in captured northern ports. Through five years of war, the German armed forces had lost over 3 million men killed, 263,000 of them in the west, since D-day. The United States lost 135,576 dead in Western Europe, while Britain, Canada, France, and other Allies incurred after D-day approximately 60,000 military deaths.

Unlike in World War I, when the United States had come late on the scene and provided only those forces to swing the balance of power to the Allied side, the American contribution to the reconquest of Western Europe had been predominant, not   in manpower but as a true arsenal of democracy. American factories produced for the British almost three times more lend-lease materials than for the Russians, including 185,000 vehicles, 12,000 tanks, and enough planes to equip four tactical air forces, and for the French, all weapons and equipment for 8 divisions and 1 tactical air force, plus partial equipment for 3 more divisions.

Although strategic air power had failed to prove the decisive instrument many had expected, it was a major factor in the Allied victory, as was the role of Allied navies, for without control of the sea lanes, there could have been no build-up in Britain and no amphibious assaults. It was nonetheless true that the application of the power of ground armies finally broke the German ability and will to resist.

While the Germans had developed a flying bomb and later a supersonic missile, the weapons with which both sides fought the war were in the main much improved versions of those that had been present in World War I—the motor vehicle, the airplane, the machine gun, indirect fire artillery, the tank. The difference lay in such accouterments as excellent radio communications and in a new sophistication, particularly in terms of mobility, that provided the means for rapid exploitation that both sides in World War I had lacked.

From North Africa to the Elbe, U.S. Army generalship proved remarkably effective. Such field commanders as Bradley, Devers, Clark, Hodges, Patton, Simpson, Patch, and numerous corps and division commanders would stand beside the best that had ever served the nation. Having helped develop Army doctrine during the years between the two great wars, these same men put the theories to battlefield test with enormous success. Some indication of the magnitude of the responsibilities they carried is apparent from the fact that late in the war General Bradley as commander of the 12th Army Group had under his command four field armies, 12 corps, and 48 divisions, more than 1,300,000 men, the largest exclusively American field command in U.S. history.

These commanders throughout displayed a steady devotion to the principles of war. Despite sometimes seemingly insurmountable obstacles of weather, terrain, and enemy concentration, they were consistently able to achieve the mass, mobility, and firepower to avoid a stalemate, maintaining the principles of the objective and the offensive and exploiting the principle of maneuver to the fullest. On many occasions they achieved surprise, most notably in the amphibious assaults and at the Rhine. They were themselves taken by surprise twice, in central Tunisia and in the Ardennes, yet in both cases they recovered quickly. Economy of force was particularly evident in Italy, and simplicity was nowhere better demonstrated than in the Normandy landings, despite a complexity inherent in the size and diversity of the invasion forces. From the first, unity of command was present in every campaign, not just at the tactical level but also in the combined staff system that afforded the U.S. and Britain a unity of command and purpose never approached on the Axis side.

CHAPTER 23

World War II: The War Against Japan

In World War II, for the first time, the United States had to fight a war on two fronts. Though the central strategic principle governing allocation of resources to the two fronts provided for concentrating first on the defeat of the European Axis, on the American side this principle was liberally interpreted, permitting conduct of an offensive war against Japan as well as against Germany in the years 1943–45. The U.S. Fleet, expanding after its initial setback at Pearl Harbor much as the Army had, provided the main sinews for an offensive strategy in the Pacific, although the Army devoted at least one-third of its resources to the Pacific war, even at the height of war in Europe. In sum, the United States proved capable, once its resources were fully mobilized, of successfully waging offensives on two fronts simultaneously—a development the Japanese had not anticipated when they launched their attack on Pearl Harbor.

Japan's Strategy

Japan entered World War II with limited aims and with the intention of fighting a limited war. Its principal objectives were to secure the resources of Southeast Asia and much of China and to establish a "Greater East Asia Co-Prosperity Sphere" under Japanese hegemony. In 1895 and in 1905 Japan had gained important objectives without completely defeating China or Russia and in 1941 Japan sought to achieve its hegemony over East Asia in similar fashion. The operational strategy the Japanese adopted to start war, however, doomed their hopes of limiting the conflict. Japan believed it necessary to destroy or neutralize American striking power in the Pacific—the U.S. Pacific Fleet at Pearl Harbor and the U.S. Far East Air Force in the Philippines—before moving southward and eastward to occupy Malaya, the Netherlands Indies, the Philippines, Wake Island, Guam, the Gilbert Islands, Thailand, and Burma. Once in control of these areas, the Japanese intended to establish a defensive perimeter stretching from the Kurile Islands south through Wake, the Marianas, the Carolines, and the Marshalls and Gilberts to Rabaul on New Britain. From

MAP 42

THE PACIFIC AREAS

1 AUGUST 1942

0   500   1000
STATUTE MILES ON THE EQUATOR

Rabaul the perimeter would extend westward to northwestern New Guinea and would encompass the Indies, Malaya, Thailand, and Burma. Japan thought that the Allies would wear themselves out in fruitless frontal assaults against the perimeter and would ultimately settle for a negotiated peace that would leave it in possession of most of its conquests. (*Map 42*)

The Japanese were remarkably successful in the execution of their offensive plan and by early 1942 had reached their intended perimeter. But they miscalculated the effect of their surprise attack at Pearl Harbor which unified a divided people and aroused the United States to wage a total, not a limited, war. As a result Japan lost, in the long run, any chance of conducting the war on its own terms. The Allies, responding to their defeats, sought no negotiated peace, but immediately began to seek means to strike back. In February and March 1942 small carrier task forces of the Pacific Fleet hit the Marshalls, Wake, and Marcus, and bombers from Australia began to harass the Japanese base at Rabaul. In April Army bombers, flying off a naval carrier, delivered a hit-and-run raid on Tokyo. Meanwhile, the United States began to develop and fortify a line of communications across the southern Pacific to Australia and to strengthen the defenses of the "down-under" continent itself. These new bases, along with Alaska, Hawaii, and India, also strengthened during the period, could become the launching points for counteroffensives. And once the Allies became strong enough to threaten the Japanese defensive perimeter from several directions the Japanese would lose the advantage of interior lines, and with it the strategic initiative, for Japan did not have and could not produce the means to defend and hold at all points.

Perceiving their danger, the Japanese in a second phase offensive tried to sever the Allied lines of communications to Australia and to expand their perimeter in the Pacific. In the spring of 1942 they pushed southeast from Rabaul to Guadalcanal and Tulagi in the Solomons, and seized Attu and Kiska in the Aleutians. But they failed in their main effort to take Midway Island, northwest of Hawaii, and in the naval battles of the Coral Sea and Midway in May and June they lost the bulk of their best naval pilots and planes. Midway was the turning point, for it redressed the naval balance in the Pacific and gave the Allies the strategic initiative. The Japanese, with the mobility of their carrier striking forces curtailed, abandoned plans to cut the Allied South Pacific life line and turned instead to strengthening their defensive perimeter, planning to wage a protracted war of attrition in the hope of securing a negotiated peace.

Guadalcanal and Papua: The First Offensives

After Midway the U.S. Joint Chiefs, responsible for direction of the war in the Pacific, almost naturally turned to the elimination of the threat to their line of communications in the south as the objective of their first offensive. In so doing, they gave to American strategy in the Pacific a twist unanticipated in prewar planning, which had always presupposed that the main offensive in any war against Japan would be made directly across the Central Pacific from Hawaii toward the Philippines. The Joint Chiefs on July 2 directed Allied forces in the South and Southwest Pacific Areas to begin a series of operations aimed at the ultimate reduction of the Japanese stronghold at Rabaul on New Britain Island, thus establishing Allied control of the Bismarck Archipelago.

The campaign would consist of three stages or tasks. In Task One, forces of the South Pacific Area (under Vice Adm. Robert L. Ghormley until November 1942 and thereafter under Admiral William F. Halsey) would seize base sites in the southern Solomons. In Task Two, South Pacific forces would advance up the ladder of the Solomons while Southwest Pacific forces (under General MacArthur) would move up the north coast of New Guinea as far as Lae and Salamaua. In Task Three, the forces of the two theaters would converge on Rabaul and clear the rest of the Bismarck Archipelago. Task One was to be conducted under the general supervision of Admiral Chester W. Nimitz, whose vast Pacific Ocean Areas command included the North, Central, and South Pacific Areas as subtheaters. Tasks Two and Three would be executed under the strategic direction of General MacArthur. The Joint Chiefs of Staff, reserving to themselves final control of the assignment of tasks, allocation of resources, and timing of operations, would provide, in effect, unified command over Nimitz and MacArthur.

The offensive began on August 7, 1942, when the 1st Marine Division landed on Guadalcanal and nearby islands in the southern Solomons. The Japanese, taking full advantage of interior lines from their bases at Rabaul and Truk, reacted vigorously. Six times from August to the end of November they challenged American naval superiority in the South Pacific in a series of sharp surface engagements. Air battles were almost daily occurrences for a month or more after the landings, and the Japanese sent in strong ground reinforcements, gambling and ultimately losing substantial air and naval resources in the effort to hold Guadalcanal. The Americans had to reinforce heavily, deploying naval power, planes, soldiers, and marines in the battle at the expense of other theaters. Before the island was secured in November, another Marine

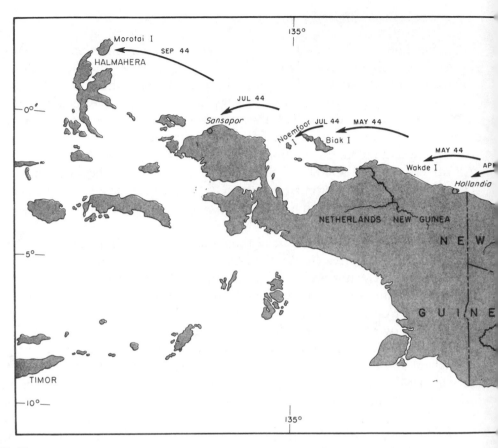

MAP 43

division (the 2d), two Army divisions (25th and American), and one separate regiment, to mention only the major ground combat elements, had been thrown into the battle. The last act came in February 1943, when the 43d Division moved into the Russell Islands, thirty-five miles northwest of Guadalcanal. On Guadalcanal and in the Russells, American forces then began to construct major air and logistical bases for further advances.

A Japanese overland drive toward Port Moresby in New Guinea had meanwhile forced General MacArthur to begin an offensive of his own—the Papua Campaign. (*Map 43*) During the late summer the Japanese had pushed across the towering Owen Stanley Mountains toward Port Moresby from the Buna-Gona area on New Guinea's northeastern coast, and by mid-September were only twenty miles from their objective. Australian ground forces drove the

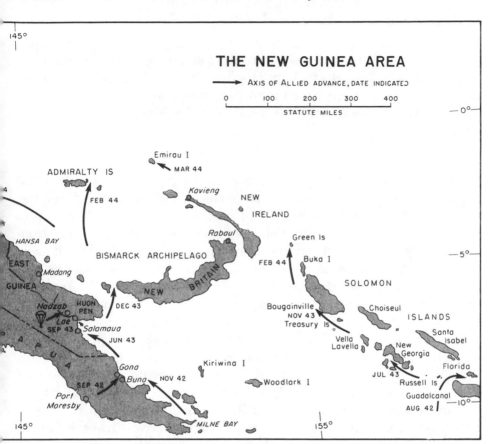

THE NEW GUINEA AREA

Japanese back to the north coast, where they strongly entrenched themselves around Buna and Gona. It took 2 Australian divisions, 1 U.S. Army division (32d), and another U.S. Army regiment almost four months of bitter fighting to dislodge the Japanese. Casualties were high, but as at Guadalcanal the Allied forces learned much about jungle fighting, the importance of air power, and the need for thorough logistical preparation. They also discovered that the Japanese soldier, though a skillful, stubborn, and fanatic foe, could be defeated. The myth of Japanese invincibility was forever laid to rest in the jungles of Guadalcanal and Papua.

After Papua and Guadalcanal the tempo of operations in the South and Southwest Pacific Areas slowed while General MacArthur and Admiral Halsey gathered resources and prepared bases for the next phase. The Japanese, in turn, undertook to reinforce their main bases in New Guinea and the northern Solomons. In March 1943 they attempted to send a large convoy to Lae in New Guinea but, in the Battle of the Bismarck Sea, lost some 3,500 troops and much valuable shipping, principally to Army land-based aircraft. During the following months Rabaul-based planes, reinforced by carrier planes flown in from the Carolines, sought unsuccessfully to knock out American air power in the southern Solomons.

Search for a Strategy

Meanwhile, in the spring and summer of 1943, a strategy for the defeat of Japan began to take shape within Allied councils. The major Allied objective was control of the South China Sea and a foothold on the coast of China, so as to sever Japanese lines of communications southward and to establish bases from which Japan could first be subjected to intensive aerial bombardment and naval blockade and then, if necessary, invaded. The first plans for attaining this objective envisioned Allied drives from several different directions—by American forces across the Pacific along two lines, from the South and Southwest toward the Philippines and from Hawaii across the Central Pacific; and by British and Chinese forces along two other lines, the first a land line through Burma and China and the second a sea line from India via the Netherlands Indies, Singapore, and the Strait of Malacca into the South China Sea. Within the framework of this tentative long-range plan, the U.S. Joint Chiefs fitted their existing plans for completion of the campaign against Rabaul, and a subsequent advance to the Philippines, and developed a plan for the second drive across the Central Pacific. They also, in 1942 and 1943, pressed the Chinese and British to get a drive under way in Burma to reopen the supply line to China in phase with their Pacific advances, offering extensive air and logistical support.

The North Pacific line running from Alaska through the Kuriles to the northernmost Japanese island of Hokkaido also beckoned in early 1943 as a possible additional avenue of approach to Japan. The Joint Chiefs decided, however, that although the Japanese perimeter should be pushed back in this area, the foggy, cold North Pacific with its rock-bound and craggy islands was not a profitable area in which to undertake a major offensive. In May 1943 the U.S. 7th Division went ashore on Attu and, after three weeks of costly fighting through icy muck and over wind-swept ridges in a cold, almost constant fog, destroyed the Japanese garrison. In August a combined American-Canadian expedition landed on Kiska, some distance away, only to find that the Japanese had evacuated the island three weeks earlier. With the Japanese perimeter pushed back to the Kuriles the Allied advance stopped, and further operations were limited to nuisance air raids against these Japanese-held islands. Ground forces used in the attacks on Attu and Kiska were redeployed to the Central Pacific, and some of the defensive forces deployed in Alaska were also freed for employment elsewhere.

Prospects of an advance through China to the coast faded rapidly in 1943. At the Casablanca Conference in January the Combined Chiefs agreed on an ambitious operation, called ANAKIM, to be launched in the fall of 1943 to retake Burma and reopen the supply line to China. ANAKIM was to include a British amphibious assault on Rangoon and an offensive into central Burma, plus an American-sponsored Chinese offensive in the north involving convergence of forces operating from China and India. ANAKIM proved too ambitious; even limited offensives in Southeast Asia were postponed time and again for lack of adequate resources. By late 1943 the Americans had concluded that their Pacific forces would reach the China coast before either British or Chinese forces could come in through the back door. At the SEXTANT Conference late in 1943 the Combined Chiefs agreed that the main effort against Japan should be concentrated in the Pacific along two lines of advance, with operations in the North Pacific, China, and Southeast Asia to be assigned subsidiary roles.

In this strategy the two lines of advance in the Pacific—the one across the Central Pacific via the Gilberts, Marshalls, Marianas, Carolines, and Palaus toward the Philippines or Formosa (Taiwan) and the other in the Southwest Pacific via the north coast of New Guinea to the Vogelkop and thence to the southern Philippines—were viewed as mutually supporting. (*Map 44*) Although the Joint Chiefs several times indicated a measure of preference for the Central Pacific as the area of main effort, they never established any real priority between the two lines, seeking instead to retain a flexibility that would permit striking blows along either line as opportunity offered. The Central Pacific route promised to force a naval showdown with the Japanese and, once the Marianas were secured, to provide bases from which the U.S. Army Air Forces' new B-29 bombers could strike the Japanese home islands. The Southwest Pacific route was shorter, if existing bases were taken into consideration, and offered more opportunity to employ land-based air power to full advantage. The target area for both drives, in the strategy approved at SEXTANT, was to be the Luzon-Formosa-China coast area. Within this area the natural goal of the Southwest Pacific drive was the Philippines, but that of the Central Pacific drive could be either the Philippines or Formosa. As the drives along the two lines got under way in earnest in 1944, the choice between the two became the central strategic issue.

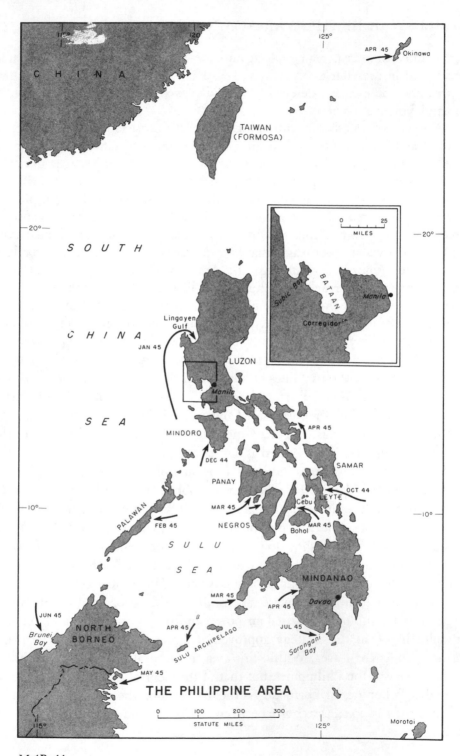

APR 45 Okinawa

C H I N A

TAIWAN
(FORMOSA)

—20°—

S O U T H

C H I N A

S E A

Lingayen
Gulf

JAN 45

LUZON

Manila

MINDORO

DEC 44

SAMAR

PANAY

OCT 44

LEYTE

MAR 45

Cebu

PALAWAN

FEB 45

NEGROS

MAR 45

Bohol

—10°—

S U L U

S E A

MINDANAO

MAR 45

Davao

APR 45

JUN 45

NORTH
BORNEO

Brunei
Bay

APR 45

B

SULU ARCHIPELAGO

JUL 45

Sarangani
Bay

MAY 45

THE PHILIPPINE AREA

0   100   200   300
STATUTE MILES

Morotai

0   25
MILES

Subic Bay

B A T A A N

Manila

Corregidor

MAP 44

Cartwheel: The Encirclement of Rabaul

In June 1943 MacArthur and Halsey resumed their offensive to reduce the Japanese stronghold at Rabaul—a prerequisite to further advances along the Southwest Pacific axis toward the Philippines. The plan for the campaign provided for a carefully phased series of operations in each theater, each designed to secure a strategic position where air cover could be provided for further advances. The first of the series started in late June when MacArthur landed American troops on the Woodlark and Kiriwina Islands off eastern New Guinea and at Nassau Bay on the New Guinea coast, and Halsey's forces made their first landings on the New Georgia group in the Central Solomons. From these beginnings the operations proceeded up the ladder of the Solomons, along the coast of New Guinea, and across the straits to New Britain Island generally as scheduled, despite strong Japanese reaction.

In the Solomons by early August Army forces under Halsey had secured New Georgia with its important Munda airfield, but the campaign was not completed until October when U.S. and New Zealand troops occupied Vella Lavella, between New Georgia and Bougainville. At the end of October, New Zealanders and U.S. marines landed on Treasury and Choiseul Islands to secure bases for the assault on Bougainville; that assault got under way on November 1 when marines landed, followed soon after by the Army's 37th Division. In each phase of the Solomons campaign, the Japanese sought unsuccessfully to contest Allied air and naval supremacy, to land reinforcements, and to launch strong counterattacks against Allied beachheads, losing in the effort both planes and combat ships they could ill afford to spare. Air and naval losses suffered in the Solomons crippled the Japanese Fleet for months to come and helped to pave the way for the successful Central Pacific drive that got under way in November. With the repulse of the Japanese counterattack on Bougainville, by the end of November security of the American beachhead on that island was assured, permitting the development of a major American air base. With the taking of Bougainville, the main part of the South Pacific Area's task in Operation CARTWHEEL was completed.

MacArthur's forces meanwhile continued their offensives, with Australian troops carrying most of the burden in New Guinea. In early September the U.S. Army's 503d Parachute Regiment, in the first airborne operation of the Pacific war, seized an airfield at Nadzab, inland from Lae and Salamaua. Australian troops cleared Lae and Salamaua by mid-September and, flown into Nadzab, moved on to the Huon peninsula. Elements of the U.S. 32d Division landed at the western end of the peninsula in January 1944 in an attempt to trap a large Japanese force, but by the time Australian and American units had sealed the western exits to the peninsula most of the Japanese had escaped northwest to Hansa Bay and Wewak.

In the meantime, MacArthur and Halsey had assembled the forces to launch a final offensive toward Rabaul, but the Joint Chiefs decided that the actual seizure of that objective would be too costly in terms of men, equipment, and time. They preferred to encircle Rabaul, neutralize it by air bombardment, and push on to seize an offensive base farther west, in the Admiralty Islands. A new series of operations toward these ends started in MacArthur's theater on December 15, 1943, when U.S. Army units landed on the south coast of western New Britain, and on the 26th, the 1st Marine Division landed on the north coast. In mid-February 1944 New Zealand troops of the South Pacific Area secured an air base site on Green Island, north of Rabaul, and on the last day of the month MacArthur began landing the 1st Cavalry Division (an infantry unit retaining its former designation) on the Admiralties, closing the western and northwestern approaches to Rabaul. Marines under Halsey seized a final air base site on Emirau, north of Rabaul, on March 20, while Marine and Army units under MacArthur secured additional positions in western and central New Britain from March to May 1944. The major Japanese base at Rabaul, with its 100,000-man garrison, was as effectively out of the war as if it had been destroyed. In the process of encircling Rabaul, the Allies had also left to wither on the vine another important Japanese base at Kavieng on New Ireland, north of Rabaul.

In the last phase of the campaign against Rabaul, a pattern developed that came to characterize much of the war in the Pacific. The Allies would mount no frontal attacks against strongly entrenched Japanese forces if they could avoid it; they would not advance island by island across a vast ocean studded with myriad atolls and island groups. Rather, they would advance in great bounds, limited only by the range of land-based air cover or the availability of carrier-based air support. The Allies would deceive and surprise the Japanese; they would bypass major strongpoints and leave them reduced to strategic and tactical impotence.

The Central Pacific Drive Begins

The necessity for relying primarily on support of land-based aircraft curtailed the length of the jumps in the South and Southwest Pacific in 1943. The Navy's limited supply of aircraft carriers could not be employed to best advantage in the narrow waters around New Guinea and the Solomons. By mid-1943, however, new larger and faster carriers of the *Essex* class (27,000 tons) and lighter carriers of the *Independence* class (11,000 tons) were joining the Pacific

Fleet. Around these new carriers Admiral Nimitz built naval task forces tailored in each case to the particular operation at hand. The task forces consisted of a mix of carriers, destroyers, cruisers, battleships, submarines, minesweepers, and support craft. In the broad expanses of the Central Pacific, these air carrier task forces could provide both air and naval support for far longer leaps forward, while the entire Pacific Fleet stood ready to confront the main Japanese Fleet at any time it chose to give battle.

The Central Pacific drive got under way on November 20, 1943, when Nimitz sent Army and Marine forces to the Gilbert Islands to seize bases from which to support subsequent jumps into the Marshalls. Troops and supplies for the Gilberts loaded at Hawaii on newly developed assault shipping and sailed more than 2,000 miles to be set ashore by specially designed landing craft and amphibian vehicles. Makin, the Army objective, fell to the 27th Division after four days of hard fighting. Tarawa, where the 2d Marine Division went ashore, proved a bloody affair that provided a stiff test for American amphibious doctrine, techniques, and equipment. Naval gunfire vessels and carrier-based aircraft provided support during and after the assault.

The advance to the Gilberts disclosed that U.S. forces had not entirely mastered certain aspects of amphibious warfare, especially naval gunfire support, co-ordination of air support, and ship-to-shore communications. But valuable lessons were learned that, added to the earlier experiences of the South and Southwest Pacific Areas, established a pattern of island warfare which represented one of the major tactical developments of the war. First, air and naval forces isolated an objective and softened its defenses; simultaneously, joint forces would attack or feint toward other islands to deceive the Japanese. The approach of convoys carrying the ground assault forces to the main objective signaled the opening of final, intensive air and naval bombardment of the landing beaches. Whenever practicable, small forces occupied neighboring islands as sites for land-based artillery. Under cover of all these supporting fires, the landing forces moved from ship to shore in echelons, or waves, rocket-firing landing craft in the lead and amphibian tanks and tractors following to carry the assault troops directly onto the beaches and inland. Finally came landing craft with more infantry and with tanks, artillery, and supporting troops. Supplies followed rapidly as the assault forces secured and expanded the beachhead. Amphibious techniques were refined and modified to some extent after the Gilberts, but the lessons learned there made it unnecessary to effect any radical changes in amphibious doctrine throughout the rest of the war.

The Japanese did not react strongly to the loss of the Gilberts, and at the end of January 1944 Nimitz' Army and Marine forces moved into the eastern and central Marshalls to seize Majuro and Kwajalein. The strength employed in this operation proved so preponderant and Japanese defenses so weak that Nimitz was able to accelerate his next advance by two and a half months, and on February 17 landed Marine and Army units on Eniwetok Atoll in the western Marshalls. Concurrently, he conducted a long-awaited carrier strike against Truk in the central Carolines, considered Japan's key bastion in the Central Pacific. The raid revealed that the Japanese had virtually abandoned Truk as a naval base, and the capture of the atoll, set for June, no longer appeared necessary. Nimitz then drew up plans to invade the Marianas in mid-June and move on to the western Carolines and Palaus in mid-September, again accelerating the pace of the advance.

Acceleration of the Pacific Drive

General MacArthur had also pushed forward the Southwest Pacific Area's timetable. Having landed in the Admiralties a month ahead of his original schedule, he proposed to cancel operations against Hansa Bay and Wewak on the northeast coast of New Guinea in favor of a jump to Hollandia and Aitape, on the north-central coast, in April, two months earlier than previously planned. He would then continue northwestward along the coast in a campaign entailing the steady extension of land-based air cover by the seizure of successive air base sites until he reached the Vogelkop, at the eastern end of New Guinea, and then proceed to Mindanao, southernmost of the Philippine Islands.

The Joint Chiefs, quickly seizing the fruits of their strategy of opportunism, on March 12, 1944, rearranged the schedule of major Pacific operations. They provided for the assault by MacArthur's forces on Hollandia and Aitape in April with the support of a carrier task force from the Pacific Fleet, to be followed by Nimitz's move into the Marianas in June and into the Palaus in September. While Nimitz was employing the major units of the Pacific Fleet in these ventures, MacArthur was to continue his advance along the New Guinea coast with the forces at his disposal. In November, he was again to have the support of main units of the Pacific Fleet in an assault on Mindanao. Refusing yet to make a positive choice of what was to follow, the Joint Chiefs directed MacArthur to plan for the invasion of Luzon and Nimitz to plan for the invasion of Formosa early in 1945.

The March 12 directive served as a blueprint for an accelerated drive in the Pacific in the spring and summer of 1944. On April 22 Army forces under MacArthur landed at Hollandia and Aitape. At neither place was the issue ever in doubt, although during July the Japanese who had been bypassed at Wewak launched an abortive counterattack against Aitape. Protected by land-based aircraft from Hollandia, MacArthur's Army units next jumped 125 miles northwest on May 17 to seize another air base site at Wakde Island, landing first on the New Guinea mainland opposite the chief objective. A ground campaign of about a month and a half ensued against a Japanese division on the mainland, but, without waiting for the outcome of the fight, other Army troops carried the advance northwestward on May 27 another 180 miles to Biak Island.

As this point the wisdom of conducting twin drives across the Pacific emerged. The Japanese Navy was preparing for a showdown battle it expected to develop off the Marianas in June. MacArthur's move to Biak put land-based planes in position to keep under surveillance and to harry the Japanese Fleet, which was assembling in Philippine waters before moving into the Central Pacific. Reckoning an American-controlled Biak an unacceptable threat to their flank, the Japanese risked major elements of their fleet to send strong reinforcements to Biak in an attempt to drive MacArthur's forces off the island. They also deployed to bases within range of Biak about half their land-based air strength from the Marianas, Carolines, and Palaus—planes upon which their fleet depended for support during the forthcoming battle off the Marianas.

After two partially successful attempts to reinforce Biak, the Japanese assembled for a third try enough naval strength to overwhelm local American naval units; but just as the formidable force was moving toward Biak the Japanese learned the U.S. Pacific Fleet was off the Marianas. They hastily assembled their naval forces and sailed northwestward for the engagement known as the Battle of the Philippine Sea. Having lost their chance to surprise the U.S. Navy, handicapped by belated deployment, and deprived of anticipated land-based air support, the Japanese suffered another shattering naval defeat. This defeat, which assured the success of the invasions of both Biak and the Marianas, illustrates well the interdependence of operations in the two Pacific areas. It also again demonstrated that the U.S. Pacific Fleet's carrier task forces were the decisive element in the Pacific war.

Army and Marine divisions under Nimitz landed on Saipan in the Marianas on June 15, 1944, to begin a bloody three-week battle for control of the island. Next, on July 21, Army and Marine units invaded Guam, 100 miles south of Saipan, and three days later marines moved on to Tinian Island. An important turning point of the Pacific war, the American seizure of the Marianas brought the Japanese home islands within reach of the U.S. Army Air Forces' B-29 bombers, which in late November began to fly missions against the Japanese homeland.

At Biak Japanese resistance delayed capture of the best airfield sites until late June. On July 2, MacArthur's Army forces moved on to Noemfoor Island, ninety miles to the west, in a combined parachute-amphibious operation designed to broaden the base of the Southwest Pacific's air deployment. On July 30 the 6th Division continued on to the northwestern tip of New Guinea to secure another air base, and on September 15 MacArthur landed the reinforced 31st Division on Morotai Island, between New Guinea and Mindanao in the Philippines. On the same day Nimitz sent the 1st Marine Division ashore on Peleliu in the southern Palaus, and on the 17th the 81st Division from Nimitz' command landed on Angaur, just south of Peleliu. A regimental combat team of the 81st Division secured Ulithi Atoll, midway between Peleliu and the Marianas, without opposition on September 23.

With these landings the approach to the Philippines was virtually completed. The occupation of Morotai proved easy, and the island provided airfields for the support of advances into the Philippines and Indies. The Pacific Fleet employed Ulithi as a forward anchorage. Hard fighting dragged on in the Palaus through November, but as the result of another acceleration in the pace of Pacific operations these islands never played the role originally planned for them.

In twin drives, illustrative of the principles of maneuver, objective, economy of force, surprise, and mass, the Allied forces of the Pacific had arrived in mid-September 1944 at the threshold of their strategic objective, the Luzon-Formosa-China coast triangle. In seven months MacArthur's forces had moved forward nearly 1,500 miles from the Admiralties to Morotai; in ten months Nimitz' forces had advanced over 4,500 miles from Hawaii to the Palaus. The time had now arrived when a final choice had to be made of the main objective in the target area.

The Decision To Invade Luzon

During the summer of 1944, as the battles raged along both lines of advance, the strategic debate over the choice of Luzon versus Formosa also waxed hot. General MacArthur argued fervently that the proper course was to move through the Philippines to Luzon, cutting the Japanese lines of communications southward, establishing a base for bombardment and invasion of Japan, and fulfilling a solemn national obligation to liberate the Philippine people. Admiral Ernest J. King, Chief of Naval Operations, just as adamantly insisted that the war could be shortened by directing the Pacific advance from the Marianas and Palaus toward Formosa, the China coast, and Japan proper, seizing only the essential positions in the southern and central Philippines necessary to render air support for these advances. The arguments for Formosa were cogent enough. Its strategic position made it a better island steppingstone to the China coast or the Japanese home islands, a position from which Japanese communications to the south could be cut more effectively than from Luzon, and a closer-in position from which to conduct strategic bombardment. But it also could prove to be a more difficult position to take, and Nimitz did not have in his theater sufficient Army supporting and service troops, without reinforcement, to sustain a land campaign on the island. It might be difficult, too, to mount an invasion of Formosa as long as the Japanese could, from strong positions on Luzon, interfere with the Allied line of communications. Another consideration involved the real value of a foothold on the China coast. By the early fall of 1944, air base sites in east China from which the Allies had hoped to support Pacific operations and bomb Japan appeared irretrievably lost, and the Marianas already provided bases for the B–29's almost as close to Tokyo as Formosa. The need to seize and develop a port on the China coast thus lost much of its urgency, and the argument that Formosa was the best steppingstone to China became less compelling. Then, too, a successful invasion of either Luzon or Formosa required some concentration of forces from the two theaters. It was far easier to shift highly mobile naval resources in Nimitz' theater to the Philippines than it was to redeploy Army troops from the Southwest Pacific to support Nimitz' invasion of Formosa and the jump to the China coast with which he hoped to follow it.

At the time of the Morotai and Palaus landings, MacArthur's plans for invasion of the Philippines called for a preliminary assault in southern Mindanao on November 15, 1944, to secure air bases for the support of a larger attack at Leyte, in the east-central Philippines, on December 20. He would follow this with a large-scale assault on Lingayen Gulf in February 1945. Nimitz meanwhile planned to mount an invasion of Yap in the Carolines in October 1944 and then would prepare to launch his attack on Formosa as soon afterward as the elements of the Pacific Fleet required for operations in the southern and central Philippines could be returned. Obviously, there had to be a choice between Luzon and Formosa, for the Pacific Fleet would be required to support either operation.

The course of events went far to dictate the final choice. In mid-September Admiral Halsey's carrier task forces providing strategic support for the Morotai and Palaus operations struck the central and southern Philippines. Halsey found Japanese air strength unexpectedly weak and uncovered few signs of significant ground or naval activity. On the basis of Halsey's reports, MacArthur and Nimitz proposed to the Joint Chiefs a move directly to Leyte in October, bypassing Mindanao. Nimitz agreed to divert to the Leyte invasion the 3-division corps then mounting out of Hawaii for the assault against Yap. The Joint Chiefs quickly approved the new plan, and the decision to invade Leyte two months ahead of schedule gave MacArthur's arguments to move onto Luzon almost irresistible force. MacArthur now reported that he could undertake the invasion of Luzon in December 1944, whereas all the planners' estimates indicated that resources for an invasion of Formosa—particularly service troops and shipping— could not be readied before February 1945 at the earliest. Nimitz proposed to shift the Central Pacific attack northward against Iwo Jima in the Bonins in January 1945 and then against Okinawa and other islands in the Ryukyus early in March. On October 3, Admiral King bowing to the inevitable, accepted the new plans and the Joint Chiefs issued directives to MacArthur for the invasion of Luzon on December 20 and to Nimitz for the invasion of Iwo Jima and Okinawa early in 1945.

Pacific strategy had been cast into almost its final mold. In the end, the China coast objective disappeared entirely from planning boards. Final plans for the defeat of Japan envisaged gradual tightening of the ring by blockade and bombardment from the Marianas, Philippines, and Ryukyus with an invasion of the home islands to be mounted from these bases.

The Philippines Campaign

The main assault at Leyte took place on October 20, 1944, as four Army divisions landed abreast in the largest amphibious operation yet conducted in the Pacific. Vice Adm. Thomas C. Kinkaid, MacArthur's naval commander, controlled the amphibious phases, including naval gunfire support and close air support by planes based on escort carriers. Ground forces were under Lt. Gen. Walter Krueger, commanding the U.S. Sixth Army; land-based air forces of the Southwest Pacific Area in general support were commanded by Lt. Gen. George C. Kenney. MacArthur himself exercised unified command over the air, ground, and naval commanders. The fast carrier task forces of the Pacific Fleet, providing strategic support, operated under the control of Admiral Halsey, who reported to Nimitz, not MacArthur. There was no provision for unified naval command, and Halsey's orders were such that he could make his principal mission the destruction of the Japanese Fleet rather than the support of MacArthur's entry into the Philippines.

The Japanese had originally planned to make their stand in the Philippines on Luzon, but the invasion of Leyte moved them to reconsider, since they now decided that the entire Philippine Archipelago would be strategically lost if the

Unloading Supplies on a Leyte Beach

U.S. Army secured a foothold in the central islands. They therefore began sending ground reinforcements to Leyte; increased their land-based air strength in the Philippines in the hope of destroying Allied shipping in Leyte Gulf and maintaining local air superiority; and dispatched their remaining naval strength to Leyte Gulf to destroy Kinkaid's invasion fleet and to block Allied access to the Philippines. The ensuing air-naval Battle of Leyte Gulf was the most critical moment of the campaign, and proved one of the most decisive actions of the Pacific war.

Admiral Halsey, without consulting MacArthur or Kinkaid, pulled the bulk of his carrier forces northward to intercept part of the Japanese Fleet, leaving Leyte Gulf open to other Japanese Fleet units. Gallant, desperate action by Kinkaid's old battleships and escort carrier planes turned back the Japanese in the gulf, assuring the safety of the landing forces. It had been a close thing, clearly demonstrating the dangers of divided command. In the end, however, the combined operations of Kinkaid's and Halsey's forces virtually eliminated the Japanese Navy as a factor in the Pacific war.

With the Leyte beaches secure, U.S. Army units proceeded to destroy the Japanese ground forces. Miserable weather bogged down the pace of operations, made supply difficult, delayed airfield construction, curtailed air support, and permitted the Japanese to continue to ship reinforcements to the island. The reinforcement program came to a sudden halt early in December when the 77th Division executed an amphibious envelopment on Leyte's west coast,

GENERAL MACARTHUR AND MEMBERS OF HIS STAFF *wading ashore at Leyte.*

and by late December the Sixth Army had secured the most important sections of the island, those required for air and logistical bases. Japanese troops in the mountains of northwestern Leyte continued organized resistance well into the spring of 1945, occupying the energies of large portions of Lt. Gen. Robert L. Eichelberger's newly formed Eighth Army.

While the fight on Leyte continued, MacArthur's forces moved on to Luzon only slightly behind schedule. The first step of the Luzon Campaign was the seizure of an air base in southwestern Mindoro, 150 miles south of Manila, on December 15, 1944, two Army regiments accomplishing the task with ease. The invasion of Luzon itself started on January 9, 1945, when four Army divisions landed along the shores of Lingayen Gulf. Command arrangements were similar to those at Leyte, and again fast carrier task forces under Halsey operated in general support and not under MacArthur's control. Within three days five Army divisions, a separate regimental combat team, two artillery groups, an armored group, and supporting service units were ashore and had begun a drive down the Central Plains of Luzon toward Manila. The Japanese were incapable of naval intervention at Lingayen Gulf, and their most significant reaction was to throw a number of kamikaze (suicide plane) attacks against Kinkaid's naval forces for four days.

General Tomoyuki Yamashita, commanding Japanese forces in the Philippines, did not intend to defend the Central Plains—Manila Bay region, the strategic prize of Luzon. Knowing he would receive no reinforcements and believing the issue in the Philippines had been decided at Leyte, he sought only to pin down major elements of MacArthur's forces in the hope of delaying Allied progress toward Japan. For this purpose he moved the bulk of his troops into mountain strongholds, where they could conduct a protracted, bloody defensive campaign. But Japanese naval forces on Luzon, only nominally under Yamashita, decided to ignore this concept in favor of defending Manila and Manila Bay. Thus, when U.S. Army units reached Manila on February 3, it took them a month of bitter building-to-building fighting to root out the Japanese. Meanwhile, operations to clear Manila Bay had begun with a minor amphibious landing at the southern tip of Bataan on February 15. The next day a combined parachute-amphibious assault, involving two Army regiments, initiated a battle to clear Corregidor Island. Other forces cleared additional islands in Manila Bay and secured the south shore. By mid-March the bay was open for Allied shipping, but an immense salvage and repair job was necessary before the Allies could fully exploit Manila's excellent port facilities.

The reinforced 38th Division had landed meanwhile near Subic Bay and had cut across the base of Bataan peninsula to prevent the Japanese from holing up on Bataan as had MacArthur's forces three years earlier. The 11th Airborne Division undertook both amphibious and parachute landings in southern Luzon to start clearing that region, and the 158th Regimental Combat Team made an amphibious assault in southeastern Luzon to secure the Bicol peninsula. Turning against the Japanese mountain strongholds, MacArthur continued to pour reinforcements onto Luzon, and the land campaign there ultimately evolved into the largest of the Pacific war. MacArthur committed to Luzon ten divisions, two regiments of another division, and three separate regimental combat teams. Guerrillas also played a large role. One guerrilla unit came to substitute for a regularly constituted division, and other guerrilla forces of battalion and regimental size supplemented the efforts of the Army units. Moreover, the loyal and willing Filipino population immeasurably eased the problems of supply, construction, and civil administration.

Except for a strong pocket in the mountains of north central Luzon, organized Japanese resistance ended by late June 1945. The rugged terrain in the north, along with rainy weather, prevented Krueger's Sixth Army from applying its full strength to the reduction of this pocket. Eichelberger's Eighth Army took over responsibility for operations on Luzon at the end of June and continued the pressure against Yamashita's force in the last-stand area, but they held out there until the end of the war.

While Sixth Army was destroying Japanese forces on Luzon, Eighth Army ultimately employed five divisions, portions of a sixth division, a separate

U.S. PARATROOPERS DROPPING ON CORREGIDOR

regimental combat team, and strong guerrilla units in its campaign to re-conquer the southern Philippines. This effort began when a regimental combat team of the 41st Division landed on Palawan Island on February 28, 1945. Here engineers built an air base from which to help cut Japan's line of communications to the south and to support later advances in the southern Philippines and the Indies. On March 10, another regimental combat team of the 41st, later reinforced, landed near Zamboanga in southwestern Mindanao, and soon thereafter Army units began moving southwest toward Borneo along the Sulu Archipelago. In rapid succession Eighth Army units then landed on Panay, Cebu, northwestern Negros, Bohol, central Mindanao, southeastern Negros, northern Mindanao, and finally at Sarangani Bay in southern Mindanao, once intended as the first point of re-entry into the Philippines. At some locales bitter fighting raged for a time, but the issue was never in doubt and organized Japanese resistance in the southern Philippines had largely collapsed by the end of May. Mopping up continued to the end of the war, with reorganized and re-equipped guerrilla forces bearing much of the burden.

The last offensives in the Southwest Pacific Area started on May 1 when an Australian brigade went ashore on Tarakan Island, Borneo. Carried to the beaches by landing craft manned by U.S. Army engineers, the Australians had air support from fields on Morotai and in the southern Philippines. On June 10 an Australian division landed at Brunei Bay, Borneo, and another Australian division went ashore at Balikpapan on July 1 in what proved to be the final amphibious assault of the war.

Iwo Jima and Okinawa

Since slow-base development at Leyte had forced MacArthur to delay the Luzon invasion from December to January, Nimitz in turn had to postpone his target dates for the Iwo Jima and Okinawa operations, primarily because the bulk of the naval resources in the Pacific—fast carrier task forces, escort carrier groups, assault shipping, naval gunfire support vessels, and amphibious assault craft—had to be shifted between the two theaters for major operations. The alteration of schedules again illustrated the interdependence of the Southwest and Central Pacific Areas.

The Iwo Jima assault finally took place on February 19, 1945, with the 4th and 5th Marine Divisions, supported by minor Army elements, making the landings. The 3d Marine Division reinforced the assault, and an Army regiment ultimately took over as island garrison. The marines had to overcome fanatic resistance from firmly entrenched Japanese, who held what was probably the strongest defensive system American forces encountered during the Pacific war, and it took a month of bloody fighting to secure the island. In early March a few crippled B–29's made emergency landings on Iwo; by the end of the month an airfield was fully operational for fighter planes. Later, engineers constructed a heavy bomber field and another fighter base on the island.

The invasion of the Ryukyus began on March 26 when the 77th Division landed on the Kerama Islands, fifteen miles west of Okinawa, to secure a forward naval base, a task traditionally assigned to marines. On April 1 the 7th and 96th Divisions and the 2d and 6th Marine Divisions executed the assault on the main objective, Okinawa. Two more Army divisions and a Marine infantry regiment later reinforced it. Another amphibious assault took place on April 16, when the 77th Division seized Ie Shima, four miles west of Okinawa, and the final landing in the Ryukyus came on June 26, when a small force of marines went ashore on Kume Island, fifty miles west of Okinawa. Ground forces at Okinawa were first under the U.S. Tenth Army, Lt. Gen. Simon B. Buckner commanding. When General Buckner was killed on June 18, Marine Lt. Gen. Roy S. Geiger took over until General Joseph W. Stilwell assumed command on the 23d.

The Japanese made no attempt to defend the Okinawa beaches, but instead fell back to prepared cave and tunnel defenses on inland hills. Bitterly defending every inch of ground, the Japanese continued organized resistance until late June. Meanwhile, Japanese suicide planes had inflicted extensive damage on Nimitz' naval forces, sinking about 25 ships and damaging nearly 165 more in an unsuccessful attempt to drive Allied naval power from the western Pacific. Skillful small unit tactics, combined with great concentrations of naval, air, and artillery bombardment, turned the tide of the ground battle on Okinawa itself. Especially noteworthy was the close support that naval gunfire vessels provided the ground forces and the close air support furnished by Army, Navy, and Marine aircraft.

Capture of Okinawa and other positions in the Ryukyus gave the Allies both air and naval bases within easy striking distance of Japan. By early May fighter planes from Okinawa had begun flights over Japan, and as rapidly as fields became available bombers, including units from the Southwest Pacific Area, came forward to mount attacks in preparation for the invasion of the home islands. The forward anchorages in the Ryukyus permitted the Pacific Fleet to keep in almost continuous action against Japanese targets. The Ryukyus campaign had brought Allied forces in the Pacific to Japan's doorstep.

The American Effort in China, Burma, and India

While American forces in the Pacific, under the unified direction of the U.S. Joint Chiefs of Staff, made spectacular advances, the Allied effort in Southeast Asia bogged down in a mire of conflicting national purposes. The hopes Americans held, in the early stages of the war, that Chinese manpower and bases would play a vitally important role in the defeat of Japan were doomed to disappointment. Americans sought to achieve great aims on the Asiatic mainland at small cost, looking to the British in India and the Chinese, with their vast reservoirs of manpower, to carry the main burden of ground conflict. Neither proved capable of exerting the effort the Americans expected of them.

Early in 1942 the United States had sent General Stilwell to the Far East to command American forces in China, Burma, and India and to serve as Chief of Staff and principal adviser to Chiang Kai-shek, the leader of Nationalist China and Allied commander of the China theater. Stilwell's stated mission was "to assist in improving the efficiency of the Chinese Army." The Japanese conquest of Burma, cutting the last overland supply route to China, frustrated Stilwell's designs, for it left a long and difficult airlift from Assam to Kunming over the high peaks of the Himalayas as the only remaining avenue for the flow of supplies. The Americans assumed responsibility for the airlift, but its development was slow, hampered by a scarcity of transport planes, airfields, and trained pilots. Not until late in 1943 did it reach a monthly capacity of 10,000 tons, and in the intervening months few supplies flowed into China. The economy of the country continually tottered on the brink of collapse, and the Chinese Army, although it was a massive force on paper, remained ill organized, ill equipped, poorly led, and generally incapable of offensive action.

Stilwell thought that the only solution was to retake Burma and reopen the land supply line to China, and this became the position of the U.S. Joint Chiefs of Staff. To achieve the goal Stilwell undertook the training and equipping of a Chinese force in India that eventually consisted of three divisions, and sought to concentrate a much larger force in Yunnan Province in China and to give it offensive capability. With these two Chinese forces he hoped to form a junction in north Burma, thus re-establishing land communications between China and India. Stilwell's scheme became part of the larger plan, ANAKIM, that had been approved by the Combined Chiefs of Staff at the Casablanca Conference. Neither the British nor the Chinese, however, had any real enthusiasm for ANAKIM, and in retrospect it seems clear that its execution in 1943 was beyond the capabilities of forces in the theater. Moreover, Chiang was quite dilatory in concentrating a force in Yunnan; Maj. Gen. Claire L. Chennault, commanding the small American air force in China, urged that the Hump air line should be used to support an air effort in China, rather than to supply Chinese ground forces. Chennault promised amazing results at small cost, and his proposals attracted President Roosevelt as well as the British and the Chinese. As an upshot, at the TRIDENT Conference in May 1943, the amphibious operation against Rangoon was canceled and a new plan for operations emerged that stressed Chennault's air operations and provided for a lesser ground offensive in central and northern Burma. Under this concept a new road would be built from Ledo in Assam Province, India, to join with the trace of the old Burma Road inside China. The Americans assumed responsibility for building the Ledo Road in the rear of Chinese forces advancing from India into Burma.

Logistical difficulties in India, however, again delayed the opening of any land offensive and kept the airlift well below target figures. Until the supply line north from Calcutta to the British and Chinese fronts could be improved— and this job took well over a year—both air and ground operations against the Japanese in Burma were handicapped. In October 1943 Chinese troops under Stilwell did start to clear northern Burma, and in the spring of 1944 a U.S. Army unit of regimental size, Merrill's Marauders, spearheaded new offensives to secure the trace for the overland road. But Myitkyina, the key point in the Japanese defenses in north Burma, did not fall until August 2 and by that time the effort in Burma had been relegated to a subsidiary role.

After the SEXTANT Conference in late 1943, in fact, the American staff no longer regarded it as probable that the overland route to China could be opened in time to permit Chinese forces to drive to the coast by the time American forces advancing across the Pacific reached there. While the Americans insisted on continuing the effort to open the Ledo Road, they now gave first priority to an air effort in China in support of the Pacific campaigns. The Army Air Forces, in May 1944, started to deploy the first of its B–29 groups to airfields in East China to commence bombing of strategic targets in Korea, Manchuria, and Japan. At the same time, Chennault's Fourteenth Air Force was directed to stockpile supplies for missions in support of Pacific forces as they neared the China coast. Again these projects proved to be more than could be supported over the Hump air line, particularly since transports had also to be used to supply the ground effort of both British and Chinese forces. Then the Japanese reacted strongly to the increased air effort and launched a ground offensive that overran most of the existing fields and proposed air base sites in east China. Both air and ground resources inside China had to be diverted to oppose the Japanese advance. The B–29's were removed to India in January 1945, and two months later were sent to Saipan where the major strategic bombing offensive against Japan was by that time being mounted. In sum, the air effort in China without the protection of an efficient Chinese Army fulfilled few of the goals proclaimed for it.

To meet the crisis in east China, President Roosevelt urged Chiang to place his U.S. supported armies under the command of General Stilwell; Chiang eventually refused and asked for Stilwell's recall, a request the President honored. In September 1944, Maj. Gen. Albert C. Wedemeyer replaced Stilwell as Chief of Staff to Chiang and commander of American forces in the China Theater; a separate theater in India and Burma was created with Lt. Gen. Dan I. Sultan as its commanding general. The command issue was dropped and the American strategy in China became simply one of trying to realize at least something from previous investments without additional commitments.

Ironically enough, it was in this phase, after the Pacific advances had outrun those in Southeast Asia, that objects of the 1942 strategy were realized, in large part because the Japanese, hard-pressed everywhere, were no longer able to support their forces in Burma and China adequately. British and Chinese forces advanced rapidly into Burma in the fall of 1944, and, on January 27, 1945, the junction between Chinese forces advancing from India and Yunnan finally took place, securing the trace of the Ledo Road. To the south, the British completed the conquest of central Burma and entered Rangoon from the north early in May. The land route to China was thus finally secured on all sides, but the Americans had already decided that they would develop the Ledo Road only as a one-way highway, though they did expand the airlift to the point where, in July 1945, it carried 74,000 tons into China.

With increased American supply support, Wedemeyer was able to make more progress in equipping and training the Chinese Army. Under his tutelage the Chinese were able to halt the Japanese advance at Chihchiang in April 1945, and, as the Japanese began to withdraw in order to prepare a citadel defense of their home islands, Wedemeyer and the Chinese laid plans to seize a port on the Chinese coast. The war came to an end, however, before this operation even started and before the training and equipping of a Chinese Army was any-where near completion. Chiang's forces commenced the reoccupation of their homeland still, for the most part, ill equipped, ill organized, and poorly led.

The Japanese Surrender

During the summer of 1945, Allied forces in the Pacific had stepped up the pace of their air and naval attacks against Japan. In June and July carrier-based planes of the U.S. Pacific Fleet and U.S. Army Air Forces planes from the Marianas, Iwo Jima, and Okinawa struck the Japanese home islands contin-uously. During July Pacific Fleet surface units bombarded Japan's east coast, and in the same month a British carrier task force joined in the attack. Planes from the Philippines hit Japanese shipping in the South China Sea and extended their strikes as far as Formosa and targets along the South China coast. American submarines redoubled their efforts to sweep Japanese shipping from the sea and sever the shipping lanes from Japan to the Indies and Southeast Asia. Throughout the war, in fact, submarines had preyed on Japanese merchant and combat vessels, playing a major role in isolating Japan from its conquests and thereby drastically reducing Japan's ability to wage war.

After Germany's surrender in May the United States embarked upon a huge logistical effort to redeploy more than a million troops from Europe, the United States, and other inactive theaters to the Pacific. The aim was to complete the redeployment in time to launch an invasion of Japan on November 1, and the task had to be undertaken in the face of competing shipping demands for demobilization of long-service troops, British redeployment, and civil relief in Europe. By the time the war ended, some 150,000 men had moved directly from Europe to the Pacific, but a larger transfer from the United States across the Pacific had scarcely begun. In the Pacific, MacArthur and Nimitz had been sparing no effort to expand ports and ready bases to receive the expected influx and to mount invasion forces. The two commanders were also completing plans

ATOMIC CLOUD OVER NAGASAKI

for the invasion of Japan. In the last stage of the war, as all forces converged on Japan, the area unified commands were replaced by an arrangement that made MacArthur commander of all Army forces in the Pacific and Nimitz commander of all Navy forces.

By midsummer of 1945 most responsible leaders in Japan realized that the end was near. In June, those favoring peace had come out in the open, and Japan had already dispatched peace feelers through the Soviet Union, a country it feared might also be about to enter the war despite the existence of a non-aggression treaty between the two nations. As early as the Tehran Conference in late 1943 Stalin had promised to enter the war against Japan, and it was agreed at Yalta in February 1945 that the USSR would do so three months after the defeat of Germany. At the Potsdam Conference in July 1945 the Soviet Union reaffirmed its agreement to declare war on Japan. At this conference the United States and Britain, with China joining in, issued the famed Potsdam Declaration calling upon Japan to surrender promptly, and about the same time President Truman decided to employ the newly tested atomic bomb against Japan in the event of continued Japanese resistance.

Despite the changing climate of opinion in Japan, the Japanese did not immediately accept the terms of the Potsdam Declaration. Accordingly, on August 6 a lone American B–29 from the Marianas dropped an atomic bomb on Hiroshima; on the 9th the Soviet Union came into the war and attacked Japanese forces in Manchuria; and on the same day another B–29 dropped a second atomic bomb on Nagasaki. The next day Japan sued for peace, and, with the signing of surrender terms aboard the USS *Missouri* in Tokyo Bay on September 2, the bitter global war came to an end.

Retrospect

In winning the Pacific war the Allies had found it unnecessary to press home their attacks and destroy the Japanese military forces except for the

Japanese Fleet. By the end of the war Japan's Navy had virtually ceased to exist; Japanese industry had been so hammered by air bombardment that Japan's ability to wage war was seriously reduced; and U.S. submarine and air actions had cut off sources of raw material. At the time of the surrender Japan still had 2,000,000 men under arms in the homeland and was capable of conducting a tenacious ground defense; about 3,000 Japanese aircraft were also operational. Nevertheless, the Japanese could hardly have continued the war for more than a few months. On the other hand, the fact that an invasion was not necessary certainly spared many American lives.

The great arbiter of the Pacific war had been American industrial power, which produced a mighty war machine. Out of this production had come the Pacific Fleet, a potent force that could overcome the vast reaches of the Pacific upon which the Japanese had depended so heavily as a defensive advantage. The decisive combat element of the fleet was the fast carrier task force, which carried the war deep into Japanese territory and supported advances far beyond the range of land-based aircraft. Land-based air power also played a decisive part. When carriers were not available to support offensives, it was land-based aviation that measured the distance of each forward move. Land-based aviation proved important as well in providing close support for ground operations, while aerial supply operations and troop movements contributed greatly to the success of the Allied campaigns.

Both naval and air forces were dependent upon shore bases, and the war in the Pacific demonstrated that even in a predominantly naval-air theater, ground combat forces are an essential part of the offensive team. The Japanese had also been dependent upon far-flung bases, so that much of the Allied effort during the war had gone into the seizure or neutralization of Japan's bases. Thus, the Pacific war was in large measure a war for bases. On the other hand, the U.S. Pacific Fleet, in one of the greatest logistical developments of the war, went far in the direction of carrying its bases with it by organizing fleet trains of support vessels that were capable of maintaining the fleet at sea over extended periods.

Another important facet of the Pacific war was the development and employment of amphibious assault techniques, repeatedly demonstrating the need for unified command. Air, ground, and naval teamwork, supremely important in the struggle against Japan, occasionally broke down, but the success of the Allied campaigns illustrates that all three elements achieved it to a large degree. Strategic air bombardment in the Pacific, designed to cripple Japan's industrial capacity, did not get under way until well along in 1945. The damage inflicted on Japanese cities was enormous, but the effect, as in the case of the bomber offensive against Germany, remains unsettled, though the bombardment finally brought home to the Japanese people that the war was lost. The submarine played a vital role in reducing Japan's capabilities by taking a huge toll of Japanese shipping and by helping to cut Japan off from the resources of Southeast Asia.

In the final analysis Japan lost because the country did not have the means to fight a total war against the combination of industrial, air, naval, and human resources represented by the United States and its Allies. Admiral Isoroku Yamamoto, commander of the Japanese Fleet at the outbreak of the war, put his finger on the fatal weakness of the Japanese concept of the war, when he stated: "It is not enough that we should take Guam and the Philippines, or even Hawaii and San Francisco. We should have to march into Washington and sign the treaty in the White House." This the Japanese could never do, and because they could not they had to lose the war.

CHAPTER 24

Peace Becomes Cold War, 1945–1950

The United States did not return to its prewar isolationism after World War II. The balance of power in Europe and Asia and the safety of ocean distances east and west that made isolation possible had vanished, the balance upset by the war, the protection of oceans eliminated by advances in air transportation and weaponry. There was now little inclination to dispute the essential rightness of the position espoused by Woodrow Wilson after World War I that the nations of the world were interdependent, the peace indivisible. "We are participants," Wilson had said, "whether we would or not, in the life of the world. We are partners with the rest. What affects mankind is inevitably our affair as well as the affair of the nations of Europe and of Asia." Indeed, in the years immediately following World War II, full participation in world events became a governing dynamic of American life.

In the immediate wake of the war the hopes of the American Government and people rested in the United Nations Organization formed at San Francisco in 1945 to provide a world program of collective security. The fifty countries signing the U.N. Charter agreed to employ ". . . effective collective measures for the prevention and removal of threats to the peace and for the suppression of acts of aggression . . .," including the use of armed force if peaceful measures failed. A U.N. Security Council received authority to determine when the peace was threatened and what counteraction was to be taken and to call on member states to furnish military formations when armed force was deemed necessary. Founder members of the United Nations included the United States, Union of Soviet Socialist Republics, United Kingdom, China, and France; each of them received permanent representation on the Security Council and the power of veto over any council action. Since the United Nations' effectiveness depended largely upon the full cooperation of these five countries, the primary objective of American foreign policy as the postwar era opened was to continue and strengthen the solidarity those nations had displayed during the war.

A clear responsibility of U.S. membership in the United Nations was to maintain sufficient military power to permit an effective contribution to any U.N. force that might be necessary. Other than this, it was difficult, in the immediate aftermath of war, to foresee national security requirements in the changed world and, consequently, to know the proper shape of a military establishment to meet them. The immediate task was to demobilize the great war machine assembled during the war and, at the same time, maintain occupation troops in conquered and liberated territories. Beyond this lay the problems of deciding the size and composition of the postwar armed forces and of establishing the machinery through which national security policy would be determined and the military establishment governed.

Demobilization

The Army and Navy had worked separately during the war to determine what their postwar strengths should be and had produced plans for an orderly demobilization. The Navy developed a program for 600,000 men, 370 combat and 5,000 other ships, and 8,000 aircraft. The Army Air Forces was equally specific, setting its sights on becoming a separate service with 400,000 members, 70 air wings, and a complete organization of supporting units. The Army initially established as an over-all postwar goal a Regular and Reserve structure capable of mobilizing four million men within a year of any future outbreak of war; later it set the strength of the active ground and air forces at one and a half million. Demobilization plans called for the release of troops on an individual basis, each man receiving point credit for length of service, combat participation and awards, time spent overseas, and parenthood. The shipping available to bring overseas troops home and the capacity to process discharges were considered in setting the number of points determining eligibility for release, with the whole scheme aimed at producing a systematic transition to a peacetime military structure.

Pressure for faster demobilization from an articulate public, the Congress, and the troops themselves upset the plans for an orderly demobilization. The Army, which felt the greatest pressure, responded by easing the eligibility requirement and releasing half its eight million troops by the end of 1945. Early in 1946, when the Army cut down the return of troops from abroad in order to meet its overseas responsibilities, a crescendo of protest greeted the move, including troop demonstrations in the Philippines, China, England, France, Germany, Hawaii, and even California. The public cry diminished only after the Army more than halved its remaining strength during the first six months of 1946.

President Truman, determined to balance the national budget, meanwhile developed and through fiscal year 1950 employed a "remainder method" of calculating military budgets, subtracting all other expenditures from revenues before recommending a military appropriation. The dollar ceiling applied for fiscal year 1947 dictated a new maximum Army strength of just over one million. To reach it, the Army issued no more draft calls and released all postwar draftees along with the remaining troops eligible for demobilization. By June 30, 1947, the Army was a volunteer body of 684,000 ground troops and 306,000 airmen. (The Navy was meanwhile reduced to a strength of 484,000, the Marine Corps to 92,000.) It was still a large peacetime Army, but shortages of capable maintenance troops resulted in a widespread deterioration of equipment, and remaining Army units, understrength and infused with briefly trained replacements, were only shadows of the efficient organizations they had been at the end of the war.

Unification

While demobilization proceeded, civil and military officials alike wrestled with the task of reorganizing the national security system to cope with a changed world. The basic need, long recognized and proved anew by World War II, was unified control at the national level and at major military command levels. During the war this control had been accomplished through temporary arrangements. After the war, some permanent merger of ground, air, and naval forces under the authority of a single civilian member of the President's cabinet and the establishment of a statutory body where all plans and policies bearing on national security could be integrated seemed necessary. After long arguments over the degree of central authority to be imposed on the armed forces and over roles and missions to be assigned each service, the National Security Act of 1947 was passed as a first effort to achieve these ends.

The principal creations of the act were a National Security Council and a National Military Establishment. The latter, though not an executive department of the Federal government, was headed by a civilian Secretary of Defense with cabinet rank. The Air Force became a separate service equal with the Army and Navy; and all three were designated as executive departments and headed by civilian secretaries who, though they lacked cabinet rank, had direct access to the President.

Members of the National Security Council included the Secretary of State, Secretary of Defense, the three service secretaries, and heads of other governmental agencies as appointed by the President. One of the appointees was the Chairman of the National Security Resources Board, an agency also established by the act to handle the problems of industrial, manpower, and raw material mobilization in support of an over-all national strategy. In theory, the National

Security Council was to develop co-ordinated diplomatic, military, and industrial plans; recommend integrated national security policies to the President; and guide the execution of those policies approved. In practice, because the responsibility was inherently so complicated, the council would produce something less than precise policy determinations.

The national military establishment included the Departments of the Army, Navy, and Air Force and the Office of the Secretary of Defense. The Secretary of Defense exercised general direction over the three departments. The Joint Chiefs of Staff, composed of the military chiefs of the three services, became a statutory body seated in the Office of the Secretary of Defense and functioned as the principal military advisers to the President, the National Security Council, and the Secretary of Defense. They were also responsible for formulating joint military plans, establishing unified commands in various areas of the world, and giving strategic directon to those commands. Under this dispensation, unified commands were established by mid-1950 in the Far East, the Pacific, Alaska, the Caribbean, and Europe. Within each, at least theoretically, Army, Navy, and Air Force troops were under commanders of their respective services and under the overall supervision of a commander in chief designated from one of the services by the Joint Chiefs. But it would take some time for the principle of unity of command to be completely applied in all areas.

Under the Security Act, each military service retained much of its former autonomy since it was administered within a separate department. Interservice accord on roles and missions negotiated in 1948 by James V. Forrestal, the first Secretary of Defense, tended to harden the separation. The Army received primary responsibility for conducting operations on land, for supplying anti-aircraft units to defend the United States against air attack, and for providing occupation and security garrisons overseas. The Navy, besides remaining responsible for surface and submarine operations, retained control of its sea-based aviation and of the Marine Corps with its organic aviation. The new Air Force received jurisdiction over strategic air warfare, air transport, and combat air support of the Army.

The signal weakness of the act, however, was not that it left the armed forces more federated than unified, but that the Secretary of Defense, empowered to exercise only general supervision, could do little more than encourage cooperation among the departments. Furthermore, the direct access to the President given the three service secretaries tended to confuse the lines of authority. These faults prompted an amendment to the act in 1949 by which the National Military Establishment was converted into an executive department and renamed the Department of Defense. The Departments of the Army, Navy, and Air Force were reduced from executive departments to military departments within the Department of Defense; a chairman without vote was added to the Joint Chiefs; and the Secretary of Defense received the appropriate responsibility and authority to make him truly the central figure in co-ordinating the activities of the three services. In extension of civilian control, the three service secretaries retained authority to administer affairs within their respective departments; and the departments remained the principal operating agencies for administering, training, and supporting their respective forces.

Unification also touched the military school system, although each service continued to conduct courses to meet its own specialized needs. Three schools were opened to educate senior officers of all the services and selected civilians: an Armed Forces Staff College to train selected officers in planning and executing joint military operations, an Industrial College of the Armed forces to instruct senior officers in the many aspects of mobilizing the nation's resources for war, and a National War College to develop selected officers and civilians for duties connected with the execution of national policy.

A new Uniform Code of Military Justice applying to all the armed forces was enacted by Congress in May 1950. This code, besides prescribing uniformity, reduced the severities of military discipline in the interest of improving the lot of the individual serviceman. In another troop matter, part of a larger effort in the area of civil rights, President Truman directed the armed forces to eliminate all segregation of troops by race. The Navy and the Air Force abolished their all-Negro units by June 1950, whereas the Army, with more Negro members than its sister services, would take some four years longer to desegregate.

Occupation

Throughout demobilization about half the Army's diminishing strength remained overseas, the bulk involved in the occupation of Germany and Japan. Another large force was in liberated Korea, along with a Soviet force, both armies having sent units to accept the surrender of Japanese troops stationed there and to occupy the country.

Under a common occupation policy developed principally in conferences at Yalta and Potsdam in 1945, the Allied Powers assumed joint sovereign authority over Germany. American, British, Soviet, and French forces occupied separate zones, and national matters came before an Allied Control Council composed of he commanders of the four occupation armies. Berlin, itself lying deep in the Soviet zone in eastern Germany, was similarly divided and governed.

In the American zone, Army occupation troops proceeded rapidly with disarmament, demilitarization, and the eradication of Nazi influence from German life. American officials meanwhile participated as members of an International Military Tribunal which tried 22 major leaders of the Nazi party, sentencing 12 to death, imprisoning 7, and acquitting 3. An Office of Military Government supervised German civil affairs within the American zone, working increasingly through German local, state, and zonal agencies which military government officials staffed with men who were politically reliable. A special U.S. Constabulary, organized by the Army as demobilization cut away the strength of units in Germany, operated as a mobile police force.

Each of the other occupying powers organized its zone along similar lines. But the Allied Control Council, which could act only by unanimous agreement, failed to achieve unanimity on such nationwide matters as central economic administrative agencies, political parties, labor organizations, foreign and internal trade, currency, and land reform. USSR demands and dissents were chiefly responsible for the failures. Each zone inevitably became a self-contained administrative and economic unit, and some two years after the German surrender very little progress had been made toward the reconstruction of German national life. The eventual result, first taking shape in September 1949, was a divided Germany: the Federal Republic of Germany in the area of the American, British, and French zones; a Communist government in the Soviet zone in the east.

The occupation of Japan proceeded along different lines as a result of President Truman's insistence that the whole of Japan come under American control. Largely because the war in the Pacific had been primarily an American war, the President secured Allied approval of General of the Army Douglas MacArthur as Supreme Commander, Allied Powers, for the occupation of Japan. A Far East Advisory Commission representing the eleven nations that had fought against Japan was seated in Washington; and a branch of that body, with representatives from the United States, Great Britain, China, and the USSR, was located in Tokyo. These provided forums for Allied viewpoints or occupation policies, but the real power rested in General MacArthur.

Unlike Germany, Japan retained its government, which, under the supervision of General MacArthur's occupation troops, disarmed the nation rapidly and without incident. An International Military Tribunal similar to the one that functioned in Germany tried twenty-five high military and political officials, sentencing seven to death. MacArthur meanwhile encouraged reforms to alter the old order of government in which the emperor claimed power by divine right and exercised rule through an oligarchy of military, bureaucratic, and economic cliques. By mid-1947, the free election of a new Diet and a thorough revision of the nation's constitution began the transformation of Japan into a constitutional democracy with the emperor's role limited to that of a constitutional monarch. The way was thus open for the ultimate restoration of Japan's sovereignty.

West of the Japanese islands, on the peninsula of Korea jutting out from the central Asian mainland, the course of occupation resembled that in Germany. USSR forces, following their brief campaign against the Japanese in Manchuria, had moved into Korea from the north in August 1945. U.S. Army forces, departing their last battleground on Okinawa, entered from the south a month later. The 38th parallel of north latitude crossing the peninsula at its waist was set as the boundary between forces as the two nations released Korea from forty years of Japanese rule, the Americans accepting the Japanese surrender south of the line, the Soviets above it.

According to wartime agreements, Korea was to receive full independence following a period of Allied military occupation during which native leadership was to be regenerated and the country's economy rehabilitated. Very quickly the 38th parallel represented a complication in restoring Korea's sovereignty. For while the parallel had been designated only as a boundary between forces, the Soviets considered it a permanent delineation between occupation zones. This interpretation, as in Germany, ruptured the administrative and economic unity of the country.

Hope of removing this obstacle rose when the United States presented the problem during a meeting of foreign ministers at Moscow in December 1945. The ministers agreed that a joint U.S.-USSR commission would develop a provisional Korean government and that a four-power trusteeship composed of the United States, the Soviet Union, the United Kingdom, and China would guide the provisional government for a maximum of five years. But in the meetings of the commission, the Soviet members revealed a willingness to reunite Korea only if the provisional government was Communist-dominated. Persistent Soviet demands to this end were matched by equally persistent American refusals. The resulting impasse finally prompted the United States to lay the whole Korean question before the General Assembly of the United Nations in September 1947.

The Rise of a New Opponent

Soviet intransigence, as demonstrated in Germany, in Korea, and in other areas, dashed American hopes for Great Power unity. The USSR, Winston Churchill warned in a speech at Fulton, Missouri, early in 1946, was lowering an "iron curtain" across the European continent. It successfully, and quickly, drew eastern Germany, Poland, Hungary, Rumania, Bulgaria, Yugoslavia, and Albania behind that curtain. In Greece, where political and economic disorder led to civil war, the rebels received support from Albania, Bulgaria, and Yugoslavia. In the Near East, the Soviets kept a grip on Iran by holding troops placed there during the war beyond the time specified in the wartime arrangement. They also tried to intimidate Turkey into giving them special privileges in connection with the strategic Dardanelles. In Asia, besides insisting on full control in northern Korea, the USSR, it appeared, had turned Manchuria over to the Chinese Communists under Mao Tse-tung and was encouraging Mao in his renewed effort to wrest power from Chiang Kai-shek and the Kuomintang government.

Whatever the impulse behind the Soviet drive, whether it was a search for national security or a desire to promote Communist world revolution in keeping with Marxist doctrine, the USSR strategy appeared to be one of expansion. The United States could see no inherent limits to the outward push. Each Communist gain, it seemed, would serve as a springboard from which to try another; and a large part of the world, still suffering from the ravages of war, offered tempting opportunities for further Soviet expansion. The American response was a policy of containment, of blocking any extension of Communist influence. But, viewing the European continent as the main area of Soviet expansion, the United States at first limited its containment policy to western Europe and the Mediterranean area and attempted other solutions to the problem in Asia.

China, in any case, presented a dilemma. On the one hand, it was doubtful that Chiang Kai-shek could defeat the Communists with aid short of direct American participation in the civil war. Such participation was considered unacceptable. On the other hand, an attempt, through the efforts of General of the Army George C. Marshall following his Army retirement, to negotiate an end to the war on terms that would place the Kuomintang in full authority proved futile. The United States, consequently, adopted the attitude of "letting the dust settle." Part of the basis for this attitude was a prevalent American view that the Chinese Communist revolt was more Chinese than Communist, that its motivation was nationalistic, not imperialistic. Hence, though the dust appeared to be settling in favor of the Chinese Communists by the end of 1948, there was some hope that American-Chinese friendship could be restored whenever and however the conflict ended.

Next door in Korea, the division between north and south had become a reality by the end of 1948. After the Korean problem was referred to the United Nations, that body sent a commission to supervise free elections throughout the peninsula. But USSR authorities, declaring the U.N. project illegal, refused the commission entry above the 38th parallel. The U.N. then sponsored an elected government in the southern half of the peninsula, which in August 1948 became the Republic of Korea (South Korea). The Soviets countered during the following month by establishing a Communist government, the Democratic People's Republic of Korea (North Korea), above the parallel. Three months later, they announced the withdrawal of their occupation forces. The United States followed suit, withdrawing its troops by mid-1949 except for an advisory group left behind to help train the South Korean armed forces.

In the main arena in western Europe and in the Mediterranean area, blunt diplomatic exchanges finally produced a withdrawal of Soviet forces from Iran. But it was around American economic strength that the United States constructed a basic containment strategy, a resort based on judgment that the American monopoly on atomic weapons would cause the USSR to forgo direct military aggression in favor of exploiting civil strife in those countries prostrated by the war. The American strategy hence was to provide economic assistance to friends and former enemies alike to alleviate the conditions of distress conducive to Communist expansion.

To ease the situations in Turkey and Greece, President Truman in 1947 obtained $400 million from Congress with which to assist those two countries. "I believe," the President declared, "that it must be the policy of the United States to support free peoples who are resisting attempted subjugation by armed minorities or by outside pressures . . . that we must assist free peoples to work out their own destinies in their own way . . . that our help should be primarily through economic and financial aid which is essential to economic stability and orderly political processes." This philosophy, to become well known as the Truman Doctrine, was limited in application at the time, but it was destined to have wide significance for it, in effect, placed the United States in the position of opposing Communist expansion in any part of the world.

A broader program of economic aid followed. General Marshall, who became Secretary of State in January 1947, proposed that economic recovery in Europe be pursued as a single task, not nation by nation, and that the resources of European countries be combined with American aid within a single program. This "Marshall Plan" drew an immediate response wherein sixteen nations (who also considered the needs and resources of western Germany) devised a four-year European Recovery Program incorporating their resources and requiring some $16 billion from the United States. The Congress balked when President Truman first asked for approval of the program but appropriated funds for the first year in April 1948, after the USSR had engineered a *coup d'etat* that placed a Communist government in power in Czechoslovakia. The USSR, though invited in a last effort to promote Great Power unity, had refused to participate in the program and discouraged the initial interest displayed by some countries within its sphere of influence. In further counteraction, the Soviet Union in October 1947 had organized the Cominform, a committee for co-ordinating Communist parties in Europe whose aim was to fight the Marshall Plan as "an instrument of American imperialism."

Meanwhile, to protect the Western Hemisphere against Communist intrusion, the United States in September 1947 helped devise the Inter-American Treaty of Reciprocal Assistance (Rio Treaty), the first regional arrangement for collective defense under provisions of the U.N. Charter. Eventually signed by all twenty-one American republics, the treaty served notice that armed aggression against one signatory would be considered an attack upon all. Responses, by independent choice of each signatory, could range from severance of diplomatic relations through economic sanctions to military counteraction.

In March 1948, a second regional arrangement, the Brussels Treaty, drew five nations of western Europe—Great Britain, France, Belgium, the Nether-lands, and Luxembourg—into a long-term economic and military alliance. The signatories received encouragement from President Truman, who declared before the Congress his confidence ". . . that the determination of the free countries of Europe to protect themselves will be matched by an equal determi-nation on our part to help them. . . ." Senator Arthur H. Vandenberg of Michigan followed with a resolution, passed in the Senate in June 1948, author-izing the commitment of American military strength to regional alliances such as the Brussels Treaty.

Out of all of this grew the real basis of postwar international relations: West versus East, anti-Communists against Communists, those nations aligned with the United States confronting those assembled under the leadership of the Soviet Union, a cold war between power blocs. Leadership of the western bloc fell to the United States, since the fortunes of war had left it the only western power with sufficient resources to take the lead in containing Soviet expansion.

The Trends of Military Policy

Although pursued as a program of economic assistance, the American policy of containment nonetheless needed military underwriting. Containment, first of all, was a defensive measure. The USSR, moreover, had not completely de-mobilized. On the contrary, it was maintaining over four million men under arms, keeping armament industries in high gear, and rearming some of its satellites. Hence, containment needed the support of a military policy of deterrence, of a military strategy and organizational structure possessing sufficient strength and balance to discourage any Soviet or Soviet-supported military aggression.

Postwar military policy, however, did not develop as a full response to the needs of containment. For one reason, mobilization in the event of war, not the maintenance of ready forces to prevent war, was the traditional and current trend of American peacetime military thinking. A principal feature of mobilization planning was an effort to install universal military training. This effort was a particular response to technological advances which had eliminated the grace of time and distance formerly permitting the nation to mobilize its untrained citizenry after a threat of war became real, and which therefore posed a need for a huge reservoir of trained men. Late in 1945, President Truman asked the Congress for legislation requiring male citizens to undergo a year of military training (not *service*) upon reaching the age of eighteen or after completing high school. Universal military training quickly became the subject of wide debate. Objections ranged from mild criticism that it was ". . . a system in which the American mind finds no pleasure" to its denunciation as a "Nazi program." Regardless of the President's urgings, studies that produced further justification, and various attempts to make the program more palatable, the Congress over the five years following the President's first proposal refused to act on the controversial issue.

Without universal military training, the provision of trained strength with which to reinforce a nucleus of Regular forces at mobilization depended almost entirely upon the older system of using civilian components. This Reserve strength, like that of the Regular forces, was affected by limited funds. Enrollment in the National Guard and Reserves of all three services at mid-1950 totaled over two and a half million. But, owing in large part to restricted budgets, members in active training numbered less than one million. The bulk of this active strength rested in the Army's National Guard and Organized Reserve Corps. The National Guard, with 325,000 members, included twenty-seven understrength divisions. The active strength of the Organized Reserve Corps, some 186,000, was vested mainly in a multitude of small combat support and service units, these, too, generally understrength. A final source of trained strength was the Reserve Officers' Training Corps program, in which at midterm in fiscal year 1950 about 219,000 high school and college students were enrolled.

Also inhibiting a response to the military needs of containment was the influence of World War II, above all, the advent of the atomic bomb. The tendency was to consider the American nuclear monopoly as the primary deterrent to direct Soviet military action and to think only in terms of total war. Obversely, the possibility of lesser conflicts in which the bomb would be neither politically nor militarily relevant was almost completely disregarded.

Budgetary limitations to a great extent governed the size of the armed forces. From the figure reached at the end of demobilization, the total strength of active forces gradually decreased under the limited appropriations. The Army, Navy, and Marine Corps suffered losses in strength, whereas the Air Force actually grew somewhat larger. About a third of the Air Force constituted the Strategic Air Command, whose heavy bombers armed with atomic bombs represented the main deterrent to Soviet military aggression. Louis A. Johnson, who became Secretary of Defense in March 1949, gave full support to a defense based primarily on strategic air power, largely because of his dedication to economy. Intent on ridding the Department of Defense of what he considered "costly war-born spending habits," Secretary Johnson reduced defense expenditures below even the restrictive ceilings in President Truman's recommendations. As a result, by mid-1950 the Air Force, with 411,000 members, was barely able to maintain forty-eight air wings. The Navy, with a strength of 377,000, had 670 ships in its active fleet and 4,300 operational aircraft. In the Marine Corps, which had 75,000 men, the battle units amounted to skeletons of two divisions and two air wings. The Army, down to 591,000 members, had its combat strength vested in ten divisions and five regimental combat teams. The constabulary in Germany was equal to another division.

As evident in the strength reductions, mobilization strategy, and heavy reliance on the atomic bomb and strategic air power, the idea of deterring aggression through balanced ready forces had little place in the development of postwar military policy. The budgetary limitations made clear that military policy, caught as it often is between conflicting domestic pressures and foreign challenges, had responded more to domestic interests; and the roles played by traditional thinking and the influence of World War II invite the observation that, while foreign policy was being adjusted to a new opponent and a new kind of conflict, military policy was being developed mainly with earlier enemies and an all-out war in mind.

The Army of 1950

As the Army underwent its postwar reduction, from 8 million men and 89 divisions in 1945 to 591,000 men and 10 divisions in 1950, it also underwent numerous structural changes. At the department level, changes were made in

1946 to restore the General Staff to its prewar position. The principal adjustment toward this end was the elimination of the very powerful Operations Division (OPD), where control of wartime operations had been centralized. The prewar structure of the General Staff was restored with five coequal divisions under new names: Personnel and Administration; Intelligence; Organization and Training; Service, Supply and Procurement; and Plans and Operations. Also in 1946, Headquarters, Army Service Forces, was abolished, and the administrative and technical services serving under that headquarters during the war regained their prewar status as departmental agencies. In 1948, Army Ground Forces was redesignated Army Field Forces.

These and other organizational changes instituted or planned over the first five postwar years became a matter of statute with passage of an Army Reorganization Act in 1950. The act confirmed the power of the Secretary of the Army to administer departmental affairs. Under him, the Army Chief of Staff was responsible for the Army's readiness and operational plans, and for carrying out, worldwide, the approved plans and policies of the department. He had the assistance of general and special staffs whose size and composition could be adjusted as requirements changed. Below the Chief of Staff, the Chief of Army Field Forces was directly responsible for developing tactical doctrine, for controlling the Army school system, and for supervising the field training of Army units. Most of the training and schools were conducted within six Continental Army Areas into which the United States was divided.

Under the new act, the Secretary of the Army received authority to determine the number and strength of the Army's combat arms and services. Three combat arms—infantry, armor, and artillery—received statutory recognition. The last represented a merger of the old field artillery, coast artillery, and antiaircraft artillery. Armor was made a continuation of another older arm, now eliminated, the cavalry. The services numbered fourteen and included The Adjutant General's Corps, Army Medical Service, Chaplains Corps, Chemical Corps, Corps of Engineers, Finance Corps, Inspector General's Corps, Judge Advocate General's Corps, Military Police Corps, Ordnance Corps, Quartermaster Corps, Signal Corps, Transportation Corps, and Women's Army Corps. Army Aviation, designated neither arm nor service, existed as a quasi arm equipped with small fixed-wing craft and helicopters.

The better Army troops at mid-1950 were among a large but diminishing group of World War II veterans. The need to obtain replacements quickly during demobilization, the distractions and relaxed atmosphere of occupation duty, and a postwar training program less demanding than that of the war years impeded the combat readiness of newer Army members. The new Uniform Code of Military Justice, because it softened military discipline, was considered in some quarters as likely to blunt the Army's combat ability even more.

Half the Army's major combat units were deployed overseas. Of the ten divisions, four infantry divisions were part of the Far East Command on occupation duty in Japan. Another infantry division was with the European Command in Germany. The remaining five were in the United States, constituting a General Reserve ιo meet emergency assignments. These included two airborne infantry divisions, two infantry divisions, and an armored division. All ten had undergone organizational changes, most of them prompted by the war experience. Under new tables of organization and equipment, the firepower and mobility of a division received a boost through the addition of a tank battalion and an antiaircraft battalion and through a rise in the number of pieces in each artillery battery from four to six. At regimental level, the cannon and antitank companies of World War II days were dropped; the new tables added a tank company, 4.2-inch mortar company, and 57-mm. and 75-mm. recoilless rifles. The postwar economies, however, had forced the Army to skeletonize its combat units. Nine of the 10 divisions were far understrength, infantry regiments had only 2 of the normal 3 battalions, most artillery battalions had only 2 of the normal 3 firing batteries, and organic armor was generally lacking. No unit had its wartime complement of weapons, and those weapons on hand as well as other equipment were largely worn leftovers from World War II. None of the combat units, as a result, came anywhere near possessing the punch conceived under the new organizational design.

The Cold War Intensifies

The deterioration in military readiness through mid-1950 proceeded in the face of a worsening trend in international events, especially from mid-1948 forward. In Germany, in further protest against western attempts to establish a national government, and in particular against efforts to institute currency reforms in Berlin, the USSR in June 1948 moved to force the Americans, British, and French out of the capital by blockading the road and rail lines through the Soviet occupation zone over which troops and supplies from the west reached the Allied sectors of the city. General Lucius D. Clay, the American military governor, countered by devising an airlift in which U.S. Army and U.S. Air Force troops, with some help from the British, loaded and flew in food, fuel, and other necessities to keep the Allied sectors of Berlin supplied. The success of the airlift and a telling counterblockade in which shipments of goods formerly reaching the Soviet sector from western Germany were shut off finally moved the Soviets to lift the blockade in May 1949.

Meanwhile, in April 1949, the United States joined the North Atlantic Treaty Organization (NATO), a military alliance growing out of the Brussels Treaty. NATO joined the United States with Canada and ten western European nations under terms by which ". . . an armed attack against one or more of them . . . shall be considered an attack against them all," a provision specifically aimed at discouraging a Soviet march in Europe. The signatories agreed to earmark forces for service under NATO direction. In the United States, the budgetary restrictions, mobilization strategy, and continuing emphasis on air power and the bomb handicapped military commitment to the alliance. An effort at the time by some officials to increase the nation's conventional forces against the possibility of a conflict in which atomic retaliation would be an excessive answer was defeated by the basic budget ceiling and Secretary of Defense Johnson's ardent economy drive. Through NATO membership, nevertheless, the United States certified that it would fight if necessary to protect common Allied interests in Europe and thus enlarged the policy of containment beyond the economic realm.

Concurrently with negotiations leading to the NATO alliance, the National Security Council reconsidered the whole course of postwar military aid. Under different programs, some of them continuations of World War II aid, the United States was by 1949 providing military equipment and training assistance to Greece, Turkey, Iran, China, Korea, the Philippines, and the Latin American republics. The National Security Council recommended and President Truman proposed to the Congress that all existing programs, including those conceived for NATO members, be combined into one. The result was the Mutual Defense Assistance Program of October 1949. The Department of the Army, made executive agency for the program, sent each recipient country a military assistance advisory group. Composed of Army, Navy, and Air Force sections, each advisory group assisted its host government in determining the amount and type of aid needed and helped train the armed forces of each country in the use and tactical employment of matériel received from the United States.

A new and surprising turn came in the late summer of 1949 when, from two to three years ahead of western bloc estimates, an explosion over Siberia announced Soviet possession of an atomic weapon. On the heels of the USSR's achievement, the civil war in China ended in favor of the Chinese Communists. Chiang Kai-shek was forced to withdraw to the island of Taiwan (Formosa) in December 1949. Two months later, Communist China and the USSR negotiated a treaty of mutual assistance, an ominous event for the rest of Asia.

The loss of the nuclear monopoly prompted a broad review of the entire political and strategic position of the United States, a task carried out at top staff levels in the National Security Council, Department of State, and Department of Defense. A special National Security Council committee at the same time considered the specific problem posed by the Soviet achievement. Out of the committee effort came a decision to intensify research already begun on the development of a hydrogen bomb to assure the United States the lead in the field of nuclear weapons. Out of the broader review, completed in April 1950, came recommendations for a large expansion of American military, diplomatic, and economic efforts to meet the changed world situation. The planning staffs in the Department of Defense began at once to translate the military recommendations into force levels and budgets. There remained the question of whether the plans when completed would persuade President Truman to lift the ceiling on military appropriations, but as a result of events in Asia this question was never put to the test.

After the Communist victory in China, the United States applied its policy of containment in Asia. In January 1950, Dean G. Acheson, who a year earlier had become Secretary of State, publicly defined the U.S. "defense line" in Asia as running south from the Aleutian Islands to Japan, to the Ryukyu Islands, and then to the Philippines. This delineation raised a question about Taiwan and Korea, which lay outside the line. These areas were not completely disregarded. Secretary Acheson pointed out that if they were attacked, ". . . the initial reliance must be on the people attacked to resist it and then upon the commitments of the entire world under the Charter of the United Nations." The question was whether the Communist bloc would construe this statement as a definite American commitment to help defend Taiwan and Korea if they came under attack.

In the case of Korea, the question would be answered in June 1950 following the armed invasion of the Republic of Korea by forces of the Soviet satellite above the 38th parallel. Until then, with the emergence of a bipolar world, the USSR and its satellites on one side, the United States and its allies on the other, the United States had responded with a policy of containing the political ambitions of the Communist bloc with the objective of deterring an outbreak of war. But by mid-1950 the United States had not yet backed that policy with a matching military establishment.

CHAPTER 25

The Korean War, 1950–1953

After the USSR installed a Communist government in North Korea in September 1948, that government promoted and supported an insurgency in South Korea in an attempt to bring down the recognized government and gain jurisdiction over the entire Korean peninsula. Not quite two years later, after the insurgency showed signs of failing, the northern government undertook a direct attack, sending the North Korea People's Army south across the 38th parallel before daylight on Sunday, June 25, 1950. The invasion, in a narrow sense, marked the beginning of a civil war between peoples of a divided country. In a larger sense, the cold war between the Great Power blocs had erupted in open hostilities.

The Decision for War

The western bloc, especially the United States, was surprised by the North Korean decision. Although intelligence information of a possible June invasion had reached Washington, the reporting agencies judged an early summer attack unlikely. The North Koreans, they estimated, had not yet exhausted the possibilities of the insurgency and would continue that strategy only.

The North Koreans, however, seem to have taken encouragement from the U.S. policy which left Korea outside the U.S. "defense line" in Asia and from relatively public discussions of the economies placed on U.S. armed forces. They evidently accepted these as reasons to discount American counteraction, or their sponsor, the USSR, may have made that calculation for them. The Soviets also appear to have been certain the United Nations would not intervene, for in protest against Nationalist China's membership in the U.N. Security Council and against the U.N.'s refusal to seat Communist China, the USSR member had boycotted council meetings since January 1950 and did not return in June to veto any council move against North Korea.

Moreover, Kim Il Sung, the North Korean Premier, could be confident that his army, a modest force of 135,000, was superior to that of South Korea. Koreans who had served in Chinese and Soviet World War II armies made up a large part of his force. He had 8 full divisions, each including a regiment of artillery; 2 divisions at half strength; 2 separate regiments; an armored brigade with 120

Soviet T34 medium tanks; and 5 border constabulary brigades. He also had 180 Soviet aircraft, mostly fighters and attack bombers, and a few naval patrol craft.

The Republic of Korea (ROK) Army had just 95,000 men and was far less fit. Raised as a constabulary during occupation, it had not in its later combat training under a U.S. Military Advisor Group progressed much beyond company-level exercises. Of its eight divisions, only four approached full strength. It had no tanks and its artillery totaled eighty-nine 105-mm. howitzers. The ROK Navy matched its North Korean counterpart, but the ROK Air Force had only a few trainers and liaison aircraft. U.S. equipment, war-worn when furnished to South Korean forces, had deteriorated further, and supplies on hand could sustain combat operations no longer than fifteen days. Whereas almost $11 million in matériel assistance had been allocated to South Korea in fiscal year 1950 under the Mutual Defense Assistance Program, Congressional review of the allocation so delayed the measure that only a trickle of supplies had reached the country by June 25, 1950.

The North Koreans quickly crushed South Korean defenses at the 38th parallel. The main North Korean attack force next moved down the west side of the peninsula toward Seoul, the South Korean capital, thirty-five miles below the parallel, and entered the city on June 28. (*Map 45*) Secondary thrusts down the peninsula's center and down the east coast kept pace with the main drive. The South Koreans withdrew in disorder, those troops driven out of Seoul forced to abandon most of their equipment because the bridges over the Han River at the south edge of the city were prematurely demolished. The North Koreans halted after capturing Seoul, but only briefly to regroup before crossing the Han.

In Washington, where a 14-hour time difference made it June 24 when the North Koreans crossed the parallel, the first report of the invasion arrived that night. Early on the 25th, the United States requested a meeting of the U.N. Security Council. The council adopted a resolution that afternoon demanding an immediate cessation of hostilities and a withdrawal of North Korean forces to the 38th parallel.

In independent actions on the night of the 25th, President Truman relayed orders to General of the Army Douglas MacArthur at MacArthur's Far East Command headquarters in Tokyo, Japan, to supply ROK forces with ammunition and equipment, evacuate American dependents from Korea, and survey conditions on the peninsula to determine how best to assist the republic further. The President also ordered the U.S. Seventh Fleet from its current location in Philippine and Ryukyu waters to Japan. On the 26th, in a broad interpretation of a U.N. Security Council request for "every assistance" in supporting the June 25

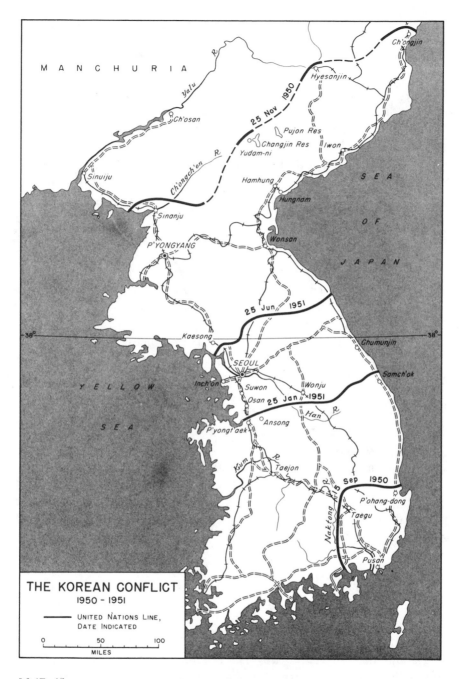

MANCHURIA

Yalu R.

Ch'osan

25 Nov 1950

Ch'ongjin

Hyesanjin

Pujon Res
Changjin Res
Yudam-ni

Iwon

Ch'ongch'on R.

SEA

Sinuiju

Hamhung

OF

Sinanju

Hungnam

JAPAN

P'YONGYANG

Wonsan

25 Jun 1951

38°   38°

Kaesong

Chumunjin

SEOUL

Samch'ok

YELLOW

Inch'on

Suwon   Wonju

Osan   25 Jan 1951

SEA

P'yongt'aek

Ansong

Han R.

Kum R.

Taejon

15 Sep 1950

P'ohang-dong

Naktong R.

Taegu

Pusan

THE KOREAN CONFLICT
1950 - 1951

━━━ United Nations Line,
      Date Indicated

0   50   100

MILES

MAP 45

resolution, President Truman authorized General MacArthur to use air and naval strength against North Korean targets below the 38th parallel. The President also redirected the bulk of the Seventh Fleet to Taiwan, where by standing between the Chinese Communists on the mainland and the Nationalists on the island it could discourage either one from attacking the other and thus prevent a widening of hostilities.

When it became clear on June 27 that North Korea would ignore the U.N. demands, the U.N. Security Council, again at the urging of the United States, asked U.N. members to furnish military assistance to help South Korea repel the invasion. President Truman immediately broadened the range of U.S. air and naval operations to include North Korea and authorized the use of U.S. Army troops to protect Pusan, Korea's major port at the southeastern tip of the peninsula. MacArthur meanwhile had flown to Korea and, after witnessing failing ROK Army efforts in defenses south of the Han River, recommended to Washington that a U.S. Army regiment be committed in the Seoul area at once and that this force be built up to two divisions. President Truman's answer on June 30 authorized MacArthur to use all forces available to him.

Thus the United Nations for the first time since its founding reacted to aggression with a decision to use armed force. The United States would accept the largest share of the obligation in Korea but, still deeply tired of war, would do so reluctantly. President Truman later described his decision to enter the war as the hardest of his days in office. But he believed that if South Korea was left to its own defense and fell, no other small nation would have the will to resist aggression, and Communist leaders would be encouraged to override nations closer to U.S. shores. The American people, conditioned by World War II to battle on a grand scale and to complete victory, would experience a deepening frustration over the Korean conflict, brought on in the beginning by embarrassing reversals on the battlefield.

South to the Naktong

Ground forces available to MacArthur included the 1st Cavalry Division and the 7th, 24th, and 25th Infantry Divisions, all under the Eighth U.S. Army in Japan, and the 29th Regimental Combat Team on Okinawa. All the postwar depreciations had affected them. Their maneuverability and firepower were sharply reduced by a shortage of organic units and by a general understrength among existing units. Some weapons, medium tanks in particular, could scarcely be found in the Far East, and ammunition reserves amounted to only a 45-day supply. By any measurement, MacArthur's ground forces were unprepared for battle. His air arm, Far East Air Forces (FEAF), moreover, was organized for air defense, not tactical air support. Most FEAF planes were short-range jet interceptors not meant to be flown at low altitudes in support of ground operations. Some F–51's in storage in Japan and more of these World War II planes in the United States would prove instrumental in meeting close air support needs. Naval Forces, Far East, MacArthur's sea arm, controlled only five combat ships and a skeleton amphibious force, although reinforcement was near in the Seventh Fleet.

When MacArthur received word to commit ground units, the main North Korean force already had crossed the Han River. By July 3, a westward enemy attack had captured a major airfield at Kimpo and the Yellow Sea port of Inch'on. Troops attacking south repaired a bridge so that tanks could cross the Han and moved into the town of Suwon, twenty-five miles below Seoul, on the 4th.

The speed of the North Korean drive coupled with the unreadiness of American forces compelled MacArthur to disregard the principle of mass and commit units piecemeal to trade space for time. Where to open a delaying action was clear, for there were few good roads in the profusion of mountains making up the Korean peninsula, and the best of these below Seoul, running on a gentle diagonal through Suwon, Osan, Taejon, and Taegu to the port of Pusan in the southeast, was the obvious main axis of North Korean advance. At MacArthur's order, two rifle companies, an artillery battery, and a few other supporting units of the 24th Division moved into a defensive position astride the main road near Osan, ten miles below Suwon, by dawn on July 5. MacArthur later referred to this 540-man force, called Task Force Smith, as an "arrogant display of strength." Another kind of arrogance to be found at Osan was a belief that the North Koreans might ". . . turn around and go back when they found out who was fighting."

Coming out of Suwon in a heavy rain, a North Korean division supported by thirty-three tanks reached and with barely a pause attacked the Americans around 8:00 a.m. on the 5th. The North Koreans lost 4 tanks, 42 men killed, and 85 wounded. But the American force lacked antitank mines, the fire of its recoilless rifles and 2.36-inch rocket launchers failed to penetrate the T34 armor, and its artillery quickly expended the little antitank ammunition that did prove effective. The rain canceled air support, communications broke down, and the task force was, under any circumstances, too small to prevent North Korean infantry from flowing around both its flanks. By midafternoon, Task Force Smith was pushed into a disorganized retreat with over 150 casualties and the loss of all equipment save small arms. Another casualty was American morale as word of the defeat reached other units of the 24th Division then moving into delaying positions below Osan.

The next three delaying actions, though fought by larger forces, had similar results. In each case, North Korean armor or infantry assaults against the front of the American position were accompanied by an infantry double envelopment. By July 13, the 24th Division was forced back on Taejon, sixty miles below Osan, where it initially took position along the Kum River above the town. Clumps of South Korean troops by then were strung out west and east of the division to help delay the North Koreans.

Fifty-three U.N. members meanwhile signified support of the Security Council's June 27 action and twenty-nine of these made specific offers of assistance. Ground, air, and naval forces eventually sent to assist South Korea would represent twenty U.N. members and one nonmember nation. The United States, Great Britain, Australia, New Zealand, Canada, Turkey, Greece, France, Belgium, Luxembourg, the Netherlands, Thailand, the Philippines, Colombia and Ethiopa would furnish ground combat troops. India, Sweden, Norway, Denmark, and Italy (the non-United Nations country) would furnish medical units. Air forces would arrive from the United States, Australia, Canada, and the Union of South Africa; naval forces would come from the United States, Great Britain, Australia, Canada, and New Zealand.

The wide response to the council's call pointed out the need for a unified command. Acknowledging the United States as the major contributor, the U.N. Security Council on July 7 asked it to form a command into which all forces would be integrated and to appoint a commander. In the evolving command structure, President Truman became executive agent for the U.N. Security Council. The National Security Council, Department of State, and Joint Chiefs of Staff participated in developing the grand concepts of operations in Korea. In the strictly military channel, the Joint Chiefs issued instructions through the Army member to the unified command in the field, designated the United Nations Command (UNC) and established under General MacArthur.

MacArthur superimposed the headquarters of his new command over that of his existing Far East Command. Air and naval units from other countries joined the Far East Air Forces and Naval Forces, Far East, respectively. MacArthur assigned command of ground troops in Korea to the Eighth Army under Lt. Gen. Walton H. Walker, who established headquarters at Taegu on July 13, assuming command of all American ground troops on the peninsula and, at the request of South Korean President Syngman Rhee, of the ROK Army. When ground forces from other nations reached Korea, they too passed to Walker's command.

U.S. Medium Tank M4A3 *on a South Korean village road.*

Between July 14 and 18, MacArthur moved the 25th and 1st Cavalry Divisions to Korea after cannibalizing the 7th Division to strengthen those two units. By then, the battle for Taejon had opened. New 3.5-inch rocket launchers hurriedly airlifted from the United States proved effective against the T34 tanks, but the 24th Division lost Taejon on July 20 after two North Korean divisions established bridgeheads over the Kum River and encircled the town. In running enemy roadblocks during the final withdrawal from town, Maj. Gen. William F. Dean, the division commander, took a wrong turn and was captured some days later in the mountains to the south. When repatriated some three years later, he would learn that for his exploits at Taejon he was one of 131 servicemen awarded the Medal of Honor during the war (Army 78, Marine Corps 42, Navy 7, and Air Force 4).

While pushing the 24th Division below Taejon, the main North Korean force split, one division moving south to the coast, then turning east along the lower coast line. The remainder of the force continued southeast beyond Taejon toward Taegu. Southward advances by the secondary attack forces in the central and eastern sectors matched the main thrust, all clearly aimed to converge on Pusan. North Korean supply lines grew long in the advance, and less and less tenable under heavy UNC air attacks. FEAF meanwhile achieved air superiority, indeed air supremacy, and UNC warships wiped out North Korean naval

TROOPS KEEPING A LOOKOUT *as phosphorous shells fall on enemy-held territory.*

opposition and clamped a tight blockade on the Korean coast. These achievements and the arrival of the 29th Regimental Combat Team from Okinawa on July 26 notwithstanding, American and South Korean troops steadily gave way. American casualties rose above 6,000 and South Korean losses reached 70,000. By the beginning of August, General Walker's forces held only a small portion of southeastern Korea.

Alarmed by the rapid loss of ground, Walker ordered a stand along a 140-mile line arching from the Korea Strait to the Sea of Japan west and north of Pusan. His U.S. divisions occupied the western arc, basing their position on the Naktong River. South Korean forces, reorganized by American military advisers into two corps headquarters and five divisions, defended the northern segment. A long line and few troops kept positions thin in this "Pusan Perimeter." But replacements and additional units now entering or on the way to Korea would help relieve the problem, and fair interior lines of communications radiating from Pusan allowed Walker to move troops and supplies with facility.

Raising brigades to division status and conscripting large numbers of recruits, many from overrun regions of South Korea, the North Koreans over the next month and a half committed thirteen infantry divisions and an armored division against Walker's perimeter. But the additional strength failed to compensate for the loss of some 58,000 trained men and much armor suffered in the advance to the Naktong. Nor in meeting the connected defenses of the perimeter did enemy commanders recognize the value of massing forces for decisive penetration at one point. They dissipated their strength instead in piecemeal attacks at various points along the Eighth Army line.

Close air support played a large role in the defense of the perimeter. But the Eighth Army's defense really hinged on a shuttling of scarce reserves to block a gap, reinforce a position, or counterattack wherever the threat appeared greatest at a given moment. Timing was the key, and General Walker proved a master of it. His brilliant responses prevented serious enemy penetrations and inflicted telling losses that steadily drew off North Korean offensive power. His own strength meanwhile was on the rise. By mid-September, he had over 500 medium tanks. Replacements arrived in a steady flow and additional units came in: the 5th Regimental Combat Team from Hawaii, the 2d Infantry Division and 1st Provisional Marine Brigade from the United States, and a British infantry brigade from Hong Kong. Thus, as the North Koreans lost irreplaceable men and equipment, UNC forces acquired an offensive capability.

North to the Parallel

Against the gloomy prospect of trading space for time, General MacArthur, at the entry of U.S. forces into Korea, had perceived that the deeper the North Koreans drove, the more vulnerable they would become to an amphibious envelopment. He began work on plans for such a blow almost at the start of hostilities, favoring Inch'on, the Yellow Sea port halfway up the west coast, as the landing site. Just twenty-five miles east lay Seoul where Korea's main roads and rail lines converged. A force landing at Inch'on would have to move inland only a short distance to cut North Korean supply routes, and the recapture of the capital city also could have a helpful psychological impact. Combined with a general northward advance by the Eighth Army, a landing at Inch'on could produce decisive results. Enemy troops retiring before the Eighth Army would be cut off by the amphibious force behind them or be forced to make a slow and difficult withdrawal through the mountains farther east.

Though pressed in meeting Eighth Army troop requirements, MacArthur was able to shape a two-division landing force. He formed the headquarters

THE INCH'ON LANDING

of the X Corps from members of his own staff, naming his chief of staff, Maj. Gen. Edward M. Almond, as corps commander. He rebuilt the 7th Division by giving it high priority on replacements from the United States and by assigning it 8,600 South Korean recruits. The latter measure was part of a larger program, called the Korean Augmentation to the United States Army, in which South Korean troops were placed among almost all American units. At the same time, he acquired from the United States the greater part of the 1st Marine Division, which he planned to fill out with the Marine brigade currently in the Pusan Perimeter. The X Corps, with these two divisions, was to make its landing as a separate force, not as part of the Eighth Army.

MacArthur's superiors and the Navy judged the Inch'on plan dangerous. Naval officers considered the extreme Yellow Sea tides, which range as much as thirty feet, and narrow channel approaches to Inch'on as big risks to shipping. Marine officers saw danger in landing in the middle of a built-up area and in having to scale high sea walls to get ashore. The Joint Chiefs of Staff anticipated serious consequences if Inch'on were strongly defended since MacArthur would be committing his last major reserves at a time when no more General Reserve units in the United States were available for shipment to the

Far East. Four National Guard divisions had been federalized on September 1, but none of these was yet ready for combat duty; and, while the draft and call-ups of members of the Organized Reserve Corps were substantially increasing the size of the Army, they offered MacArthur no prospect of immediate reinforcement. But MacArthur was willing to accept the risks.

In light of the uncertainties MacArthur's decision was a remarkable gamble, but if results are what count his action was one of exemplary boldness. The X Corps swept into Inch'on on September 15 against light resistance and, though opposition stiffened, steadily pushed inland over the next two weeks. One arm struck south and seized Suwon while the remainder of the corps cleared Kimpo Airfield, crossed the Han, and fought through Seoul. MacArthur, with dramatic ceremony, returned the capital city to President Rhee on September 29.

General Walker meanwhile attacked out of the Pusan Perimeter on September 16. His forces gained slowly at first; but on September 23, after the portent of Almond's envelopment and Walker's frontal attack became clear, the North Korean forces broke. The Eighth Army, by then organized as four corps, two U.S. and two ROK, rolled forward in pursuit, linking with the X Corps on September 26. About 30,000 North Korean troops escaped above the 38th parallel through the eastern mountains. Several thousand more bypassed in the pursuit hid in the mountains of South Korea to fight as guerrillas. But by the end of September the North Korea People's Army ceased to exist as an organized force anywhere in the southern republic.

North to the Yalu

President Truman, to this point, frequently had described the American-led effort in Korea as a "police action," a euphemism for war that produced both criticism and amusement. But the President's term was an honest reach for perspective. Determined to halt the aggression, he was equally determined to limit hostilities to the peninsula and to avoid taking steps that would prompt Soviet or Chinese participation. By western estimates, Europe with its highly developed industrial resources, not Asia, held the high place on the Communist schedule of expansion; hence, the North Atlantic Treaty Organization (NATO) alliance needed the deterrent strength that otherwise would be drawn off by a heavier involvement in the Far East.

On this and other bases, a case could be made for halting MacArthur's forces at the 38th parallel. In re-establishing the old border, the UNC had met the U.N. call for assistance in repelling the attack on South Korea. In an early statement, Secretary of State Acheson had said the United Nations was intervening ". . . solely for the purpose of restoring the Republic of Korea to its status prior to the invasion from the north." A halt, furthermore, would be consistent with the U.S. policy of containment.

There was, on the other hand, substantial military reason to carry the war into North Korea. Failure to destroy the 30,000 North Korean troops who had escaped above the parallel and an estimated 30,000 more in northern training camps, all told the equivalent of six divisions, could leave South Korea in little better position than before the start of hostilities. Complete military victory, by all appearances within easy grasp, also would achieve the longstanding U.S. and U.N. objective of reunifying Korea. Against these incentives had to be balanced warnings of sorts against a UNC entry into North Korea from both Communist China and the USSR in August and September. But these were counted as attempts to discourage the UNC, not as genuine threats to enter the war, and on September 27 President Truman authorized MacArthur to send his forces north, provided that by the scheduled time there had been no major Chinese or Soviet entry into North Korea and no announcement of intended entry. As a further safeguard, MacArthur was to use only Korean forces in extreme northern territory abutting the Yalu River boundary with Manchuria and that in the far northeast along the Tumen River boundary with the USSR. Ten days later, the U.N. General Assembly voted for the restoration of peace and security throughout Korea, thereby giving tacit approval to the UNC's entry into North Korea.

On the east coast, Walker's ROK I Corps crossed the parallel on October 1 and rushed far north to capture Wonsan, North Korea's major seaport, on the 10th. The ROK II Corps at nearly the same time opened an advance through central North Korea; and on October 9, after the United Nations sanctioned crossing the parallel, Walker's U.S. I Corps moved north in the west. Against slight resistance, the U.S. I Corps cleared P'yongyang, the North Korean capital city, on October 19 and in five days advanced to the Ch'ongch'on River within fifty miles of the Manchurian border. The ROK II Corps veered northwest to come alongside. To the east, past the unoccupied spine of the axial Taebaek Mountains, the ROK I Corps by October 24 moved above Wonsan, entering Iwon on the coast and approaching the huge Changjin Reservoir in the Taebaeks.

The outlook for the UNC in the last week of October was distinctly optimistic, despite further warnings emanating from Communist China. Convinced by all reports, including one from MacArthur during a personal conference at Wake Island on October 15, that the latest Chinese warnings were more saber-rattling bluffs, President Truman revised his instructions to MacArthur only to the extent that if Chinese forces should appear in Korea MacArthur should continue his advance if he believed his forces had a reasonable chance of success.

In hopes of ending operations before the onset of winter, MacArthur on October 24 ordered his ground commanders to advance to the northern border as rapidly as possible and with all forces available. In the west, the Eighth Army sent several columns toward the Yalu, each free to advance as fast and as far as possible without regard for the progress of the others. The separate X Corps earlier had prepared a second amphibious assault at Wonsan but needed only to walk ashore since the ROK I Corps had captured the landing area. General Almond, adding the ROK I Corps to his command upon landing, proceeded to clear northeastern Korea, sending columns up the coast and through the mountains toward the Yalu and the Changjin Reservoir. In the United States, a leading newspaper expressed the prevailing optimism with the editorial comment that "Except for unexpected developments . . . we can now be easy in our minds as to the military outcome."

UNC forces moved steadily along both coasts, and one interior ROK regiment in the Eighth Army zone sent reconnaissance troops to the Yalu at the town of Ch'osan on October 26. But almost everywhere else the UNC columns encountered stout resistance and, on October 25, discovered they were being opposed by Chinese. "Unexpected developments" had occurred.

In the X Corps zone, Chinese stopped a ROK column on the mountain road leading to the Changjin Reservoir. American marines relieved the South Koreans and by November 6 pushed through the resistance within a few miles of the reservoir, whereupon the Chinese broke contact. In the Eighth Army zone, the first Chinese soldier was discovered among captives taken on October 25 by South Koreans near Unsan northwest of the Ch'ongch'on River. In the next eight days, Chinese forces dispersed the ROK regiment whose troops had reached the Yalu, severely punished a regiment of the 1st Cavalry Division when it came forward near Unsan, and forced the ROK II Corps into retreat on the Eighth Army right. As General Walker fell back to regroup along the Ch'ongch'on, Chinese forces continued to attack until November 6, then, as in the X Corps sector, abruptly broke contact.

At first it appeared that individual Chinese soldiers, possibly volunteers, had reinforced the North Koreans. By November 6, three divisions (10,000 men each) were believed to be in the Eighth Army sector and two divisions in the X Corps area. The estimate rose higher by November 24, but not to a point denying UNC forces a numerical superiority nor to a figure indicating full-scale Chinese intervention.

Some apprehension over a massive Chinese intervention grew out of knowledge that a huge Chinese force was assembled in Manchuria. The interrogation of captives, however, did not convince the UNC that there had been a large Chinese commitment; neither did aerial observation of the Yalu and the ground below the river; and the voluntary withdrawal from contact on 6 November seemed no logical part of a full Chinese effort. General MacArthur felt that the auspicious time for intervention in force had long passed; the Chinese would hardly enter when North Korean forces were ineffective rather than earlier when only a little help might have enabled the North Koreans to conquer all of South Korea. He appeared convinced, furthermore, that the United States would respond with all power available to a massive intervention and that this certainty would deter Chinese leaders who could not help but be aware of it. In an early November report to Washington, he acknowledged the possibility of full intervention, but pointed out that ". . . there are many fundamental logical reasons against it and sufficient evidence has not yet come to hand to warrant its immediate acceptance." His reports by the last week of the month indicated no change of mind.

Intelligence evaluations from other sources were similar. As of November 24, the general view in Washington was that ". . . the Chinese objective was to obtain U.N. withdrawal by intimidation and diplomatic means, but in case of failure of these means there would be increasing intervention. Available evidence was not considered conclusive as to whether the Chinese Communists were committed to a full-scale offensive effort." In the theater, the general belief was that future Chinese operations would be defensive only, that the Chinese units in Korea were not strong enough to block a UNC advance, and that UNC airpower could prevent any substantial Chinese reinforcement from crossing the Yalu. UNC forces hence resumed their offensive. There was, in any event MacArthur said, no other way to obtain ". . . an accurate measure of enemy strength. . . ."

In northeastern Korea, the X Corps, now strengthened by the arrival of the 3d Infantry Division from the United States, resumed its advance on November 11. In the west, General Walker waited until the 24th to move the Eighth Army forward from the Ch'ongch'on while he strengthened his attack force and improved his logistical support. Both commands made gains. Part of the U.S. 7th Division, in the X Corps zone, actually reached the Yalu at the town of Hyesanjin. But during the night of November 25 strong Chinese attacks hit the Eighth Army's center and right; on the 27th the attacks engulfed the leftmost forces of the X Corps at the Changjin Reservoir; and by the 28th UNC positions began to crumble.

U.S. Troops Entering Hyesanjin

MacArthur now had a measure of Chinese strength. Around 200,000 Chinese of the XIII Army Group stood opposite the Eighth Army. With unexcelled march and bivouac discipline, this group, with eighteen divisions plus artillery and cavalry units, had entered Korea undetected during the last half of October. The IX Army Group with twelve divisions next entered Korea, moving into the area north of the Changjin Reservoir opposite the X Corps. Hence, by November 24 more than 300,000 Chinese combat troops were in Korea.

"We face an entirely new war," MacArthur notified Washington on November 28. On the following day he instructed General Walker to make whatever withdrawals were necessary to escape being enveloped by Chinese pushing hard and deep through the Eighth Army's eastern sector, and ordered the X Corps to pull into a beachhead around the east coast port of Hungnam, north of Wonsan.

The New War

In the Eighth Army's withdrawal from the Ch'ongch'on, a strong road-block set below the town of Kunu-ri by Chinese attempting to envelop Walker's forces from the east caught and severely punished the U.S. 2d Division, last away from the river. Thereafter, at each reported approach of enemy forces, General Walker ordered another withdrawal before any solid contact could be made. He abandoned P'yongyang on December 5, leaving 8,000 to 10,000 tons of supplies and equipment broken up or burning inside the city. By December 15, he was completely out of contact with the Chinese and was back at the 38th parallel where he began to develop a coast-to-coast defense line.

In the X Corps' withdrawal to Hungnam, the center and rightmost units experienced little difficulty. But the 1st Marine Division and two battalions of the 7th Division retiring from the Changjin Reservoir encountered Chinese positions overlooking the mountain road leading to the sea. After General Almond sent Army troops inland to help open the road, the Marine-Army force completed its move to the coast on December 11. General MacArthur briefly visualized the X Corps beachhead at Hungnam as a "geographic threat" that could deter Chinese to the west from deepening their advance. Later, with prompting from the Joint Chiefs, he ordered the X Corps to withdraw by sea and proceed to Pusan, where it would become part of the Eighth Army. Almond started the evacuation on the 11th, contracting his Hungnam perimeter as he loaded troops and matériel aboard ships in the harbor. With little interference from enemy forces, he completed the evacuation and set sail for Pusan on Christmas Eve.

On the day before, General Walker was killed in a motor vehicle accident while traveling north from Seoul toward the front. Lt. Gen. Matthew B. Ridgway hurriedly flew from Washington to assume command of the Eighth Army. After conferring in Tokyo with MacArthur, who instructed General Ridgway to hold a position as far north as possible but in any case to maintain the Eighth Army intact, the new army commander reached Korea on the 26th.

Ridgway himself wanted at least to hold the Eighth Army in its position along the 38th parallel and if possible to attack. But his initial inspection of the front raised serious doubts. The Eighth Army, he learned, was clearly a dispirited command, a result of the hard Chinese attacks and the successive withdrawals of the past month. He also discovered much of the defense line to be thin and weak. The Chinese XIII Army Group meanwhile appeared to be massing in the west for a push on Seoul, and twelve reconstituted North Korean divisions seemed to be concentrating for an attack in the central region. From all evidence available, the New Year holiday seemed a logical date on which to expect the enemy's opening assault.

Holding the current line, Ridgway judged, rested both on the early commitment of reserves and on restoring the Eighth Army's confidence. The latter, he believed, depended mainly on improving leadership throughout the command. But it was not his intention to start "lopping off heads." Before he would relieve any commander, he wanted personally to see the man in action, to know that the relief would not adversely affect the unit involved, and indeed to be sure he had a better commander available. For the time being, he intended to correct deficiencies in leadership by working "on and through" the incumbent corps and division commanders.

To strengthen the line, he committed the 2d Division to the central sector where positions were weakest, even though that unit had not fully recovered from losses in the Kunu-ri roadblock, and pressed General Almond to quicken the preparation of the X Corps whose forces needed refurbishing before moving to the front. Realizing that time probably was against him, he also ordered his western units to organize a bridgehead above Seoul, one deep enough to protect the Han River bridges, from which to cover a withdrawal below the city should an enemy offensive compel a general retirement.

Enemy forces opened attacks on New Year's Eve, directing their major effort toward Seoul. When the offensive gained momentum, Ridgway ordered his western forces back to the Seoul bridgehead and pulled the rest of the Eighth Army to positions roughly on line to the east. After strong Chinese units assaulted the bridgehead, he withdrew to a line forty miles below Seoul. In the west, the last troops pulled out of Seoul on January 4, 1951, demolishing the Han bridges on the way out, as Chinese entered the city from the north.

Only light Chinese forces pushed south of the city and enemy attacks in the west diminished. In central and eastern Korea, North Korean forces pushed an attack until mid-January. When pressure finally ended all along the front, reconnaissance patrols ordered north by Ridgway to maintain contact encountered only light screening forces, and intelligence sources reported that most enemy units had withdrawn to refit. It became clear to Ridgway that a primitive logistical system permitted enemy forces to undertake offensive operations for no more than a week or two before they had to pause for replacements and new supplies, a pattern he exploited when he assigned his troops their next objective. Land gains, he pointed out, would have only incidental importance. Primarily, Eighth Army forces were to inflict maximum casualties on the enemy with minimum casualties to themselves. "To do this," Ridgway instructed, "we must wage a war of maneuver—slashing at the enemy when he withdraws and fighting delaying actions when he attacks."

Whereas Ridgway was now certain his forces could achieve that objective, General MacArthur was far less optimistic. Earlier, in acknowledging the Chinese intervention, he had notified Washington that the Chinese could drive the UNC out of Korea unless he received major reinforcement. At the time, however, there was still only a slim reserve of combat units in the United States. Four more National Guard divisions were being brought into federal service to build up the General Reserve, but not with commitment in Korea in mind. The main concern in Washington was the possibility that the Chinese entry into Korea was only one part of a USSR move toward global war, a concern great enough to lead President Truman to declare a state of national emergency on December 16. Washington officials, in any event, considered Korea no place to become involved in a major war. For all of these reasons, the Joint Chiefs of Staff notified MacArthur that a major build-up of UNC forces was out of the question. MacArthur was to stay in Korea if he could, but should the Chinese drive UNC forces back on Pusan, the Joint Chiefs would order a withdrawal to Japan.

Contrary to the reasoning in Washington, MacArthur meanwhile proposed four retaliatory measures against the Chinese: blockade the China coast, destroy China's war industries through naval and air attacks, reinforce the troops in Korea with Chinese Nationalist forces, and allow diversionary operations by Nationalist troops against the China mainland. These proposals for escalation received serious study in Washington but were eventually discarded in favor of sustaining the policy of confining the fighting to Korea.

Interchanges between Washington and Tokyo next centered on the timing of a withdrawal from Korea. MacArthur believed Washington should establish all the criteria of an evacuation, whereas Washington wanted MacArthur first to provide the military guidelines on timing. The whole issue was finally settled after General J. Lawton Collins, Army Chief of Staff, visited Korea, saw that the Eighth Army was improving under Ridgway's leadership, and became as confident as Ridgway that the Chinese would be unable to drive the Eighth Army off the peninsula. "As of now," General Collins announced on January 15, "we are going to stay and fight."

Ten days later, Ridgway opened a cautious offensive, beginning with attacks in the west and gradually widening them to the east. The Eighth Army advanced slowly and methodically, ridge by ridge, phase line by phase line, wiping out each pocket of resistance before moving farther north. Enemy forces fought back vigorously and in February struck back in the central region. During that counterattack, the 23d Regiment of the 2d Division successfully defended the town of Chipyong-ni against a much larger Chinese force, a victory that to Ridgway symbolized the Eighth Army's complete recovery of its fighting spirit. After defeating the enemy's February effort, the Eighth Army again advanced steadily, recaptured Seoul by mid-March, and by the first day of spring stood just below the 38th parallel.

Intelligence agencies meanwhile uncovered evidence of rear area offensive preparations by the enemy. In an attempt to spoil those preparations, Ridgway opened an attack on April 5 toward an objective line, designated Kansas, roughly ten miles above the 38th parallel. After the Eighth Army reached Line Kansas, he sent a force toward an enemy supply area just above Kansas in the west-central zone known as the Iron Triangle. Evidence of an imminent enemy offensive continued to mount as these troops advanced. As a precaution, Ridgway on April 12 published a plan for orderly delaying actions to be fought when and if the enemy attacked, an act, events proved, that was one of his last as commander of the Eighth Army.

Plans being written in Washington in March, had they been carried out, well might have kept the Eighth Army from moving above the 38th parallel toward Line Kansas. For as a gradual development since the Chinese intervention, the United States and other members of the UNC coalition by that time were willing, as they had not been the past autumn, to accept the clearance of enemy troops from South Korea as a suitable final result of their effort. On March 20, the Joint Chiefs notified MacArthur that a Presidential announcement was being drafted which would indicate a willingness to negotiate with the Chinese and North Koreans to make "satisfactory arrangements for concluding the fighting," and which would be issued "before any advance with major forces north of 38th Parallel." Before the President's announcement could be made, however, MacArthur issued his own offer to enemy commanders to discuss an end to the fighting, but it was an offer that placed the UNC in the role of victor and which indeed sounded like an ultimatum. "The enemy . . . must by now be painfully aware," MacArthur said in part, "that a decision of the United Nations to depart from its tolerant effort to contain the war to the area of Korea, through an expansion of our military operations to its coastal areas and interior bases, would doom Red China to the risk of imminent military collapse." President Truman considered the statement at cross-purposes with the one he was to have issued and so canceled his own. Hoping the enemy might sue for an armistice if kept under pressure, he permitted the question of crossing the 38th parallel to be settled on the basis of tactical considerations. Thus it became Ridgway's decision; and the parallel would not again assume political significance.

President Truman had in mind, after the March episode, to relieve MacArthur but had yet to make a final decision when the next incident occurred. On April 5, Joseph W. Martin, Republican leader in the House of Representatives, rose and read MacArthur's response to a request for comment on an address Martin had made suggesting the use of Nationalist Chinese forces to open a second front. In that response, MacArthur said he believed in "meeting force with maximum counterforce," and that the use of Nationalist Chinese forces fitted that belief. Convinced, also, that ". . . if we lose this war to Communism in Asia the fall of Europe is inevitable, win it and Europe most probably would avoid war . . . ," he added that there could be " . . . no substitute for victory . . ." in Korea.

President Truman could not accept MacArthur's open disagreement with and challenge of national policy. There were also grounds for a charge of insubordination, since MacArthur had not cleared his March 24 statement or his response to Representative Martin with Washington, contrary to a Presidential directive issued in December requiring prior clearance of all releases touching on national policy. Concluding that MacArthur was ". . . unable to give his wholehearted support to the policies of the United States government and of the United Nations in matters pertaining to his official duties," President Truman recalled MacArthur on April 11 and named General Ridgway as successor. MacArthur returned to the United States to receive the plaudits of a nation shocked by the relief of one of its greatest military heroes. Before the Congress and the public he defended his own views against those of the Truman Administration. The controversy stirred up was to endure for many months, but in the end the nation accepted the fact that, whatever the merit of MacArthur's arguments, the President as Commander in Chief had a right to relieve him.

Before transferring from Korea to Tokyo, General Ridgway on April 14 turned over the Eighth Army to Lt. Gen. James A. Van Fleet. Eight days later twenty-one Chinese and nine North Korean divisions launched strong attacks in western Korea and lighter attacks in the east, with the major effort aimed at Seoul. General Van Fleet withdrew through successive delaying positions to previously established defenses a few miles north of Seoul where he finally contained the enemy advance. When enemy forces withdrew to refurbish, Van Fleet laid plans for a return to Line Kansas but then postponed the countermove when his intelligence sources indicated he had stopped only the first effort of the enemy offensive.

Enemy forces renewed their attack after darkness on May 15. Whereas Van Fleet had expected the major assault again to be directed against Seoul, enemy forces this time drove hardest in the east central region. Adjusting units to place more troops in the path of the enemy advance and laying down tremendous amounts of artillery fire, Van Fleet halted the attack by May 20 after the enemy had penetrated thirty miles. Determined to prevent the enemy from assembling strength for another attack, he immediately ordered the Eighth Army forward. The Chinese and North Koreans, disorganized after their own attacks, resisted only where their supply installations were threatened. Elsewhere, the Eighth Army advanced with almost surprising ease and by May 31 was just short of Line Kansas. The next day Van Fleet sent part of his force toward Line Wyoming whose seizure would give him control of the lower portion of the Iron Triangle. The Eighth Army occupied both Line Kansas and the Wyoming bulge by mid-June.

Since the Kansas-Wyoming line traced ground suitable for a strong defense, it was the decision in Washington to hold that line and wait for a bid for armistice negotiations from the Chinese and North Koreans, to whom it should be clear by this time that their committed forces lacked the ability to conquer South Korea. In line with this decision, Van Fleet began to fortify his positions. Enemy forces meanwhile used the respite from attack to recoup heavy losses and to develop defenses opposite the Eighth Army. The fighting lapsed into patrolling and small local clashes.

The Static War

On June 23, 1951, Jacob Malik, the USSR delegate to the United Nations, announced in New York during a broadcast of the U.N. radio program, "The Price of Peace," that the USSR believed the war in Korea could be settled. "Discussions," he said, "should be started between the belligerents for a cease-fire and an armistice. . . ." When Communist China endorsed Malik's proposal over Peiping radio, President Truman authorized General Ridgway to arrange armistice talks with his enemy counterpart. Through an exchange of radio messages both sides agreed to open negotiations on July 10 at the town of Kaesong, in territory which was then no-man's-land in the west but which would become a neutral area.

At the first armistice conference the two delegations agreed that hostilities would continue until an armistice agreement was signed. Except for brief, violent episodes, however, action along the front would never regain the momentum of the first year. By July 26, the two armistice delegations fixed the points to be settled in order to achieve an armistice. But then the enemy delegates began to delay negotiations, to gain time, it seemed, in which to strengthen their military forces, and thus also to strengthen their bargaining position. In any case, the enemy delegation continued to delay and finally broke off negotiations on August 22.

General Van Fleet, at that juncture, opened limited-objective attacks. In east-central Korea, he sent forces toward terrain objectives five to seven miles above Line Kansas—among them places named the Punchbowl, Bloody Ridge, and

Heartbreak Ridge—to drive enemy forces from positions that favored an attack on Line Kansas. These objectives were won by the last week of October. In the west, Van Fleet's forces struck northwest on a forty-mile front to secure a new line three to four miles beyond the Wyoming line in order to protect important supply roads that lay only a short distance behind the existing western front. The new line was reached by October 12.

These successes may have had an influence on the enemy, who agreed to return to the armistice conference table. Negotiations resumed on October 25, this time at Panmunjom, a tiny settlement seven miles southeast of Kaesong. Hope for an early armistice grew on November 27 when the two delegations agreed that a line of demarcation during an armistice would be the existing line of contact provided an armistice agreement was reached within thirty days. Hence, while both sides awaited the outcome of negotiations, fighting during the remainder of 1951 tapered off to patrol clashes, raids, and small battles for possession of outposts in no-man's-land. The first tactical use of helicopters by U.S. forces occurred about this time when almost a thousand marines were lifted to a front-line position and a like number returned to the rear.

Discord over several issues, including the exchange of prisoners of war, prevented an armistice agreement within the stipulated thirty days. The prisoner of war quarrel heightened in January 1952 after UNC delegates proposed to give captives a choice in repatriation proceedings, maintaining that those prisoners who did not wish to return to their homelands could be simply "set at liberty" according to the Geneva Conventions of 1949. The enemy representatives protested vigorously. While argument continued, both sides tacitly extended the November 27 provisions for a line of demarcation. This had the effect of holding battle action to the pattern of the thirty-day waiting period.

By May 1952 the two delegations were completely deadlocked on the repatriation issue. On the 7th of that month inmates of UNC Prison Camp No. 1 on Koje-do, an island off the southern coast, on orders smuggled to them from North Korea managed to entice the U.S. camp commander to a compound gate, drag him inside, and keep him captive. The strategy, which became clear in subsequent prisoner demands, was to trade the U.S. officer's life and release for UNC admissions of inhumane treatment of captives, including alleged cruelties during previous screenings of prisoners in which a large number of prisoners refused repatriation. The obvious objective was to discredit the voluntary repatriation stand taken by the UNC delegation at Panmunjom.

Although a new camp commander obtained his predecessor's release, in the process he signed a damaging statement including an admission that ". . . there have been instances of bloodshed where many prisoners of war have been killed and wounded by U.N. Forces." There was no change in the UNC stand on repatriation but the statement was widely exploited by the Communists at Panmunjom and elsewhere for its propaganda value.

Amid the Koje-do trouble, General Ridgway received transfer orders placing him in command of NATO forces in Europe. General Mark W. Clark became the new commander in the Far East, with one less responsibility than Mac-Arthur and Ridgway had carried. On April 28 a peace treaty with Japan had gone into effect, restoring Japan's sovereignty and thus ending the occupation. Faced immediately with the Koje-do affair, General Clark had the impression of walking ". . . into something that felt remarkably like a swinging door. . . ." He immediately repudiated the prison camp commander's statement. Moving swiftly, he placed Brig. Gen. Haydon L. Boatner in charge of the camp with instructions to move the prisoners into smaller, more manageable compounds and to institute other measures that would eliminate the likelihood of another uprising. General Boatner completed the task on June 10.

While argument over repatriation went on at Panmunjom, action at the front continued as a series of artillery duels, patrols, ambushes, raids, and bitter contests for outpost positions. But for all the furious and costly small-scale battles that took place, the lines remained substantially unchanged at the end of 1952. The armistice conference meanwhile went into an indefinite recess in October with the repatriation issue still unresolved.

In November, the American people elected a Republican President, Dwight D. Eisenhower. An issue in the campaign had been the war in Korea, over which there was a growing popular discontent, in particular with the lack of progress toward an armistice. In a campaign pledge to "go to Korea," Eisenhower implied that if elected he would attempt to end the war quickly. Consequently, when the President-elect in early December fulfilled his promise to visit Korea, there was indeed some expectation of a dramatic change in the conduct of the war. General Clark went so far as to prepare detailed estimates of measures necessary to obtain a military victory. But it quickly became clear that Eisenhower, like President Truman, preferred to seek an honorable armistice. As he would write later, however, the President-elect did decide to let Communist authorities know that if satisfactory progress toward an armistice was not forthcoming, ". . . we intended to move decisively without inhibition in our use of weapons, and would no longer be responsible for confining hostilities to the Korean peninsula." Immediately after taking office, President Eisenhower made sure this word reached Moscow, Peiping, and P'yongyang.

In the hope of prompting a resumption of armistice negotiations, General Clark in February 1953 proposed to his enemy counterpart that the two sides exchange sick and wounded prisoners. But there was no response and no break in the deadlock at Panmunjom by spring. At the front, where in February Lt. Gen. Maxwell D. Taylor had replaced General Van Fleet as the Eighth Army commander, the battle action continued in the mold of the previous year. The break finally came near the end of March, about three weeks after the death of Josef Stalin, when enemy armistice delegates not only replied favorably to General Clark's proposal that sick and wounded captives be exchanged but also suggested that this exchange perhaps could ". . . lead to the smooth settlement of the entire question of prisoners of war." With that, the armistice conference resumed in April. An exchange of sick and wounded prisoners was carried out that same month; and before the middle of June, the prisoner repatriation problem was settled through agreement that each side would have an opportunity to persuade those captives refusing return to their homelands to change their minds.

The pace of battle quickened in May when Chinese forces launched regimental attacks against outposts guarding approaches to the Eighth Army's main line in the west. A large battle flared on June 10 when three Chinese divisions penetrated two miles through a South Korean position in central Korea before being contained. That engagement could have been the last of the war since the terms of an armistice by then were all but complete. But on June 18 ROK President Rhee, who from the beginning had objected to any armistice that left Korea divided, ordered the release of North Korean prisoners who had refused repatriation. Within a few days most of these North Korean captives "broke out" of prison camp and disappeared among a co-operative South Korean populace. Since the captives had been guarded by South Korean troops, UNC officials disclaimed responsibility for the break, but the enemy armistice delegates denounced the action as a serious breach of faith. It took more than a month to repair the damage done by Rhee's order.

Enemy forces used this delay to wrest more ground from UNC control, attacking on July 13 and driving a wedge eight miles deep in the Eighth Army's central sector. General Taylor deployed units to contain the shoulders and point of the wedge, then counterattacked. But he halted his attack force on July 20 short of the original line since by that date the armistice delegations had come to a new accord and needed only to work out a few small details. Taylor's order to halt ended the last major battle of the war.

After a week of dealing with administrative matters, each chief delegate signed the military armistice agreement at Panmunjom at 10:00 a.m. on July 27. General Clark and the enemy commanders later affixed their signatures at their respective headquarters. As stipulated in the agreement, all fighting stopped twelve hours after the first signing, at 10:00 p.m., July 27, 1953. When the final casualty report for the thirty-seven months of fighting was prepared, total UNC casualties reached over 550,000, including almost 95,000 dead. U.S. losses numbered 142,091, of whom 33,629 were killed, 103,284 wounded, and 5,178 missing or captured. U.S. Army casualties alone totaled 27,704 dead, 77,596 wounded, and 4,658 missing or captured. The bulk of these casualties occurred during the first year of the fighting. The estimate of enemy casualties, including prisoners, exceeded 1,500,000, of which 900,000, almost two-thirds, were Chinese.

The Aftermath

By the terms of the armistice, the line of demarcation between North and South Korea closely approximated the front line as it existed at the final hour. (*Map 46*) Slanting as the line did from a point on the west coast fifteen miles below the 38th parallel northeastward to an east coast anchor forty miles above the parallel, the demarcation represented a relatively small adjustment of the

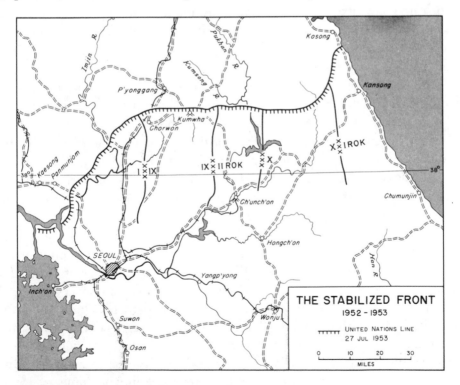

MAP 46

prewar division. Within three days of the signing of the armistice, each opposing force withdrew two kilometers from this line to establish a demilitarized zone that was not to be trespassed.

The armistice provisions forbade either force to bring additional troops or new weapons into Korea, although replacement one for one and in kind was permissible. To oversee the enforcement of all armistice terms and to negotiate settlements of any violations of them, a Military Armistice Commission composed of an equal number of officers from each side was established. This body was assisted by a Neutral Nations Supervisory Commission whose members came from Sweden, Switzerland, Czechoslovakia, and Poland. Representatives of those same countries, with India furnishing an umpire and custodial forces, formed a Neutral Nations Repatriation Commission to handle the disposition of prisoners refusing repatriation. Finally, a provision of the armistice recommended that the belligerent governments convene a political conference to negotiate a final settlement of the whole Korean question.

By September 6, all prisoners wishing to be repatriated had been exchanged. From the UNC returnees came full details of brutally harsh treatment in enemy prison camps and of an extensive Communist indoctrination program, of "brainwashing" techniques, designed to produce prisoner collaboration. Several hundred U.S. returnees were investigated on charges of collaborating with the enemy, but few were convicted.

The transfer of nonrepatriates to the Neutral Nations Repatriation Commission was undertaken next. In the drawn out and troublesome procedure that followed, few of the prisoners changed their minds as officials from both sides attempted to convince former members of their respective commands that they should return home. Of twenty-three Americans who at first refused repatriation, two decided to return. On February 1, 1954, the Neutral Nations Repatriation Commission dissolved itself after releasing the last of the nonrepatriates as civilians free to decide their own destinations.

The main scene then shifted to Geneva, Switzerland, where the political conference recommended in the armistice agreement convened on April 26. There was a complete impasse from the beginning: the representatives of UNC member nations wanted to reunify Korea through elections supervised by the United Nations; the Communist delegation refused to recognize the U.N.'s authority to deal with the matter. The conference on Korea closed June 15, 1954, with the country still divided and with opposing forces, although their guns remained silent, still facing each other across the demilitarized zone. The prognosis was that this situation would continue for some time to come.

The Geneva impasse leaving Korea divided essentially along the prewar line could scarcely be viewed as merely re-establishing the land's *status quo ante bellum*. For by the end of the war, the ROK Army had grown to a well-organized force of sixteen divisions and was scheduled to raise four more divisions, a force North Korea's resources would be strained to match. Within days of the armistice, moreover, South Korea had a mutual security pact with the United States and a first installment, $200 million, of promised American economic aid.

The war's impact reached far beyond Korea. Despite criticism of the armistice by those who agreed with General MacArthur that there was "no substitute for victory," the UNC had upheld the U.N. principle of suppressing armed aggression. True, the U.N. Security Council had been able to enlist forces under the U.N. banner in June 1950 only in the absence of the USSR veto. Nevertheless, the UNC success strengthened the possibility of keeping or restoring peace through the U.N. machinery.

More far reaching was the war's impact on the two Great Power blocs. The primary result for the western bloc was a decided strengthening of the NATO alliance. Virtually without military power in June 1950, NATO could call on fifty divisions and strong air and naval contingents by 1953, a build-up directly attributable to the increased threat of general war seen in the outbreak of hostilities in Korea. With further reinforcement in the NATO forecast at the end of the Korean War, USSR armed aggression in western Europe became unlikely. For the east, the major result was the emergence of Communist China as a Great Power. A steady improvement in the Chinese army and air force during the war gave China a more powerful military posture at war's end than when it had intervened; and its performance in Korea, despite vast losses, won China respect as a nation to be reckoned with not only in Asian but in world affairs.

Outside these direct impacts of the war, the relative positions of west and east also had been affected during the war years by the development of thermonuclear devices. The United States exploded its first such device in 1952, the USSR in August 1953. The exact consequences of all these changes were incalculable. But it was certain that the cold war would continue and that both power blocs would face new challenges and new responses.

CHAPTER 26

The Army and the New Look

Conditioned to the military decisiveness of World Wars I and II, Americans of the twentieth century found the frustration of fighting three years for a stalemate a new experience. Yet most were relieved to see the end of Korean hostilities despite the realization that the signing of the armistice merely marked the transition back to the cold war. The shooting and killing stopped, but the tension continued.

The war had clearly demonstrated that the United States was the only nation in a position to offer determined resistance to Communist expansion. The old era of reliance upon allies to bear the first brunt of battle while the country prepared for war had passed. If the United States intended to continue its policy of Communist containment, it was evident that it would have to depend increasingly upon American forces in being to meet the challenges. The cost in manpower and resources of maintaining large, well-prepared military forces in peacetime promised to be high, since there was little prospect in 1953 of attaining U.S. foreign policy objectives through diplomacy alone.

Acceptance of military power as an indispensable and open partner in the conduct of foreign relations represented a basic change in the American approach to international affairs. Previously the nation had mobilized its latent military strength only under the threat of conflict. For the most part, its wars had been fought as crusades, with overtones of strong emotional and moral support. The post-Korean situation demanded a different response—the sustained and disciplined use of military power against Communist opponents who had always regarded the use of force as a logical and necessary extension of politics. Yet, with remarkably little debate, the American people accepted the new military role and revealed a willingness to shoulder the heavy responsibilities that attended leadership of the free world.

Massive Retaliation and the New Look

With the end of hostilities, the Eisenhower administration could devote more attention to the task of determining the nation's future strategy and the military forces necessary to carry it out. The President and his advisers, torn between pressures generated by worldwide commitments and the desire to cut back defense spending, came up with a policy that placed major emphasis on nuclear air power. The Korean War was to be regarded as an aberration and American land forces would not be committed again to fight conventional battles with the Communist hordes in Asia unless it became necessary in the national interest.

As Secretary of State John Foster Dulles put it:

> The basic decision was to depend primarily upon a great capacity to retaliate, instantly, by means and at places of our choosing. Now the Department of Defense and the Joint Chiefs of Staff can shape our military establishment to fit what is our policy, instead of having to try to be ready to meet the enemy's many choices. That permits of a selection of military means instead of a multiplication of means. As a result, it is now possible to get, and share, more basic security at less cost.

In an effort to regain the strategic initiative through the use of strong and selective responses, Mr. Dulles had sought to raise the threshold of war to a higher level. Since the responses relied heavily upon American nuclear superiority, the doctrine soon came to be known as massive retaliation.

Unlike previous postwar periods, no drastic dismantling of the defense industrial mobilization base took place. The ever-present Russian threat made rearmament a continuous process dependent upon a mobilization base that could be rapidly expanded if the deterrent failed. With the new stress on nuclear capabilities, the armed forces took on a "new look" in the mid-fifties. The Air Force increased its strategic bombing forces, the Navy concentrated its efforts on development of the Polaris nuclear missile, which could be launched from submarines or other ships, and the Army sought to perfect tactical nuclear weapons to support the soldier on the battlefield.

In the absence of experience in waging nuclear war, strategic planning had to evolve in a historical vacuum. National security policy guidance in the post-Korean period, therefore, was issued in general terms, and disputes quickly arose over the types and numbers of the forces required to carry out the policy. Frequently the Secretary of Defense found it difficult to reconcile the differences of opinion among the military chiefs. The end result was hardly surprising. A House Appropriations Committee report noted: "Each service, it would seem, is striving to develop and acquire an arsenal of weapons complete in itself to carry out any and all possible missions."

Since the military budget was divided vertically by service rather than on a functional basis, the annual allocation of funds was attended by some bitterness. As the Air Force's share of the budget increased in the mid-fifties to procure expensive bombers and missiles and as the United States' capability to wage less than general nuclear war decreased, opposition to the massive retaliation policy mounted. The Army Chief of Staff, General Ridgway, upon his retirement in June 1955, expressed his doubts cogently. As Soviet nuclear strength grew, General Ridgway maintained, a situation of nuclear parity would come into being, where neither side would have an advantage. Soviet strategy could then be directed toward creating situations that would preclude the use of nuclear weapons on a worldwide basis. If this should happen, the American military forces then in being would not be strong enough to meet the lesser Soviet challenge. General Ridgway put the case bluntly: "The present United States preoccupation with preparations for general war has limited the military means available for cold war to those which are essentially by-products or leftovers from the means available for general war."

Ridgway's plea for balanced forces capable of coping with general or limited war was supported by his successor, General Maxwell D. Taylor, and taken up by a number of prominent scholars. During the remainder of the decade the debates over general versus limited war, nuclear versus conventional war, and various combinations thereof were waged in Congress, in the universities, and in printed media. Not until the latter part of the decade, when the Soviet Union's nuclear parity with the United States had become clear, did some of the leading supporters of the use of nuclear weapons begin to concede that such a war would result in mutual extermination and that a resort to nuclear weapons should become "the *last* and not the only recourse" of the nation.

The NATO Build-up

While the word battles raged, the strategy of nuclear war had profoundly affected the conduct of American foreign policy and the posture of the U.S. armed forces. Even during the latter stages of the Korean War, the major American build-up had taken place in Europe rather than in the Far East. Fears that the Soviet Union might take advantage of American involvement in Korea to launch an offensive on the Continent had spurred the United States to increase its lone Army division to five divisions by the end of the war. Through the Mutual Defense Assistance Program, the United States had also helped strengthen the NATO ground, air, and naval forces. During this period NATO adopted a "forward defense" strategy which contemplated defending Germany as far east of the Rhine as possible.

The conclusion of the Korean War, the death of Stalin, and the launching of another Soviet peace movement shortly thereafter, all combined to alter conditions in Europe. With tensions temporarily lessened, the NATO build-up slowed down to ease the economic drain upon the United States and its allies and the main effort shifted to the development of the infrastructure—the construction of roads, airfields, and depot areas and the improvement of communications. At the same time the United States began to press its allies to integrate the NATO forces and to rearm the West Germans. Despite strong Communist opposition to the revival of West German military forces, the NATO nations in 1954 approved the formation of an army of twelve divisions.

To redress further the imbalance between Communist and NATO ground forces, American nuclear scientists had produced a growing variety of tactical nuclear warheads that could be fitted to artillery shells and missiles. As these weapons became available, NATO planning was based on the assumption that a Soviet attack would be met by tactical nuclear weapons.

Control of all nuclear devices and weapons remained with the United States political leadership, and America's refusal to share this exclusive control by consultation with its allies occasioned some discontent within the alliance, especially on the part of the French and the British. Both of these allies decided to develop their own nuclear weapons and delivery systems to lessen their dependence upon the United States.

Continental Defense

In the meantime, the Soviet Union developed an intercontinental jet bomber and hydrogen bombs that could be carried in planes. It began to arm its ground forces with tactical nuclear weapons and pushed ahead with the production of long-range missiles. By 1955 the fierce Soviet-American competition and the growth of nuclear stockpiles that could obliterate cities and industrial complexes were causing mounting concern. At a summit conference at Geneva during the summer, the American and Soviet representatives made clear that they fully recognized that a full-scale nuclear war could lead only to mutual suicide. Although the arms race went on unabated, there was a slight relaxation of tension and a growing feeling that neither the United States nor the Soviet Union would resort to general nuclear war unless its own survival was threatened.

Early in 1956 the Russian premier, Nikita Khrushchev, gave an even clearer sign that the Soviet Union was shifting its tactics again. Qualifying to some extent Lenin's thesis that war between Communists and capitalists was inevitable, he indicated that the two worlds could coexist on a competitive basis. However, he made clear that the Soviet Union would still take part in or sponsor wars against the United States and other free world nations. Lest the western nations misunderstand the new peaceful coexistence, Khrushchev warned that the Communists still supported "wars of liberation" to free peoples from colonialism and imperialism and that the ceaseless struggle with capitalism would still be carried on by means other than full-scale warfare between the two countries.

Despite the symptoms of a possible thaw in East-West relations, the United States speeded its efforts to protect the American people in the event of another sudden freeze. Construction of a defensive perimeter in the form of a series of radar warning stations was completed in 1957. In co-operation with the Canadian Government, the distant early warning (DEW) radar net was built across northern Canada and Alaska, supplementing other radar lines in central and southern Canada. Radar outposts in the Aleutians, radar towers and picket boats in the Atlantic, and airborne early warning craft provided additional protection.

Operational responsibility for the direction of the overall air defense fell under the Continental Air Defense Command with the Air Force acting as executive agent for the Secretary of Defense. To assist the interceptor squadrons, the Army contributed ground antiaircraft defense support and developed the first operational antiaircraft missile—the Nike Ajax—with greater range and accuracy than conventional shells. Later and more sophisticated members of the Nike family were fitted with nuclear warheads for greater destructive power, and the Army also developed the Hawk missile to defend against low-flying aircraft. Antiaircraft missile sites grew up around vital defense areas across the nation, and complex control centers had to be established to co-ordinate the missile defense system.

The Missile Era

Although the United States had keyed its efforts to the strategic bomber, the development of missiles for offense proceeded apace. Gradually, the range and efficiency of the missiles increased as new designs and improved fuels emerged. The Army was developing its Jupiter and the Air Force its Thor—both intermediate-range, 1,500-mile missiles—during the mid-fifties, and the Air Force was working on the Atlas and Titan 5,000-mile intercontinental ballistic missiles (ICBM's).

Since, under the roles and missions agreement, the Army was responsible for point defense and the Air Force for area defense, the Army development of intermediate-range missiles eventually led to a jurisdictional dispute. In 1956 the Secretary of Defense ruled that the Air Force should take charge of all land-based intermediate- and long-range missiles, but the Army was allowed to finish the development and testing of the Jupiter. Progress on missiles was steady, but the sense of urgency had lessened somewhat by 1957.

Fresh impetus came from the Soviet Union. The Russians sent aloft an operational ICBM and then followed with a spectacular launching of the first Sputnik satellite in October 1957, revealing a rocket thrust far in excess of anything the United States could then produce. The Soviet feat caused the United States to review its missile programs in order to narrow the rocket-booster gap. To sustain morale, several small American satellites using the Jupiter and Vanguard boosters were launched in 1958, but it would take considerable time to construct engines equaling those already developed by the Russians.

The beginning of the ICBM era and the attendant exploration of space by unmanned and manned vehicles had serious military implications. As soon as the developmental problems could be overcome, the United States and the Soviet Union could build up stockpiles on land and in the future could also arm space stations. The threat of giant, nuclear weapons poised and then irretrievably launched at the nervous touch of a button thousands of miles from the target was a frightening prospect. If the two nations were to act like "two scorpions in a bottle," each certain that the other wished to destroy him, the inclination to push the button first might, in a period of crisis, become overwhelming. Later on, during the Kennedy Administration, the United States sense of responsibility was emphasized by the careful avoidance of a first-strike policy.

Since every new weapon evoked an antiweapon, the Army became responsible for the development of an anti-ICBM and pushed the research and testing of the Nike series for this role. A running debate quickly broke out over the capabilities of the Nike or any missile to protect the United States against a saturation ICBM attack. The technical difficulties and the tremendous expense of attempting to devise an absolute defense against nuclear attack were bound, however, to have a deterrent effect on both sides; as long as neither could be sure of warding off major disaster, there would be little inclination to risk a direct confrontation.

Another part of the ICBM controversy centered about a continued need for American military bases and garrisons in various overseas areas. Under defense agreements with friendly nations, the United States had put airfields and missile sites within striking range of the Soviet Union and Communist China during the decade following World War II. The costs of maintaining these overseas bases and the troops to man them had begun to concern officials in the Congress and the Executive Branch. The advent of long-range missiles that could be launched from the continental United States or from submarines offered some new alternatives, but it would take time to test and put them into operation.

Challenges and Responses

The domination of the fifties by the nuclear threat tended to cast a shadow over developments in other areas. Although the United States did not want to become involved in limited war and was wary of the risks inherent in nuclear confrontation, international challenges arose and had to be met—some by the provision of military and economic aid and others by the dispatch of combat forces.

In an effort to strengthen the military capabilities of friendly and neutral nations in Latin America, the Middle East, Asia, and Europe to resist aggression and subversion, the United States continued the military assistance programs (MAP's) initiated under President Truman before the Korean War. American commitments to provide military aid, advisory groups, and military missions around the world burgeoned despite the concomitant drive to curtail military expenditures.

In such places as Korea, two Army divisions continued to man positions south of the demilitarized zone and the United States provided substantial military assistance to build up South Korean armed forces. Although the Communists broke the uneasy truce many times during the fifties, none of the violations generated renewed hostilities.

Prudence underlined the American approach to the crisis in Indochina in 1954. The United States was willing to give military supplies and equipment and economic aid to the French, but in the absence of support from its allies refused to commit American troops or to carry out bombings to support the French in their battle at Dien Bien Phu. The American leadership and people were reluctant to become embroiled again on the Asian continent so soon after the Korean experience.

After the Geneva Conference of 1954 set up the two Vietnams, the United States was a chief sponsor of the Southeast Asia Treaty Organization, which was launched in early 1955 with Australia, France, New Zealand, Pakistan, the Philippines, Thailand, the United Kingdom, and the United States as charter members. The treaty was a collective defense arrangement calling for mutual help and consultation to resist overt Communist aggression or other acts threatening internal security.

Taiwan and Southeast Asia became the chief trouble spots in 1954. Heavy Chinese Communist bombardment of Nationalist garrison positions on the tiny offshore islands of Quemoy and Matsu seemed to presage a move to take over those outposts. Since the loss of the islands could have opened the way for an invasion of Taiwan, the United States through a Congressional Joint Resolution in 1955 empowered the President to act if the Communists sought to seize the outposts.

In the summer of 1958 the bombardments of Quemoy and Matsu again became severe and the Communist Chinese interdicted the Nationalist supply service to the islands. To defeat the artillery blockade, U.S. ships convoyed the supply vessels and Nationalist aircraft were armed with American missiles. As the tension mounted, a U.S. Composite Air Strike Force moved to Taiwan to strengthen the Nationalist defenses in the event of a Communist invasion. But the Communist Chinese evidently were not prepared to risk war at that time and again slackened their artillery fire. By the end of the year the crisis had passed but the two islands remained vulnerable to a renewed attack.

In Southeast Asia Communist pressure abated yet did not cease after the Geneva settlement in 1954. In the small state of Laos the Communist Pathet Lao in the post-Geneva period had established control of several border provinces abutting North Vietnam and China in order to resist attempts of the government to unite the country. In 1956 the government and the Pathet Lao signed a peaceful coexistence agreement, but efforts to integrate the two forces failed.

Since the United States provided total support for the 25,000-man Laotian Army, the differences between the government and the Pathet Lao became a small part of the larger quarrel between East and West. Open warfare broke out in 1959 in Laos, but neither side could gain the upper hand, despite the military aid given by the Soviet Union and North Vietnam and by the United States.

The serious concern of other nations over the escalation of the Soviet and American assistance programs and the possibility of a direct confrontation in Laos led to behind-the-scenes attempts to convene a conference to consider neutralizing the country. The warring factions in Laos also seemed in early 1961 to be more favorably disposed to this kind of solution. But until the new U.S. administration took office, the likelihood of an immediate settlement was rather remote, and in the meantime both American and Soviet aid and advisory efforts continued.

While the tension in the Far East persisted along the Communist periphery and could be traced, for the most part, to basic East-West conflicts, the problems that arose in the Middle East during the fifties stemmed mainly from resurgent nationalism and Arab hostility toward the Jewish state of Israel. To shore up the West's defenses in the area, the United States sponsored but did not sign the Baghdad Pact of 1955, although it did become a member of several of the pact's major committees in 1956 and 1957. The signatories of the pact included the United Kingdom, Turkey, Iran, Iraq, and Pakistan, all pledging co-operation for their mutual security and defense, and the United States continued to provide military assistance to members of the pact.

Although the United States did not become militarily involved in the Suez crisis of 1956, Congress, at the President's request, adopted in January 1957 a Joint Resolution that came to be known as the Eisenhower Doctrine. It pledged American military assistance to nations in the Middle East that were endangered by Communist aggression and empowered the President to use the armed forces for this purpose.

American action in the Middle East came in the following year. In early 1958 factions favoring Egyptian leader Gamal Abdel Nasser became active in Lebanon, Jordan, and Iraq. Rebellion broke out in Lebanon and in mid-July the King of Iraq was assassinated and an Iraqi Republic under pro-Nasser leadership was set up. The President of Lebanon and the King of Jordan quickly requested assistance for their own governments.

Less than twenty-four hours later, naval units from the U.S. Sixth Fleet arrived offshore and a battalion of marines landed near Beirut, the Lebanese capital. Within two days additional marines were sent by land and sea and the Army began to move airborne, tank, and combat engineer troops to Lebanon to stabilize the situation. By early August the U.S. forces had reached a total of over 5,800 marines and 8,500 soldiers. Navy warships stood off the Lebanese coast and a U.S. composite Air Strike Force moved into Turkey in support of the ground forces. Meanwhile, the British had responded to Jordan's request for help and had dispatched airborne troops to bolster Jordan's armed forces. U.S. aircraft airlifted supplies to the British forces and the Jordanian population. The prompt U.S. and British actions having enabled the Lebanese and Jordanian Governments to restore order, all American forces were withdrawn by October. Both Lebanon and Jordan received special U.S. military assistance to help build up their defense forces and prevent internal outbreaks.

The Iraqi revolt had other repercussions. After Iraq withdrew from the Baghdad Pact in early 1959, a new arrangement became mandatory. When the Central Treaty Organization (CENTO) was established in August, the United States accepted membership on the economic, military, and antisubversion committees along with other acts of participation such as the attendance by the American Secretary of State at the meetings of the CENTO foreign ministers and the attendance of the United States Ambassador to Turkey at other important CENTO meetings in Ankara; it had already concluded separate defense treaties with Turkey, Iran, and Pakistan earlier in the year.

Closer to home, the United States did not intervene in the Cuban rebellion that had broken out in 1958. The United States watched the revolt of Fidel Castro and his followers carefully, and when the Batista government was overthrown the next year, recognized the Castro regime. During the remaining two years of the Eisenhower administration, Castro moved steadily into the Communist camp and U.S.-Cuba relations deteriorated. American military and economic assistance to Cuba was cut off in 1960 to be replaced by arms and other aid from the Soviet Union and Communist China. The situation had so worsened on the eve of the Kennedy inauguration that diplomatic relations were severed completely. Cuba openly charged that the United States was preparing to commit aggression against the island republic to overthrow Castro's government.

The Military Budget

As American commitments reached around the globe and U.S. forces and assistance were dispatched to comply with the agreements concluded during the fifties, it appeared that the nation was more likely to become involved in local wars than in a general conflict. Yet the military budgets following the Korean War had emphasized, for the most part, deterrence of a general nuclear war rather than the contingencies of brush-fire operations.

It was hardly surprising that the Eisenhower administration should seek to cut defense spending after the high outlays during the Korean War, but to some critics it appeared that military policy was being determined by the fixed budget ceilings adopted by the President and his advisers rather than by the requirements of national defense. In any event, the decision to rely heavily upon strategic air power rather than on ground forces soon created an imbalance in the military budget and in the distribution of military forces. In 1953 the Army had a strength of over a million and a half men and had 20 combat divisions—8 in the Far East, 5 in Europe, and 7 in the United States. Of the over $34 billion in military funds voted by Congress for fiscal year 1954, the Army was allocated close to $13 billion.

The lower postwar defense ceilings adopted by the National Security Council in 1953 envisioned sharp manpower cuts, and the Joint Chiefs of Staff came up with a long-range program to trim over 600,000 men from the armed forces over the next four years. While most of the reduction would be absorbed by the ground forces, the air and naval forces would also experience personnel cuts.

By 1958 the manpower adjustments had taken place. The Army had shrunk to 15 divisions and less than 900,000 men. Only 2 reduced-strength divisions remained in Korea and 1 in Hawaii; the deployment of divisions in Europe and the United States held firm at 5 and 7, respectively, but several of the latter were also at reduced strength. New obligational funds for the Army for fiscal year 1959 were slightly more than $9 billion, about 22 percent of the total military budget for one year.

The high costs of deterring nuclear war were evident. Despite administration efforts to hold down military spending, the defense budget climbed from $34 billion in fiscal year 1954 to over $41 billion for fiscal year 1959. Much of the expense could be traced to the intricate air and missile weapons systems needed to carry out and defend against nuclear attack. Not only were the systems costly to procure, but they also became obsolescent almost overnight as the fast pace of technology produced newer and better models. In addition, the complex mechanisms required highly trained personnel who had to be given costlier schooling, training equipment, and higher pay. Under the circumstances, much of the military procurement budget was devoted to the nuclear threat with relatively little allocated to provide for the possibility of limited, conventional war.

Defense Reorganization

The perennial service disputes over strategy, force levels, and funds did little to promote the effective unification and rapid decision-making that the United States required. In response to Congressional criticism the President decided in 1958 to strengthen further the authority of the Secretary of Defense, to lessen the autonomy of the military departments, and to provide a more direct chain of command from the President to the unified commands. The reorganization was approved by the Congress in August, bringing with it a number of sweeping changes.

Henceforth the system of using the military departments as executive agents for operations was abolished. Almost all of the active combat forces were to be placed under unified commands with the chain of command to them running from the President and the Secretary of Defense through the Joint Chiefs of Staff. The Secretary of Defense also received greater freedom to transfer functions within the services, and a Defense Directorate of Research and Development was set up to supervise the research and development programs of all the services. At the JCS level, the Joint Staff was enlarged but specifically directed not to operate or to organize as an over-all armed forces general staff. An effort was also made to free the members of the JCS themselves from some of their routine service duties by permitting them to delegate more authority and duties to their Vice Chiefs.

Under the reorganization the services remained in control of training, equipping, and organizing the forces for unified commands and of developing, under the general supervision of the Secretary of Defense, the weapons and equipment they would need. The services also retained control of all units and individuals not assigned to unified commands and provided logistical support to all their troops, whether in unified commands or not.

The act of 1958 marked the end of one major aspect of the traditional role of the military departments, since they no longer had any part in the direction of combat operations. The JCS and the unified commands were to occupy stage center, while the Secretary of Defense and his assistants were to exercise tighter control of service functions through increasing budgetary and management supervision.

Within the services internal reorganizations had already been carried out by 1958 to improve efficiency of operations and to adjust to the changes necessitated by the threat of nuclear war. In 1955, the Army had replaced the Army Field Forces with the Continental Army Command (CONARC) in an effort to cut down the number of commands reporting directly to the Chief of Staff. CONARC was given responsibility for the six U.S. armies and the Military District of Washington, as well as for certain other units, activities, and installations. Among the chief functions assigned CONARC were supervising the training of the active Army and Reserves, planning for development of the future Army and its equipment, and planning and conducting the ground defenses of the United States.

The Dual Capability Army

The need to adjust to the nuclear threat had a deep impact upon the Army, since it had to be prepared for both conventional and nuclear war. Although the old tactical organization seemed inadequate to meet a nuclear attack, no historical experience factors existed around which to develop a new organization. The tremendous destructive power of nuclear weapons argued that military forces could no longer be massed for offensives of great duration. Since nuclear battlefields would presumably be of great breadth and depth, there would be no point in attempting to hold a solid front; the enemy could easily penetrate the line with nuclear weapons and inflict heavy casualties upon the defenders.

One recourse was to establish a checkerboard pattern with mobile, well-armed units in alternate squares. In the event of attack, either on offense or defense, the mobile units could quickly concentrate, carry out their missions, and just as rapidly disperse before a nuclear counterattack might be launched. The key to success would lie in highly trained troops, equipped with weapons providing a high ratio of firepower and carried by fast and reliable ground and air vehicles. Other essential items would be first-class communications, dependable intelligence on the enemy's dispositions, and an efficient logistics system for resupply of the combat forces. The development of these capabilities, it was hoped, would enable the Army to produce units that could cope with both nuclear and conventional war.

The major tactical reorganization to meet the new conditions began in 1956 when the first pentomic divisions and missiles commands were set up to furnish the mobile units and fire support deemed necessary for nuclear war. The old triangular infantry and airborne divisions were replaced by an organization consisting of five battle groups, each a self-contained force capable of independent operations. Manned by 13,500 men instead of about 17,000, the pentomic divisions were directly supported by artillery and missiles that could employ conventional or nuclear warheads, while the heavier long-range missiles were concentrated in the missile commands. The armored divisions required less drastic overhauling, since they were better adapted to the requisite pattern of mobility and dispersion. By 1958 all of the Regular Army divisions had been reorganized; the National Guard and Reserve divisions did not complete their change-over until 1960.

The seven divisions stationed in the United States constituted the strategic reserve. Four of these—two airborne and two infantry—were designated in 1957 the Strategic Army Corps (STRAC) and were maintained in a high state of readiness for quick deployment in event of an emergency. The other three were earmarked as STRAC reinforcements and as a training base for expansion of Army forces should the crisis become prolonged or develop into a full-scale war.

To provide the weapons and equipment for the nuclear Army, scientists, engineers, and designers, among others, combined to produce a steady stream of new or improved items. From rifles, mortars, semiautomatic and automatic weapons, and recoilless rifles at the company level to powerful rockets, missiles, and artillery in the support commands, more efficient instruments of war were fashioned to increase the firepower of the combat forces. Whole new families of surface-to-surface and surface-to-air missiles emerged, with both short- and long-range capabilities. With the emphasis on mobility, even the larger and heavier weapons and equipment were designed to be air-transportable.

A program to produce ground and air vehicles with the necessary battlefield mobility led to the development of armored personnel carriers, such as the M113 with aluminum armor, that could move troops rapidly to the scene of operations while providing greater protection for the individual soldier. Since

GUIDED MISSILES AT SELFRIDGE AIR FORCE BASE

highways and bridges might be damaged or destroyed, dual-capability amphibious vehicles that could travel on rough terrain and swim across rivers and
swamps freed the fighting units from total dependence upon roads. Also, transportable bridges and bridge-laying equipment were designed to help speed
movement of land-bound vehicles like the new, diesel-powered M60 battle tank
that became operational in 1960. The M60 weighed over fifty-two tons, had a
cruising range of 300 miles, and mounted a 105-mm. turret gun.

Perhaps the most dramatic efforts to increase the Army's mobility occurred
in the field of aviation. To secure both firepower and maneuverability, the Army
pushed its development of helicopters and low-speed fixed-wing aircraft. The
versatile helicopter had already been used in Korea to move troops and supplies,
conduct reconnaissance, and evacuate casualties. Some of the new fixed-wing
planes were designed for short take-off and landing to increase their value in
forward areas and to carry pay loads of over three tons; others were to conduct
visual, photographic, and electronic surveillance missions over the battlefield
and behind enemy lines. Experiments were also initiated on vertical take-off and
landing aircraft that would combine the advantages of the helicopter's small
operating area requirements with the greater speed of the fixed-wing plane.

In co-ordinating the employment of increased mobility and firepower, the role of communications mounted in importance. Whether the pentomic units operated independently over large areas or quickly concentrated for a major attack, light but reliable radio equipment was essential. The advent of the space age spurred communications research, since the space capsules required that a large number of intricate recording and transmitting instruments be fitted into an extremely limited area. A dramatic breakthrough in miniaturization of component parts helped solve the problem. With tiny transistors replacing bulky tubes, radio equipment became lighter, smaller, and more reliable. Sets could be redesigned to be carried by the individual soldier, in light vehicles, or in aircraft, to ease the command problems involved in exercising control in fluid situations.

Tactical communications was only one facet of the technological advances of the fifties stemming from miniaturization. The ponderous early computers began to give way to smaller versions capable of storing more information and retrieving it more swiftly. In time, the Army found more and more areas where computers could be usefully employed. From the co-ordination of information on approaching air targets and the direction of weapons fire to the storage and retrieval of personnel and logistics data, computers assumed an ever-growing number of functions throughout the Army.

The storage and quick retrieval of information made the computer a valuable intelligence tool as well. To secure the data needed to feed the machines required developing new families of surveillance equipment that could detect the presence of enemy forces, weapons, and supply concentrations. More sophisticated radar and sonar instruments emerged for picking up and identifying objects on land, at sea, and in the air. To aid ground-based and airborne surveillance, infrared, acoustic, and seismic devices were put into use to supplement improved and highly accurate cameras and the side-looking radar carried by planes to locate enemy concentrations by day and night under all weather conditions.

Once the foe had been spotted and operations got under way, the Army logistics system would have to have methods and means for furnishing supplies and equipment to the troops on the nuclear battlefield. Since nuclear wars would, it was expected, be short, the armed forces would have to rely upon munitions in being rather than on future production, leaving no time for the American war machine to gear up and outstrip its enemies a year or two after the outbreak of hostilities. Instead the United States would have to prestock depots at home and in vital overseas areas while at the same time avoiding large concentration of war matériel in ports or other ideal targets for nuclear weapons.

Support for combat troops would have to be keyed to minimum essential requirements. Furnishing the minimum essential requirements in itself presented problems that were by no means completely solved. By rapidly processing requisitions in electronic computers, using fast naval vessels and air transport, delivering over the beaches by means of roll-on-roll-off ships and aerial tramways instead of through ports, and employing cross-country vehicles to steer clear of reliance on road nets, the logistics planners hoped to provide adequate support to the front-line troops.

Despite the influx of new weapons, tactics, machines, and equipment, the basic strength of the American armed forces remained dependent upon the caliber of the personnel. With the reductions after the conclusion of the Korean armistice enabling the bulk of the Reserves called into service for the war to return to civilian life, the military services again contained a high proportion of career officers and men.

Just as the logistics planners had to contend with the concept that a nuclear war would have to be fought with current stocks, the personnel planners soon decided that it would have to be fought with forces in being. Mobilizing and training civilians for a year or two as in past wars would no longer be practicable; they would not become available in time to influence military operations in a nuclear war. Only military forces in being and a well-trained, ready reserve could be expected to participate in the fighting.

Retaining the more capable officers and enlisted men became of greater importance as the technological advances of the fifties gave the armed services a growing inventory of complex weapons and equipment. Developing, operating, and maintaining the new items demanded administrators with scientific or engineering backgrounds and skilled technicians with considerable schooling. If the services were going to allocate funds for long and expensive training courses, they wanted to assure that the graduates would remain in uniform at least until the investment paid off. Since the graduates would be qualified to fill well-paid positions in rapidly expanding occupational areas, the services had to compete with attractive civilian offers.

Yet the situation was not without hope, for the advantages of a military career were many. The twenty-year retirement option was a strong inducement to many who had already served ten years or more. Among fringe benefits that made military life more attractive were free family medical care, and post exchange, commissary, and recreational and educational facilities. In most places the pre-World War II cleavage between the civilian and military communities had begun to disappear and military careers had gained more prestige, both because large numbers of civilians had served in World War II and in

Korea and because many areas had become dependent upon military spending for subsistence. The large post-Korea military establishment thus cut across social lines, while the large defense budgets affected every walk of American economic life.

In one respect, however, a military career had become less attractive. As a steady inflation set in after Korea, military pay had not kept pace with civilian salaries. With more and more talented military personnel shedding their uniforms to take on more lucrative civilian jobs, Congress in 1958 brought military salaries into closer correlation with civilian positions of similar responsibilities and also enabled the services to award proficiency pay for highly skilled personnel. Increased retirement benefits, approved at the same time, added to Social Security benefits, which had become available in early 1957, enabled the services to improve their competitive position considerably and to retain a higher percentage of the best-qualified officers and men.

The Reserve Forces

Despite the progress made in retention, the Army could not rely entirely upon a voluntary recruitment to fill its manpower requirements. During the Korean War, Congress had passed legislation placing a theoretical "military obligation" on all physically and mentally qualified males between the ages of 18½ and 26 for a total of 8 years of combined active and Reserve military duty. The Reserve was divided into two categories, the Ready Reserve, which could be ordered to duty on declaration of an emergency by the President and in numbers authorized by Congress, and the Standby Reserve, which could be ordered to duty only in war or emergency declared by Congress. To fulfill his military obligation, a young eligible male had several alternatives. By spending 5 years of his 8-year obligation on active duty or in a combination of active duty and membership in the Ready Reserve, he could transfer to the Standby Reserve for his last 3 years. Or he might join the National Guard at 18 and by rendering satisfactory service for 10 years avoid active duty unless his Guard unit was called into federal service. For college students there was also the alternative of enrolling in an ROTC course, spending 2 or 3 years on active duty and the remainder of the 8 years as a Reserve officer.

This system had many weaknesses. There was really no compulsory military obligation beyond existing selective service arrangements, and draft quotas dwindled rapidly after the end of the Korean War. Similarly, the armed services found it impossible to accommodate all ROTC graduates for their required active duty. The obligation to remain in the Reserve carried with it no compulsion either to enlist in a Reserve unit or to participate in continued training. Since enlistees in the National Guard required no prior training, Guard units had to spend most of their time drilling recruits. Thus the Reserve, while strong enough numerically, fulfilled none of the requisites for rapid mobilization in case of need, and there was no assurance that it would be kept up to strength by a steady input of young Reservists.

To remedy these faults, Congress, at the urging of the President, passed new Reserve legislation in 1955. While this act reduced the term of obligatory service for enlistees from 8 to 6 years, it imposed a requirement for active participation in Reserve training on those passing out of the armed services with an unexpired obligation. It also authorized voluntary enlistment of young men between the ages of 17 and 18½ in the Reserve up to a total of 250,000 per year. These youths would receive 6 months on active duty followed by 7½ years in the Reserve instead of a 2- or 3-year tour within a 6-year military obligation. The President was authorized, without further Congressional action, to call up to a million Ready Reservists to duty in an emergency proclaimed by him. He could also recall selected members of the Standby Reserve in the event of a national emergency declared by Congress.

It was difficult to eliminate all the weaknesses of Reserve legislation in one swoop, however, and even with a perfect bill circumstances would still have played a role in determining the outcome. In a period of irregular voluntary enlistments and restricted funds, many of the Reserve units soon fell below authorized strength. The main effort was placed upon training those units that could be mobilized and deployed in the early stages of a conflict. To fill the high priority units, Reservists were often assigned without regard to their military specialties, and imbalances that could seriously affect readiness dates increased. Many Reservists failed to keep their parent organization informed of changes in address or in Reserve status and this was especially true of members of the Ready Reserve Mobilization Reinforcement Pool which contained Reservists who did not belong to organized units. Failure to screen out the ineligibles promptly and on a regular basis caused the reinforcement pool to become clogged with deadwood that could only serve to delay a quick and efficient mobilization.

As budget cuts forced the active Army to lower its manpower ceiling, efforts were made to strengthen the Reserves. In the Reserve Forces Act of 1955 provisions were set up for a total Ready Reserve of 2,900,000 by 1970. The Army's share reached about a million and a half men in 1957—over a million in the Army Reserve and over 440,000 in the National Guard, with paid drill strengths reaching 305,000 and 422,000, respectively. At the same time, the number of

Army Reserve divisions was cut from 25 to 10 and manning levels were increased substantially to give these units a higher readiness capability, while the National Guard divisions rose from 26 to 27. Since the active Army could support only a force of 18 divisions on a manpower base of about one million men in 1957, it was evident that the Reserve forces could not come close to supporting adequately a total of 37 divisions on a paid drill strength of only 727,000. With the Reserve divisions heavily involved in training activities and suffering from equipment shortages as well, their capability to attain combat readiness quickly was open to serious question.

The Army's efforts to secure increases to correct these deficiencies, therefore, ran into mounting opposition in the late fifties from the President and his advisers. Convinced that the United States was spending about $80 million a year on sustaining Reserve units that were of little or no military value, President Eisenhower tried to cut the paid drill strength. But it proved to be extremely difficult to persuade Congress of the necessity or desirability of thoroughly reorganizing and reducing the many Reserve units scattered in Congressional districts throughout the country. The political significance of the Reserve forces could not be discounted and Congress in 1959 voted a mandatory 700,000 figure to assure that no further reductions would be made without its approval. Actually, when President Eisenhower left office two years later, the paid drill strength had climbed to over 750,000 men.

During the Eisenhower period the American public had accepted the need for large military forces in being despite its long history of antimilitarism and had shown itself willing to allocate money and troops to insure U.S. security. In assuming the responsibility and loneliness of leadership of the free world, the people had revealed a growing maturity.

CHAPTER 27

Global Pressures and the Flexible Response

When President John F. Kennedy assumed office in the opening days of 1961, the prospects for peace were not encouraging. Premier Khrushchev had been cool since an American U–2 plane gathering intelligence had been shot down over Russia in the spring of 1960. Although the possibility of a general nuclear war had receded, Soviet support of wars of national liberation had increased.

Despite the unfavorable signs President Kennedy was quite willing to renew the quest for peace. As he pointed out in his budget message of March 1961, the United States would make "efforts to explore all possibilities and to take every step to lessen tensions, to attain peaceful solutions, and to secure arms limitation." To Mr. Kennedy, diplomacy and defense were not distinct alternatives, but complemented each other.

Yet the President, well aware that the search for peace might be long, determined to give the United States a more flexible defense posture that would enable the nation to back its diplomacy with appropriate military action. The country should be strong enough to survive and retaliate after an enemy attack, on the one hand, and be able to prevent the erosion of the free world through limited war, on the other, the President informed Congress. "Any potential aggressor contemplating an attack on any part of the free world with any kind of weapons, conventional or nuclear, must know that our response will be suitable, selective, swift, and effective."

The Changing Face of the Cold War

As President Kennedy ushered in the era of flexible response, massive retaliation was officially de-emphasized. Long overdue, the shift in military policy stressed the need for ready nonnuclear forces as a deterrent to limited war. Besides, other changes under way indicated that America would need a more flexible position of strength in the days ahead.

By 1961 the tight bipolar system that had arisen after World War II and under which the United States and the Soviet Union were the only truly great powers was on the wane. No longer could the Soviet Union claim to speak for all Communists without challenge. In eastern Europe the satellite nations were pressing for more freedom of action and were eager to increase trade with the West. The Chinese Communists, on the other hand, were becoming impatient with Soviet conservatism and strongly opposed peaceful coexistence. And, in the New World, Fidel Castro was pursuing his own program of intrigue and subversion in Latin America. The Communist bloc, therefore, was in the process of splintering, with groups favoring the Soviet, Chinese, or Cuban brand of Communism emerging in many countries.

Dissent was also mounting in the West. With the success of the Marshall plan and the return of economic prosperity to western Europe during the fifties, France, West Germany, and other nations became creditor countries and were less and less dependent for the maintenance of their economies upon the United States. The return of Charles de Gaulle to power in France under a new and strong executive type of government in 1958 produced growing dissidence within the North Atlantic Treaty Organization as de Gaulle sought to recapture some of France's former glory by taking an increasingly independent role.

Outside Soviet and American circles the **presence** of a third force began to make itself felt during the fifties and early sixties. Most of the former colonial possessions in the Middle East, Asia, and Africa were granted independence in the fifteen years following World War II, and although many of them retained economic and cultural ties with the mother country they were generally reluctant to become politically involved in the East-West struggle. Since the new non-aligned nations contained about one-third of the world's population and controlled much of the earth's oil and other resources, they were courted by both sides. Many suffered, however, from basic political instability and economic weakness that made them fertile fields, first for Communist propaganda and subversion and then for wars of national liberation.

In May 1961 President Kennedy, touching on such revolutionary wars, pointed out to Congress that the great battleground of the sixties would be "the lands of the rising peoples." As the revolts to end injustice, tyranny, and exploitation broke out, he noted, the Communists had sent in arms, agitators, technicians, and propaganda to capture the rebel movements. Working behind the scenes with terrorists and saboteurs, the Communists had extended their control over large areas since World Ward II and had even broader ambitions. In such conflicts, the President had affirmed, "It is a contest of will and purpose as well as force and violence—a battle for minds and souls as well as lives and territory." The United States could not, Kennedy concluded, stand aside and passively let this fight be won by the Communists.

With half the world still in the balance, the prospects for peaceful coexistence between the United States and the Soviet Union dimmed in 1961. Insurgent movements were already disrupting Laos, Vietnam, the Congo, and Algeria and the threat of revolutionary outbreaks hung over several other countries in South America, Africa, and Asia. In most instances the Communists were abetting the insurgents and the United States was providing aid to the government forces. It was ironic, under the circumstances, that President Kennedy's first brush with the Communists should result from American support of an insurgent group.

Cuba and Berlin

During the closing days of the Eisenhower administration the United States had severed diplomatic relations with Cuba, but the presence of a Communist satellite almost within sight of the mainland remained a constant source of irritation. In April 1961 a band of Cuban exiles launched a poorly conceived invasion of the island at the Bay of Pigs with limited air and no naval support. When the people failed to rise and join the invaders, the operation collapsed and most of the invading force was taken prisoner. Since the United States had sponsored the exiles, their utter failure damaged American prestige and enhanced Fidel Castro's stature. The invasion also brought offers of Soviet help from Premier Khrushchev and dark hints that he was ready to employ Russian missile power to aid Castro.

The timing of the Cuban fiasco was particularly unfortunate, since President Kennedy was scheduled to hold a summit meeting with Khrushchev in Vienna in early June on the delicate subject of Berlin. In that divided and isolated city the growing prosperity of West Berlin contrasted sharply with the poverty and drabness of the Soviet sector and West Berlin had become as great an irritation to the Communists as Cuba was to the United States. In 1958 Khrushchev had demanded that Berlin be made a free city and threatened that unless western troops were withdrawn in six months he would conclude a separate treaty with East Germany. Although Khrushchev later backed off from this threat and even showed signs of a conciliatory attitude on Berlin, at the Vienna meeting he made a complete about-face.

Once again he informed Kennedy that unless the West accepted the Soviet position he would take unilateral action to solve the Berlin impasse. If the Soviet premier hoped to intimidate the new President in the wake of the Cuban setback, he was unsuccessful. Instead, Mr. Kennedy in July requested and received additional defense funds from Congress as well as authority to call up to 250,000 members of the Ready Reserve to active duty.

The President refrained from declaring a national emergency, which would have permitted him to bring up to a million Reserve members back to federal service; he did not wish to panic either the American public or the Soviet Union by a huge mobilization. On the other hand, he determined to strengthen the conventional armed forces in the event that Soviet pressure at Berlin demanded a gradual commitment of American military power.

During August, tension heightened as thousands of refugees crossed from East to West Berlin, and the Communists took the drastic step of constructing a high wall about their sector to block further losses. As the situation grew worse, the President decided in September to increase American troops in Europe and to call up some Reserve personnel and units to strengthen the continental U.S. forces. By October almost 120,000 reserve troops, including two National Guard divisions, had been added to the active Army, and the Regular troop strength had been increased by more than 80,000.

The partial American mobilization and the quick reinforcement of Europe with U.S. ground, air, and naval units were accompanied by strong efforts to bring the military personnel and equipment remaining in the United States to a high degree of readiness. Accelerated training and production prepared and outfitted the new and the Reserve troops as quickly as possible. In the event that an emergency should arise in Europe, extra equipment was shipped there to be held in storage for units that might have to be air-transported from the United States in a hurry.

As the Soviet Union became aware that the Berlin challenge would be met swiftly and firmly, it began to ease the pressure again. The new administration had passed its first test. By mid-1962 the Reserve forces called up were returned to civil life, but the Regular increases were retained.

The next Soviet ploy was less direct but more dangerous than the Berlin threat. After the Bay of Pigs invasion, the Soviet Union had dispatched military advisers and equipment to the Castro forces in Cuba, ostensibly to help them repel any future attacks. In the summer of 1962, however, rumors that the Soviet assistance might include offensive weapons such as medium-range bombers, and possibly medium-range ballistic missiles as well, increased. Not until mid-October could the conclusive photographic proof of the presence of the missiles in Cuba be obtained. With the pictures in hand, Mr. Kennedy quickly took steps aimed at getting these offensive weapons removed from the island.

The President made it clear that the United States would retaliate against the Soviet Union with nuclear weapons if any Cuban missiles were used against an American nation. The Strategic Air Command's heavy bombers went on a 15-minute alert status with some aircraft aloft at all times. To buttress the defense of the southeastern states closest to Cuba, fighter-interceptor squadrons and Hawk and Nike missile battalions moved in to supplement the local air defense forces. At sea Polaris-equipped submarines left for preassigned stations in case the Soviet Union decided to use the occasion for a nuclear showdown.

On October 22 President Kennedy announced that he would seek the endorsement of the Organization of American States (OAS) for a quarantine on all offensive military equipment being shipped to Cuba, tighten surveillance of the island, and reinforce the U.S. naval base at Guantánamo. With OAS approval, the quarantine went into effect two days later. Meanwhile dependents had been removed from Guantánamo and marines had been lifted by air and sea to defend the base. The Army began to move over 30,000 troops, including the 1st Armored Division, and over 100,000 tons of equipment into the southeastern states to meet the emergency.

As the Navy's Second Fleet started to enforce the quarantine on October 25, hundreds of Air Force and Navy planes conducted surveillance missions over the Atlantic and Caribbean to locate and track ships that might be carrying offensive weapons to Cuba. The continued activity at missile construction sites in Cuba had now placed the world on the brink of its first nuclear war.

The possibility of a clash between American warships and Soviet merchantmen carrying offensive war items to Cuba added to existing tensions. As the crisis mounted in intensity, however, the Soviet Union ordered such ships to return home and no incidents occurred. In the meantime a dramatic series of messages between Mr. Kennedy and Premier Khrushchev, and the Soviet Union finally agreed on the 28th to dismantle and remove the offensive weapons from Cuba. During the next three weeks the sites were gradually evacuated and the missile systems and technicians were loaded on Soviet ships. Negotiations for the removal of the Russian bombers were completed in November and they were shipped out of Cuba in early December. Although the quarantine ended on November 20, many air units remained on duty stations to continue surveillance missions in the area to insure that the sites remained inactive. Army forces deployed during the crisis did not return to their home bases until shortly before Christmas.

For the second time in two years the Soviet Union had demonstrated that it was unwilling to risk nuclear war. With the ending of the Cuban missile crisis, Soviet attempts to challenge the United States directly began to subside and Soviet interest centered increasingly upon support of so-called wars of liberation.

For the United States, Berlin and Cuba marked the beginning of the flexible response era, as the American reaction ranged from limited and conventional measures to the threat of general war.

Detente in Europe

The aftermath of Berlin and Cuba produced several unexpected developments. Evidently convinced that further testing of the American leadership might be unwise, the Soviet Union adopted a more conciliatory attitude in its propaganda and indicated that at long last it might be willing to conclude a nuclear test ban treaty. In view of the long history of fruitless negotiation over nuclear controls, the Soviet move was a promising breakthrough.

Under the provisions of the accord ratified in the fall of 1963, the Soviet Union, the United Kingdom, and the United States agreed not to conduct nuclear explosions in space, in the atmosphere, or underwater; underground explosions were permissible as long as no radioactive material reached the surface. Although the treaty was weakened by the failure of France to ratify or adhere to it, it marked the first major agreement between the Soviet Union and the United States since the Austrian peace treaty of 1955.

The explanation for Soviet co-operation with the West in the sixties, however limited, may have resulted partly from the growing independence of Communist China. The Chinese had never embraced the concept of peaceful coexistence with the capitalist countries and their criticism of what their leaders claimed was too soft a line by Moscow to the West had mounted. As the Sino-Soviet split widened, the Soviet Union adopted a less threatening role in Europe, and the shift had far-reaching effects upon the carefully built-up alliance system designed to guard western Europe against Soviet aggression.

The defense system of the North Atlantic Treaty Organization had been constructed around the American strategic deterrent, but the credibility of the U.S. determination to defend western Europe in the face of a growing Soviet nuclear power that might devastate the United States itself had come into serious question. Under President Kennedy and, after his assassination in November 1963, under President Lyndon B. Johnson, the United States made several efforts to reassure its NATO allies of American good faith. The reinforcement of U.S. conventional forces in Europe at the time of the Berlin crisis provided NATO with more options in responding to Communist pressure. In 1963 the United States assigned three Polaris submarines to the U.S. European Command and suggested that a multilateral naval force be established but the idea was dropped in 1965.

By that time it was becoming clear that General de Gaulle intended to disengage France militarily from NATO. The French cut the ties gradually by participating less and less in NATO exercises, while the French nuclear strike force slowly expanded. In early 1966 de Gaulle served notice that all NATO troops in the country would have to depart. All remaining French forces would be relieved from NATO command during 1966, de Gaulle stated, but France would not quit the alliance. The French president maintained that conditions in Europe had changed since 1949 and the threat to the West from the Soviet Union had lessened.

The military disassociation of France from NATO was unfortunate, since the chief headquarters and many of elaborate lines of communications supporting the forward military forces were in France. When representations to the French proved fruitless, however, the exodus of NATO troops got under way in mid-1966. Supplies and equipment were relocated at bases in the United Kingdom, Belgium, Germany, and the Netherlands. In early 1967 Supreme Headquarters, Allied Powers Europe (SHAPE), moved to Belgium, the U.S. European Command shifted its headquarters to Germany, and the Allied Command Central Europe as well as the ground command was transferred to the Netherlands.

Changes within the alliance had been slow. Despite the fact that the concept of massive retaliation had been discredited except as a last resort, it was not until 1967 that a strategy of flexible response was officially adopted. Apparently the Soviet Union also had decided that nuclear warfare offered only the bleak prospect of mutual destruction. In late 1969 the Soviet Union joined the United States in a series of Strategic Arms Limitations Talks in Finland to explore ways and means of stopping the nuclear arms race and of beginning seriously the task of disarmament. Progress was slow because of the many technical points that had to be settled, but at least a start was made.

In the meantime, however, the United States proceeded with its plans to deploy its ballistic missile defense system, using the NIKE–X program, with the long-range Spartan and the short-range Sprint missiles, as its base. The Safeguard System, as it eventually came to be known, envisioned a phased installation of the missiles, radars, and computers at key sites across the country by the mid-seventies. Although the Safeguard System was limited and was regarded as a thin line of defense, President Richard M. Nixon was reluctant to halt site development and construction of the missile complexes until an agreement was reached in the Strategic Arms Limitation Talks. Thus, despite considerable Congressional and public opposition, work on the first two bases in Montana and North Dakota was initiated in 1970.

The Growing Commitment in Underdeveloped Areas

The American policy of containment met its most serious challenge in Southeast Asia as the Communist revolutionary wars to take over Laos and South Vietnam picked up momentum in the early sixties. Taking advantage of the political instability in these countries, the Communists had built up their political and military organizations and gradually brought large segments of the rural areas under their control. Efforts by the governments to regain these areas through military operations had been largely unsuccessful despite the presence of American advisers and the provision of military equipment and supplies.

The struggle to keep Laos and South Vietnam out of the Communist camp, American diplomats and advisers soon discovered, was complex. After decades under French rule, many Indochinese leaders were willing to accept American assistance but unenthusiastic about instituting political and economic reforms that might lessen their newly won power.

The situation in Laos mirrored the American frustration. Until 1961 the United States supported the pro-West military leaders with aid and advice, but the efforts of these leaders to unify the country by force had failed and three different factions controlled segments of the country. As conditions steadily worsened, President Kennedy decided to recognize a coalition government in a neutral Laos. Fourteen nations signed a declaration in July 1962 confirming the independence and neutrality of Laos, which pledged itself to enter into no military alliance as well as to clear all foreign troops from the country. While the future of Laos remained clouded, a coalition government was preferable to a Communist takeover. By the end of 1962 over 600 American advisers and technicians stationed in Laos had left the country.

The concern over Communist activity in Laos and Vietnam also involved Thailand in mid-1962. To deter Communist expansion and to **protect** the territorial integrity of Thailand under its obligations to the Southeast Asia Treaty Organization, the United States set up a joint task force at the request of the Thai government. As Communist troops maneuvered not far from the Thai border, a reinforced battalion of marines was quickly transported to Thailand and was followed by a battle group of the 25th Infantry Division. Army signal, engineer, transportation, and other service troops moved in to support the U.S. combat forces and to provide training and advice for Thai units. The quick response so strengthened the Thai government's position that the Communist threat abated during the remainder of the year, enabling first the Marine and then the Army troops to withdraw. Many of the American service support forces, however, remained to assist in Thai training and logistical support programs. As the war in Vietnam intensified in the mid-sixties, the roads, airfields, depots, and communications constructed and maintained by U.S. forces in Thailand became extremely valuable in supporting the American effort in Vietnam.

Trouble in the Caribbean

Although Europe and Asia remained the critical areas in the **policy** of Communist containment, American interest in Caribbean developments increased sharply after Cuba's defection from the West. When a military revolt in April 1965 to oust the civilian junta in the Dominican **Republic** was followed by a military counterrevolution, the United States monitored the situation closely.

As both factions sought to gain control of the government machinery, the capital city of Santo Domingo became a bloody battleground and all semblance of law and order vanished. Concern over the immediate threat to American lives rose as diplomatic efforts to restore peace failed. First to **provide** protection for U.S. nationals and subsequently to insure that the Communists did not get another foothold in the Caribbean, President Johnson sent Marine Corps and then Army airborne troops to Santo Domingo to stabilize the situation.

Less than seventy-two hours after alert, two battalions of the 82d Airborne Division from Fort Bragg, North Carolina, air-landed at a field east of Santo Domingo and fanned out toward the city. They were soon reinforced by four additional airborne battalions with support units. In the meantime, Marine troops consolidated their hold on the western portion of Santo Domingo. Since the forces of the rebels, the so-called Constitutionalists, were concentrated in the southern part of town, Lt. Gen. Bruce Palmer, Jr., the American ground force commander, carried out a night operation to link up the Army and Marine units and to separate the warring factions. Using three airborne battalions for the action, Palmer had the first move into the easternmost sector, then **passed** the other two through the first to secure a corridor. With **surprising** ease and speed, the 82d Airborne's troops crossed the city and joined with the marines, thus creating a buffer zone between the two fighting forces.

By the end of the first week in May all nine battalions of the 82d Airborne Division and four battalions of marines were in the Dominican Republic. With supporting forces the total number of American troops soon reached a **peak** of about 23,000. They patrolled the streets of Santo Domingo, maintained law and order, and distributed food, water, and medical **supplies** to both sides. The quick landings in force and the establishment of the buffer zone made further fighting on a large scale impossible. With stalemate the alternative, the adversaries began a series of negotiations that lasted until September.

The U.S. intervention in the Dominican Republic became the subject of spirited discussion in the United States and abroad. Despite unfavorable public reaction to the intervention in some Latin American countries, the Organization of American States did ask its members to send troops to the Dominican Republic to help restore order. Six members—Brazil, Costa Rica, El Salvador, Honduras, Nicaragua, and Paraguay—eventually dispatched forces and joined the United States in forming the first inter-American force ever established in the Western Hemisphere. Although American troops constituted the largest contingent of the force, Lt. Gen. Hugo Panasco Alvim of Brazil was named commander in May and General Palmer became his deputy to emphasize the international composition of the force. Some U.S. troop withdrawals began almost immediately after the Latin American units arrived.

The acceptance of a provisional government by both sides in early September relieved much of the tension in the Dominican Republic, and by the end of 1965 all but three battalions of the 82d had returned to the United States. After elections in mid-1966, the last U.S. and Latin American elements pulled out in September, ending the 16-month intervention. Although the legality and the unilateral nature of the U.S. action have been challenged, there is little doubt but that the intervention saved lives and restored law and order in the Dominican Republic.

Civil Rights and Civil Disturbances

Within the United States itself, meanwhile, racial tensions growing out of the civil rights movement had dictated the use of troops in civil disturbances on a scale reminiscent of the labor troubles of the late nineteenth century. The first and most dramatic use of federal troops came in September 1957 when President Eisenhower dispatched a battle group of the 101st Airborne Division to Little Rock and federalized the entire Arkansas National Guard to enforce a court order permitting nine Negro students to attend Central High School. The paratroopers successfully dispersed the mob that had gathered at the school and stabilized the situation. Some weeks later they turned over the task of protecting the Negro students to the Arkansas National Guard, which kept about 400 members on federal duty at Little Rock until the end of the school year. The incident marked the first time a President had exercised his power to call the militia into federal service to control a domestic disturbance since 1867, and it was one of the few times in American history that a Chief Executive used either Regular troops or the National Guard in the face of opposition from a state's governor.

Other instances of the same sort followed in the administrations of Presidents Kennedy and Johnson. When, in September 1962, the governor of Mississippi attempted to block the court-ordered registration of James H. Meredith, a Negro, at the University of Mississippi at Oxford, President Kennedy first sought to enforce the law by using federal marshals. When riots broke out on the campus during the night before the registration of Meredith and the marshals were unable to control the mob, President Kennedy federalized the Mississippi National Guard and ordered active Army troops, some already standing by at Memphis, Tennessee, to Oxford. Eventually some 20,000 active Army troops and 10,000 federalized Guardsmen were deployed during the crisis, with 12,000 men in the immediate area and the remainder standing by at other stations. With the military forces in firm control the tension rapidly subsided and the number of troops was scaled down, although as at Little Rock some federal protection had to be provided throughout the school year.

Bombings and other racially motivated incidents in Birmingham, Alabama, in May 1963 forced President Kennedy to send Regular troops to Alabama bases. Later that year an integration crisis, first at the University of Alabama and then in the public schools of several Alabama cities, led him to federalize the entire Alabama Guard, although he used only part of it. In 1965 President Johnson employed both Regulars and Guardsmen to protect civil rights marchers along the route from Selma to Montgomery.

A riot in Rochester, New York, in 1964, and a far more serious one in the Watts district of Los Angeles in 1965, with killing, looting, and burning on a large scale, drew attention to the fact that the problem was not confined to the South. Restoration of order in the city required the efforts of 13,400 California Guardsmen as well as city and state law enforcement officers.

Racial disturbances continued to occur during the next two years, with particularly serious outbreaks in 1966 in Chicago, Cleveland, Cicero, Illinois, and San Francisco. They increased sharply in 1967 when more than fifty cities reported disorders during the first nine months of the year. These ranged from minor disturbances to the extremely serious disorders of Newark and Detroit, both of which occurred in July. Aside from state and local law enforcement officers, only the National Guard in its state capacity was used in the Newark riot, whereas in the destructive Detroit outbreak the governor of Michigan not only used the National Guard but also requested and, after some delay, obtained federal troops. This was the first time since the Detroit riot of 1943, when the Michigan National Guard was overseas, that a governor had requested federal assistance to put down a civil disturbance. During the Detroit riot of 1967 the task force commander had over 10,000 Guardsmen and 5,000 Regulars under his command and deployed nearly 10,000 men before the crisis passed.

TROOPS GUARDING A RIOT-TORN AREA OF DETROIT

Since disorders were occurring with greater frequency, President Johnson on July 28, 1967 appointed a National Advisory Commission on Civil Disorders for the purpose of investigating the causes and possible cures, with Governor Otto Kerner of Illinois as it chairman. The Kerner Commission, as it came to be know, concluded in its report early in 1968 that "our Nation is moving toward two societies, one black and one white—separate and unequal." The events recently experienced called attention to the racial imbalance in the National Guard and led to more training for both the Regular Army and the Guard as well as to more sophisticated planning by the Army in preparation for possible future disturbances.

The assassination of Dr. Martin Luther King, Jr., in Memphis, Tennessee, on April 4, 1968 produced a wave of rioting, looting, and burning in cities across the country, and the National Guard was used by the states in many places to subdue the rioters. Federal intervention was required in the troubled cities of Washington, Chicago, and Baltimore where the government used both federalized Guardsmen and Regular troops, deploying over 40,000 men in these three cities alone. Only a portion of the forces was committed to control rioting.

On April 22, 1968 in the wake of the riots, the Army established a new agency in the Office of the Chief of Staff, the Directorate for Civil Disturbance

Planning and Operations. Designed to provide command facilities for the Army's role as the agent of the Department of Defense in civil disturbance matters, the agency became the Directorate of Military Support on September 1, 1970.

Although the years immediately following 1968 produced no great racial disturbance, they did see the continuation of a series of large and small antiwar demonstrations in which federal and National Guard troops were employed. In October 1967 a large demonstration against the war took place at the Pentagon. The government had assembled protective forces that included 236 marshals, some of whom had been at Oxford, Mississippi, in 1962, and a military force which, including troops actually operational at the Pentagon and those in reserve, totaled around 10,000 men. Massive antiwar rallies were staged in Washington in November 1969 and May 1970, but these were generally peaceful; federal troops were positioned in the capital area but not used. Student protests against the Cambodian operations of 1970, however, led to tragedy at Kent State University in Ohio. National Guardsmen, under provocation from some students, fired upon the demonstrators, killing four, including two women, and wounding a dozen others.

The Kent State incident and another at Jackson State College in Mississippi involving students and police led to the appointment of the President's Commission on Campus Unrest, headed by former governor of Pennsylvania, William W. Scranton. The Scranton Commission found that campus unrest reflected the crisis over the war and related matters that gripped the nation.

An extended antiwar protest in the nation's capital took place in April and May 1971. A peaceful and impressive demonstration by Vietnam veterans was followed by an attempt on the part of youthful demonstrators on May Day to tie up Washington traffic and prevent government workers from reaching their jobs. The government deployed about 2,000 National Guardsmen, who were sworn in as special policemen, 3,000 Marines, and 8,600 troops of the Regular Army. The police and troops guarded highways and bridges and kept the traffic moving despite minor efforts by the demonstrators to carry out their plans.

Secretary McNamara and the New Management System

The operational activities of the armed forces during the Kennedy and Johnson administrations reflected but one portion of the wide range of problems confronting the nation's civilian and military leaders. At the same time, changes of far-reaching importance were being carried out in less publicized areas.

The primacy of the heavy manned bomber as the nation's main instrument of nuclear deterrence had come into question after the Korean War and finally ended in the sixties. President Kennedy and his Secretary of Defense, Robert S. McNamara, followed the trend of the Eisenhower **period** and missiles gradually replaced some of the strategic bombers. For fixed wing aircraft, the sixties saw the end of a cycle that began in Korea and the restoration of their support role.

For the ground forces, Vietnam brought about a reaffirmation that in conventional and limited wars the ground units bear the brunt of battle. The steady decline of the Army during the Eisenhower years was dramatically reversed in 1961 as the Army grew in numbers and its portion of the defense budget increased.

Within the Department of Defense, exercise of the more extensive authority granted the Secretary of Defense by the reorganization act of 1958 had begun. When Mr. McNamara became secretary in 1961, he accelerated the process.

President Kennedy gave McNamara two instructions: develop the force structure necessary to meet American military requirements, without regard to arbitrary or predetermined budget ceilings, and procure and operate the necessary force at the lowest possible cost. In accordance with McNamara's concept of centralized planning the Joint Chiefs of Staff, assisted by the services, continued to establish the military plans and force requirements deemed necessary to support U.S. national security policies. The forces, however, were now separated according to function, such as **strategic** retaliation, general purpose, and reserve, and placed in what was called a program package. When McNamara received these packages, he considered whether each one contained balanced forces and resources to accomplish its function, correlated the costs and the effectiveness of the weapon systems involved, and then forwarded the approved packages in the annual budget for Presidential and Congressional action. To provide assistance in long-range planning, a five-year projection of all forces, weapon systems, and defense activities, together with the cost, was also drawn up yearly for McNamara's endorsement.

Initially the Kennedy administration had three basic defense goals: to strengthen the strategic retaliatory forces; to build up the conventional forces so that a flexible response could be made to lesser challenges; and to improve the over-all effectiveness and efficiency of the defense effort. To attain the first objective, intercontinental ballistic missiles in hardened sites and Polaris nuclear-equipped submarines were added to provide the United States with the capability of retaliating in force in the event of a Soviet nuclear attack.

The second goal gained quick impetus from the Berlin crisis as Army strength alone rose from 860,000 to over 1,060,000 in 1961 and the Navy and the Air Force conventional forces also made modest gains. Although the National Guard units called up for the crisis were released in mid-1962, the Army was authorized in the meantime to activate two Regular divisions, for a total of sixteen, and to retain a permanent strength of 970,000 men. The influx of men allowed many units to remedy understrengths, and the additional funds allocated during the build-up permitted the procurement of new equipment and weapons to modernize the Army. As the Army budget rose from $10.1 billion to $12.4 billion in fiscal years 1961 and 1962, almost half the increase was allocated to the purchase of new vehicles, aircraft, missiles, and other equipment.

Seeking greater efficiency and reduced costs for the defense effort, Secretary McNamara instituted changes in organization and procedures utilizing the latest management techniques and computer systems. He established firm control over the services through close budget supervision, and gradually centralized under the Office of the Secretary of Defense many activities formerly administered separately by one of the services. Since a great number of supply items and related services were in common use throughout the Defense Department, he established the Defense Supply Agency in 1961. The agency assumed control of the five old and three new commodity single managerships, and of the Defense Traffic Management Service, as well as functions relating to cataloging and standardization. To the Defense Supply Agency fell the management, purchase, and distribution of items such as food, petroleum products, and medical, automotive, and construction supplies at the wholesale level. Centralization permitted mass buying at competitive prices, the establishment of tighter inventory controls through the use of computers, the standardization of items to eliminate duplication, and the consolidation of supply installations.

Tied in closely with the objectives in setting up the Defense Supply Agency was the launching of a five-year defense cost reduction program in 1962. Designed to cut procurement and logistics costs throughout the Defense Department, the program had three main goals: to buy only what was needed, with no frills; to purchase at the lowest sound price after competitive bidding whenever possible; and to decrease operating costs.

Centralization rather than cost reduction was the prime aim in setting up the Defense Intelligence Agency in 1961. Mr. McNamara had directed that all defense intelligence operations should be co-ordinated at a higher level and that one office should prepare his intelligence estimates.

The effects of the 1958 reorganization were most noticeable in the decision-making process. By maintaining close watch over such matters as budget and finance, manpower, logistics, and research and engineering, the Secretary of

Defense tightened civilian control over the services and carried unification much further than any of his predecessors. One of the moves designed to improve unified action was Secretary McNamara's creation of the U.S. Strike Command in 1961. By combining the Army's Strategic Army Corps with the Air Force's Tactical Air Command, the new command had combat-ready ground and air support forces that could be deployed quickly to meet contingencies or to reinforce overseas units. The Army and Air Force components of Strike Command remained under the control of their own services until an emergency arose, then passed to the operational control of Strike Command.

Army Reorganization

In view of the changes in organization and procedures at the Defense Department level, it was not surprising that the Secretary of Defense should also direct a thorough review of the Army's organization in 1961. A broad reorganization plan, approved by the President in early 1962 under the authority of Reorganization Act of 1958, called for major shifts in the tasks performed by the Department of the Army Staff and the technical services. The Army Staff became primarily responsible for planning and policy, leaving the execution of decisions to the field commands. In an effort to organize the Army along more functional lines, centralize such matters as personnel, training, and research and development activities, and integrate supply operations, most of the technical services were abolished. The statutory offices of the Chief Chemical Officer, the Chief of Ordnance, and The Quartermaster General were completely eliminated. The Chief Signal Officer and the Chief of Transportation continued to perform their duties as special staff officers rather than as chiefs of services. The Chief Signal Officer later regained a place on the General Staff when he became Assistant Chief of Staff for Communications-Electronics in 1967, but the Chief of Transportation's activities were absorbed by the Deputy Chief of Staff for Logistics in 1964. The Chief of Engineers retained his special status only with respect to civil functions; his military functions were placed under the general supervision of the Deputy Chief of Staff for Logistics until 1969, when he was again accorded independent status. Among the technical services, only The Surgeon General emerged with his position intact after the reorganization.

In the administrative services, The Adjutant General and the Chief of Finance also lost their statutory status and became special staff officers; later, in 1967, the Office of the Chief of Finance was discontinued as a special staff agency and its functions were transferred to the Office of the Comptroller of the Army. A new Office of Personnel Operations was established on the special staff level to provide central control for the career development and assignment of all military personnel. Officers of the technical and administrative services retained their branch designations but the management of their careers, with certain exceptions, was taken over by the Office of Personnel Operations. Although many of the most important Quartermaster functions were given to the Defense Supply Agency, a new Chief of Support Services assumed responsibility for such matters as graves registration and burials, commissaries, and clothing and laundry facilities.

Most of the operating functions lost by the Army Staff and the technical services were allocated to the U.S. Continental Army Command and to two new commands—the U.S. Army Materiel Command (USAMC) and the U.S. Army Combat Developments Command (USACDC). Continental Army Command became responsible for almost all of the Army schools and for the training of all individuals and units in the United States, but lost its test and evaluation mission to Army Materiel Command and turned over combat development activities to Combat Developments Command.

The Army Materiel Command took over many of the tasks formerly assigned to the technical services and set up subcommands to handle them. It assumed operating responsibility for research, development, testing, production, procurement, storage, maintenance, and distribution of matériel on a wholesale basis.

To the Combat Developments Command went the mission of developing organizational and operational doctrine, matériel objectives and qualitative requirements, war games and field experimentation, and cost effectiveness studies. This command was to provide answers to questions on how the Army was to be organized and equipped and how it was to fight in the field.

The transfer of functions began in the spring of 1962 and the new commands became operational in the summer. During the following year other major changes affecting staff responsibilities took place. In January 1963 the Office of Reserve Components was established to exercise general supervision over all plans, policies, and programs concerning the National Guard and Reserve forces. The statutory responsibility of the Chief, National Guard Bureau, to advise the Chief of Staff on National Guard affairs and to serve as the channel of communications between the Army and the states adjutants general was not altered by the creation of the new agency. The Chief, Army Reserve, however, did lose his control of the Reserve officers training program, which was transferred to the Office of Reserve Components in February and later to the Deputy Chief of Staff for Personnel in 1966.

Since the Deputy Chief of Staff for Military Operations (DCSOPS) had become heavily involved in planning for joint operations, the Army in the spring of 1963 created an Assistant Chief of Staff for Force Development to assure adequate attention to affairs that primarily concerned the Army. To prepare the Army force plans and structures in consonance with requirements developed by DCSOPS and with manpower and budget limitations as well became the main task of the new office; DCSOPS remained the principal adviser to the Chief of Staff on all joint matters and also retained responsibility for strategic planning and the employment of combat-ready Army troops.

As it turned out, neither the new Assistant Chief of Staff for Force Development nor the Army Comptroller had sufficient authority to manage the Army's resources or to integrate the proliferating automatic data processing systems. Gradually the responsibility for co-ordinating these shifted to the secretariat of the General Staff, which became almost a "superstaff." To provide for centralized direction and control of resource management programs, including management information systems, force planning, and weapons system analysis, the Army in February 1967 established the Office of the Assistant Vice Chief of Staff, to be headed by a lieutenant general. The new office under the Vice Chief of Staff would have authority to manage the various programs and the secretariat could return to its normal duties.

Tactical Readjustment for Flexible Response

The reorganization of the Army staff was accompanied by a major overhaul of the tactical organization. In practice the pentomic division had proved to be weak in staying power and needed more men to be capable of sustained combat. In 1961 the Army revised the divisional structure to provide a better balance between mobility and firepower and to insure greater flexibility.

Under the Reorganization Objective Army Division (ROAD) concept the Army began in early 1962 to form four types of division—infantry, armor, airborne, and mechanized—each with a common base and three brigade headquarters. The base contained a headquarters company, a military police company, a reconnaissance squadron, division artillery, and a battalion each of engineer, signal, medical, supply and transportation, and maintenance troops. In the combat mix of the ROAD division the Army attained flexibility, since the numbers and types of battalions could be varied at will to carry out different missions. An infantry division might ordinarily have eight infantry and two armor battalions with a total strength of 16,000 men, but could control up to fifteen battalions if the need arose. When terrain permitted, more armor or mechanized elements could be added; in the swamps or jungles, the accent could be placed upon the infantry battalions.

The first ROAD divisions were the newly reactivated 1st Armored and 5th Infantry (Mechanized) Divisions, which were tested during 1962. When the concept worked out well, the Army in 1963 began to convert the remaining fourteen active divisions and to reorganize the National Guard and Army Reserve divisions under ROAD. The active and Reserve reorganizations were completed in mid-1964.

The search for mobility sparked another tactical innovation in 1962 when an Army board compared ground and air vehicles in terms of cost and efficiency. The board recommended that new air combat and transport units be formed. The concept of an air assault division employing air-transportable weapons and aircraft-mounted rockets to replace artillery involved the delicate question of Air Force and Army missions, but Mr. McNamara decided to give it a thorough test.

Organized in February 1963, the 11th Air Assault Division was successfully tested for two years. By the spring of 1965 the situation in Vietnam offered an opportunity to demonstrate its capabilities for mobility in rough terrain. In July the division was inactivated and the personnel and equipment used to reorganize the 1st Cavalry Division under the air mobile concept at Fort Benning, Georgia. The 2d Infantry Division took over the personnel and equipment left by the 1st Cavalry Division in Korea; an exchange of divisional colors and the repainting of divisional insignia accomplished the switch. The new airmobile division had an authorized strength of 15,787 men, 428 helicopters, and 1,600 road vehicles (half the number of an infantry division). Although the number of rifles and automatic weapons in the division was the same as in an infantry division, the supporting weapons were lighter. The direct support artillery was moved by helicopter and had no vehicular prime movers. Instead of a general support artillery battalion, the airmobile division used an aerial rocket artillery battalion. Since all equipment was designed to move by air, the division total weight was only 10,000 tons, less than a third of an infantry division's.

The development of the air assault division provided fresh impetus to the dramatic growth of Army aviation. Although Army–Air Force agreements and decisions at Defense Department level during the fifties had generally been designed to restrict the size and weight of Army aircraft and their area of operations, the Army had pushed ahead vigorously in its research and development program. Concentrating heavily in the rotary-wing field, the Army by

1960 had built up its inventory to over 5,500 aircraft, almost half of them helicopters.

The versatility of rotary-wing aircraft made them ideal for observation and reconnaissance, medical evacuation, and command and control missions. Under the service roles and missions agreement all of these activities were permissible for the Army when conducted in the battlefield area. But the Army expansion into the development of larger craft that could be used for transporting large loads of troops and supplies and the subsequent arming of helicopters raised questions concerning the proper role to be played by the two services.

A reassessment of missions and roles in 1966 placed the larger transports that the Army had developed with the Air Force. Insofar as helicopters were concerned, however, the Army maintained primacy, partly because of the demonstrated ability of rotary-wing aircraft to support land combat operations and partly because the Army had been farsighted in its research and development effort. Although the Army inventory of fixed-wing aircraft slipped slightly in the ensuing years, the number of helicopters, spurred by the demands of the war in Vietnam, soared from about 2,700 in 1966 to about 9,500 by mid-1971.

The Vietnam War also accelerated the development and introduction of many improved and new Army aircraft models. Among the new additions were the HueyCobra, a gunship armed with combinations of rockets, 7.62-mm. miniguns, and machine guns, and the Cayuse observation helicopter. Later versions of the Mohawk fixed-wing observation plane, the Chinook medium transport helicopter, and the Iroquois (Huey UH–1) light transport helicopter, among others, incorporated technological advances and tactical adaptations that greatly improved their value in field operations. One of the new aircraft, the Cheyenne, the first helicopter designed as a weapons system to provide fire support to ground troops, experienced technical difficulties in 1969 and had to undergo further modification and testing.

New weapon systems, vehicles, and equipment and new organizations to provide better support and greater flexibility for the fighting forces continued to emerge in bewildering rapidity during the sixties. The technological developments in air and ground vehicles promoted mobility, while the advances in communications facilitated the exercise of command and control and the gathering of intelligence. To handle the great number of men and to keep track of the countless items of supply, complex and efficient computer systems were put into operation. Along with sophistication of equipment came the training of qualified men to operate and maintain the machines and weapons and the development of an elaborate and responsive logistics system to provide the parts, fuel, and ammunition to keep them in action.

The Army school system furnished the bulk of the basic technical training, although civilian manufacturers frequently supplied specialists to demonstrate to and instruct military units in the **operation** and maintenance of new products. Army schools had to keep abreast of the latest technological developments, therefore, and to turn our soldiers who would be able to use new items to the best advantage. The man behind the gun or machine became all the more important as the weapons and engines grew deadlier and more efficient.

In the environment of the sixties professional skills had to be resharpened continually, but the expanding role of the soldier required other talents as well. In the underdeveloped areas of the world, battlefield **proficiency** was only part of the task. Military victories might gain real estate, but if they failed to win the subsequent support of the local population they were of little consequence. In counterinsurgency operations the important objective was to convince the people in the countryside of the central government's interest and concern for their safety and welfare and to earn their loyalty and confidence—the only victory with any permanent meaning.

Civic action and counterinsurgency operations were not new to the Army for they had played a dominant role in the opening of the American West and the pacification of the Philippines. During the occupation of Germany and Japan after World War II civic action programs had done much to improve the relations between the American military and the peoples of those countries; broad economic assistance and political and educational reorientation, combined with a willingness to co-operate on the **part** of the German and **Japanese** people and their leaders, had simplified the problem of reconstituting civil authority. In underdeveloped countries the task was usually much more difficult, since communications were poor and the bonds between the central authority and the rural areas were seldom strong. Special forces, capable of operating independently and of reaching to the grass roots, were required to counter insurgency in such places.

Although the Army had trained small units in psychological warfare, unconventional warfare, and counterinsurgency operations during the fifties, President Kennedy's personal interest in the field gave the **program** a significant boost in 1961. The Special Forces expanded sharply from 1,500 to 9,000 men in a year and continued to grow until 1969. Even more important, new emphasis in Army schools and camps provided all soldiers with basic instruction in counterinsurgency techniques.

The Special Forces helped train local forces to fight guerrillas and taught them skills essential to strengthening the nation internally. Special Forces Groups were oriented toward specific geographic areas and given language training to facilitate their operations in the field. Each group was augmented with aviation, engineer, medical, civil affairs, intelligence, communications, psychological warfare, military police, or other elements that could be tailored for an assignment. Individual members of each team sent out could be trained also in other skills to increase their versatility. Working on a person-to-person basis, the Special Forces strove to improve the image of the government armed forces and to foster co-operative attitudes among the rural people.

Special warfare training was also given to the Reserve forces to keep them current with counterinsurgency developments and the measures necessary to counteract internal aggression and subversion. One phase of this training—crowd and riot control tactics—became of particular importance because of the growing threat of civil disturbance.

The Reserve Forces and the Draft

Concerned over the expenditure of defense funds for Reserves that were long on numbers but short on readiness, Mr. McNamara ordered a thorough analysis of the status and functions of the Reserve forces during the early sixties. Maintaining a force of 400,000 National Guardsmen and 300,000 Army Reserves on a paid drill status, for instance, made little sense unless these backup forces could step in quickly in a crisis and replace the regular strategic reserve. The performance of the Army National Guard and Army Reserve units called up for the Berlin crisis in 1961 had demonstrated that the Army Reserve forces could not, with the level of support and training at that time, become ready for combat in less than four to nine months. In light of current military requirements, the time lag was considered excessive.

In the spring of 1962 Mr. McNamara announced a plan that the Army had developed to reduce and realign the Army National Guard and to lower the paid drill strength of the Army Reserve. Considerable opposition from Congress and many state officials led him to defer action on the reduction, but he carried out the realignment the following year, eliminating in the process four National Guard and four Reserve divisions as well as hundreds of smaller units.

At the close of 1964 the Secretary of Defense proposed a far more drastic reorganization of the Reserves to bring them into balance with contingency war plans. His contention was that the dual National Guard–Army Reserve management system was duplicative and that by consolidating units the paid drill strength could be trimmed from 700,000 to 550,000, and 15 National Guard and 6 Reserve divisions for which there were considered to be no military requirements would be eliminated under the secretary's proposal. The reorganization plan would place all units under the National Guard; only individuals would be carried in the U.S. Army Reserve.

The storm of protest from Congress, the states, and the Reserve associations was quick and long-lived. While the debate went on, McNamara sought to achieve partial implementation of his reorganization goal by ordering the inactivation of Army Reserve units that were not required for contingency war plans. Despite strong Congressional opposition, the excess units, which include all 6 Army Reserve combat divisions and a total of 751 company and detachment size units, were eliminated by the end of 1965. In the fall of 1967, after concessions had been made by both Congress and the Department of Defense, a mutually acceptable reorganization plan that met Secretary McNamara's basic reorganization objectives was approved. Under the new structure, which was full implemented by the end of May 1968 the Army Reserve retained organized units, but its paid drill strength was reduced from 300,000 to 260,000. Only three U.S. Army Reserve combat brigades were included; the remainder were training and support units. Army National Guard strength remained at slightly over 400,000 men, but the division total was lowered from 23 to 8, while the number of separate brigades was raised from 7 to 18. All units in the new force structure were to be manned at 93 percent or better of wartime strength and were to be fully supported with technicians, equipment, repair parts, and other essentials.

To help obtain the men to fill the Reserve units, legislation had been passed in September 1963 revising the Reserve Forces Act of 1955. The new law provided for direct enlistment—an optional feature of the 1955 act—and the term of obligated service was reduced from eight to six years. The length of the initial tour became more flexible, generally ranging from four to seven months, depending upon the particular military skill involved. Under this Reserve enlistment program, recruits could be given longer periods of initial active duty to train them to fill the requirements for more highly skilled specialists.

The ROTC program was revised in 1964 to improve the flow of qualified Reserve officers into both the active Army and the Reserve components. The four-year senior program at colleges and universities was strengthened by the addition of scholarship provisions, and a two-year program was added for students who had been unable to complete the first two years of ROTC and who had undergone at least six weeks of field training to qualify them for entrance into the advanced course (last two years). Congress also authorized the other military departments to establish a junior ROTC program at qualified public and private secondary schools, beginning in 1966. While most newly commissioned National Guard officers were products of state-operated officer candidate schools, ROTC from 1965 to 1970 continued to be the primary source of new officers for both the Regular Army and the Army Reserve. Cutbacks in active Army officer requirements for fiscal year 1971 indicated that a growing number of ROTC graduates would not be required to perform a two-year active duty stint, but would be released to the Army National Guard or the Army Reserve after three to six months of active duty for training. Recent reductions in the number enrolled in the ROTC program reflect the changeover of the ROTC basic course from required to elective status in many participating institutions, reduced draft pressure, prospects for an all-volunteer army, and antimilitary activities on the college campuses.

Although the Army build-up for the war in Vietnam increased the pressures for a Reserve call-up to replace the Regular troops and draftees sent overseas, the Johnson administration decided in July 1965 not to call up the Reserve forces to meet the Army's immediate needs for additional manpower. The President may have been influenced by dissatisfaction caused by the Berlin call-up, the restrictions usually set by the Congress on the length of the Reserve tour of active duty, and the desire to retain the Ready Reserves as an emergency force. To cover the void in the Army's ability to meet other contingencies created by utilization of active Army assets to supply initial Vietnam requirements and the cadres for newly formed units, a Selected Reserve Force for quick response was established in August 1965, using elements of 8 Army National Guard divisions and some backup units from the Army Reserve. The Selected Reserve Force contained over 150,000 men—about 119,000 National Guardsmen and 31,000 Army Reservists— and consisted of 3 divisions and 6 separate brigades with combat and service support units. All units were authorized to maintain 100 percent strength, received extra training, and were given priority in equipment allocation. To relieve Selected Reserve Force personnel of the burden of additionally prescribed training assemblies—100 annually as compared to the normal 48—the force was reorganized during 1968 and the additional training requirements were reduced. The force was abolished in September of 1969.

By early 1968 the strain placed on active forces in meeting the continuing Vietnam build-up, keeping up other worldwide deployments, and maintaining a strategic reserve had become so great that these tasks could not longer be met through reliance upon increased draft calls. The urgency of the situation was underscored by Communists provocations in Korea and the enemy's *Tet* offensive in Vietnam. To alleviate the situation President Johnson directed the Secretary of Defense on April 11, 1968 to mobilize units and individuals of the Ready Reserve for a period not to exceed twenty-four months. This smallest of the three partial mobilizations since the end of World War II brought into federal service 34 Army National Guard units and 42 Army Reserve units with a combined strength of 17,415. An additional 2,459 members of the Individual Ready Reserve—the new designation for the Ready Reserve Mobilization Replacement Pool—were ordered to active duty as fillers for the activated units and to meet critical active Army shortages. Of the 76 units mobilized, 43 went to Vietnam and the remaining 33 were assigned to the Strategic Army Forces. As in earlier mobilizations, failure to attain peacetime training objectives and the shortages of equipment proved major problems that generally prevented the mobilized units from meeting postmobilization readiness objectives. But **despite** these short-comings, the partial mobilization of 1968 proved to be the most successful to date, and forces were provided for both the refurbishment of the strategic reserve and Vietnam deployments much earlier than would have been possible if new units had been started from scratch. The last of the mobilized Reserve component units was returned to reserve status in December 1969.

Three months later selected Army National Guard and Reserve units were once again ordered into federal service. On March 18, 1970 New York City mail carriers began an unauthorized work stoppage that threatened to halt essential mail services. President Nixon declared a national emergency on the 23d, thus paving the way for a partial mobilization of the Ready Reserves that began the next day. A total of more than 18,000 National Guard and Army Reserve members participated with other Regular and Reserve forces in assisting U.S. postal authorities in getting the mails through. The postal workers soon returned to work, and by April 3 the last of the mobilized reservists were returned to civilian status.

The phase-down of U.S. military operations in Vietnam and the accompanying cutbacks in active force levels caused renewed reliance to be **placed** on reserve forces. As early as November 1968 Congress, concerned that the Reserve components were not being adequately provided for, **passed** the Reserve forces "Bill of Rights." Signed into law by President Johnson in December, the act placed upon the service secretaries the responsibility for providing the support needed to develop Reserve forces capable of attaining peacetime training goals and the responsibility for meeting approved mobilization readiness objectives. The act also established the position of Assistant Secretary for Manpower and Reserve Affairs within each of the military departments and gave statutory status to the position of Chief of the Army Reserve. In August 1970 Secretary of Defense Melvin R. Laird emphatically affirmed that the Reserve components would be **prepared to provide** the units and individuals required to augment the active forces during the initial phases of any future expansion.

By mid-1971 the Army's Reserve components had substantially recovered from the turbulence associated with the reorganization and partial mobilization of 1968. Defense Department plans for yet another reorganization, designed to bring the Reserve components troop program into consonance with new organizational concepts emanating from the Vietnam experience, were under way but they did not involve the loss of any major units.

Since the President had elected not to call up the Reserve forces in the early stages of the build-up, the main burden of meeting the Army's need for additional manpower in Vietnam had fallen upon the Selective Service system. Increased draft calls and voluntary enlistments rather than a resort to the Reserves swelled the Army strength from 970,000 in mid-1965 to over 1,500,000 in 1968. The Army's divisions increased from sixteen to nineteen during this period and Army appropriations rose from $12 billion in fiscal year 1965 to almost $25 billion in fiscal year 1969.

Reliance upon Selective Service to meet the growing requirements of the Army when large Reserve forces were available drew critical comments from both Congress and the public. This would have been true whether the choice had been made by draft board or lottery, or whether it had been based on physical, marital, or educational status. The nub of the matter was that some were selected while others stayed home. On the other hand, there was no practicable way to change this state of affairs, since the armed forces could not use, nor did they need, all those young men eligible for military service. The four-year extension of the draft law in 1967 attempted to eliminate some of the imbalance, and the introduction of a lottery system in late 1969 helped to alleviate the lot of the potential draftee by limiting the period during which he could be selected to one year, but the basic problem remained. The unpopularity of the war in Vietnam among certain members of the draft age group rose as the conflict dragged on, and evidenced itself in a rising number of antiwar demonstrations, draft card burnings, and efforts to avoid military service. Such a climate was not calculated to bring forth enough volunteers to make the draft unnecessary.

CHAPTER 28

The U.S. Army in Vietnam

The Vietnam War was the legacy of France's failure to suppress nationalist forces in Indochina as it struggled to restore its colonial dominion after World War II. Led by Ho Chi Minh, a Communist-dominated revolutionary movement—the Viet Minh—waged a political and military struggle for Vietnamese independence that frustrated the efforts of the French and resulted ultimately in their ouster from the region.

The U.S. Army's first encounters with Ho Chi Minh were brief and sympathetic. During World War II, Ho's anti-Japanese resistance fighters helped to rescue downed American pilots and furnished information on Japanese forces in Indochina. U.S. Army officers stood at Ho's side in August 1945 as he basked in the short-lived satisfaction of declaring Vietnam's independence. Five years later, however, in an international climate tense with ideological and military confrontation between Communist and non-Communist powers, Army advisers of the newly formed U.S. Military Assistance Advisory Group (MAAG), Indochina, were aiding France against the Viet Minh. With combat raging in Korea and mainland China recently fallen to the Communists, the war in Indochina now appeared to Americans as one more pressure point to be contained on a wide arc of Communist expansion in Asia. By underwriting French military efforts in Southeast Asia, the United States enabled France to sustain its economic recovery and to contribute, through the North Atlantic Treaty Organization (NATO), to the collective defense of western Europe.

Provided with aircraft, artillery, tanks, vehicles, weapons, and other equipment and supplies—a small portion of which they distributed to an anti-Communist Vietnamese army they had organized—the French did not fail for want of equipment. Instead, they put American aid at the service of a flawed strategy that sought to defeat the elusive Viet Minh in set-piece battles, but neglected to cultivate the loyalty and support of the Vietnamese people. Too few in number to provide more than a veneer of security in most rural areas, the French were unable to suppress the guerrillas or to prevent the underground Communist shadow government from reappearing whenever French forces left one area to fight elsewhere.

The battle of Dien Bien Phu epitomized the shortcomings of French strategy. Located near the Laotian border in a rugged valley of remote northwestern

Vietnam, Dien Bien Phu was not a congenial place to fight. Far inland from coastal supply bases and with roads vulnerable to the Viet Minh, the base depended almost entirely on air support. The French, expecting the Viet Minh to invade Laos, occupied Dien Bien Phu in November 1953 in order to force a battle. Yet they had little to gain from an engagement. Victory at Dien Bien Phu would not have ended the war; even if defeated, the Viet Minh would have retired to their mountain redoubts. And no French victory at Dien Bien Phu would have reduced Communist control over large segments of the population. On the other hand, the French had much to lose, in manpower, equipment, and prestige.

Their position was in a valley, surrounded by high ground that the Viet Minh quickly fortified. While bombarding the besieged garrison with artillery and mortars, the attackers tunneled closer to the French positions. Supply aircraft that successfully ran the gauntlet of intense antiaircraft fire risked destruction on the ground from Viet Minh artillery. Eventually, supplies and ammunition could be delivered to the defenders only by parachute drop. As the situation became critical, France asked the United States to intervene. Believing that the French position was untenable and that even massive American air attacks using small nuclear bombs would be futile, General Matthew B. Ridgway, the Army Chief of Staff, helped to convince President Dwight D. Eisenhower not to aid them. Ridgway also opposed the use of U.S. ground forces, arguing that such an effort would severely strain the Army and possibly lead to a wider war in Asia.

The fall of Dien Bien Phu on 7 May 1954, as peace negotiations were about to start in Geneva, hastened France's disengagement from Indochina. On 20 July, France and the Viet Minh agreed to end hostilities and to divide Vietnam temporarily into two zones at the 17th parallel. (*Map 47*) In the North, the Viet Minh established a Communist government, with its capital at Hanoi. French forces withdrew to the South, and hundreds of thousands of civilians, most of whom were Roman Catholics, accompanied them. The question of unification was left to be decided by an election scheduled for 1956.

The Emergence of South Vietnam

As the Viet Minh consolidated control in the North, Ngo Dinh Diem, a Roman Catholic of mandarin background, sought to assert his authority over the chaotic conditions in the South in hopes of establishing an anti-Communist state. A onetime minister in the French colonial administration, Diem enjoyed a reputation for honesty. He had resigned his office in 1933 and had taken no part in the tumultuous events that swept over Vietnam after the

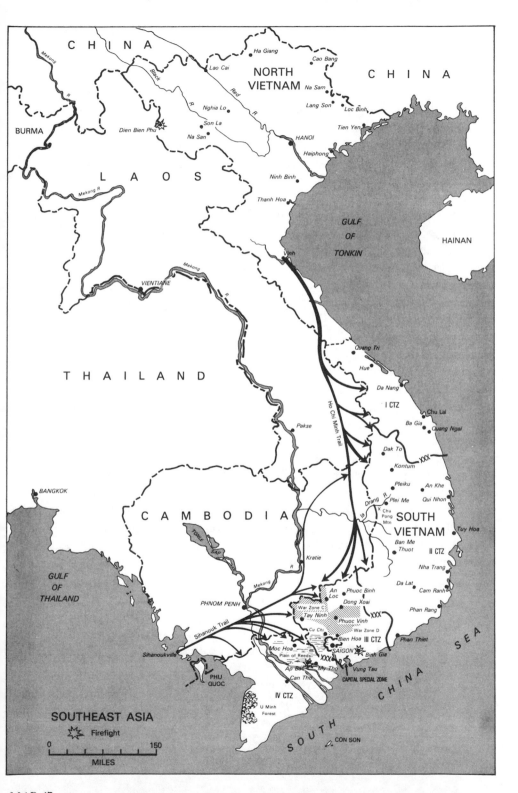

C H I N A

• Ha Giang

Lao Cai

NORTH
VIETNAM

• Cao Bang

C H I N A

Na Sam

Nghia Lo •

Lang Son

Loc Binh •

Son La •

Dien Bien Phu ☆

Tien Yen •

Na San •

HANOI •

BURMA

Haiphong

L A O S

Ninh Binh •

Thanh Hoa •

Vinh •

GULF

OF

TONKIN

HAINAN

VIENTIANE

Mekong R

T H A I L A N D

Quang Tri •

Hue •

Da Nang →

I CTZ

Chu Lai •

Pakse •

Ba Gia • Quang Ngai

Dak To •

XXX

Kontum •

B A N G K O K

Pleiku •

An Khe •

Plei Me •

Qui Nhon •

Drang R

Ia

X Chu
Pong
Mtn

SOUTH
VIETNAM

Tuy Hoa •

Ho Chi Minh Trail

C A M B O D I A

Ban Me
Thuot •

II CTZ

Nha Trang •

Kratie •

Da Lat •

Cam Ranh •

GULF

OF

THAILAND

Mekong
R

An
Loc • • Phuoc Binh

Dong Xoai

Phan Rang •

PHNOM PENH •

War Zone C
Tay Ninh

XXX

Phan Thiet •

Sihanouk Trail

Cu Chi •

Phuoc Vinh •

War Zone D

Sihanoukville •

Moc Hoa •

Bien Hoa • III CTZ

Plain of Reeds

SAIGON ☆ • Binh Gia

XXX

PHU
QUOC

Ap Bac • • My Tho

Vung Tau •

Can Tho •

CAPITAL SPECIAL ZONE

SOUTHEAST ASIA

IV CTZ

☆ Firefight

U Minh
Forest

0   150

S O U T H   C H I N A   S E A

MILES

CON SON

MAP 47

war. Diem returned to Saigon in the summer of 1954 as premier with no political following except his family and a few Americans. His authority was challenged, first by the independent Hoa Hao and Cao Dai religious sects and then by the Binh Xuyen, an organization of gangsters that controlled Saigon's gambling dens and brothels and had strong influence with the police. Rallying an army, Diem defeated the sects and gained their grudging allegiance. Remnants of their forces, however, fled to the jungle to continue their resistance, and some, at a later date, became the nucleus of Communist guerrilla units.

Diem was also challenged by members of his own army, where French influence persisted among the highest ranking officers. But he weathered the threat of an army coup, dispelling American doubts about his ability to survive in the jungle of Vietnamese politics. For the next few years, the United States commitment to defend South Vietnam's independence was synonymous with support for Diem. Americans now provided advice and support to the Army of the Republic of Vietnam (ARVN); at Diem's request, they replaced French advisers throughout his nation's military establishment.

As the American role in South Vietnam was growing, U.S. defense policy was undergoing review. Officials in the Eisenhower administration believed that wars like those in Korea and Vietnam were too costly and ought to be avoided in the future. "Never again" was the rallying cry of those who opposed sending U.S. ground forces to fight a conventional war in Asia. Instead, the Eisenhower administration relied on the threat or use of massive nuclear retaliation to deter or, if necessary, to defeat the armies of the Soviet Union or Communist China. The New Look, as this policy was called, emphasized nuclear air power at the expense of conventional ground forces. If deterrence failed, planners envisioned the next war as a short, violent nuclear conflict of a few days' duration, conducted with forces in being. Ground forces were relegated to a minor role, and mobilization was regarded as an unnecessary luxury. In consequence, the Army's share of the defense budget decreased, the modernization of its forces was delayed, and its strength was reduced by 40 percent—from 1,404,598 in 1954 to 861,964 in 1956.

A strategy dependent on one form of military power, the New Look was sharply criticized by soldiers and academics alike. Unless the United States was willing to risk destruction, critics argued, the threat of massive nuclear retaliation had little credibility. General Ridgway and his successor, General Maxwell D. Taylor, were vocal opponents. Both advocated balanced forces to enable the United States to cope realistically with a variety of military contingencies. The events of the late 1950's appeared to support their demand for flexibility. The United States intervened in Lebanon in 1956 to restore political stability there. Two years later an American military show of force in the Straits of Taiwan helped to dampen tensions between Communist China and the Nationalist Chinese Government on Formosa. Both contingencies underlined the importance of avoiding any fixed concept of war.

Advocates of the flexible response doctrine foresaw a meaningful role for the Army as part of a more credible deterrent and as a means of intervening, when necessary, in limited and small wars. They wished to strengthen both conventional and unconventional forces; to improve strategic and tactical mobility; and to maintain troops and equipment at forward bases, close to likely areas of conflict. They placed a premium on highly responsive command and control, to allow a close meshing of military actions with political goals. The same reformers were deeply interested in the conduct of brush-fire wars, especially among the underdeveloped nations. In the so-called third world, competing cold war ideologies and festering nationalistic, religious, and social conflicts interacted with the disruptive forces of modernization to create the preconditions for open hostilities. Southeast Asia was one of several such areas identified by the Army. Here the United States' central concern was the threat of North Vietnamese and perhaps Chinese aggression against South Vietnam and other non-Communist states.

The United States took the lead in forming a regional defense pact, the Southeast Asia Treaty Organization (SEATO), signaling its commitment to contain Communist encroachment in the region. Meanwhile the 342 American advisers of MAAG, Vietnam (which replaced MAAG, Indochina, in 1955), trained and organized Diem's fledgling army to resist an invasion from the North. Three MAAG chiefs—Lt. Gens. John W. O'Daniel, Samuel T. Williams, and Lionel C. McGarr—reorganized South Vietnam's light mobile infantry groups into infantry divisions, compatible in design and mission with U.S. defense plans. The South Vietnamese Army, with a strength of about 150,000, was equipped with standard Army equipment and given the mission of delaying the advance of any invasion force until the arrival of American reinforcements. The residual influence of the army's earlier French training, however, lingered in both leadership and tactics. The South Vietnamese had little or no practical experience in administration and the higher staff functions, from which the French had excluded them.

The MAAG's training and reorganization work was often interrupted by Diem's use of his army to conduct "pacification" campaigns to root out stay-behind Viet Minh cadre. Hence responsibility for most internal security was transferred to poorly trained and ill-equipped paramilitary forces, the Civil Guard and Self-Defense Corps, which numbered about 75,000. For the most part, the Viet Minh in the South avoided armed action and subscribed to a political action program in anticipation of Vietnam-wide elections in 1956, as stipulated by the Geneva Accords. But Diem, supported by the United States, refused to hold elections, claiming that undemocratic conditions in the North precluded a fair contest. (Some observers thought Ho Chi Minh sufficiently popular in the South to defeat Diem.) Buoyed by his own election as President in 1955 and by the adulation of his American supporters, Diem's political strength rose to its apex. While making some political and economic reforms, he pressed hard his attacks on political opponents and former Viet Minh, many of whom were not Communists at all but patriots who had joined the movement to fight for Vietnamese independence.

By 1957 Diem's harsh measures had so weakened the Viet Minh that Communist leaders in the South feared for the movement's survival there. The southerners urged their colleagues in the North to sanction a new armed struggle in South Vietnam. For self-protection, some Viet Minh had fled to secret bases to hide and form small units. Others joined renegade elements of the former sect armies. From bases in the mangrove swamps of the Mekong Delta, in the Plain of Reeds near the Cambodian border, and in the jungle of War Zones C and D northwest of Saigon, the Communists began to rebuild their armed forces, to re-establish an underground political network, and to carry out propaganda, harassment, and terrorist activities. As reforms faltered and Diem became more dictatorial, the ranks of the rebels swelled with the politically disaffected.

The Rise of the Viet Cong

The insurgents, now called the Viet Cong, had organized several companies and a few battalions by 1959, the majority in the Delta and the provinces around Saigon. As Viet Cong military strength increased, attacks against the paramilitary forces, and occasionally against the South Vietnamese Army, became more frequent. Many were conducted to obtain equipment, arms, and ammunition, but all were hailed by the guerrillas as evidence of the government's inability to protect its citizens. Political agitation and military activity also quickened in the Central Highlands, where Viet Cong agents recruited among the Montagnard tribes. In 1959, after assessing conditions in the South, the leaders in Hanoi agreed to resume the armed struggle, giving it equal weight with political efforts to undermine Diem and reunify Vietnam. To attract the growing number of anti-Communists opposed to Diem, as well as to provide a democratic facade for administering the party's policies in areas controlled by the Viet Cong, Hanoi in December 1960 created the National Liberation Front of South Vietnam.

The revival of guerrilla warfare in the South found the advisory group, the South Vietnamese Army, and Diem's government ill prepared to wage an effective campaign. In their efforts to train and strengthen Diem's army, U.S. advisers had concentrated on meeting the threat of a conventional North Vietnamese invasion. The ARVN's earlier antiguerrilla campaigns, while seemingly successful, had been carried out against a weak and dormant insurgency. The Civil Guard and Self-Defense Corps, which bore the brunt of the Viet Cong's attacks, were not under the MAAG's purview and proved unable to cope with the audacious Viet Cong. Diem's regime, while stressing military activities, neglected political, social, and economic reforms. American officials disagreed over the seriousness of the guerrilla threat, the priority to be accorded political or military measures, and the need for special counterguerrilla training for the South Vietnamese Army. Only a handful of the MAAG's advisers had personal experience in counterinsurgency warfare.

Yet the U.S. Army was not a stranger to such conflict. Americans had fought insurgents in the Philippines at the turn of the century, conducted a guerrilla campaign in Burma during World War II, helped the Greek and Philippine Governments to subdue Communist insurgencies after the war, and studied the French failure in Indochina and the British success in Malaya. The Army did not, however, have a comprehensive doctrine for dealing with insurgency. For the most part, insurgent warfare was equated with the type of guerrilla or partisan struggles carried out during World War II behind enemy lines in support of conventional operations. This viewpoint reduced antiguerrilla warfare to providing security against enemy partisans operating behind friendly lines.

Almost totally lacking was an appreciation of the political and social dimensions of insurgency and its role in the larger framework of revolutionary war. Insurgency meant above all a contest for political legitimacy and power—a struggle between contending political cultures over the organization of society. Most of the Army advisers and Special Forces who were sent to South Vietnam in the early 1960's were poorly prepared to wage such a struggle. A victory for counterinsurgency in South Vietnam would require Diem's government not only to outfight the guerrillas, but to compete successfully with their efforts to organize the population in support of the government's cause.

The Viet Cong thrived on their access to and control of the people, who formed the most important part of their support base. The population provided both economic and manpower resources to sustain and expand the insurgency; the people of the villages served the guerrillas as their first line of resistance against government intrusion into their "liberated zones" and bases. By comparison with their political effort, the strictly military aims of the Viet Cong were secondary. The insurgents hoped not to destroy government forces—although they did so when weaker elements could be isolated and defeated—but by limited actions to extend their influence over the population. By mobilizing the population, the Viet Cong compensated for their numerical and material disadvantages. The rule of thumb that ten soldiers were needed to defeat one guerrilla reflected the insurgents' political support rather than their military superiority. For the Saigon government, the task of isolating the Viet Cong from the population was difficult under any circumstances and impossible to achieve by force alone.

Viet Cong military forces varied from hamlet and village guerrillas, who were farmers by day and fighters by night, to full-time professional soldiers. Organized into squads and platoons, part-time guerrillas had several military functions. They gathered intelligence, passing it on to district or provincial authorities; they proselytized, propagandized, recruited, and provided security for local cadres. They reconnoitered the battlefield, served as porters and guides, created diversions, evacuated wounded, and retrieved weapons. Their very presence and watchfulness in a hamlet or village inhibited the population from aiding the government.

By contrast, the local and main force units consisted of full-time soldiers, most often recruited from the area where the unit operated. Forming companies and battalions, local forces were attached to a village, district, or provincial headquarters. Often they formed the protective shield behind which a Communist Party cadre established its political infrastructure and organized new guerrilla elements at the hamlet and village levels. As the link between guerrilla and main force units, local forces served as a reaction force for the former and as a pool of replacements and reinforcements for the latter. Having limited offensive capability, local forces usually attacked poorly defended, isolated outposts or weaker paramilitary forces, often at night and by ambush. Main force units were organized as battalions, regiments, and—as the insurgency matured—divisions. Subordinate to provincial, regional, and higher commands, such units were the strongest, most mobile, and most offensive-minded of the Viet Cong forces; their mission often was to attack and defeat a specific South Vietnamese unit.

Missions were assigned and approved by a political officer who, in most cases, was superior to the unit's military commander. Party policy, military discipline, and unit cohesion were inculcated and reinforced by three-man party cells in every unit. Among the insurgents, war was always the servant of policy.

As the Viet Cong's control over the population increased, their military forces grew in number and size. Squads and platoons became companies, companies formed battalions, and battalions were organized into regiments. This process of creating and enlarging units continued as long as the Viet Cong had a base of support among the population. After 1959, however, infiltrators from the North also became important. Hanoi activated a special military transportation unit to control overland infiltration along the Ho Chi Minh Trail through Laos and Cambodia. Then a special naval unit was set up to conduct sea infiltration. At first, the infiltrators were southern-born Viet Minh soldiers who had regrouped north after the French Indochina War. Each year until 1964, thousands returned south to join or to form Viet Cong units, usually in the areas where they had originated. Such men served as experienced military or political cadres, as technicians, or as rank-and-file combatants wherever local recruitment was difficult.

When the pool of about 80,000 so-called regroupees ran dry, Hanoi began sending native North Vietnamese soldiers as individual replacements and reinforcements. In 1964 the Communists started to introduce entire North Vietnamese Army (NVA) units into the South. Among the infiltrators were senior cadres, who manned the expanding Viet Cong command system—regional headquarters, interprovincial commands, and the Central Office for South Vietnam (COSVN), the supreme military and political headquarters. As the southern branch of the Vietnamese Communist Party, COSVN was directly subordinate to the Central Committee in Hanoi. Its senior commanders were high-ranking officers of North Vietnam's Army. To equip the growing number of Viet Cong forces in the South, the insurgents continued to rely heavily on arms and supplies captured from South Vietnamese forces. But, increasingly, large numbers of weapons, ammunition, and other equipment arrived from the North, nearly all supplied by the Sino-Soviet bloc.

From a strength of approximately 5,000 at the start of 1959, the Viet Cong's ranks grew to about 100,000 at the end of 1964. The number of infiltrators alone during that period was estimated at 41,000. The growth of the insurgency reflected not only North Vietnam's skill in infiltrating men and weapons, but South Vietnam's inability to control its porous borders, Diem's failure to develop a credible pacification program to reduce Viet Cong influence in the countryside, and the South Vietnamese Army's difficulties in reducing long-standing Viet Cong bases and secret zones. Such areas not only facilitated infiltration, but were staging areas for operations; they contained training camps, hospitals, depots, workshops, and command centers. Many bases were in remote areas seldom visited by the army, such as the U Minh Forest or the Plain of Reeds. But others existed in the heart of populated areas, in the "liberated zones." There Viet Cong forces, dispersed among hamlets and villages, drew support from the local economy. From such centers the Viet Cong expanded their influence into adjacent areas that were nominally under Saigon's control.

A New President Takes Charge

Soon after John F. Kennedy became President in 1961, he sharply increased military and economic aid to South Vietnam to help Diem defeat the growing insurgency. For Kennedy, insurgencies (or "wars of national liberation" in the parlance of Communist leaders) were a challenge to international security every bit as serious as nuclear war. The administration's approach to both extremes of conflict rested on the precepts of the flexible response. Regarded as a form of "sub-limited" or small war, insurgency was treated largely as a military problem—conventional war writ small—and hence susceptible to resolution by timely and appropriate military action. Kennedy's success in applying calculated military pressures to compel the Soviet Union to remove its offensive missiles from Cuba in 1962 reinforced the administration's disposition to deal with other international crises, including the conflict in Vietnam, in a similar manner.

Though an advance over the New Look, his policy also had limitations. Long-term strategic planning tended to be sacrificed to short-term crisis management. Planners were all too apt to assume that all belligerents were rational and that the foe subscribed as they did to the seductive logic of the flexible response. Hoping to give the South Vietnamese a margin for success, Kennedy periodically authorized additional military aid and support between 1961 and November 1963, when he was assassinated. But potential benefits were nullified by the absence of a clear doctrine and a coherent operational strategy for the conduct of counterinsurgency, and by chronic military and political shortcomings on the part of the South Vietnamese.

The U.S. Army played a major role in Kennedy's "beef up" of the American advisory and support efforts in South Vietnam. In turn, that role was made possible in large measure by Kennedy's determination to increase the strength and capabilities of Army forces for both conventional and unconventional operations. Between 1961 and 1964 the Army's strength rose from about 850,000 to nearly a million men, and the number of combat divisions grew from eleven to sixteen. These increases were backed up by an ambitious program to modernize Army equipment and, by stockpiling supplies and equipment at forward bases, to increase the deployability and readiness of Army combat forces. The build-up, however, did not prevent the call-up of 120,000 Reservists to active duty in the summer of 1961, a few months after Kennedy assumed office. Facing renewed Soviet threats to force the Western Powers out of Berlin, Kennedy mobilized the Army to reinforce NATO, if need be. But the mobilization revealed serious shortcomings in Reserve readiness and produced a swell of criticism and complaints from Congress and Reservists alike. Although Kennedy sought to remedy the deficiencies that were exposed and set in motion plans to reorganize the Reserves, the unhappy experience of the Berlin Crisis was fresh in the minds of national leaders when they faced the prospect of war in Vietnam a few years later.

Facing trouble spots in Latin America, Africa, and Southeast Asia, Kennedy took a keen interest in the U.S. Army's Special Forces, believing that their skills in unconventional warfare were well suited to countering insurgency. During his first year in office, he increased the strength of the Special Forces from about 1,500 to 9,000 and authorized them to wear a distinctive green beret. In the same year he greatly enlarged their role in South Vietnam. First under the auspices of the Central Intelligence Agency and then under a military commander, the Special Forces organized the highland tribes into the Civilian Irregular Defense Group (CIDG) and in time sought to recruit other ethnic groups and sects in the South as well. To this scheme, underwritten almost entirely by the United States, Diem gave only tepid support. Indeed, the civilian irregulars drew strength from groups traditionally hostile to Saigon. Treated with disdain by the lowland Vietnamese, the Montagnards developed close, trusting relations with their Army advisers. Special Forces detachment commanders frequently were the real leaders of CIDG units. This strong mutual bond of loyalty between adviser and highlander benefited operations, but some tribal leaders sought to exploit the special relationship to advance Montagnard political autonomy. On occasion, Special Forces advisers found themselves in the awkward position of mediating between militant Montagnards and South Vietnamese officials who were suspicious and wary of the Americans' sympathy for the highlanders.

Through a village self-defense and development program, the Special Forces aimed initially to create a military and political buffer to the growing Viet Cong influence in the Central Highlands. Within a few years, approximately 60,000 highlanders had enlisted in the CIDG program. As their participation increased, so too did the range of Special Forces activities. In addition to village defense programs, the Green Berets sponsored offensive guerrilla activities and border surveillance and control measures. To detect and impede the Viet Cong, camps were established astride infiltration corridors and near enemy base areas, especially along the Cambodian and Laotian borders. But the camps themselves were vulnerable to enemy attack and, despite their presence, infiltration continued. At times, border control diverted tribal units from village defense, the original heart of the CIDG program.

By 1965, as the military situation in the highlands worsened, many CIDG units had changed their character and begun to engage in quasi-conventional military operations. In some instances, irregulars under the leadership of Army Special Forces stood up to crack enemy regiments, offering much of the military resistance to enemy efforts to dominate the highlands. Yet the Special Forces—despite their efforts in South Vietnam and in Laos, where their teams helped to train and advise anti-Communist Laotian forces in the early 1960's—did not provide an antidote to the virulent insurgency in Vietnam. Long-standing animosities between Montagnard and Vietnamese prevented close, continuing co-operation between the South Vietnamese Army and the irregulars. Long on promises but short on action to improve the lot of the Montagnards, successive South Vietnamese regimes failed to win the loyalty of the tribesmen. And the Special Forces usually operated in areas that were remote from the main.Viet Cong threat to the heavily populated and economically important Delta and coastal regions of the country.

Besides the Special Forces, the Army's most important contribution to the fight was the helicopter. Neither Kennedy nor the Army anticipated the rapid growth of aviation in South Vietnam when the first helicopter transportation company arrived in December 1961. Within three years, however, each of South Vietnam's divisions and corps was supported by Army helicopters, with the faster, more reliable and versatile UH–1 (Huey) replacing the older CH–21. In addition to transporting men and supplies, helicopters were used to reconnoiter, to evacuate wounded, and to provide command and control. The Vietnam conflict became the crucible in which Army airmobile and air assault tactics evolved. As armament was added—first machine gun–wielding door-gunners, and later rockets and mini-guns—armed helicopters began to protect troop carriers against antiaircraft fire, to suppress enemy fire around landing zones during air assaults, and to deliver fire support to troops on the ground.

Army fixed-wing aircraft also flourished. Equipped with a variety of detection devices, the OV–1 Mohawk conducted day and night surveillance of Viet Cong bases and trails. The Caribou, with its sturdy frame and ability to land and take off on short, unimproved airfields, proved ideal to supply remote camps.

Army aviation revived old disagreements with the Air Force over the roles and missions of the two services and the adequacy of Air Force close air

ARMY CH–21 HELICOPTER TRANSPORTS TROOPS *to enter battle near Saigon.*

support. The expansion of the Army's own "air force" nevertheless continued, abetted by the Kennedy administration's interest in extending airmobility to all types of land warfare, from counterinsurgency to the nuclear
battlefield. Secretary of Defense Robert S. McNamara himself encouraged
the Army to test an experimental air assault division. During 1963 and 1964
the Army demonstrated that helicopters could successfully replace ground
vehicles for mobility and provide fire support in lieu of ground artillery. The
result was the creation in 1965 of the 1st Cavalry Division (Airmobile)—the
first such unit in the Army. In South Vietnam the helicopter's effect on
organization and operations was as sweeping as the influence of mechanized
forces in World War II. Many of the operational concepts of airmobility,
rooted in cavalry doctrine and operations, were pioneered by helicopter units
between 1961 and 1964, and later adopted by the new airmobile division and
by all Army combat units that fought in South Vietnam.

In addition to Army Special Forces and helicopters, Kennedy greatly
expanded the entire American advisory effort. Advisers were placed at the
sector (provincial) level and were permanently assigned to infantry battalions
and certain lower echelon combat units; additional intelligence advisers were

U.S. ADVISER PLANS OPERATIONS WITH SOUTH VIETNAMESE TROOPS

sent to South Vietnam. Wide use was made of temporary training teams in psychological warfare, civic action, engineering, and a variety of logistical functions. With the expansion of the advisory and support efforts came demands for better communications, intelligence, and medical, logistical, and administrative support, all of which the Army provided from its active forces, drawing upon skilled men and units from U.S.-based forces. The result was a slow, steady erosion of its capacity to meet worldwide contingency obligations. But if Vietnam depleted the Army, it also provided certain advantages. The war was a laboratory in which to test and evaluate new equipment and techniques applicable to counterinsurgency—among others, the use of chemical defoliants and herbicides, both to remove the jungle canopy that gave cover to the guerrillas and to destroy his crops. As the activities of all the services expanded, U.S. military strength in South Vietnam increased from under 700 at the start of 1960 to almost 24,000 by the end of 1964. Of these, 15,000 were Army and a little over 2,000 were Army advisers.

Changes in American command arrangements attested to the growing commitment. In February 1962 the Joint Chiefs of Staff established the United States Military Assistance Command, Vietnam (USMACV), in Saigon as the senior American military headquarters in South Vietnam, and appointed General Paul D. Harkins as commander (COMUSMACV). Harkins reported to the Commander in Chief, Pacific (CINCPAC), in Hawaii, but because of high-level interest in South Vietnam, enjoyed special access to military and civilian leaders in Washington as well. Soon MACV moved into the advisory effort hitherto directed by the Military Assistance Advisory Group. To simplify the advisory chain of command, the latter was disestablished in May 1964, and MACV took direct control. As the senior Army commander in South Vietnam, the MACV commander also commanded Army support units; for day-to-day operations, however, control of such units was vested in the corps and division senior advisers. For administrative and logistical support Army units looked to the U.S. Army Support Group, Vietnam (later the U.S. Army Support Command), which was established in mid-1962.

Though command arrangements worked tolerably well, complaints were heard in and out of the Army. Some officials pressed for a separate Army component commander, who would be responsible both for operations and for logistical support—an arrangement enjoyed by other services in South Vietnam. Airmen tended to believe that an Army command already existed, disguised as MACV. They believed that General Harkins, though a joint commander, favored the Army in the bitter interservice rivalry over the roles and missions of aviation in South Vietnam. Some critics thought his span of control excessive, for Harkins' responsibility extended to Thailand, where Army combat units had deployed in 1962, aiming to overawe Communist forces in neighboring Laos. The Army undertook several logistical projects in Thailand, and Army engineers, signalmen, and other support forces remained there after combat forces withdrew in the fall of 1962.

While the Americans strengthened their position in South Vietnam and Thailand, the Communists tightened their grip in Laos. In 1962 agreements on that small, land-locked nation were signed in Geneva requiring all foreign military forces to leave Laos. American advisers, including hundreds of Special Forces, departed. But the agreements were not honored by North Vietnam. Its army, together with Laotian Communist forces, consolidated their hold on areas adjacent to both North and South Vietnam through which passed the network of jungle roads called the Ho Chi Minh Trail. As a result, it became easier to move supplies south to support the Viet Cong in the face of the new dangers embodied in U.S. advisers, weapons, and tactics.

Counterinsurgency Falters

At first the enhanced mobility and firepower afforded the South Vietnamese Army by helicopters, armored personnel carriers, and close air support surprised and overwhelmed the Viet Cong. Saigon's forces reacted more quickly to insurgent attacks and penetrated many Viet Cong areas. Even more threatening to the insurgents was Diem's strategic hamlet program, launched in late 1961. Diem and his brother Ngo Dinh Nhu, an ardent sponsor of the program, hoped to create thousands of new, fortified villages, often by moving peasants from their existing homes. Hamlet construction and defense were the responsibility of the new residents, with paramilitary and ARVN forces providing initial security while the peasants were recruited and organized. As security improved, Diem and Nhu hoped to enact social, economic, and political reforms which, when fully carried out, would constitute Saigon's revolutionary response to Viet Cong promises of social and economic betterment. If successful, the program might destroy the insurgency by separating and protecting the rural population from the Viet Cong, threatening the rebellion's base of support.

By early 1963, however, the Viet Cong had learned to cope with the army's new weapons and more aggressive tactics and had begun a campaign to eliminate the strategic hamlets. The insurgents became adept at countering helicopters and slow-flying aircraft and learned the vulnerabilities of armored personnel carriers. In addition, their excellent intelligence, combined with the predictability of ARVN's tactics and pattern of operations, enabled the Viet Cong to evade or ambush government forces. The new weapons the United States had provided the South Vietnamese did not compensate for the stifling influence of poor leadership, dubious tactics, and inexperience. The much publicized defeat of government forces at the Delta village of Ap Bac in January 1963 demonstrated both the Viet Cong's skill in countering ARVN's new capabilities and the latter's inherent weaknesses. Faulty intelligence, poorly planned and executed fire support, and overcautious leadership contributed to the outcome. But Ap Bac's significance transcended a single battle. The defeat was a portent of things to come. Now able to challenge ARVN units of equal strength in quasi-conventional battles, the Viet Cong were moving into a more intense stage of revolutionary war.

As the Viet Cong became stronger and bolder, the South Vietnamese Army became more cautious and less offensive-minded. Government forces became reluctant to respond to Viet Cong depredations in the countryside, avoided night operations, and resorted to ponderous sweeps against vague military objectives, rarely making contact with their enemies. Meanwhile, the Viet Cong concentrated on destroying strategic hamlets, showing that they considered the settlements, rather than ARVN forces, the greater danger to the insurgency. Poorly defended hamlets and outposts were overrun or subverted by enemy agents who infiltrated with peasants arriving from the countryside.

The Viet Cong's campaign was aided by Saigon's failures. The government built too many hamlets to defend. Hamlet militia varied from those who were poorly trained and armed to those who were not trained or armed at all. Fearing that weapons given to the militia would fall to the Viet Cong, local officials often withheld arms. Forced relocation, use of forced peasant labor to construct hamlets, and tardy payment of compensation for relocation were but a few reasons why peasants turned against the program. Few meaningful reforms took place. Accurate information on the program's true condition and on the decline in rural security was hidden from Diem by officials eager to please him with reports of progress. False statistics and reports misled U.S. officials, too, about the progress of the counterinsurgency effort.

If the decline in rural security was not always apparent to Americans, the lack of enlightened political leadership on the part of Diem was all too obvious. Diem habitually interfered in military matters—bypassing the chain of command to order operations, forbidding commanders to take casualties, and appointing military leaders on the basis of political loyalty rather than competence. Many military and civilian appointees, especially province and district chiefs, were dishonest and put career and fortune above the national interest. When Buddhist opposition to certain policies erupted into violent antigovernment demonstrations in 1963, Diem's uncompromising stance and use of military force to suppress the demonstrators caused some generals to decide that the President was a liability in the fight against the Viet Cong. On 1 November, with American encouragement, a group of reform-minded generals ousted Diem, who was murdered along with his brother.

Political turmoil followed the coup. Emboldened, the insurgents stepped up operations and increased their control over many rural areas. North Vietnam's leaders decided to intensify the armed struggle, aiming to demoralize the South Vietnamese Army and further undermine political authority in the South. As Viet Cong military activity quickened, regular North Vietnamese Army units began to train for possible intervention in the war. Men and equipment continued to flow down the Ho Chi Minh Trail, with North Vietnamese conscripts replacing the dwindling pool of southerners who had belonged to the Viet Minh.

Setting the Stage for Confrontation

The critical state of rural security that came to light after Diem's death again prompted the United States to expand its military aid to Saigon. General Harkins and his successor General William C. Westmoreland urgently strove to revitalize pacification and counterinsurgency. Army advisers helped their Vietnamese counterparts to revise national and provincial pacification plans. They retained the concept of fortified hamlets as the heart of a new national counterinsurgency program, but corrected the old abuses, at least in theory. To help implement the program, Army advisers were assigned to the subsector (district) level for the first time, becoming more intimately involved in local pacification efforts and in paramilitary operations. Additional advisers were assigned to units and training centers, especially those of the Regional and Popular Forces (formerly called the Civil Guard and Self-Defense Corps). All Army activities, from aviation support to Special Forces, were strengthened in a concerted effort to undo the effects of years of Diem's mismanagement.

At the same time, American officials in Washington, Hawaii, and Saigon began to explore ways to increase military pressure against North Vietnam. In 1964 the South Vietnamese launched covert raids under MACV's auspices. Some military leaders, however, believed that only direct air strikes against North Vietnam would induce a change in Hanoi's policies by demonstrating American determination to defend South Vietnam's independence. Air strike plans ranged from immediate massive bombardment of military and industrial targets to gradually intensifying attacks spanning several months.

The interest in using air power reflected lingering sentiment in the United States against involving American ground forces once again in a land war on the Asian continent. Many of President Lyndon B. Johnson's advisers—among them General Maxwell D. Taylor, who was appointed Ambassador to Saigon in mid-1964—believed that a carefully calibrated air campaign would be the most effective means of exerting pressure against the North and, at the same time, the method least likely to provoke intervention by China. Taylor thought conventional Army ground forces ill suited to engage in day-to-day counterinsurgency operations against the Viet Cong in hamlets and villages. Ground forces might, however, be used to protect vital air bases in the South and to repel any North Vietnamese attack across the demilitarized zone, which separated North from South Vietnam. Together, a more vigorous counterinsurgency effort in the South and military pressure against the North might buy time for Saigon to put its political house in order, boost flagging military and civilian morale, and strengthen its military position in the event of a negotiated peace. Taylor and Westmoreland, the senior U.S. officials in South Vietnam, agreed that Hanoi was unlikely to change its course unless convinced that it could not succeed in the South. Both recognized that air strikes were neither a panacea nor a substitute for military efforts in the South.

As each side undertook more provocative military actions, the likelihood of a direct military confrontation between North Vietnam and the United States increased. The crisis came in early August 1964 in the international waters of the Gulf of Tonkin. North Vietnamese patrol boats attacked U.S. naval vessels engaged in surveillance of North Vietnam's coastal defenses. The Americans promptly launched retaliatory air strikes. At the request of President Johnson, Congress overwhelmingly passed the Southeast Asia Resolution—the so-called Gulf of Tonkin Resolution—authorizing all actions necessary to protect American forces and to provide for the defense of the nation's allies in Southeast Asia. Considered by some in the administration as the equivalent of a declaration of war, this broad grant of authority encouraged Johnson to expand American military efforts within South Vietnam, against North Vietnam, and in Southeast Asia at large.

By late 1964, both sides were poised to increase their stake in the war. Regular NVA units had begun moving south and stood at the Laotian frontier, on the threshold of crossing into South Vietnam's Central Highlands. U.S. air and naval forces stood ready to renew their attacks. On 7 February 1965, Communist forces attacked an American compound in Pleiku in the Central Highlands and a few days later bombed American quarters in Qui Nhon. The United States promptly bombed military targets in the North. A few weeks later, President Johnson approved ROLLING THUNDER, a campaign of sustained, direct air strikes of progressively increasing strength against military and industrial targets in North Vietnam. Signs of intensifying conflict appeared in South Vietnam as well. Strengthening their forces at all echelons, from village guerrillas to main force regiments, the Viet Cong quickened military activity in late 1964 and in the first half of 1965. At Binh Gia, a village forty miles east of Saigon in Phuoc Tuy Province, a multiregimental Viet Cong force—possibly the *1st Viet Cong Infantry Division*—fought and defeated several South Vietnamese battalions.

Throughout the spring the Viet Cong sought to disrupt pacification and oust the government from many rural areas. The insurgents made deep inroads in the central coastal provinces and withstood government efforts to reduce their influence in the Delta and in the critical provinces around Saigon. Committed to static defense of key towns and bases, government forces were unable or unwilling to respond to attacks against rural communities. In late spring and early summer, strong Communist forces sought a major military victory over the South Vietnamese Army by attacking border posts and highland camps. The enemy also hoped to draw government forces from populated areas, to weaken pacification further. By whipsawing war-weary ARVN forces between coast and highland and by inflicting a series of damaging defeats against regular units, the enemy hoped to undermine military morale and popular confidence in the Saigon government. And by accelerating the dissolution of government military forces, already racked by high desertions and casualties, the Communists hoped to compel the South Vietnamese to abandon the battlefield and seek an all-Vietnamese political settlement that would compel the United States to leave South Vietnam.

By the summer of 1965, the Viet Cong, strengthened by several recently infiltrated NVA regiments, had gained the upper hand over government forces in some areas of South Vietnam. With U.S. close air support and the aid of Army helicopter gunships, Saigon's forces repelled many enemy attacks, but suffered heavy casualties. Elsewhere highland camps and border outposts had to be abandoned. ARVN's cumulative losses from battle deaths and desertions amounted to nearly a battalion a week. Saigon was hard pressed to find men to replenish these heavy losses and completely unable to match the growth of Communist forces from local recruitment and infiltration. Some American officials doubted whether the South Vietnamese could hold out until ROLLING THUNDER created pressures sufficiently strong to convince North Vietnam's leaders to reduce the level of combat in the South. General Westmoreland and others believed that U.S. ground forces were needed to stave off an irrevocable shift of the military and political balance in favor of the enemy.

For a variety of diplomatic, political, and military reasons, President Johnson approached with great caution any commitment of large ground combat forces to South Vietnam. Yet preparations had been under way for some time. In early March 1965, a few days after ROLLING THUNDER began, American marines went ashore in South Vietnam to protect the large airfield at Da Nang—a defensive security mission. Even as they landed, General Harold K. Johnson, Chief of Staff of the Army, was in South Vietnam to assess the situation. Upon returning to Washington, he recommended a substantial increase in American military assistance, including several combat divisions. He wanted U.S. forces either to interdict the Laotian panhandle to stop infiltration or to counter a growing enemy threat in the central and northern provinces.

But President Johnson sanctioned only the dispatch of additional marines to increase security at Da Nang and to secure other coastal enclaves. He also authorized the Army to begin deploying nearly 20,000 logistical troops, the main body of the 1st Logistical Command, to Southeast Asia. (Westmoreland had requested such a command in late 1964.) At the same time, the President modified the marines'mission to allow them to conduct offensive operations close to their bases. A few weeks later, to protect American bases in the vicinity of Saigon, Johnson approved sending the first Army combat unit, the 173d Airborne Brigade (Separate), to South Vietnam. Arriving from Okinawa in early May, the brigade moved quickly to secure the air base at Bien Hoa, just northeast of Saigon. With its arrival, U.S. military strength in South Vietnam passed 50,000. Despite added numbers and expanded missions, American ground forces had yet to engage the enemy in full-scale combat.

Indeed, the question of how best to use large numbers of American ground forces was still unresolved on the eve of their deployment. Focusing on population security and pacification, some planners saw U.S. combat forces concentrating their efforts in coastal enclaves and around key urban centers and bases. Under this plan, such forces would provide a security shield behind which the Vietnamese could expand the pacification zone; when required, American combat units would venture beyond their enclaves as mobile reaction forces.

This concept, largely defensive in nature, reflected the pattern established by the first Army combat units to enter South Vietnam. But the mobility and offensive firepower of U.S. ground units suggested their use in remote, sparsely populated regions to seek out and engage main force enemy units as they infiltrated into South Vietnam or emerged from their secret bases. While secure coastal logistical enclaves and base camps still would be required, the weight of the military effort would be focused on the destruction of enemy military units. Yet even in this alternative, American units would serve indirectly as a shield for pacification activities in the more heavily populated lowlands and Delta. A third proposal had particular appeal to General Johnson. He wished to employ U.S. and allied ground forces across the Laotian panhandle to interdict enemy infiltration into South Vietnam. Here was a more direct and effective way to stop infiltration than the use of air power. Encumbered by military and political problems, the idea was revived periodically but always rejected. The pattern of deployment that actually developed in South Vietnam was a compromise between the first two concepts.

For any type of operations, secure logistical enclaves at deep-water ports (Cam Ranh Bay, Nha Trang, Qui Nhon, for example) were a military necessity. In such areas combat units arrived and bases developed for regional logistical complexes to support the troops. As the administration neared a decision on combat deployment, the Army began to identify and ready units for movement overseas and to prepare mobilization plans for Selected Reserve forces. The dispatch of Army units to the Dominican Republic in May 1965 to forestall a leftist take-over caused only minor adjustments to the build-up plans. The episode nevertheless showed how unexpected demands elsewhere in the world could deplete the strategic reserve, and it underscored the importance of mobilization if the Army was to meet worldwide contingencies and supply trained combat units to Westmoreland as well.

The prospect of deploying American ground forces also revived discussions of allied command arrangements. For a time, Westmoreland considered placing South Vietnamese and American forces under a single commander, an arrangement similar to that of U.S. and South Korean forces during the Korean War. In the face of South Vietnamese opposition, however, the idea was dropped. Arrangements with other allies were varied. Americans in South Vietnam were joined by combat units from Australia, New Zealand, South Korea, Thailand, and by noncombat elements from several other nations. Westmoreland entered into separate agreements with each commander in turn; the compacts ensured close co-operation with MACV, but fell short of giving Westmoreland command over the allied forces.

While diversity marked these arrangements, Westmoreland strove for unity within the American build-up. As forces began to deploy to South Vietnam, the Army again sought to elevate the U.S. Army, Vietnam (USARV), to a full-fledged Army component command with responsibility for combat operations. But Westmoreland successfully warded off the challenge to his dual role as unified commander of MACV and Army commander. For the remainder of the war, USARV performed solely in a logistical and administrative capacity; unlike MACV's air and naval component commands, the Army component did not exercise operational control over combat forces, special forces, or field advisers. However, through its logistical, engineer, signal, medical, military police, and aviation commands, all established in the course of the build-up, USARV commanded and managed a support base of unprecedented size and scope.

Despite this victory, unity of command over the ground war in South Vietnam eluded Westmoreland, as did over-all control of U.S. military operations in support of the war. Most air and naval operations outside of South Vietnam, including ROLLING THUNDER, were carried out by the Commander in Chief, Pacific, and his air and naval commanders from his headquarters thousands of miles away in Hawaii. This patchwork of command arrangements contributed to the lack of a unified strategy, the fragmentation of operations, and the pursuit of parochial service interests to the detriment of the war effort. No single American commander had complete authority or responsibility to fashion an over-all strategy or to co-ordinate all military aspects of the war in Southeast Asia. Furthermore, Westmoreland labored under a variety of political and operational constraints on the use of the combat forces he did command. Like the Korean War, the struggle in South Vietnam was complicated by enemy sanctuaries and by geographical and political restrictions on allied operations. Ground forces were barred from operating across South Vietnam's borders into Cambodia, Laos, or North Vietnam, although the border areas of those countries were vital to the enemy's war effort. These factors narrowed Westmoreland's freedom of action and detracted from his efforts to make effective use of American military power.

Groundwork for Combat: Build-up and Strategy

On 28 July 1965, President Johnson announced plans to deploy additional combat units and to increase American military strength in South Vietnam to 175,000 by year's end. The Army already was preparing hundreds of units for duty in Southeast Asia, among them the newly activated 1st Cavalry Division (Airmobile). Other combat units—the 1st Brigade, 101st Airborne Division, and all three brigades of the 1st Infantry Division—were either ready to go or already on their way to Vietnam. Together with hundreds of support and logistical units, these combat units constituted the first phase of the build-up during the summer and fall of 1965.

At the same time, President Johnson decided not to mobilize any Reserve units. The President's decision profoundly affected the manner in which the Army supported and sustained the build-up. To meet the call for additional combat forces and to obtain manpower to enlarge its training base and to maintain a pool for rotation and replacement of soldiers in South Vietnam, the Army had to increase its active strength, over the next three years, by nearly 1.5 million men. Necessarily, it relied on larger draft calls and voluntary enlistments, supplementing them with heavy draw downs of experienced soldiers from units in Europe and South Korea and extensions of some tours of duty to retain specialists, technicians, and cadres who could train recruits or round out deploying units. Combat units assigned to the strategic reserve were used to meet a large portion of MACV's force requirements, and Reservists were not available to replace them. Mobilization could have eased the additional burden of providing noncommissioned officers (NCO's) and officers to man the Army's growing training bases. As matters stood, requirements for experienced cadres competed with the demands for seasoned leaders in units deploying to South Vietnam.

The personnel turbulence caused by competing demands for the Army's limited manpower was intensified by a one-year tour of duty in South Vietnam. A large number of men was needed to sustain the rotational base, often necessitating the quick return to Vietnam of men with critical skills. The heightened demand for leaders led to accelerated training programs and the lowering of standards for NCO's and junior officers. Moreover, the one-year tour deprived units in South Vietnam of experienced leadership. In time, the infusion of less-seasoned NCO's and officers contributed to a host of morale problems that afflicted some Army units. At a deeper level, the administration's decision against calling the Reserves to active duty sent the wrong signal to friends and enemies alike, implying that the nation lacked the resolution to support an effort of the magnitude needed to achieve American objectives in South Vietnam.

Hence the Army began to organize additional combat units. Three light infantry brigades were activated, and the 9th Infantry Division was reactivated. In the meantime the 4th and 25th Infantry Divisions were alerted for deployment to South Vietnam. With the exception of a brigade of the 25th, all of the combat units activated and alerted during the second half of 1965 deployed to South Vietnam during 1966 and 1967. By the end of 1965, U.S. military strength in South Vietnam had reached 184,000; a year later it stood at 385,000; and by the end of 1967 it approached 490,000. Army personnel accounted for nearly two-thirds of the total. Of the Army's eighteen divisions, at the end of 1967, seven were serving in South Vietnam.

Facing a deteriorating military situation, Westmoreland in the summer of 1965 planned to use his combat units to blunt the enemy's spring-summer offensive. As they arrived in the country, Westmoreland moved them into a defensive arc around Saigon and secured bases for the arrival of subsequent units. His initial aim was defensive—to stop losing the war and to build a structure that could support a later transition to an offensive campaign. As additional troops poured in, Westmoreland planned to seek out and defeat major enemy forces. Throughout both phases, the South Vietnamese, relieved of major combat tasks, were to refurbish their forces and conduct an aggressive pacification program behind the American shield. In a third and final stage, as enemy main force units were driven into their secret zones and bases, Westmoreland hoped to achieve victory by destroying those sanctuaries and shifting the weight of the military effort to pacification, thereby at last subduing the Viet Cong throughout rural South Vietnam.

The fulfillment of this concept rested not only on the success of American efforts to find and defeat enemy forces, but on the success of Saigon's pacification program. In June 1965 the last in a series of coups that followed Diem's overthrow brought in a military junta headed by Lt. Gen. Nguyen Van Thieu as Chief of State and Air Vice Marshal Nguyen Cao Ky as Prime Minister. The new government provided the political stability requisite for successful pacification. Success hinged also on the ability of the U.S. air campaign against the North to reduce the infiltration of men and material, dampening the intensity of combat in the South and inducing Communist leaders in Hanoi to alter their long-term strategic goals. Should any strand of this threefold strategy—the campaign against Communist forces in the South, Saigon's pacification program, and the air war in the North—falter, Westmoreland's prospects would become poorer. Yet he was directly responsible for only one element, the U.S. military effort in the South. To a lesser degree, through American advice and assistance to the South Vietnamese forces, he also influenced Saigon's efforts to suppress the Viet Cong and to carry out pacification.

Army Operations in III and IV Corps, 1965–1967

Centered on the defense of Saigon, Westmoreland's concept of operations in the III Corps area had a clarity of design and purpose that was not always apparent elsewhere in South Vietnam. (*Map 48*) Nearly two years would pass before U.S. forces could maintain a security belt around the capital and at the same time attack the enemy's bases. But Westmoreland's ultimate aims and the difficulties he would encounter were both foreshadowed by the initial combat operations in the summer and fall of 1965.

Joined by newly arrived Australian infantrymen, the 173d Airborne Brigade during June began operations in War Zone D, a longtime enemy base north of Saigon. Though diverted several times to other tasks, the brigade gained experience in conducting heliborne assaults and accustomed itself to the rigors of jungle operations. It also established a pattern of operations that was to grow all too familiar. Airmobile assaults, often in the wake of B–52 air strikes, were followed by extensive patrolling, episodic contact with the Viet Cong, and withdrawal after a few days' stay in the enemy's territory. In early November the airborne soldiers uncovered evidence of the enemy's recent and hasty departure—abandoned camps, recently vacated tunnels, and caches of food and supplies. However, the Viet Cong, by observing the brigade, began to formulate plans for dealing with the Americans.

On 8 November, moving deeper into War Zone D, the brigade encountered the first significant resistance. A multibattalion Viet Cong force attacked at close quarters and forced the Americans into a tight defensive perimeter. Hand-to-hand combat ensued as the enemy tried to "hug" Ameri-

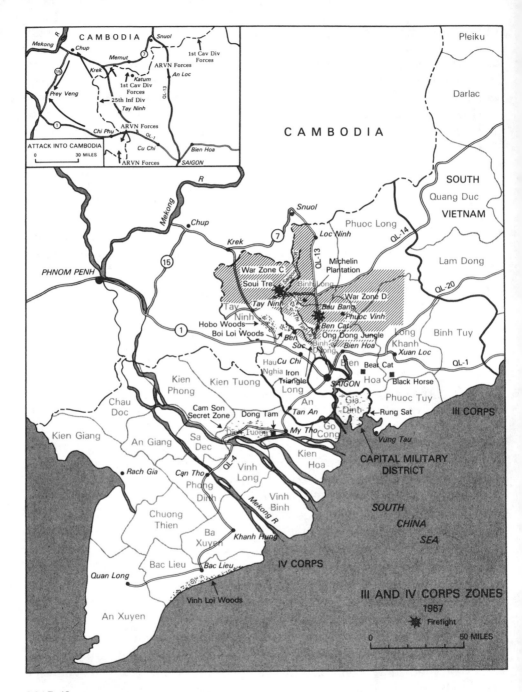

Inset map (top left):

CAMBODIA

Mekong
R
Chup
Snuol
Memut
7
1st Cav Div
Forces
Krek
ARVN Forces
An Loc
15
Katum
1st Cav Div
Forces
Prey Veng
25th Inf Div
Tay Ninh
QL-13
1
Chi Phu
ARVN Forces
QL-1
Cu Chi
Bien Hoa
SAIGON
ARVN Forces

ATTACK INTO CAMBODIA

0   30 MILES

Main map labels:

Pleiku

CAMBODIA

SOUTH

Quang Duc

VIETNAM

Darlac

Mekong
R
Chup
Snuol
Phuoc Long
Loc Ninh
QL-14
7
Krek
QL-13
15
Michelin
Plantation
Lam Dong
PHNOM PENH
War Zone C
Soui Tre
Binh Long
War Zone D
QL-20
Tay
Ninh
Tay Ninh
Bau Bang
Phuoc Vinh
Hobo Woods
Ben Cat
Boi Loi Woods
Ong Dong Jungle
Long
Khanh
Binh Tuy
Ben
Suc
Binh
Duong
Bien Hoa
Xuan Loc
Hau
Cu Chi
Bien
Hoa
Bear Cat
QL-1
Nghia
Iron
Triangle
SAIGON
Black Horse
Long
An
Gia
Dinh
Phuoc Tuy
Kien
Phong
Kien Tuong
Tan An
Rung Sat
III CORPS
Chau
Doc
Cam Son
Secret Zone
Dong Tam
An An
My Tho
Go
Cong
Vung Tau
Kien Giang
An Giang
Sa
Dec
Dinh Tuong
CAPITAL MILITARY
DISTRICT
Kien
Hoa
Rach Gia
Can Tho
QL-4
Vinh
Long
SOUTH
Phong
Dinh
Vinh
Binh
Mekong R
CHINA
Chuong
Thien
Ba
Xuyen
Khanh Hung
SEA
Bac Lieu
Bac Lieu
IV CORPS
Quan Long
Vinh Loi Woods

III AND IV CORPS ZONES
1967
✴ Firefight

0   50 MILES

An Xuyen

MAP 48

can soldiers to prevent the delivery of supporting air and artillery fire. Unable to prepare a landing zone to receive reinforcements or to evacuate casualties, the beleaguered Americans withstood repeated enemy assaults. At nightfall the Viet Cong ceased their attack and withdrew under cover of darkness. Next morning, when reinforcements arrived, the brigade pursued the enemy, finding evidence that he had suffered heavy casualties. Such operations inflicted losses but failed either to destroy the enemy's base or to prevent him from returning to it later on.

Like the airborne brigade, the 1st Infantry Division initially divided its efforts. In addition to securing its base camps north of Saigon, the division helped South Vietnamese forces clear an area west of the capital in the vicinity of Cu Chi in Hau Nghia Province. Reacting to reports of enemy troop concentrations, units of the division launched a series of operations in the fall of 1965 and early 1966 that entailed quick forays into the Ho Bo and Boi Loi woods, the Michelin Rubber Plantation, the Rung Sat swamp, and War Zones C and D. In Operation MASTIFF, for example, the division sought to disrupt Viet Cong infiltration routes between War Zones C and D that crossed the Boi Loi woods in Tay Ninh Province, an area that had not been penetrated by government forces for several years.

But defense of Saigon was the first duty of the "Big Red One" as well as of the 25th Infantry Division, which arrived in the spring of 1966. The 1st Division took up a position protecting the northern approaches, blocking Route 13 from the Cambodian border. The 25th guarded the western approaches, chiefly Route 1 and the Saigon River. The two brigades of the 25th Division served also as a buffer between Saigon and the enemy's base areas in Tay Ninh Province. Westmoreland hoped, however, that the 25th Division would loosen the insurgents' tenacious hold on Hau Nghia Province as well. Here American soldiers found to their amazement that the division's camp at Cu Chi had been constructed atop an extensive Viet Cong tunnel complex. Extending over an area of several miles, this subterranean network, one of several in the region, contained hospitals, command centers, and storage sites. The complex, though partially destroyed by Army "tunnel rats," was never completely eliminated and lasted for the duration of the war. The 25th Division worked closely with South Vietnamese Army and paramilitary forces throughout 1966 and 1967 to foster pacification in Hau Nghia and to secure its own base. But suppressing insurgency in Hau Nghia proved as difficult as eradicating the tunnels at Cu Chi.

As the number of Army combat units in Vietnam grew larger, Westmoreland established two corps-size commands, I Field Force in the II Corps area and II Field Force in the III Corps area. Reporting directly to the

MACV commander, the field force commander was the senior Army tactical commander in his area and the senior U.S. adviser to ARVN forces there. Working closely with his South Vietnamese counterpart, he co-ordinated ARVN and American operations by establishing territorial priorities for combat and pacification efforts. Through his deputy senior adviser, a position established in 1967, the field force commander was able to keep abreast both of the activities of U.S. sector (province) and subsector (district) advisers and of the progress of Saigon's pacification efforts. A similar arrangement was set up in I Corps, where the commander of the III Marine Amphibious Force was the equivalent of a field force commander. Only in IV Corps, in the Mekong Delta where few American combat units served, did Westmoreland choose not to establish a corps-size command. There the senior U.S. adviser served as COMUSMACV's representative; he commanded Army advisory and support units, but no combat units.

Although Army commanders in III Corps were eager to seek out and engage enemy main force units in their strongholds along the Cambodian border, operations at first were devoted to base and area security and to clearing and rehabilitating roads. The 1st Infantry Division's first major encounter with the Viet Cong occurred in November as division elements carried out a routine road security operation along Route 13, in the vicinity of the village of Bau Bang. Trapping convoys along Route 13 had long been a profitable Viet Cong tactic. Ambushed by a large, well-entrenched enemy force, division troops reacted aggressively and mounted a successful counter-attack. But the road was by no means secured; close to enemy bases, the Cambodian border, and Saigon, Route 13 would be the site of several major battles in years to come.

Roads were a major concern of U.S. commanders. In some operations, infantrymen provided security as Army engineers improved neglected routes. Defoliants and the Rome plow—a bulldozer modified with sharp front blades—removed from the sides of important highways the jungle growth that provided cover for Viet Cong ambushes. Road-clearing operations also contributed to pacification by providing peasants with secure access to local markets. In III Corps, with its important road network radiating from Saigon, ground mobility was as essential as airmobility for the conduct of military operations. Lacking as many helicopters as the airmobile division, the 1st and 25th Infantry Divisions, like all Army units in South Vietnam, strained the resources of their own aviation support units and of other Army aviation units providing area support to obtain the maximum airmobile capacity for each operation. Nevertheless, on many occasions the Army found itself road bound.

A Typical Search and Destroy Operation *using armored personnel carriers.*

Road and convoy security was also the original justification for introducing Army mechanized and armor units into South Vietnam in 1966. At first Westmoreland was reluctant to bring heavy mechanized equipment into South Vietnam, for it seemed ill suited either to counterinsurgency operations or to operations during the monsoon season, when all but a few roads were impassable. Armor advocates pressed Westmoreland to reconsider his policy. Operation Circle Pines, carried out by elements of the 25th Infantry Division in the spring of 1966, successfully combined an infantry force and an armor battalion. This experience, together with new studies indicating a greater potential for mechanized forces, led Westmoreland to reverse his original policy and request deployment of the 11th Armored Cavalry Regiment, with its full complement of tanks, to Vietnam.

Arriving in III Corps in the last half of 1966, the regiment set up base at Xuan Loc, on Route 1 northeast of Saigon in Long Khanh Province. In addition to assuming an area support mission and strengthening the eastern approaches to Saigon as part of Westmoreland's security belt around the capital, squadrons of the regiment supported Army units throughout the corps zone, often "homesteading" with other brigades or divisions.

Route security, however, was only the first step in carving out a larger role for Army mechanized forces. Facing an enemy who employed no armor, American mechanized units, often in conjunction with airmobile assaults, acted both as blocking or holding forces and as assault or reaction forces, where terrain permitted. "Jungle bashing," as offensive armor operations were sometimes called, had its uses but also its limitations. The intimidating presence of tanks and personnel carriers was often nullified by their cumbersomeness and noise, which alerted the enemy to an impending attack. The Viet Cong also took countermeasures to immobilize tracked vehicles. Crude tank traps, locally manufactured mines (often made of plastic to thwart discovery by metal detectors), and well-aimed rocket or recoilless rifle rounds could disable a tank or personnel carrier. Together with the dust and tropical humidity, such weapons placed a heavy burden on Army maintenance units. Yet mechanized units brought the allies enhanced mobility and firepower and often were essential to counter ambushes or destroy an enemy force protected by bunkers.

As Army strength increased in III Corps, Westmoreland encouraged his units to operate farther afield. In early 1966 intelligence reports indicated that enemy strength and activity were increasing in many of his base areas. In two operations during the early spring of 1966, units of the 1st and 25th Divisions discovered Viet Cong training camps and supply dumps, some of the sites honeycombed with tunnels. But they failed to engage major enemy forces. As Army units made the deepest penetration of War Zone C since 1961, all signs pointed to the foe's hasty withdrawal into Cambodia. An airmobile raid failed to locate the enemy's command center, COSVN. (COSVN, in fact, was fragmented among several sites in Tay Ninh Province and in nearby Cambodia.) Like the 173d Airborne Brigade's operations, the new attacks had no lasting effects.

By May 1966 an ominous build-up of enemy forces, among them NVA regiments that had infiltrated south, was detected in Phuoc Long and Binh Long Provinces in northern III Corps. U.S. commanders viewed the build-up as a portent of the enemy's spring offensive, plans for which included an attack on the district town of Loc Ninh and on a nearby Special Forces camp. The 1st Division responded, sending a brigade to secure Route 13. But the threat to Loc Ninh heightened in early June, when regiments of the *9th Viet Cong Division* took up positions around the town. The arrival of American reinforcements apparently prevented an assault. About a week later, however, an enemy regiment was spotted in fortified positions in a rubber plantation adjacent to Loc Ninh. Battered by massive air and artillery strikes, the regiment was dislodged and its position overrun, ending the threat. Americans recorded other successes, trapping Viet Cong ambushers in a counterambush, securing Loc Ninh, and spoiling the enemy's spring offensive. But if the enemy still underestimated the mobility and firepower that U.S. commanders could bring to bear, he had learned how easily Americans could be lured away from their base camps.

By the summer of 1966 Westmoreland believed he had stopped the losing trend of a year earlier and could begin the second phase of his general campaign strategy. This entailed aggressive operations to search out and destroy enemy main force units, in addition to continued efforts to improve security in the populated areas of III Corps. In Operation ATTLEBORO he sent the 196th Infantry Brigade and the 3d Brigade, 4th Infantry Division, to Tay Ninh Province to bolster the security of the province seat. Westmoreland's challenge prompted COSVN to send the *9th Viet Cong Division* on a "countersweep," the enemy's term for operations to counter allied search and destroy tactics. Moving deeper into the enemy's stronghold, the recently arrived and inexperienced 196th Infantry Brigade sparred with the enemy. Then an intense battle erupted, as elements of the brigade were isolated and surprised by a large enemy force. Operation ATTLEBORO quickly grew to a multidivision struggle as American commanders sought to maintain contact with the Viet Cong and to aid their own surrounded forces. Within a matter of days, elements of the 1st and 25th Divisions, the 173d Airborne Brigade, and the 11th Armored Cavalry Regiment had converged on War Zone C. Control of ATTLEBORO passed in turn from the 196th to the 1st Division and finally to the II Field Force, making it the first Army operation in South Vietnam to be controlled by a corps-size headquarters. With over 22,000 U.S. troops participating, the battle had become the largest of the war. Yet combat occurred most often at the platoon and company levels, usually at night. As the number of American troops increased, the *9th Viet Cong Division* shied away, withdrawing across the Cambodian border. Then Army forces departed, leaving to the Special Forces the task of detecting the enemy's inevitable return.

As the threat along the border abated, Westmoreland turned his attention to the enemy's secret zones near Saigon, among them the so-called Iron Triangle in Binh Duong Province. Harboring the headquarters of *Military Region IV*, the Communist command that directed military and terrorist activity in and around the capital, this stronghold had gone undisturbed for several years. Westmoreland hoped to find the command center, disrupt Viet Cong activity in the capital region, and allow South Vietnamese forces to accelerate pacification and uproot the stubborn Viet Cong political organization that flourished in many villages and hamlets.

Operation CEDAR FALLS began on 8 January 1967 with the objectives of destroying the headquarters, interdicting the movement of enemy forces into the major war zones in III Corps, and defeating Viet Cong units encamped there. Like ATTLEBORO before it, CEDAR FALLS tapped the manpower and resources of nearly every major Army unit in the corps area. A series of preliminary maneuvers brought Army units into position. Several air assaults sealed off the Iron Triangle, exploiting the natural barriers of the rivers that formed two of its boundaries. Then American units began a series of sweeps to push the enemy toward the blocking forces. At the village of Ben Suc, long under the sway of the insurgents, sixty helicopters descended into seven landing zones in less than a minute. Ben Suc was surrounded, its entire population evacuated, and the village and its tunnel complex destroyed. But insurgent forces had fled before the heliborne assault. As CEDAR FALLS progressed, U.S. troops destroyed hundreds of enemy fortifications, captured large quantities of supplies and food, and evacuated other hamlets. Contact with the enemy was fleeting. Most of the Viet Cong, including the high-level cadre of the regional command, had escaped, sometimes infiltrating through allied lines.

By the time Army units left the Iron Triangle, MACV had already received reports that Viet Cong and NVA regiments were returning to War Zone C in preparation for a spring offensive. This time Westmoreland hoped to prevent Communist forces from escaping into Cambodia, as they had done in ATTLEBORO. From forward field positions established during earlier operations, elements of the 25th and 1st Divisions, the 196th Infantry Brigade, and the 11th Armored Cavalry Regiment launched JUNCTION CITY, moving rapidly to establish a cordon around the war zone and to begin a new sweep of the base area. As airmobile and mechanized units moved into positions on the morning of 21 February 1967, elements of the 173d Airborne Brigade made the only parachute drop of the Vietnam War—and the first combat airborne assault since the Korean War—to establish a blocking position near the Cambodian border. Then other U.S. units entered the horseshoe-shaped area of operations through its open end.

Despite the emphasis on speed and surprise, Army units did not encounter many enemy troops at the outset. As the operation entered its second phase, however, American forces concentrated their efforts in the eastern portion of War Zone C, close to Route 13. Here several violent battles erupted, as Communist forces tried to isolate and defeat individual units and possibly also to screen the retreat of their comrades into Cambodia. On 19 March a mechanized unit of the 9th Infantry Division was attacked and nearly overrun along Route 13 near the battered village of Bau Bang. The combined firepower of armored cavalry, supporting artillery, and close air support finally caused the enemy to break contact. A few days later, at Fire Support Base GOLD, in the vicinity of Soui Tre, an infantry and artillery battalion of the 25th Infantry engaged the *272d Viet Cong Regiment*. Behind an intense, walking mortar barrage, enemy troops breached GOLD's defensive perimeter and rushed into the base. Man-to-man combat ensued. A complete disaster was averted when Army artillerymen lowered their howitzers and fired, directly into the oncoming enemy, Beehive artillery rounds that contained hundreds of dartlike projectiles. The last major encounter with enemy troops during JUNCTION CITY occurred at the end of March, when elements of two Viet Cong regiments, the *271st* and the *70th* (the latter directly subordinate to COSVN) attacked a battalion of the 1st Infantry Division in a night defensive position deep in War Zone C, near the Cambodian border. The lopsided casualties—over 600 enemy killed in contrast to 10 Americans—forcefully illustrated once again the U.S. ability to call in overwhelmingly superior fire support by artillery, armed helicopters, and tactical aircraft.

Thereafter, JUNCTION CITY became a pale shadow of the multidivision effort it had been at its outset. Most Army units were withdrawn, either to return to their bases or to participate in other operations. The 196th Infantry Brigade was transferred to I Corps to help replace Marine forces sent north to meet a growing enemy threat near the demilitarized zone. Contacts with enemy forces in this final phase were meager. Again a planned Viet Cong offensive had been aborted; the enemy himself escaped, though not unscathed.

In the wake of JUNCTION CITY, MACV's attention reverted to the still critical security conditions around Saigon. The 1st Infantry Division returned to War Zone D to search for the *271st Viet Cong Regiment* and to disrupt the insurgents' lines of communications between War Zones C and D. Despite two major contacts, the main body of the regiment eluded its American pursuers. Army units again returned to the Iron Triangle between April and July 1967, after enemy forces were detected in their old stronghold. Supplies and documents were found in quantities even larger than those discovered in CEDAR FALLS. Once again, however, encounters with the Communists were fleeting. The enemy's reappearance in the Iron Triangle and War Zone D, combined with rocket and mortar attacks on U.S. bases around Saigon, heightened Westmoreland's concern about the security of the capital. When the 1st Infantry Division's base at Phuoc Vinh and the Bien Hoa Air Base were attacked in mid-1967, the division mounted operations into the Ong Dong jungle and the Vinh Loi woods. Other operations swept the jungles and villages of Bien Hoa Province and sought once again to support pacification in Hau Nghia Province.

These actions pointed up a basic problem. The large, multidivision operations into the enemy's war zones produced some benefits for the pacification campaign; by keeping enemy main force regiments at bay, Westmoreland impeded their access to heavily populated areas and prevented them from reinforcing Viet Cong provincial and district forces. Yet when American units were shifted to the border, the local Viet Cong units gained a measure of relief. Westmoreland faced a strategic dilemma: he could not afford to keep substantial forces away from their bases for more than a few months at a time without jeopardizing local security. Unless he received additional forces, Westmoreland would always be torn between two operational imperatives. By the summer of 1967, MACV's likelihood of receiving more combat troops, beyond those scheduled to deploy during the latter half of the year and in early 1968, had become remote. In Washington the administration turned down his request for an additional 200,000 men.

Meanwhile, however, the 9th Infantry Division and the 199th Infantry Brigade arrived in South Vietnam. Westmoreland stationed the brigade at Bien Hoa, where it embarked on FAIRFAX, a year-long operation in which it worked closely with a South Vietnamese ranger group to improve security in Gia Dinh Province, which surrounded the capital. Units of the brigade "paired off" with South Vietnamese rangers and, working closely with paramilitary and police forces, sought to uproot the very active Viet Cong local forces and destroy the enemy's political infrastructure. Typical activities included ambushes by combined forces; cordon and search operations in villages and hamlets, often in conjunction with the Vietnamese police; psychological and civic action operations; surprise road blocks to search for contraband and Viet Cong supporters; and training programs to develop proficient military and local self-defense capabilities.

Likewise, the 9th Infantry Division set up bases east and south of Saigon. One brigade deployed to Bear Cat; another set up camp at Tan An in Long An Province, south of Saigon, where it sought to secure portions of Route 4, an important north-south highway connecting Saigon with the rice-rich lower Delta. Further south, the 2d Brigade, 9th Infantry Division, established its base at Dong Tam in Dinh Tuong Province in IV Corps. Located in the midst of rice paddies and swamps, Dong Tam was created by Army engineers with sand dredged from the My Tho River. From this 600-acre base, the brigade began a series of riverine operations unique to the Army's experience in South Vietnam.

To patrol and fight in the inundated marshlands and rice paddies and along the numerous canals and waterways crossing the Delta, the Army modernized the concept of riverine warfare employed during the Civil War by Union forces on the Mississippi River and by the French during the Indochina War. The Mobile Riverine Force utilized a joint Army-Navy task force controlled by a ground commander. In contrast to amphibious operations, where control reverts to the ground commander only after the force is ashore, riverine warfare was an extension of land combat, with infantry units traveling by water rather than by trucks or tracked vehicles. Aided by a Navy river support squadron and river assault squadron, infantrymen were housed on barracks ships and supported by gunships or fire support boats called monitors. Howitzers and mortars mounted on barges provided artillery support. The 2d Brigade, 9th Infantry Division, began operations against the Cam Son Secret Zone, approximately 10 miles west of Dong Tam, in May 1967.

Meanwhile, the war of main force units along the borders waxed and waned in relation to seasonal weather cycles, which affected the enemy's pattern of logistical activity, his ability to infiltrate men and supplies from North Vietnam, and his penchant for meticulous preparation of the battlefield. By the fall of 1967, enemy activity had increased again in the base areas, and sizable forces began appearing along South Vietnam's border from the demilitarized zone to III Corps. By the year's end, American forces had returned to War Zone C to screen the Cambodian border to prevent Communist forces from re-entering South Vietnam. Units of the 25th Infantry Division that had been conducting operations in the vicinity of Saigon moved to the border. Elements of the 1st Infantry Division had resumed road-clearing operations along Route 13, but the division soon faced another major enemy effort to capture Loc Ninh. On 29 October Viet Cong units assaulted the CIDG camp and the district command post, breaching the defense perimeter. Intense air and artillery fire prevented its complete loss. Within a few hours, South Vietnamese and U.S. reinforcements reached Loc Ninh, their arrival made possible by the enemy's failure to capture the local airstrip.

When the build-up ended, ten Army battalions were positioned within Loc Ninh and between the town and the Cambodian border. During the next two days allied units warded off repeated enemy attacks as Communist forces desperately tried to score a victory. Tactical air support and artillery fire prevented the enemy from massing though he outnumbered allied forces by about ten to one. At the end of a ten-day battle, over 800 enemy were left on the battlefield, while allied deaths numbered only 50. Some 452 close air support sorties, 8 B–52 bomber strikes, and 30,125 rounds of artillery had been directed at the enemy. Once again, Loc Ninh had served as a lightning rod to attract U.S. forces to the border. The pattern of two wars—one in the villages, one on the border—continued without decision.

Army Operations in II and I Corps, 1965–1967

Spearheaded by at least three NVA regiments, Communist forces mounted a strong offensive in South Vietnam's Central Highlands during the summer of 1965, overrunning border camps and besieging some district towns. Here the enemy threatened to cut the nation in two. To meet the danger, Westmoreland proposed to introduce the newly organized Army airmobile division, the 1st Cavalry Division, with its large contingent of helicopters, directly into the highlands. Some of his superiors in Hawaii and Washington opposed this plan, preferring to secure coastal bases. Though Westmoreland contended that enclave security made poor use of U.S. mobility and offensive firepower, he was unable to overcome the fear of an American Dien Bien Phu, if a unit in the highlands should be isolated and cut off from the sea.

In the end, the deployment of Army forces to II Corps reflected a compromise. As additional American and South Korean forces arrived during 1965 and 1966, they often reinforced South Vietnamese efforts to secure coastal enclaves, usually centered on the most important cities and ports. (*Map 49*) At Phan Thiet, Tuy Hoa, Qui Nhon, Nha Trang, and Cam Ranh Bay, allied forces provided area security, not only protecting the ports and logistical complexes that developed in many of these locations, but also assisting Saigon's forces to expand the pacified zone that extended from the urban cores to the countryside.

Here, as in III Corps, Westmoreland addressed two enemy threats. Local insurgents menaced populated areas along the coastal plain, while enemy main force units intermittently pushed forward in the western highlands. Between the two regions stretched the piedmont, a transitional area in whose lush valleys lived many South Vietnamese. In the piedmont's craggy hills and jungle-covered uplands, local and main force Viet Cong units had long flourished by exacting food and taxes from the lowland population through a well-entrenched shadow government. Although the enemy's bases in the piedmont did not have the notoriety of the secret zones near Saigon, they served similar purposes, harboring units, command centers, and training and logistical facilities. Extensions of the Ho Chi Minh Trail ran from the highlands through the piedmont to the coast, facilitating the movement of enemy units and supplies from province to province. To be effective, allied operations on the coast had to uproot local units living amid the population and to eradicate the enemy base areas in the piedmont, together with the main force units that supported the village and hamlet guerrillas.

Despite their sparse population and limited economic resources, the highlands had a strategic importance equal to and perhaps greater than the

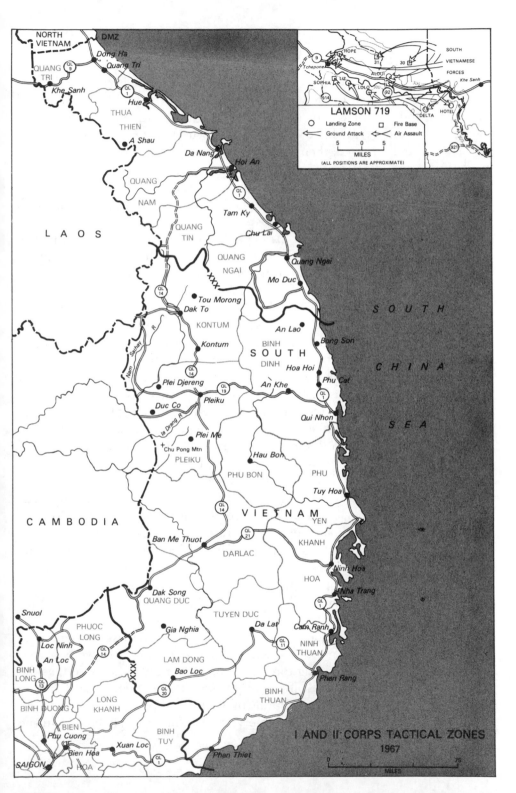

NORTH VIETNAM

DMZ

QUANG TRI

Dong Ha
Quang Tri
QL 9
Khe Sanh
Hue
QL 1
THUA THIEN
A Shau

Da Nang
Hoi An

QUANG NAM

QL 1

QUANG TIN
Tam Ky
Chu Lai

QUANG NGAI
Quang Ngai
Mo Duc

QL 14
Tou Morong
Dak To
KONTUM
An Lao
Bong Son
Kontum
SOUTH DINH
BINH DINH
Hoa Hoi
Phu Cat
QL 14
Plei Djereng
QL 19
An Khe
Duc Co
Pleiku
Qui Nhon

Plei Me
Chu Pong Mtn
PLEIKU
Hau Bon
PHU BON
PHU
Tuy Hoa

QL 14
VIETNAM
YEN
CAMBODIA
Ban Me Thuot
QL 21
KHANH
DARLAC
Ninh Hoa
HOA
Dak Song
Nha Trang
QUANG DUC
Snuol
PHUOC LONG
Gia Nghia
Da Lat
Cam Ranh
Loc Ninh
An Loc
QL 14
LAM DONG
NINH THUAN
QL 11
BINH LONG
Bao Loc
QL 13
QL 20
BINH THUAN
BINH DUONG
Phan Rang
BIEN
LONG KHANH
Phu Cuong
BINH TUY
Bien Hoa
Xuan Loc
QL 1
SAIGON
HOA
Phan Thiet

LAOS

Nam Sathay R.
Ia Drang R.

SOUTH CHINA SEA

I AND II CORPS TACTICAL ZONES
1967

0   75
MILES

LAMSON 719

○ Landing Zone   □ Fire Base
← Ground Attack   ← Air Assault

5   0   5
MILES
(ALL POSITIONS ARE APPROXIMATE)

SOUTH VIETNAMESE FORCES

HOPE
Tchepone
QL 9
SOPHIA
LIZ
ALOUI
LOLO
QL 92
Khe Sanh
DELTA
HOTEL
QL 914
QL 921
31
30

MAP 49

coastal plain. Around the key highland towns—Pleiku, Kontum, Ban Me Thuot, and Da Lat—South Vietnamese and U.S. forces had created enclaves. Allied forces protected the few roads that traversed the highlands, screened the border, and reinforced outposts and Montagnard settlements from which the irregulars and Army Special Forces sought to detect enemy cross-border movements and to strengthen tribal resistance to the Communists. Such border posts and tribal camps, rather than major towns, most often were the object of enemy attacks. Combined with road interdiction, such attacks enabled the Communists to disperse the limited number of defenders and to discourage the maintenance of outposts.

Such actions served a larger strategic objective. The enemy planned to develop the highlands into a major base area from which to mount or support operations in other areas. A Communist-dominated highlands would be a strategic fulcrum, enabling the enemy to shift the weight of his operations to any part of South Vietnam. The highlands also formed a "killing zone" where Communist forces could mass. Challenging American forces had become the principal objective of leaders in Hanoi, who saw their plans to undermine Saigon's military resistance thwarted by U.S. intervention. Salient victories against Americans, they believed, might deter a further build-up and weaken Washington's resolve to continue the war.

The 1st Cavalry Division (Airmobile) moved with its 435 helicopters into this hornet's nest in September 1965, establishing its main base at An Khe, a government stronghold on Route 19, halfway between the coastal port of Qui Nhon and the highland city of Pleiku. The location was strategic: at An Khe the division could help to keep open the vital east-west road from the coast to the highlands and could pivot between the highlands and the coastal districts, where the Viet Cong had made deep inroads. Meanwhile, the 1st Brigade, 101st Airborne Division, had begun operations in the rugged Song Con valley, about 18 miles northeast of An Khe. Here, on 18 September, one battalion ran into heavy fire from an enemy force in the tree line around its landing zone. Four helicopters were lost and three company commanders killed; reinforcements could not land because of the intense enemy fire. With the fight at close quarters, the Americans were unable to call in close air support, armed gunships, and artillery fire, except at the risk of their own lives. But as the enemy pressed them back, supporting fires were placed almost on top of the contending forces. At dusk the fighting subsided; as the Americans steeled themselves for a night attack, the enemy, hard hit by almost 100 air strikes and 11,000 rounds of artillery, slipped away. Inspection of the battlefield revealed that the Americans had unwittingly landed in the midst of a heavily bunkered enemy base.

The fight had many hallmarks of highland battles that were to come. Americans had little information about enemy forces or the area of operations; the enemy could "hug" Army units to nullify their massive advantage in firepower. In compensation, the enemy underestimated the accuracy of such fire and the willingness of U.S. commanders to call it in even when fighting at close quarters. Finally, enemy forces when pressed too hard could usually escape, and pursuit, as a rule, was futile.

Less than a month later the newly arrived airmobile division received its own baptism of combat. The North Vietnamese Army attacked a Special Forces camp at Plei Me; when it was repulsed, Westmoreland directed the division to launch an offensive to locate and destroy enemy regiments that had been identified in the vicinity of the camp. The result was the battle of the Ia Drang valley, named for a small river that flowed through the area of operations. For thirty-five days the division pursued and fought the *32d, 33d,* and *66th North Vietnamese Regiments*, until the enemy, suffering heavy casualties, returned to his bases in Cambodia.

With scout platoons of its air cavalry squadron covering front and flanks, each battalion of the division's 1st Brigade established company bases from which patrols searched for enemy forces. For several days neither ground patrols nor aero-scouts found any trace, but on 4 November the scouts spotted a regimental aid station several miles west of Plei Me. Quick reacting aero-rifle platoons converged on the site. Hovering above, the airborne scouts detected an enemy battalion nearby and attacked from UH–1B gunships with aerial rockets and machine guns. Operating beyond the range of their ground artillery, Army units engaged the enemy in an intense firefight. Again enemy troops "hugged" American forces, then broke contact as reinforcements began to arrive.

The search for the main body of the enemy continued for the next few days, with Army units concentrating their efforts in the vicinity of the Chu Pong Massif, a mountain near the Cambodian border that was believed to be an enemy base. Communist forces were given little rest, as patrols harried and ambushed them. The enemy attacked an American patrol base, Landing Zone MARY, at night, but was repulsed by the first night air assault into a defensive perimeter under fire, accompanied by aerial rocket fire.

The heaviest fighting was yet to come. As the division began the second stage of its campaign, enemy forces began to move out of the Chu Pong base. Units of the 1st Cavalry Division advanced to establish artillery bases and landing zones at the base of the mountain. Landing Zone X-RAY was one of several U.S. positions vulnerable to attack by the enemy forces that occupied the surrounding high ground. Here on 14 November began fighting that pitted three battalions against elements of two NVA regiments. Withstanding repeated mortar attacks and infantry assaults, the Americans used every means of firepower available to them—the division's own gunships, massive artillery bombardment, hundreds of strafing and bombing attacks by tactical aircraft, and earth-shaking bombs dropped by B–52 bombers from Guam—to turn back a determined enemy. The Communists lost 600 dead, the Americans 79.

Although badly hurt, the enemy did not leave the Ia Drang valley. Elements of the *66th North Vietnamese Regiment* moving east toward Plei Me encountered an American battalion on 17 November, a few miles north of X-RAY. The fight that resulted was a gory reminder of the North Vietnamese mastery of the ambush. The Communists quickly snared three U.S. companies in their net. As the trapped units struggled for survival, nearly all semblance of organized combat disappeared in the confusion and mayhem. Neither reinforcements nor effective firepower could be brought in. At times combat was reduced to valiant efforts by individuals and small units to avert annihilation. When the fighting ended that night, 60 percent of the Americans were casualties, and almost one of every three soldiers in the battalion had been killed.

Lauded as the first major American triumph of the Vietnam War, the battle of the Ia Drang valley was in truth a costly and problematic victory. The airmobile division, committed to combat less than a month after it arrived in-country, relentlessly pursued the enemy for thirty-five days over difficult terrain and defeated three NVA regiments. In part, its achievements underlined the flexibility that Army divisions had gained in the early 1960's under the Reorganization Objective Army Division (ROAD) concept. Replacing the pentomic division with its five lightly armed battle groups, the ROAD division, organized around three brigades, facilitated the creation of brigade and battalion task forces tailored to respond and fight in a variety of military situations. The newly organized division reflected the Army's embrace of the concept of flexible response and proved eminently suitable for operations in Vietnam. The helicopter was given great credit as well. Nearly every aspect of the division's operations was enhanced by its airmobile capacity. Artillery batteries were moved sixty-seven times by helicopter. Intelligence, medical, and all manner of logistical support benefited as well from the speed and flexibility provided by helicopters. Despite the fluidity of the tactical situation, airmobile command and control procedures enabled the division to move and to keep track of its units over a large area, and to accommodate the frequent and rapid changes in command arrangements as units were moved from one headquarters to another.

Yet for all the advantages that the division accrued from airmobility, its performance was not without blemish. Though the conduct of division-size airmobile operations proved tactically sound, two major engagements stemmed from the enemy's initiative in attacking vulnerable American units. On several occasions massive air and artillery support provided the margin of victory (if not survival). Above all, the division's logistical self-sufficiency fell short of expectations. It could support only one brigade in combat at a time, for prolonged and intense operations consumed more fuel and ammunition than the division's helicopters and fixed-wing Caribou aircraft could supply. Air Force tactical airlift became necessary for resupply. Moreover, in addition to combat losses and damage, the division's helicopters suffered from heavy use and from the heat, humidity, and dust of Vietnam, taxing its maintenance capacity. Human attrition was also high; hundreds of soldiers, the equivalent of almost a battalion, fell victim to a resistant strain of malaria peculiar to Vietnam's highlands.

Westmoreland's satisfaction in blunting the enemy's offensive was tempered by concern that enemy forces might re-enter South Vietnam and resume their offensive while the airmobile division recuperated at the end of November and during most of December. He thus requested immediate reinforcements from the Army's 25th Infantry Division, based in Hawaii and scheduled to deploy to South Vietnam in the spring of 1966. By the end of 1965, the division's 3d Brigade had been airlifted to the highlands and, within a month of its arrival, had joined elements of the 1st Cavalry Division to launch a series of operations to screen the border. Army units did not detect any major enemy forces trying to cross from Cambodia into South Vietnam. Each operation, however, killed hundreds of enemy soldiers and refined airmobile techniques, as Army units learned to cope with the vast territorial expanse and difficult terrain of the highlands.

In Operation MATADOR, for example, air strikes were used to blast holes in the forests, enabling helicopters to bring in heavy engineer equipment to construct new landing zones for use in future operations. Operation LINCOLN, a search and destroy operation on the Chu Pong Massif, featured combined armor and airmobile operations; air cavalry scouts guided armored vehicles of the 3d Brigade, 25th Infantry Division, as they operated in a lightly wooded area near Pleiku City. Also in LINCOLN, Army engineers, using heli-lifted equipment, in two days cleared and constructed a runway to handle C–130 air transports in an area inaccessible by road.

Despite the relative calm that followed the Ia Drang fighting, the North Vietnamese left no doubt of their intent to continue infiltration and to challenge American forces along the highland border. In February 1966

SOUTH VIETNAMESE INTERPRETER QUESTIONS CIVILIANS *about Viet Cong activities.*

enemy forces overran the Special Forces camp at A Shau, in the remote northwest corner of I Corps. The loss of the camp had long-term consequences, enabling the enemy to make the A Shau valley a major logistical base and staging area for forces infiltrating into the piedmont and coastal areas. The loss also highlighted certain differences between operational concepts of the Army and the marines. Concentrating their efforts in the coastal districts of I Corps and lacking the more extensive helicopter support enjoyed by Army units, the marines avoided operations in the highlands. On the other hand, Army commanders in II Corps sought to engage the enemy as close to the border as possible and were quick to respond to threats to Special Forces camps in the highlands. Operations near the border were essential to Westmoreland's efforts to keep main force enemy units as far as possible from heavily populated areas.

For Hanoi's strategists, however, a reciprocal relation existed between highlands and coastal regions. Here, as in the south, the enemy directed his efforts to preserving his own influence among the population near the coast, from which he derived considerable support. At the same time, he maintained a constant military threat in the highlands to divert allied forces from efforts at pacification. Like the chronic shifting of units from the neighbor-hood of Saigon to the war zones in III Corps, the frequent movement of American units between coast and border in II Corps reflected the Communist desire to relieve allied military pressure whenever guerrilla and local forces were endangered. In its broad outlines, Hanoi's strategy to cope with U.S. forces was the same employed by the Viet Minh against the French and by Communist forces in 1964 and 1965 against the South Vietnamese Army. Whether it would be equally successful remained to be seen.

The airmobile division spent the better part of the next two years fighting Viet Cong and NVA main force units in the coastal plain and piedmont valleys of Binh Dinh Province. Here the enemy had deep roots, while pacif-ication efforts were almost dead. Starting in early 1966, the 1st Cavalry Division embarked on a series of operations against the *2d Viet Cong* and the *18th* and *22d North Vietnamese Regiments* of the *3d North Vietnamese Division* (the *Yellow Star Division*). For the most part, the 1st Cavalry Division oper-ated in the Bong Son plain and the adjacent hills, from which enemy units reinforced the hamlet and village guerrillas who gathered in taxes, food, and recruits. As in the highlands, the division exploited its airmobility, using helicopters to establish positions in the upper reaches of the valleys. They sought to flush the enemy from his hiding places and drive him toward the coast, where American, South Vietnamese, and South Korean forces held blocking positions. When trapped, the enemy was attacked by ground, naval, and air fire. The scheme was a new version of an old tactical concept, the "hammer and anvil," with the coastal plain and the natural barrier formed by the South China Sea forming the anvil or killing zone. Collectively the operations became known as the Binh Dinh Pacification Campaign.

For forty-two days elements of the airmobile division scoured the An Lao and Kim Son valleys, pursuing enemy units that had been surprised and routed from the Bong Son plain. Meanwhile, Marine forces in neighboring Quang Ngai Province in southern I Corps sought to bar the enemy's escape routes to the north. The enemy units evaded the Americans, but thousands of civilians fled from the Viet Cong–dominated valleys to government-controlled areas. Although the influx of refugees taxed the government's already strained relief services, the exodus of peasants weakened the Viet Cong's infrastructure and aimed a psychological blow at the enemy's pres-tige. The Communists had failed either to confront the Americans or to protect the population over which they had gained control.

Failing to locate the fleeing enemy in the An Lao valley, units of the airmobile division assaulted another enemy base area, a group of valleys and ridges southwest of the Bong Son plain known as the Crow's Foot or the Eagle's Claw. Here some Army units sought to dislodge the enemy from his upland bases while others established blocking positions at the "toe" of each valley, where it found outlet to the plain. In six weeks over 1,300 enemy soldiers were killed. Enemy forces in northern Binh Dinh Province were temporarily thrown off balance. Beyond this, the long-term effects of the operation were unclear. The 1st Cavalry Division did not stay in one area long enough to exploit its success. Whether the Saigon government could marshal its forces effectively to provide local security and to reassert its political control remained to be seen.

Later operations continued to harass an elusive foe. Launching a new attack without the extensive preparatory reconnaissance that often alerted the enemy, Army units again surprised him in the Bong Son area but soon lost contact. The next move was against an enemy build-up in the vicinity of the Vinh Thanh Special Forces Camp. Here the Green Berets watched the "Oregon Trail," an enemy infiltration corridor that passed through the Vinh Thanh valley from the highlands to the coast. Forestalling the attack, Army units remained in the area where they conducted numerous patrols and made frequent contact with the enemy. (One U.S. company came close to being overrun in a ferocious firefight.) But again the action had little enduring effect, except to increase the enemy's caution by demonstrating the airmobile division's agility in responding to a threat.

After a brief interlude in the highlands, the division returned to Binh Dinh Province in September 1966. Conditions in the Bong Son area differed little from those the division had first encountered. For the most part, the Viet Cong rather than the Saigon government had been successful in reasserting their authority, and pacification was at a standstill. The division devoted most of its resources for the remainder of 1966 and throughout 1967 to supporting renewed efforts at pacification. In the fall of 1966, for the first time in a year, all three of the division's brigades were reunited and operating in Binh Dinh Province. Although elements of the division were occasionally transferred to the highlands as the threat there waxed and waned, the general movement of forces was toward the north. Army units increasingly were sent to southern I Corps during 1967, replacing Marine units in operations similar to those in Binh Dinh Province.

In one such operation the familiar pattern of hammer and anvil was tried anew, with some success. The 1st Cavalry Division opened with a multibattalion air assault in an upland valley to flush the enemy toward the coast, where allied ground and naval forces were prepared to bar his escape. Enemy forces had recently left their mountain bases to plunder the rice harvest and to harass South Vietnamese forces providing security for provincial elections. These units were caught with their backs to the sea. For most of October, allied forces sought to destroy the main body of a Communist regiment isolated on the coast and to seize an enemy base in the nearby Phu Cat Mountain. The first phase consisted of several sharp combat actions near the coastal hamlet of Hoa Hoi. With South Vietnamese and U.S. naval forces blocking an escape by sea, the encircled enemy fought desperately to return to the safety of his bases in the upland valleys. His plight was compounded when floods forced his troops out of their hiding places and exposed them to attacks. After heavy losses, remnants of the regiment divided into small parties that escaped through allied lines. As contacts with the enemy diminished on the coast, American efforts shifted inland, with several sharp engagements occurring when enemy forces tried to delay pursuit or to divert the allies from entering base areas. By the end of October, as the Communists retreated north and west, the running fight had accounted for over 2,000 enemy killed. Large caches of supplies, equipment, and food were uncovered, and the Viet Cong's shadow government in some coastal hamlets and villages was severely damaged, some hamlets reverting to government control for the first time in several years.

Similar operations continued through 1967 and into early 1968. In addition to offensive operations against enemy main forces, Army units in Binh Dinh worked in close co-ordination with South Vietnamese police, Regional and Popular Forces, and the South Vietnamese Army to help the Saigon government gain a foothold in villages and hamlets dominated or contested by the Communists. The 1st Cavalry Division adopted a number of techniques in support of pacification. Army units frequently participated in cordon and search operations: airmobile forces seized positions around a hamlet or village at dawn to prevent the escape of local forces or cadres, while South Vietnamese authorities undertook a methodical house-to-house search. The Vietnamese checked the legal status of residents, took a census, and interrogated suspected Viet Cong to obtain more information about the enemy's local political and military apparatus. At the same time, allied forces engaged in a variety of civic action and psychological operations; specially trained pacification cadres established the rudiments of local government and provided various social and economic services. At other times, the division might participate in "checkpoint and snatch" operations, establishing surprise roadblocks and inspecting traffic on roads frequented by the insurgents.

Although much weakened by such methods, enemy forces found opportunities to attack American units. They aimed both to win a military victory and to remind the local populace of their presence and power. An attack on Landing Zone BIRD, an artillery base on the Bong Son plain, was one such example. Taking advantage of the Christmas truce of 1966, enemy units moved into position and mounted a ferocious attack as soon as the truce ended. Although portions of the base were overrun, the onslaught was

checked when artillerymen leveled their guns and fired Beehive antiperson-
nel rounds directly into the waves of oncoming enemy troops. Likewise,
several sharp firefights occurred immediately after the 1967 *Tet* truce, when
the enemy took advantage of the cease-fire to move back among the population. This time units of the 1st Cavalry Division forced the enemy to leave the
coastal communities and seek refuge in the piedmont. As the enemy moved
across the boundary into southern I Corps, so too did units of the airmobile
division. About a month later, the 3d Brigade, 25th Infantry Division, also
moved to southern I Corps. Throughout the remainder of 1967, other Army
units transferred to either I Corps to reinforce the marines or to the highlands to meet renewed enemy threats. As the strength of American units
committed to the Binh Dinh Pacification Campaign decreased during late
1967 and early 1968, enemy activity in the province quickened as the Viet
Cong sought to reconstitute their weakened military forces and to regain a
position of influence among the local population.

In many respects, the Binh Dinh campaign was a microcosm of
Westmoreland's over-all campaign strategy. It showed clearly the intimate
relation between the war against enemy main force units and the fight for
pacification waged by the South Vietnamese, and it demonstrated the effectiveness of the airmobile concept. After two years of persistent pursuit of the
NVA's *Yellow Star Division*, the 1st Cavalry Division had reduced the combat
effectiveness of each of its three regiments. By the end of 1967, the threat to
Binh Dinh Province posed by enemy main force units had been markedly
reduced. The airmobile division's operations against the *3d North Vietnamese
Division*, as well as its frequent role in operations directly in support of
pacification, had weakened local guerrilla forces and created an environment
favorable to pacification.

The campaign in Binh Dinh also exposed the vulnerabilities of Westmoreland's campaign strategy. Despite repeated defeats at the hands of the
Americans, the three NVA regiments still existed. They contrived to find
respite and a measure of rehabilitation, building their strength anew with
recruits filtering down from the North, with others found in-country, and
with Viet Cong units consolidated into their ranks. Although much weakened, Communist forces persistently returned to areas cleared by the 1st
Cavalry Division. Even more threatening to the allied cause, Saigon's pacification efforts languished as South Vietnamese forces failed in many
instances to provide security to the villages and effective police action to root
out local Viet Cong cadres. And the government, dealing with a population
already skeptical, failed to grant the political, social, and economic benefits it
had promised.

A Cordon and Search Operation in Support of Pacification

The Highlands: Progress or Stalemate?

Moreover, the allies could not concentrate their efforts everywhere as they had in strategic Binh Dinh. The expanse of the highlands compelled Army operations there to be carried out with economy of force. During 1966 and 1967, the Americans engaged in a constant search for tactical concepts and techniques to maximize their advantages of firepower and mobility and to compensate for the constraints of time, distance, difficult terrain, and an inviolable border. Here the war was fought primarily to prevent the incursion of NVA units into South Vietnam and to erode their combat strength. In the highlands, each side pursued a strategy of military confrontation, seeking to weaken the fighting forces and will of its opponent through attrition. Each sought military victories to convince opposing leaders of the futility of continuing the contest. For the North Vietnamese, however, confrontation in the highlands had the additional purpose of relieving allied pressure in other areas, where pacification jeopardized their hold on the rural population. Of all the factors influencing operations in the highlands, the most significant may well have been the strength and success of pacification elsewhere.

For Americans, the most difficult problem was to locate the enemy. Yet Communist strategists sometimes created threats to draw in the Americans.

Recurrent menaces to Special Forces camps reflected the enemy's seasonal cycle of operations, his desire to harass and eliminate such camps, and his hope of luring allied forces into situations where he held the military advantages. Thus Army operations in the highlands during 1966 and 1967 were characterized by wide-ranging, often futile searches, punctuated by sporadic but intense battles fought usually at the enemy's initiative.

For the first few months of 1966, the Communists lay low. In May, however, a significant concentration of enemy forces appeared in Pleiku and Kontum Provinces. The 1st Brigade, 101st Airborne Division, the reserve of I Field Force, was summoned to Pleiku and subsequently moved to Dak To, a CIDG camp in northern Kontum Province, to assist a besieged South Vietnamese force at the nearby government post at Toumorong. Although the *24th North Vietnamese Regiment* had surrounded Toumorong, allied forces secured the road to Dak To and evacuated the government troops, leaving one battalion of the 101st inside the abandoned camp and one company in an exposed defensive position in the jungle a short distance beyond. On the night of 6 June a large North Vietnamese force launched repeated assaults on this lone company. Facing disaster, the commander called in air strikes on his own position to stop the enemy's human-wave attacks. Relief arrived the next morning, as additional elements of the brigade were heli-lifted to the battlefield to pursue and trap the North Vietnamese. Fighting to close off the enemy's escape routes, the Americans called in renewed air strikes, including B–52's. By 20 June enemy resistance had ended, and the NVA regiment that had begun the fighting, leaving behind dead, escaped to the safety of its Laotian base.

Although the enemy's push in Kontum Province was blunted, the siege of Toumorong was only one aspect of his summer offensive in the highlands. Suspecting that NVA forces meant to return to the Ia Drang, Westmoreland sent the 3d Brigade, 25th Infantry Division, back into the valley in May. Dividing the area into "checkerboard" squares, the brigade methodically searched each square. Small patrols set out ambushes and operated for several days without resupply to avoid having helicopters reveal their location. After several days in one square, the patrols leapfrogged by helicopter to another. Though the Americans made only light, sporadic contacts, the cumulative toll of enemy killed was equal to many short, violent battles. One significant contact was made in late May near the Chu Pong Massif. A running battle ensued, as the enemy again sought safety in Cambodia. Westmoreland now appealed to Washington for permission to maneuver Army units behind the enemy, possibly into Cambodian territory. But officials refused, fearing international repercussions, and the NVA sanctuary remained inviolate.

Yet the operation confirmed that sizable enemy forces had returned to South Vietnam and, as in the fall of 1965, were threatening the outposts at Plei Me and Duc Co. To meet the renewed threat, I Field Force sent additional Army units to Pleiku Province and launched a new operation under the 1st Cavalry Division. The action followed the now familiar pattern of extensive heli-lifts, establishment of patrol bases, and intermittent contact with an enemy who usually avoided American forces. When the Communists elected to fight, they preferred to occupy high ground; dislodging them from hilltop bunkers was a difficult task, requiring massive air and artillery support. By the time the enemy left Pleiku again at the end of August, his forces had incurred nearly 500 deaths.

Border battles continued, however, and some were sharp. When enemy forces appeared in strength around a CIDG camp at Plei Djering in October, elements of the 4th Infantry and 1st Cavalry Divisions rapidly reinforced the camp, clashing with the enemy in firefights during October and November. As North Vietnamese forces began to withdraw through the Plei Trap valley, the 1st Brigade, 101st Airborne Division, was airlifted from Phu Yen to northern Kontum to try to block their escape, but failed to trap them before they reached the border. Army operations in the highlands were continued by the 4th Infantry Division. In addition to screening the border to detect infiltration, the division constructed a new road between Pleiku and the highland outpost at Plei Djering and helped the Saigon government resettle thousands of Montagnards in secure camps. Contact with the enemy generally was light, the heaviest occurring in mid-February 1967, in an area west of the Nam Sathay River near the Cambodian border, when Communist forces unsuccessfully tried to overrun several American fire bases. Despite infrequent contacts, however, 4th Division troops killed 700 enemy over a period of three months.

In I Corps as well, the enemy seemed intent on dispersing American forces to the border regions. Heightened activity along the demilitarized zone drew marines from southern I Corps. To replace them, Army units were transferred from III and II Corps to the area vacated by the marines, among them the 196th Infantry Brigade, which was pulled out of Operation JUNCTION CITY, and the 3d Brigade, 25th Infantry Division, which had been operating in the II Corps Zone. Together with the 1st Brigade, 101st Airborne Division, these units formed Task Force OREGON, activated on 12 April 1967 and placed under the operational control of the III Marine Amphibious Force. Army infantry units were now operating in all four of South Vietnam's corps areas.

Once at Chu Lai, the Army forces supported an extensive South Vietnamese pacification effort in Quang Tin Province. To the north, along the demilitarized zone, Army heavy artillery engaged in almost daily duels with NVA guns to the north. In Quang Tri Province, the marines fought a hard twelve-day battle to prevent NVA forces from dominating the hills surrounding Khe Sanh. The enemy's heightened military activity along the demilitarized zone, which included frontal attacks across it, prompted American officials to begin construction of a barrier consisting of highly sophisticated electronic and acoustical sensors and strong point defenses manned by allied forces. Known as the McNamara Line, after Secretary of Defense Robert S. McNamara, who vigorously promoted the concept, the barrier was to extend across South Vietnam and eventually into Laos. Westmoreland was not enthusiastic about the project, for he hesitated to commit large numbers of troops to man the strongpoints and doubted that the barrier would prevent the enemy from breaching the demilitarized zone. Hence the McNamara Line was never completed.

Throughout the summer of 1967, Marine forces endured some of the most intense enemy artillery barrages of the war and fought several battles with NVA units that infiltrated across the 17th parallel. Their stubborn defense, supported by massive counterbattery fire, naval gunfire, and air attacks, ended the enemy's offensive in northern I Corps, but not before Westmoreland had to divert additional Army units as reinforcements. A brigade of the 1st Cavalry Division and South Korean units were deployed to southern I Corps to replace additional marines who had been shifted further north. The depth of the Army's commitment in I Corps was shown by Task Force OREGON's reorganization as the 23d Infantry Division (Americal). The only Army division to be formed in South Vietnam, its name echoed a famous division of World War II that had also been organized in the Pacific. If the enemy's aim was to draw American forces to the north, he evidently was succeeding.

Even as Westmoreland shifted allied forces from II Corps to I Corps, fighting intensified in the highlands. After Army units made several contacts with enemy forces during May and June, Westmoreland moved the 173d Airborne Brigade from III Corps to II Corps to serve as the I Field Force's strategic reserve. Within a few days, however, the brigade was committed to an effort to forestall enemy attacks against the CIDG camps of Dak To, Dak Seang, and Dak Pek in northern Kontum Province. Under the control of the 4th Infantry Division, the operation continued throughout the summer until the enemy threat abated. A few months later, however, reconnaissance patrols in the vicinity of Dak To detected a rapid and substantial build-up of enemy forces in regimental strength. Believing an attack to be imminent, 4th Infantry Division forces reinforced the garrison. In turn, the 173d Airborne Brigade returned to the highlands, arriving on 2 November. From 3 to 15 November enemy forces estimated to number 12,000 probed, harassed, and attacked American and South Vietnamese positions along the ridges and hills surrounding the camp. As the attacks grew stronger, more U.S. and South Vietnamese reinforcements were sent, including two battalions from the airmobile division and six ARVN battalions. By mid-November allied strength approached 8,000.

Despite daily air and artillery bombardments of their positions, the North Vietnamese launched two attacks against Dak To on 15 November, destroying two C–130 aircraft and causing severe damage to the camp's ammunition dump. Allied forces strove to dislodge the enemy from the surrounding hills, but the North Vietnamese held fast in fortified positions. The center of enemy resistance was Hill 875; here, two battalions of the 173d Airborne Brigade made a slow and painful ascent against determined resistance and under grueling physical conditions, fighting for every foot of ground. Enemy fire was so intense and accurate that at times the Americans were unable to bring in reinforcements by helicopter or to provide fire support. In fighting that resembled the hill battles of the final stage of the Korean War, the confusion at Dak To pitted soldier against soldier in classic infantry battle. In desperation, beleaguered U.S. commanders on Hill 875 called in artillery and even B–52 air strikes at perilously close range to their own positions. On 17 November American forces at last gained control of Hill 875.

The battle of Dak To was the longest and most violent in the highlands since the battle of the Ia Drang two years before. Enemy casualties numbered in the thousands, with an estimated 1,400 killed. Americans had suffered too. Approximately one-fifth of the 173d Airborne Brigade had become casualties, with 174 killed, 642 wounded, and 17 missing in action. If the battle of the Ia Drang exemplified airmobility in all its versatility, the battle of Dak To, with the arduous ascent of Hill 875, epitomized infantry combat at its most basic and the crushing effect of supporting air power.

Yet Dak To was only one of several border battles in the waning months of 1967. At Song Be and Loc Ninh in III Corps, and all along the northern border of I Corps, the enemy exposed his positions in order to confront U.S. forces in heavy fighting. By the end of 1967 the 1st Infantry Division had again concentrated near the Cambodian border, and the 25th Infantry Division had returned to War Zone C. The enemy's threat in I Corps caused Westmoreland to disperse more Army units. In the vacuum left by their departure, local Viet Cong sought to reconstitute their forces and to reassert their control over the rural population. In turn, Viet Cong revival often was a prelude to the resurgence of Communist military activity at the district and village level. Hard pressed to find additional Army units to shift from III Corps and II Corps to I Corps, Westmoreland asked the Army to accelerate deployment of two remaining brigades of the 101st Airborne Division from the United States. Arriving in December 1967, the brigades were added to the growing number of Army units operating in the northern provinces.

While allied forces were under pressure, the border battles of 1967 also led to a reassessment of strategy in Hanoi. Undeviating in their long-term aim of unification, the leaders of North Vietnam recognized that their strategy of military confrontation had failed to stop the American military build-up in the South or to reduce U.S. military pressure on the North. The enemy's regular and main force units had failed to inflict a salient military defeat on American forces. Although the North Vietnamese Army maintained the tactical initiative, Westmoreland had kept its units at bay and in some areas, like Binh Dinh Province, diminished their influence on the contest for control of the rural population. Many Communist military leaders perceived the war to be a stalemate and thought that continuing on their present course would bring diminishing returns, especially if their local forces were drastically weakened.

On the other side, Westmoreland could rightly point to some modest progress in improving South Vietnam's security and to punishing defeats inflicted on several NVA regiments and divisions. Yet none of his successes were sufficient to turn the tide of the war. The Communists had matched the build-up of American combat forces, the number of enemy divisions in the South increasing from one in early 1965 to nine at the start of 1968. Against 320 allied combat battalions, the North Vietnamese and Viet Cong could marshal 240. Despite heavy air attacks against enemy lines of infiltration, the flow of men from the North had continued unabated, even increasing toward the end of 1967.

Although the Military Assistance Command had succeeded in warding off defeat in 1965 and had gained valuable time for the South Vietnamese to concentrate their political and military resources on pacification, security in many areas of South Vietnam had improved little. Americans noted that the Viet Cong, in one district within artillery range of Saigon, rarely had any unit as large as a company. Yet, relying on booby traps, mines, and local guerrillas, they tied up over 6,000 American and South Vietnamese troops. More and more, success in the South seemed to depend not only on Westmoreland's ability to hold off and weaken enemy main force units, but on the equally important efforts of the South Vietnamese Army, the Regional and the Popular Forces, and a variety of paramilitary and police forces to pacify the countryside. Writing to President Johnson in the spring of 1967, outgoing Ambassador Henry Cabot Lodge warned that if the South Vietnamese "dribble along and do not take advantage of the success which MACV has achieved against the main force and the Army of North Viet-Nam, we must expect that the enemy will lick his wounds, pull himself together and make another attack in '68." Westmoreland's achievements, he added, would be "judged not so much on the brilliant performance of the U.S. troops as on the success in getting ARVN, RF and PF quickly to function as a first-class . . . counter-guerrilla force." Meanwhile the war appeared to be in a state of equilibrium. Only an extraordinary effort by one side or the other could bring a decision.

The Tet Offensive

The *Tet* offensive marked a unique stage in the evolution of North Vietnam's People's War. Hanoi's solution to the stalemate in the South was the product of several factors. North Vietnam's large unit war was unequal to the task of defeating American combat units. South Vietnam was becoming politically and militarily stronger, while the Viet Cong's grip over the rural population eroded. Hanoi's leaders suspected that the United States, frustrated by the slow pace of progress, might intensify its military operations against the North. (Indeed, Westmoreland had broached plans for an invasion of the North when he appealed for additional forces in 1967.) The *Tet* offensive was a brilliant stroke of strategy by Hanoi, designed to change the arena of war from the battlefield to the negotiating table, and from a strategy of military confrontation to one of talking and fighting.

Communist plans called for violent, widespread, simultaneous military actions in rural and urban areas throughout the South—a general offensive. But as always, military action was subordinate to a larger political goal. By focusing attacks on South Vietnamese units and facilities, Hanoi sought to undermine the morale and will of Saigon's forces. Through a collapse of military resistance, the North Vietnamese hoped to subvert public confidence in the government's ability to provide security, triggering a crescendo of popular protest to halt the fighting and force a political accommodation. In short, they aimed at a general uprising.

Hanoi's generals, however, were not completely confident that the general offensive would succeed. Viet Cong forces, hastily reinforced with new recruits and part-time guerrillas, bore the brunt. Except in the northern pro-

U.S. TROOPS PATROL *near Cholon during the Tet Offensive.*

vinces, the North Vietnamese Army stayed on the sidelines, poised to exploit success. While hoping to spur negotiations, Communist leaders probably had the more modest goals of reasserting Viet Cong influence and undermining Saigon's authority so as to cast doubt on its credibility as the United States' ally. In this respect, the offensive was directed toward the United States and sought to weaken American confidence in the Saigon government, discredit Westmoreland's claims of progress, and strengthen American antiwar sentiment. Here again, the larger purpose was to bring the United States to the negotiating table and hasten American disengagement from Vietnam.

The *Tet* offensive began quietly in mid-January 1968 in the remote northwest corner of South Vietnam. Elements of three NVA divisions began to mass near the Marine base at Khe Sanh. At first the ominous proportions of the build-up led the Military Assistance Command to expect a major offensive in the northern provinces. To some observers the situation at Khe Sanh resembled Dien Bien Phu, the isolated garrison where the Viet Minh had defeated French forces in 1954. Khe Sanh, however, was a diversion, an attempt to entice Westmoreland to defend yet another border post by withdrawing forces from the populated areas of the South.

While pressure around Khe Sanh increased, 85,000 Communist troops prepared for the *Tet* offensive. Since the fall of 1967, the enemy had been infiltrating arms, ammunition, and men, including entire units, into Saigon and other cities and towns. Most of these meticulous preparations went undetected, although MACV received warnings of a major enemy action to take place in early 1968. The command did pull some Army units closer to Saigon just before the attack. However, concern over the critical situation at Khe Sanh and preparations for the *Tet* holiday festivities preoccupied most Americans and South Vietnamese. Even when Communist forces prematurely attacked Kontum, Qui Nhon, Da Nang, and other towns in the northern and central provinces on 29 January, Americans were unprepared for what followed.

On 31 January combat erupted throughout the entire country. Thirty-six of 44 provincial capitals and 64 of 242 district towns were attacked, as well as 5 of South Vietnam's 6 autonomous cities, among them Hue and Saigon. Once the shock and confusion wore off, most attacks were crushed in a few days. During those few days, however, the fighting was some of the most violent ever seen in the South or experienced by many ARVN units. Though the South Vietnamese were the main target, American units were swept into the turmoil. All Army units in the vicinity of Saigon helped to repel Viet Cong attacks there and at the nearby logistical base of Long Binh. In some American compounds, cooks, radiomen, and clerks took up arms in their own defense. Military police units helped root the Viet Cong out of Saigon, and Army helicopter gunships were in the air almost continuously, assisting the allied forces.

The most tenacious combat occurred in Hue, the ancient capital of Vietnam, where the 1st Cavalry and 101st Airborne Divisions, together with marines and South Vietnamese forces, participated in the only extended urban combat of the war. Hue had a tradition of Buddhist activism, with overtones of neutralism, separatism, and anti-Americanism, and Hanoi's strategists thought that here if anywhere the general offensive–general uprising might gain a political foothold. Hence they threw North Vietnamese regulars into the battle, indicating that the stakes at Hue were higher than elsewhere in the South. House-to-house and street-to-street fighting caused enormous destruction, necessitating massive reconstruction and community assistance programs after the battle. The allies took three weeks to recapture the city. The slow, hard-won gains of 1967 vanished overnight as South Vietnamese and Marine forces were pulled out of the countryside to reinforce the city.

Yet throughout the country the South Vietnamese forces acquitted themselves well, despite high casualties and many desertions. Stunned by the attacks, civilian support for the Thieu government coalesced instead of weakening. Many Vietnamese for whom the war had been an unpleasant abstraction were outraged. Capitalizing on the new feeling, South Vietnam's leaders for the first time dared to enact general mobilization. The change from grudging toleration of the Viet Cong to active resistance provided an opportunity to create new local defense organizations and to attack the Communist infrastructure. Spurred by American advisers, the Vietnamese began to revitalize pacification. Most important, the Viet Cong suffered a major military defeat, losing thousands of experienced combatants and seasoned political cadres, seriously weakening the insurgent base in the South.

Americans at home saw a different picture. Dramatic images of the Viet

Cong storming the American Embassy in the heart of Saigon and the North Vietnamese Army clinging tenaciously to Hue obscured Westmoreland's assertion that the enemy had been defeated. Claims of progress in the war, already greeted with skepticism, lost more credibility in both public and official circles. The psychological jolt to President Johnson's Vietnam policy was redoubled when the military requested an additional 206,000 troops. Most were intended to reconstitute the strategic reserve in the United States, exhausted by Westmoreland's appeals for combat units between 1965 and 1967. But the magnitude of the new request, at a time when almost a half-million U.S. troops were already in Vietnam, cast doubts on the conduct of the war and prompted a reassessment of American policy and strategy.

Without mobilization, the United States was overcommitted. The Army could send few additional combat units to Vietnam without making deep inroads on forces destined for NATO or South Korea. The dwindling strategic reserve left Johnson with fewer options in the spring of 1968 than in the summer of 1965. His problems were underscored by heightened international tensions when North Korea captured an American naval vessel, the USS *Pueblo,* a week before the *Tet* offensive; by Soviet armed intervention in Czechoslovakia in the summer of 1968; and by chronic crises in the Mideast. In addition, Army units in the United States were needed often between 1965 and 1968 to enforce federal civil rights legislation and to restore public order in the wake of civil disturbances.

Again, as in 1967, Johnson refused to sanction a major troop levy, but he did give Westmoreland some modest reinforcements to bolster the northern provinces. Again tapping the strategic reserve, the Army sent him the 3d Brigade, 82d Airborne Division, and the 1st Brigade, 5th Infantry Division (Mechanized)—the last Army combat units to deploy to South Vietnam. In addition, the President called to active duty a small number of Reserve units, totaling some 40,000 men, for duty in Southeast Asia and South Korea, the only use of Reserves during the Vietnam War. For Westmoreland, Johnson's decision meant that future operations would have to make the best possible use of American forces, and that the South Vietnamese Army would have to shoulder a larger share of the war effort. The President also curtailed air strikes against North Vietnam to spur negotiations. Finally, on 31 March Johnson announced his decision not to seek re-election in order to give his full attention to the goal of resolving the conflict. Hanoi had suffered a military defeat, but had won a political and diplomatic victory by shifting American policy toward disengagement.

For the Army the new policy meant a difficult time. In South Vietnam, as in the United States, its forces were stretched thin. The *Tet* offensive had concentrated a large portion of the combat forces in I Corps, once a Marine preserve. A new command, the XXIV Corps, had to be activated at Da Nang, and Army logistical support, previously confined to the three southern corps zones, extended to the five northern provinces as well. While Army units reinforced Hue and the demilitarized zone, the marines at Khe Sanh held fast. Enemy pressure on the besieged base increased daily, but the North Vietnamese refrained from an all-out attack, still hoping to divert American forces from Hue. Recognizing that he could ill afford Khe Sanh's defense, Westmoreland decided to subject the enemy to the heaviest air and artillery bombardment of the war. His tactical gamble succeeded; the enemy withdrew, and the Communist offensive slackened.

The enemy nevertheless persisted in his effort to weaken the Saigon government, launching nationwide "mini-*Tet*" offensives in May and August. Pockets of heavy fighting occurred throughout the south, and Viet Cong forces again tried to infiltrate into Saigon—the last gasps of the general offensive–general uprising. Thereafter enemy forces generally dispersed and avoided contact with Americans. In turn, the allies withdrew from Khe Sanh itself in the summer of 1968. Its abandonment signaled the demise of the McNamara Line and further postponement of MACV's hopes for large-scale American cross-border operations. For the remainder of 1968, Army units in I Corps were content to help restore security around Hue and other coastal areas, working closely with the marines and the South Vietnamese in support of pacification. North Vietnamese and Viet Cong forces generally avoided offensive operations. As armistice negotiations began in Paris, both sides prepared to enter a new phase of the war.

Vietnamization

The last phase of American involvement in South Vietnam was carried out under a broad policy called Vietnamization. Its main goal was to create strong, largely self-reliant South Vietnamese military forces, an objective consistent with that espoused by U.S. advisers as early as the 1950's. But Vietnamization also meant the withdrawal of a half-million American soldiers. Past efforts to strengthen and modernize South Vietnam's Army had proceeded at a measured pace, without the pressure of diminishing American support, large-scale combat, or the presence of formidable North Vietnamese forces in the South. Vietnamization entailed three overlapping phases: redeployment of American forces and the assumption of their combat role by the South Vietnamese; improvement of ARVN's combat and support capabilities, especially firepower and mobility; and replacement of the Military Assistance Command by an American advisory group. Vietnamization had the added dimension of fostering political, social, and economic reforms to create a vibrant South Vietnamese state based on popular participation in national political life. Such reforms, however, depended on progress in the pacification program which never had a clearly fixed timetable.

The task of carrying out the military aspects of Vietnamization fell to General Creighton W. Abrams, who succeeded General Westmoreland as MACV commander in mid-1968, when the latter returned to the United States to become Chief of Staff of the Army. Although he had the aura of a blunt, hard-talking, World War II tank commander, Abrams had spent two years as Westmoreland's deputy, working closely with South Vietnamese commanders. Like Westmoreland before him, Abrams viewed the military situation after *Tet* as an opportunity to make gains in pacifying rural areas and to reduce the strength of Communist forces in the South. Until the weakened Viet Cong forces could be rebuilt or replaced with NVA forces, both guerrilla and regular Communist forces had adopted a defensive posture. Nevertheless, 90,000 NVA forces were in the South, or in border sanctuaries, waiting to resume the offensive at a propitious time.

Abrams still had strong American forces; indeed, they reached their peak strength of 543,000 in March 1969. But he was also under pressure from Washington to minimize casualties and to conduct operations with an eye toward leaving the South Vietnamese in the strongest possible military position when U.S. forces withdrew. With these considerations in mind, Abrams decided to disrupt and destroy the enemy's bases, especially those near the border, to prevent their use as staging areas for offensive operations. His primary objective was the enemy's logistical support system rather than enemy main combat forces. At the same time, to enhance Saigon's pacification efforts and improve local security, Abrams intended to emphasize small unit operations, with extensive patrolling and ambushes, aiming to reduce the enemy's base of support among the rural population.

To the greatest extent possible, he planned to improve ARVN's performance by conducting combined operations with American combat units. As the South Vietnamese Army assumed the lion's share of combat, it was expected to shift operations to the border and to assume a role similar to that performed by U.S. forces between 1965 and 1969. The Regional and Popular Forces, in turn, were to take over ARVN's role in area security and pacification support, while the newly organized People's Self-Defense Force took on the task of village and hamlet defense. Stressing the close connection between combat and pacification operations, the need for co-operation between American and South Vietnamese forces, and the importance of co-ordinating all echelons of Saigon's armed forces, Abrams propounded a "one war" concept.

ARTILLERY TRAINING *formed a part of the Vietnamization program.*

Yet even in his emphasis on combined operations and American support of pacification, Abrams' strategy had strong elements of continuity with Westmoreland's. For the first, operations in War Zones C and D in 1967 and the thrust into the A Shau valley in 1968 were ample precedents. Again, Westmoreland had laid the foundation for a more extensive U.S. role in pacification in 1967 by establishing Civil Operations Rural Development Support (CORDS). Under CORDS, the Military Assistance Command took charge of all American activities, military and civilian, in support of pacification. Abrams' contribution was to enlarge the Army's role. Under him, the U.S. advisory effort at provincial and district levels grew as the territorial forces gained in importance, and additional advisers were assigned to the Phoenix program, a concerted effort to eliminate the Communist political apparatus. Numerous mobile advisory teams helped the South Vietnamese Army and paramilitary forces to become adept in a variety of combat and support functions.

Despite all efforts, many Americans doubted whether Saigon's armed forces could successfully play their enlarged role under Vietnamization. Earlier counterinsurgency efforts had languished under less demanding circumstances, and Saigon's forces continued to be plagued with high desertions, spotty morale, and shortages of high quality leaders. Like the French before them, U.S. advisers had assumed a major role in providing and co-ordinating logistical and firepower support, leaving the Vietnamese inexperienced in the conduct of large combined-arms operations. Despite the Viet Cong's weakened condition, South Vietnamese forces also continued to incur high casualties.

Similarly, pacification registered ostensible gains in rural security and other measures of progress, but such improvements often obscured its failure to establish deep roots. The Phoenix program, despite its success in seizing low-level cadres, rarely caught hard-core, high-level party officials, many of whom survived, as they had in the mid-1950's, by taking more stringent security measures. Furthermore, the program was abused by some South Vietnamese officials, who used it as a vehicle for personal vendettas. Saigon's efforts at political, social, and economic reform likewise were susceptible to corruption, venality, and nepotism. Temporary social and economic benefits for the peasantry rested on an uncertain foundation of continued American aid, as did South Vietnam's entire economy and war effort.

Influencing all parts of the struggle was a new defense policy enunciated by Richard M. Nixon, who became President in January 1969. The "Nixon Doctrine" harkened back to the precepts of the New Look, placing greater reliance on nuclear retaliation, encouraging allies to accept a larger share of their own defense burden, and barring the use of U.S. ground forces in limited wars in Asia, unless vital national interests were at stake. Under this policy, American ground forces in South Vietnam, once withdrawn, were unlikely to return. For President Thieu in Saigon, the future was inauspicious. For the time being, large numbers of American forces were still present to bolster his country's war effort; what would happen when they departed, no one knew.

Military Operations, 1968–1969

Vietnamization began in earnest when two brigades of the U.S. Army's 9th Infantry Division left South Vietnam in July 1968, making the South Vietnamese Army responsible for securing the southern approaches to Saigon. The protective area that Westmoreland had developed around the capital was still intact. Allied forces engaged in a corps-wide counteroffensive to locate and destroy remnants of the enemy units that had participated in the *Tet* offensive, combining thousands of small unit operations, frequent sweeps through enemy bases, and persistent screening of the Cambodian border to prevent enemy main force units from returning. As the Military

Assistance Command anticipated, the Communists launched a *Tet* offensive in 1969, but a much weaker one than a year earlier. Allied forces easily suppressed the outbreaks. Meanwhile, in critical areas around Saigon pacification had begun to take hold. Such signs of progress probably resulted mainly from the attrition of Viet Cong forces during *Tet* 1968. But the vigilant screening of the border contributed to the enemy's difficulty in reaching and helping local insurgent forces.

Yet Saigon was not impregnable. With increasing frequency, enemy sappers penetrated close enough to launch powerful rocket attacks against the capital. Such incidents terrorized civilians, caused military casualties, and were a violent reminder of the government's inability to protect the population. Sometimes simultaneous attacks were conducted throughout the country. An economy-of-force measure, the attacks brought little risk to the enemy and compelled allied forces to suspend other tasks while they cleared the "rocket belts" around every major urban center and base in the country.

In the Central Highlands the war of attrition continued. Until its redeployment of 1970, the Army protected major highland population centers and kept open important interior roads. Special Forces worked with the tribal highlanders to detect infiltration and harass enemy secret zones. As in the past, highland camps and outposts were a magnet for enemy attacks, meant to lure reaction forces into an ambush or to divert the allies from operations elsewhere. Ben Het in Kontum Province was besieged from March to July of 1969. Other bases—Thien Phuoc and Thuong Duc in I Corps; Bu Prang, Dak Seang, and Dak Pek in II Corps; and Katum, Bu Dop, and Tong Le Chon in III Corps—were attacked because of their proximity to Communist strongholds and infiltration routes. In some cases camps had to be abandoned, but in most the attackers were repulsed. By the time the 5th Special Forces Group left South Vietnam in March 1971, all CIDG units had been converted to Regional Forces or absorbed by the South Vietnamese Rangers. The departure of the Green Berets brought an end to any significant Army role in the highlands.

Following the withdrawal of the 4th and 9th Divisions, Army units concentrated around Saigon and in the northern provinces. Operating in Quang Ngai, Quang Tin, and Quang Nam Provinces, the 23d Infantry Division (Americal) conducted a series of operations in 1968 and 1969 to secure and pacify the heavily populated coastal plain of southern I Corps. Along the demilitarized zone, the 1st Brigade, 5th Infantry Division (Mechanized), helped marines and South Vietnamese forces to screen the zone and to secure the northern coastal region, including a stretch of highway, the "street without joy," that was notorious from the time of the French. The

101st Airborne Division (converted to the Army's second airmobile division in 1968) divided its attention between the defense of Hue and forays into the enemy's base in the A Shau valley.

Since the 1968 *Tet* offensive, the Communists had restocked the A Shau valley with ammunition, rice, and equipment. The logistical build-up pointed to a possible NVA offensive in early 1969. In quick succession, Army operations were launched in the familiar pattern: air assaults, establishment of fire support bases, and exploration of the lowlands and surrounding hills to locate enemy forces and supplies. This time the Army met stiff enemy resistance, especially from antiaircraft guns. The North Vietnamese had expected the American forces and now planned to hold their ground.

On 11 May 1969, a battalion of the 101st Airborne Division climbing Hill 937 found the *29th North Vietnamese Regiment* waiting for it. The struggle for "Hamburger Hill" raged for ten days and became one of the war's fiercest and most controversial battles. Entrenched in tiers of fortified bunkers with well-prepared fields of fire, the enemy forces withstood repeated attempts to dislodge them. Supported by intense artillery and air strikes, Americans made a slow, tortuous climb, fighting hand to hand. By the time Hill 937 was taken, three Army battalions and an ARVN regiment had been committed to the battle. Victory, however, was ambiguous as well as costly; the hill itself had no strategic or tactical importance and was abandoned soon after its capture. Critics charged that the battle wasted American lives and exemplified the irrelevance of U.S. tactics in Vietnam. Defending the operation, the commander of the 101st acknowledged that the hill's only significance was that the enemy occupied it. "My mission," he said, "was to destroy enemy forces and installations. We found the enemy on Hill 937, and that is where we fought them."

About one month later the 101st left the A Shau valley, and the North Vietnamese were free to use it again. American plans to return in the summer of 1970 came to nothing when enemy pressure forced the abandonment of two fire support bases needed for operations there. The loss of Fire Support Base O'REILLY, only eleven miles from Hue, was an ominous sign that enemy forces had reoccupied the A Shau and were seeking to dominate the valleys leading to the coastal plain. Until it redeployed in 1971, the 101st Airborne, with the marines and South Vietnamese forces, now devoted most of its efforts to protecting Hue. The operations against the A Shau had achieved no more than Westmoreland's large search and destroy operations in 1967. As soon as the allies left, the enemy reclaimed his traditional bases.

The futility of such operations was mirrored in events on the coastal plain. Here the 23d Infantry Division fought in an area where the population had long been sympathetic to the Viet Cong. As in other areas, pacification in southern I Corps seemed to improve after the 1968 *Tet* offensive, though enemy units still dominated the piedmont and continued to challenge American and South Vietnamese forces on the coast. Operations against them proved to be slow, frustrating exercises in warding off NVA and Viet Cong main force units while enduring harassment from local guerrillas and the hostile population. Except during spasms of intense combat, as in the summer of 1969 when the American Division confronted the *1st North Vietnamese Regiment*, most U.S. casualties were caused by snipers, mines, and booby traps. Villages populated by old men, women, and children were as dangerous as the elusive enemy main force units. Operating in such conditions day after day induced a climate of fear and hate among the Americans. The already thin line between civilian and combatant was easily blurred and violated. In the hamlet of My Lai, elements of the American Division killed about two hundred civilians in the spring of 1968. Although only one member of the division was tried and found guilty of war crimes, the repercussions of the atrocity were felt throughout the Army. However rare, such acts undid the benefit of countless hours of civic action by Army units and individual soldiers and raised unsettling questions about the conduct of the war.

What happened at My Lai could have occurred in any Army unit in Vietnam in the late 1960's and early 1970's. War crimes were born of a sense of frustration that also contributed to a host of morale and discipline problems, among enlisted men and officers alike. As American forces were withdrawn by a government eager to escape the war, the lack of a clear military objective contributed to a weakened sense of mission and a slackening of discipline. The short-timer syndrome, the reluctance to take risks in combat toward the end of a soldier's one-year tour, was compounded by the "last-casualty" syndrome. Knowing that all U.S. troops would soon leave Vietnam, no soldier wanted to be the last to die. Meanwhile, in the United States harsh criticism of the war, the military, and traditional military values had become widespread. Heightened individualism, growing permissiveness, and a weakening of traditional bonds of authority pervaded American society and affected the Army's rank and file. The Army grappled with problems of drug abuse, racial tensions, weakened discipline, and lapses of leadership. While outright refusals to fight were few in number, incidents of "fragging"—murderous attacks on officers and noncoms—occurred frequently enough to compel commands to institute a host of new security measures within their cantonments. All these problems were symptoms of larger social and political forces and underlined a growing disenchantment with the war among soldiers in the field.

As the Army prepared to leave Vietnam, lassitude and war-weariness at times resulted in tragedy, as at Fire Support Base MARY ANN in 1971. There soldiers of the Americal Division, soon to go home, relaxed their security and were overrun by a North Vietnamese force. Such incidents reflected a decline in the quality of leadership among both noncommissioned and commissioned officers. Lowered standards, abbreviated training, and accelerated promotions to meet the high demand for noncommissioned and junior officers often resulted in the assignment of squad, platoon, and company leaders with less combat experience than the troops they led. Careerism and ticket-punching in officer assignments, false reporting and inflated body counts, and revelations of scandal and corruption all raised disquieting questions about the professional ethics of Army leadership. Critics indicted the tactics and techniques used by the Army in Vietnam, noting that airmobility, for example, tended to distance troops from the population they were sent to protect and that commanders aloft in their command and control helicopters were at a psychological and physical distance from the soldiers they were supposed to lead.

Cross-border Operations

With most U.S. combat units slated to leave South Vietnam during 1970 and 1971, time was a critical factor for the success of Vietnamization and pacification. Neither program could thrive if Saigon's forces were distracted by enemy offensives launched from bases in Laos or Cambodia. While Abrams' logistical offensive temporarily reduced the level of enemy activity in the South, bases outside South Vietnam had been inviolable to allied ground forces. Harboring enemy forces, command facilities, and logistical depots, the Cambodian and Laotian bases threatened the fragile progress made in the South since *Tet* 1968. To the Nixon administration, Abrams' plans to violate the Communist sanctuaries had the special appeal of gaining more time for Vietnamization and of compensating for the bombing halt over North Vietnam.

Because of their proximity to Saigon, the bases in Cambodia received first priority. Planning for the cross-border attack occurred at a critical time in Cambodia. In early 1970 Cambodia's neutralist leader, Prince Norodom Sihanouk, was overthrown by his pro-Western Defense Minister, General Lon Nol. Among Lon Nol's first actions was closing the port of Sihanouk-ville to supplies destined for Communist forces in the border bases and in South Vietnam. He also demanded that Communist forces leave Cambodia and accepted Saigon's offer to apply pressure against those located near the border. A few weeks earlier, American B–52 bombers had begun in secret to bomb enemy bases in Cambodia. By late April, South Vietnamese military units, accompanied by American advisers, had mounted large-scale ground operations across the border.

On 1 May 1970, units of the 1st Cavalry Division, the 25th Infantry Division, and the 11th Armored Cavalry followed. Cambodia became a new battlefield of the Vietnam War. Cutting a broad swath through the enemy's Cambodian bases, Army units discovered large, sprawling, well-stocked storage sites, training camps, and hospitals, all recently occupied. What Americans did not find were large enemy forces or COSVN headquarters. Only small delaying forces offered sporadic resistance, while main force units retreated to northeastern Cambodia. Meanwhile the expansion of the war produced violent demonstrations in the United States. In response to the public outcry, Nixon imposed a geographical and time limit on operations in Cambodia, enabling the enemy to stay beyond reach. At the end of June, one day short of the sixty days allotted to the operation, all advisers accompanying the South Vietnamese and all U.S. Army units had left Cambodia.

Political and military events in Cambodia triggered changes in the war as profound as those engendered by the *Tet* offensive. From a quiescent "sideshow" of the war, Cambodia became an arena for the major belligerents. Military activity increased in northern Cambodia and southern Laos as Hanoi established new infiltration routes and bases to replace those lost during the incursion. Hanoi made clear that it regarded all Indochina as a single theater of operations. Cambodia itself was engulfed in a virulent civil war.

As U.S. Army units withdrew, the South Vietnamese Army found itself in a race against Communist forces to secure the Cambodian capital of Phnom Penh. Americans provided Saigon's overextended forces air and logistical support to enable them to stabilize the situation there. The time to strengthen Vietnamization gained by the incursion now had to be weighed in the balance against ARVN's new commitment in Cambodia. To the extent that South Vietnam's forces bolstered Lon Nol's regime, they were unable to contribute to pacification and rural security in their own country. Moreover, the South Vietnamese performance in Cambodia was mixed. When working closely with American advisers, the army acquitted itself well. But when forced to rely on its own resources, the army revealed its inexperience and limitations in attempting to plan and execute large operations.

Despite ARVN's equivocal performance, less than a year later the Americans pressed the South Vietnamese to launch a second cross-border operation, this time into Laos. Although U.S. air, artillery, and logistical support would be provided, this time Army advisers would not accompany South Vietnamese forces. The Americans' enthusiasm for the operation exceeded that of their allies. Anticipating high casualties, South Vietnam's leaders were reluctant to involve their army once more in extended operations outside their country. But American intelligence had detected a North Vietnamese build-up in the vicinity of Tchepone, a logistical center on the Ho Chi Minh Trail approximately 25 miles west of the South Vietnamese border in Laos. The Military Assistance Command regarded the build-up as a prelude to an NVA spring offensive in the northern provinces. Like the Cambodian incursion, the Laotian invasion was justified as benefiting Vietnamization, but with the added bonuses of spoiling a prospective offensive and cutting the Ho Chi Minh Trail.

In preparation for the operation, Army helicopters and artillery were moved to the vicinity of the abandoned base at Khe Sanh. The 101st Airborne Division conducted a feint toward the A Shau valley to conceal the true objective. On 8 February 1971, spearheaded by tanks and with airmobile units leapfrogging ahead to establish fire support bases in Laos, a South Vietnamese mechanized column advanced down Highway 9 toward Tchepone. Operation LAM SON 719 had begun.

The North Vietnamese were not deceived. South Vietnamese forces numbering about 25,000 became bogged down by heavy enemy resistance and bad weather. The drive toward Tchepone stalled. Facing the South Vietnamese were elements of five NVA divisions, as well as a tank regiment, an artillery regiment, and at least nineteen antiaircraft battalions. After a delay of several days, South Vietnamese forces air-assaulted into the heavily bombed town of Tchepone. By that time, the North Vietnamese had counterattacked with Soviet-built T54 and T55 tanks, heavy artillery, and infantry. They struck the rear of the South Vietnamese forces strung out on Highway 9, blocking their main avenue of withdrawal. Enemy forces also overwhelmed several South Vietnamese fire support bases, depriving ARVN units of desperately needed flank protection. The South Vietnamese also lacked antitank weapons to counter the North Vietnamese armor that appeared on the Laotian jungle trails. The result was near-disaster. Army helicopter pilots trying to rescue South Vietnamese soldiers from their besieged hilltop fire bases encountered intense antiaircraft fire. Panic ensued when some South Vietnamese units ran out of ammunition. In some units, all semblance of an orderly withdrawal vanished as desperate South Vietnamese soldiers pushed the wounded off evacuation helicopters or clung to helicopter skids to reach safety. Eventually, ARVN forces punched their way out of Laos, but only after paying a heavy price.

U.S. ARTILLERY SUPPORT DURING OPERATION LAM SON 719

That the South Vietnamese Army had reached its objective of Tchepone was of little consequence. Its stay there was brief and the supply caches it discovered disappointingly small. Saigon's forces had failed to sever the Ho Chi Minh Trail; infiltration reportedly increased during LAM SON 719, as the North Vietnamese shifted traffic to roads and trails further to the west in Laos. In addition to losing nearly 2,000 men, the South Vietnamese lost large amounts of equipment during their disorderly withdrawal, and the U.S. Army lost 107 helicopters, the highest number in any one operation of the war. Supporters pointed to heavy enemy casualties and argued that equipment losses were reasonable, given the large number of helicopters used to support LAM SON 719. The battle nevertheless raised disturbing questions among Army officials about the vulnerability of helicopters in mid- or high-intensity conflict. What was the future of airmobility in any war where the enemy possessed a significant antiaircraft capability?

LAM SON 719 proved to be a less ambiguous test of Vietnamization than the Cambodian incursion. The South Vietnamese Army did not perform well in Laos. Reflecting on the operation, General Ngo Quan Truong, the commander of I Corps, noted ARVN's chronic weakness in planning for and co-ordinating combat support. He also noted that from the battalion to the division level, the army had become dependent on U.S. advisers. At the highest levels of command, he added, "the need for advisers was more acutely felt in two specific areas: planning and leadership. The basic weakness of ARVN units at regimental and sometimes division level in those areas," he continued, "seriously affected the performance of subordinate units." LAM SON 719 scored one success, forestalling a Communist spring offensive in the northern provinces; in other respects, it was a failure and an ill omen for the future.

Withdrawal: The Final Battles

As the Americans withdrew, South Vietnam's combat capability declined. The United States furnished its allies the heavier M48 tank to match the NVA's T54 tank and heavier artillery to counter North Vietnamese 130-mm. guns, though past experience suggested that additional arms and equipment could not compensate for poor skills and mediocre leadership. In fact, the weapons and equipment were insufficient to offset the reduction in U.S. combat strength. In mid-1969, for example, an aggregate of fifty-six allied combat battalions were present in South Vietnam's two northern provinces; in 1972, after the departure of most American units, only thirty battalions were in the same area. Artillery strength in the northern region declined from approximately 400 guns to 169 in the same period, and ammunition supply rates fell off as well. Similar reductions took place throughout South Vietnam, causing decreases in mobility, firepower, intelligence support, and air support. Five thousand American helicopters were replaced by about 500. American specialties —B–52 strikes, photo reconnaissance, and the use of sensors and other means of target acquisition—were drastically curtailed.

Such losses were all the more serious because operations in Cambodia and Laos had illustrated how deeply ingrained in the South Vietnamese Army the American style of warfare had become. Nearly two decades of U.S. military involvement were exacting an unexpected price. As one ARVN division commander commented, "Trained as they were through combined action with US units, the [South Vietnamese] unit commander was used to the employment of massive firepower." That habit, he added, "was hard to relinquish."

By November 1971, when the 101st Airborne Division withdrew from the South, Hanoi was planning its 1972 spring offensive. With ARVN's combat capacity diminished and nearly all U.S. combat troops gone, North Vietnam sensed an opportunity to demonstrate the failure of Vietnamization, hasten

ARVN's collapse, and revive the stalled peace talks. In its broad outlines and goals, the 1972 offensive resembled *Tet* 1968, except that the North Vietnamese Army, instead of the Viet Cong, bore the major burden of combat. The Nguyen-Hue offensive or Easter offensive began on 30 March 1972. Total U.S. military strength in South Vietnam was about 95,000, of which only 6,000 were combat troops, and the task of countering the offensive on the ground fell almost exclusively to the South Vietnamese.

Attacking on three fronts, the North Vietnamese Army poured across the demilitarized zone and out of Laos to capture Quang Tri, South Vietnam's northernmost province. In the Central Highlands, enemy units moved into Kontum Province, forcing Saigon to relinquish several border posts before government forces contained the offensive. On 2 April, Viet Cong and North Vietnamese forces struck Loc Ninh, just south of the Cambodian border on Highway 13, and advanced south to An Loc along one of the main invasion routes toward Saigon. A two-month-long battle ensued, until enemy units were driven from An Loc and forced to disperse to bases in Cambodia. By late summer the Easter offensive had run its course; the South Vietnamese, in a slow, cautious counteroffensive, recaptured Quang Tri City and most of the lost province. But the margin of victory or defeat often was supplied by the massive supporting firepower provided by U.S. air and naval forces.

The tactics of the war were changing. Communist forces now made extensive use of armor and artillery. Among the new weapons in the enemy's arsenal was the Soviet SA–7 hand-held antiaircraft missile, which posed a threat to slow-flying tactical aircraft and helicopters. On the other hand, the Army's attack helicopter, the Cobra, outfitted with TOW antitank missiles, proved effective against NVA armor at stand-off range. In their antitank role, Army attack helicopters were crucial to ARVN's success at An Loc, suggesting a larger role for helicopters in the future as part of a combined arms team in conventional combat.

Vietnamization continued to show mixed results. The benefits of the South Vietnamese Army's newly acquired mobility and firepower were dissipated as it became responsible for securing areas vacated by American forces. Improvements of territorial and paramilitary troops were offset as they became increasingly vulnerable to attack by superior North Vietnamese forces. Insurgency was also reviving. Though their progress was less spectacular than the blitzkrieg-like invasion of the South, North Vietnamese forces entered the Delta in thousands between 1969 and 1973 to replace the Viet Cong—one estimate suggested a tenfold increase in NVA strength, from 3,000 to 30,000, in this period. Here the fighting resembled that of the early

1960's, as enemy forces attacked lightly defended outposts and hamlets to regain control over the rural population in anticipation of a cease-fire. The strength of the People's Self-Defense Force, Saigon's first line of hamlet and village defense, after steady increases in 1969 and 1970, began to decline after 1971, also suggesting a revival of the insurgency in the countryside. Pursuing a strategy used successfully in the past, the North Vietnamese forced ARVN troops to the borders, exposing the countryside and leaving its protection in the hands of weaker forces.

Such unfavorable signs, however, did not disturb South Vietnam's leaders as long as they could count on continued United States air and naval support. Nixon's resumption of the bombing of North Vietnam during the Easter offensive and, for the first time, his mining of North Vietnamese ports encouraged this expectation, as did the intense American bombing of Hanoi and Haiphong in late 1972. But such pressure was intended, at least in part, to force North Vietnam to sign an armistice. If Thieu was encouraged by the display of U.S. military muscle, the course of negotiations could only have been a source of discouragement. Hanoi dropped an earlier demand for Thieu's removal, but the United States gave up its insistence on Hanoi's withdrawal of its troops from the South. In early 1973 the United States, North and South Vietnam, and the Viet Cong signed an armistice that promised a cease-fire and national reconciliation. In fact, fighting continued, but the Military Assistance Command was dissolved, remaining U.S. forces withdrawn, and American military action in South Vietnam terminated. Perhaps most important of all, American advisers—still in many respects the backbone of ARVN's command structure—were withdrawn.

Between 1973 and 1975 South Vietnam's military security further declined through a combination of old and new factors. Plagued by poor maintenance and shortages of spare parts, much of the equipment provided Saigon's forces under Vietnamization became inoperable. A rise in fuel prices stemming from a worldwide oil crisis further restricted ARVN's use of vehicles and aircraft. South Vietnamese forces in many areas of the country were on the defensive, confined to protecting key towns and installations. Seeking to preserve its diminishing assets, the South Vietnamese Army became garrison bound and either reluctant or unable to react to a growing number of guerrilla attacks that eroded rural security. Congressionally mandated reductions in U.S. aid further reduced the delivery of repair parts, fuel, and ammunition. American military activities in Cambodia and Laos, which had continued after the cease-fire in South Vietnam went into effect, ended in 1973 when Congress cut off funds. Complaining of this austerity, President Thieu noted that he had to fight a "poor man's war." Vietnamization's legacy was that South Vietnam had to do more with less.

In 1975 North Vietnam's leaders began planning for a new offensive, still uncertain whether the United States would resume bombing or once again intervene in the South. When their forces overran Phuoc Long Province, north of Saigon, without any American military reaction, they decided to proceed with a major offensive in the Central Highlands. Neither President Nixon, weakened by the Watergate scandal and forced to resign, nor his successor, Gerald Ford, was prepared to challenge Congress by resuming U.S. military activity in Southeast Asia. The will of Congress seemed to reflect the mood of an American public weary of the long and inconclusive war.

What had started as a limited offensive in the highlands to draw off forces from populated areas now became an all-out effort to conquer South Vietnam. Thieu, desiring to husband his military assets, decided to retreat rather than to reinforce the highlands. The result was panic among his troops and a mass exodus toward the coast. As Hanoi's forces spilled out of the highlands, they cut off South Vietnamese defenders in the northern provinces from the rest of the country. Other NVA units now crossed the demilitarized zone, quickly overrunning Hue and Da Nang, and signaling the collapse of South Vietnamese resistance in the north. Hurriedly established defense lines around Saigon could not hold back the inexorable enemy offensive against the capital. As South Vietnamese leaders waited in vain for American assistance, Saigon fell to the Communists on 29 April 1975.

The Post-Vietnam Army

Saigon's fall was a bitter end to the long American effort to sustain South Vietnam. Ranging from advice and support to direct participation in combat and involving nearly three million U.S. servicemen, the effort failed to stop Communist leaders from reaching their goal of unifying a divided nation. South Vietnam's military defeat tended to obscure the crucial inability of this massive military enterprise to compensate for Saigon's political shortcomings. Over a span of nearly two decades, a series of regimes failed to mobilize fully and effectively their nation's political, social, and economic resources to foster a popular base of support. North Vietnamese main force units ended the war, but local insurgency among the people of the South made that outcome possible and perhaps inevitable.

The U.S. Army paid a high price for its long involvement in South Vietnam. American military deaths exceeded 58,000, and of these about two-thirds were soldiers. The majority of the dead were low-ranking enlisted men (E–2 and E–3), young men twenty-three years old or younger, of whom approximately 13 percent were black. Most deaths were caused by small-arms fire and gunshot, but a significant portion, almost 30 percent, stemmed from mines, booby traps, and grenades. Artillery, rockets, and bombs accounted for only a small portion of the total fatalities.

If not for the unprecedented medical care that the Army provided in South Vietnam, the death toll would have been higher yet. Nearly 300,000 Americans were wounded, of whom half required hospitalization. The lives of many seriously injured men, who would have become fatalities in earlier wars, were saved by rapid helicopter evacuation direct to hospitals close to the combat zone. Here, relatively secure from air and ground attack, usually unencumbered by mass casualties, and with access to an uninterrupted supply of whole blood, Army doctors and nurses availed themselves of the latest medical technology to save thousands of lives. As one medical officer pointed out, the Army was able to adopt a "civilian philosophy of casualty triage" in the combat zone that directed the "major effort first to the most seriously injured." But some who served in South Vietnam suffered more insidious damage from the adverse psychological effects of combat or the long-term effects of exposure to chemical agents. More than a decade after the end of the war, 1,761 American soldiers remain listed as missing in action.

The war-ravaged Vietnamese, north and south, incurred the greatest losses. South Vietnamese military deaths exceeded 200,000. War-related civilian deaths in the South approached a half-million, while the injured and maimed numbered many more. Accurate estimates of enemy casualties run afoul of the difficulty in distinguishing between civilians and combatants, imprecise body counts, and the difficulty of verifying casualties in areas controlled by the enemy. Nevertheless, nearly a million Viet Cong and North Vietnamese soldiers are believed to have perished in combat through the spring of 1975.

For the U.S. Army the scars of the war ran even deeper than the grim statistics showed. Given its long association with South Vietnam's fortunes, the Army could not escape being tarnished by its ally's fall. The loss compounded already unsettling questions about the Army's role in Southeast Asia, about the soundness of its advice to the South Vietnamese, about its understanding of the nature of the war, about the appropriateness of its strategy and tactics, and about the adequacy of the counsel provided by Army leaders to national decision makers. Marked by ambiguous military objectives, defensive strategy, lack of tactical initiative, ponderous tactics, and untidy command arrangements, the struggle in Vietnam seemed to violate most of the time-honored principles of war. Many officers sought to erase

Vietnam from the Army's corporate memory, feeling uncomfortable with the ignominy of failure or believing that the lessons and experience of the war were of little use to the post-Vietnam Army. Although a generation of officers, including many of the Army's future leaders, cut their combat teeth in Vietnam, many regretted that the Army's reputation, integrity, and professionalism had been tainted in the service of a flawed strategy and a dubious ally.

CHAPTER 29

Geopolitical and Strategic Change, 1975-1996

The Armed Forces, and particularly the Army, emerged from the Vietnam War with deep scars and an uncertain future. Problems were manifold. Manpower quality was declining, morale low, drug use widespread, enlistment rates were poor, and racial relations abysmal. The NCO corps was in disarray, the officer corps undergoing a crisis of confidence, and large numbers of good men and women were leaving the service. The war had other effects as well. For over a decade budgets, thinking, and training had been focused on the conflict in Southeast Asia. As a result by 1975 training, equipment, and doctrine were increasingly outdated. While these problems affected all the services, it was the Army, most closely identified with the war in Vietnam, which suffered most seriously. To many, the situation seemed so hopeless that, in a phrase coined at the time, the nation had a "hollow army."

Yet there were many others who did not despair, and were determined to rebuild the Armed Forces. Indeed, the seeds of a rebirth of the Armed Forces, and particularly the Army, were actually planted in the waning days of the Vietnam War. The road was difficult, but the results were remarkable.

Military Reform

Even before the withdrawal of U.S. ground forces from Vietnam in 1972, the process of assessing the lessons of the war had begun. One of the prime movers in this reassessment was General Creighton Abrams, who had commanded in Vietnam from 1968 to 1972. Appointed Chief-of-Staff of the Army in 1972, Abrams was instrumental in preventing the development of a "stab in the back" mood, pushing for a realistic examination of the roots of the Vietnam debacle and the problems confronting the service. There were many problems, in personnel, equipment, doctrine, organization, direction.

If the perceived failure of the Armed Forces in Vietnam provided the impetus for their reform, it was the Arab-Israeli War of 1973 which pointed the way towards the future. The speed and lethality of operations during the brief war proved a sobering lesson to a military leadership that had been focused on "low intensity" warfare for over a decade. The war returned attention to the "main event," a Soviet Bloc offensive on the Central Front in Europe, one undertaken without a lengthy period of rising tension and military buildup. Fortunately, shortly before the Arab-Israeli War the Army had created an agency charged with looking towards the future, TRADOC, the Training and Doctrine Command, under General William E. DePuy. A systematic examination of the 1973 war and of other historical conflicts, such as the Russo-German struggle during World War II, led to the development of the 1976 edition of FM 100-5, the Army's official guidelines on "how to fight." The emphasis shifted towards a "come as you are" war, one with little or no time for preparations, and one fought by brigades and divisions. TRADOC proposed fundamental changes in the organization of combat units, to enable them to train more effectively in peace and fight more efficiently in war.

Even as this was taking place, there was simultaneously a revival of interest in military history, a trend which was fostered by new leadership at the highest levels. Military History, once a mainstay of officer training, had been neglected by the Army during the 1950s and 1960s, eras of massive retaliation and low intensity warfare with stress on management and mathematical modeling. There was an assumption that nuclear weapons and Marxist "wars of national liberation" had so altered the conduct of war that historical precedents were no longer relevant. However, those looking at the Vietnam War soon found that many of the errors made could have been avoided if historical precedents had been examined with greater care. As a result, greater stress began being laid on military history. One consequence of this was a revival of traditional wargaming in the army, using historically based models. Wargaming—historical conflict simulation—had attained considerable popularity during the years when it was neglected by professional soldiers. As the Army's interest in historical wargaming revived, it drew on the expertise of a small, but successful and experienced, body of professional specialists in the field.

Meanwhile measures were undertaken to improve the quality of the Army's personnel. Initially many of the people joining the Army under the "all volunteer" policy were of less than desirable physical, mental, and educational standards, enlisted primarily to meet recruiting goals. The Army could do little to maintain force levels. Gradually, however, as pay and benefits increased, quality of recruits improved. This permitted discipline to be tightened, drug abuse to be largely eliminated, malcontents and chronic troublemakers to be discharged, and measures taken to improve relations between the races. There was a lot of experimentation in personnel management during the 1970s. One of the most effective was introduced in 1975: the Army Training and Evalution Program. Put simply, ARTEP was a periodic test of the military skills of troops and units. Personnel unable to meet certain performance goals were discharged. Other programs included group enlistment arrangements, regional recruiting of combat units, deferred service contracts, and educational benefits packages, among others, all of which met with varying degress of success. As a result, by the late 1970s manpower quality in the Army had risen considerably. Virtually all recruits were high school graduates, the reenlistment rate had risen, morale was high, discipline was excellent, and there had been considerable improvement in personnel training, performance, efficiency, and readiness.

Training underwent fundamental changes, with the introduction of more realistic programs and the adoption of innovative technologies. This actually began during the Vietnam War. Early in the war the Navy had noticed that its pilots were not as successful in air combat as their predecessors had been in Korea and World War II. In 1969 the Navy opened its "top gun" school. At the school, pilots practiced air combat against pilots trained to fly and fight using Soviet doctrine and tactics in aircraft whose performance characteristics closely matched those of Russian equipment. The result was a marked improvement in the performance of Navy pilots. Soon afterwards the Air Force, which had been thinking along the same lines, developed its "Red Flag" program. This used electronics to simulate the performance of different weapons. Once again the combat effectiveness of pilots improved markedly. Meanwhile the Navy developed its Fleet Readiness Program, which combined computer simulation with live-action exercises. By the mid-1970s senior Army trainers were increasingly aware of the beneficial effects of these programs on personnel performance. TRADOC began work on a "live" ground combat simulation of its own. In October 1980 the Army opened the National Training Center (NTC), at Ft. Irwin in the Mohave Desert, employing the Military Integrated Laser Engagement System (MILES).

Put simply, MILES was an extremely sophisticated version of "laser tag." Special lasers were attached to weapons. Troops and vehicles were outfitted with sophisticated sensors. When a sensor detected a "hit"—whether on a soldier or a vehicle—it determined the effects and inflicted casualties accordingly, most simply by disabling the target's weapons and notifying it as to the nature of the injury, whether disabling or fatal. Battalions were regularly rotated into the NTC for maneuvers which usually involved six to ten "engagements" over a two week period. To enhance realism, units maneuvered not against other U.S.-trained and equipped units, but against the "32nd Guards Motorized Rifle Regiment." This was formed from a pair of Regular Army battalions (6th/31st Infantry and 1st/73rd Armor), which were organized and trained according to Soviet precepts and equipped with U.S. equipment modified to resemble Russian models. Since the 32nd Guards was permanently stationed at Ft. Irwin and constantly involved in simulated engagements with U.S. tank and mechanized infantry battalions, it soon became a very highly trained and effective unit (sometimes referred to as "the best Soviet motorized rifle regiment in the world"). As a result, it usually "won" most of its sham battles. But winning and losing was not the purpose of the NTC. The purpose was to improve the performance of troops and their commanders. Debriefings at the end of a tour at the NTC were brutally frank. The performance of the troops—and of their commanders—was openly discussed. This caused some stir, as commanders were not used to having their mistakes aired before subordinates, but the policy was sustained at the highest levels in the Army. To lessen the blow, units were not formally scored as "winning" or "losing." Nevertheless, informally commanders who performed poorly or even fell apart "in combat"—and there were some—or whose units performed particularly poorly, often found their future prospects hazy. It was harsh, but not so harsh as the consequences of failure in combat.

Meanwhile, the NTC began to have an effect on overall training and doctrine. As more and more units went through the program, flaws in the Army's training program became more obvious, and corrective measures were taken. In addition, by the late 1980s TRADOC had available information on literally hundreds of "engagements." The mass of data permitted the appraisal of organization and tactics to a degree not possible even in wartime, leading to important adjustments in both.

By the end of the 1980s a small version of the NTC had been established in Germany to reduce the cost of rotating troops to California, and another in Arkansas specializing in light infantry, airborne, and special operations forces. Meanwhile, the Army established a computerized version of the NTC for senior officers, the Battle Command Training Program (BCTP), which permitted them to maneuver divisions and corps in a "realistic" if virtual environment. BCTP was only one of many computerized tools, from combat simulators to electronic theater models, which could enhance the training of military personnel. To keep the simulations realistic, constant resort was made to historical precedents and the performance of U.S. and other forces in actual operations during the period, such as the Anglo-Argentine War of 1982, operations in Lebanon later that same year, and the Afghanistan War (1980-1989).

The net result of the decade of reform which followed the end of the Vietnam War was a great improvement in doctrine, training, and readiness, developments which went largely unnoticed by the public. A notable aspect of this military reform, the longest sustained reform in the history of the Armed Forces, is that it was accomplished on a relative shoestring. Public regard and support for the Armed Forces was low in the period, and the defense establishment had to justify every cent of expenditure. In achieving such significant improvements in training and performance, the Armed Forces had demonstrated an unprecedented effectiveness in managing their resources, a matter which had important payoffs when defense budgets escalated.

The "New" Cold War and the Reorganization of the Defense Establishment

During the period of the Vietnam War and the years of lean military budgets which followed, the Soviet Union undertook a determined program of military expansion. Essentially unnoticed, Russian military outlays rose markedly, and the Soviet Armed Forces virtually doubled in size in the decade following the rise of Leonid Brezhnev to primacy in the Kremlin. By the late 1970s public awareness of this trend began to develop. This led to an increase in defense outlays, beginning under President Jimmy Carter and accelerating under Ronald Reagan. The importance of increased spending on defense should not be overrated. Major portions of the new defense outlays, such as the money expended on the Strategic Defense Initiative ("Star Wars"), the B-1 and B-2 Bombers, and other experimental technologies, had no bearing on readiness, training, or operations. Of course, the additional funds provided welcome improvements in procurement, training, benefits, and other areas. What is most interesting about the way in which the services spent their money was that rather than attempt to match the Soviets man for man, ship for ship, tank for tank, and plane for plane, a policy called "Competitive Strategies" was adopted. It was a simple idea: spend on techniques and techologies with which the Russians can not compete; fight their quantity with quality. Although more ships, tanks, and planes were procured, there was much greater spending on "smart weapons," sensors, target-acquisition systems, precision guided munitions, and special warfare.

Moreover, of even greater importance than the funds to the continuing improvement in the quality of the Armed Forces was an increasing sense that broad changes were needed in the structure and organizaton of the nation's defense establishment.

Public confidence in the state of the Armed Forces was severely shaken on 24 April 1980. A joint service operation to rescue American embassy personnel held hostage by a revolutionary regime in Teheran ended in a humiliating disaster at a remote desert airstrip in Iran. A consequence of poor planning and poor interservice cooperation, the failure at Desert One caused the Joint Chiefs of Staff to create the Special Operations Review Group (SORG) in May 1980 to conduct a thorough critique of the operation. This was intended to be neither an after-action report nor a witch hunt. The SORG was specifically charged with making recommendations to improve the ability of the Armed Forces to conduct joint operations. Joint operations, the integration of elements from different services for the performance of a particular task, reached a high state of development during World War II, a situation arrived at due to dire necessity and even then only after much painful experience. Following the war, however, the traditional tendency for each of the services to go its own way reasserted itself. Desert One provided a sobering reminder that in war things have to work right from the start. It sparked great interest in improving interservice cooperation and integration, a trend enhanced with the publication in 1982 of a new edition of FM 100-5. The new edition of FM-105 established the AirLand Battle (ALB) doctrine. ALB attempted to strike a balance between maneuver warfare and attritional warfare, reintroduced the concept of operational art, the employment of forces in large scale campaigns, and established the idea of "over the horizon" warfare, projecting military power deep into the enemy's rear. The new doctrine stressed the use of psyops, deception, and special warfare, the employment of overwhelming force, and stressed "the synchronization of air, ground, and sea assets" to fight the enemy not only at the front, but in his rear. Strengthening the case for greater integration was a speech by Chief of Staff of the Army General Edward Meyer, in which he argued that as currently organized, the Armed Forces were not prepared for war and urged that the Chairman of the Joint Chiefs be given greater powers over strategy, operations, priorities, and organization. General Meyer's address sparked considerable discussion not only in the services, but also in public forums and in Congress, all of which bore fruit in 1986.

In 1983 the movement towards "jointness" received considerable impetus with the establishment of the Army-Air Force Joint Force Development Process. The new Chief of Staff of the Army General John A. Wickham and his former West Point roommate, Chief of Staff of the Air Force General Charles A. Gabriel, created this body using personnel from their existing staffs. These officers quickly identified over 30 programs in which Army and Air Force efforts seemed to be duplicative or where joint doctrines could be developed. As a result, many programs were dropped or merged, with a resulting savings in money, time, and inter-service friction. The Air Force started participating in maneuvers at the NTC, and began to develop a renewed interest in ground support.

The Armed Forces' new policies and doctrines were tested in 1983 when an American peacekeeping mission in Lebanon turned out badly. A terrorist bombing of a Marine barracks demonstrated serious failures in intelligence assessment, communications, command, and control, and in the definition of objectives. Soon afterwards came the Grenada Operation. A Cuban-supported coup installed a radical regime on the small Caribbean island. With the new government openly soliciting Cuban aid and threatening to hold hundreds of American students hostage, the Armed Forces were ordered into action. Mounted on less than a week's notice, with the troops receiving their orders only three days before going into action, the Grenada operation was swift and successful. Individually, American troops performed well. However, the operation demonstrated that there was still work to be done. Interservice rivalries had quickly reared their heads during the planning phase, and there were failures in intelligence and communications, as well as some problems in special operations.

Shortly after Grenada, the Army War College and the Air War College began a series of joint wargaming exercises. The Army also established the School of Advanced Military Studies (SAMS), designed to prepare selected officers for higher level staffs, a measure which was shortly adopted by the other services. Graduates of these programs served 18 month internships on senior staffs to refine their skills. In addition, realizing that perhaps too much attention had been focused on large scale conventional warfare (the "Central Front Fixation"), the Army reconsidered the problems of low intensity warfare. Several "light" divisions were created, including an experimental "Hi-Tech" unit, to test equipment, training, and doctrine for small wars. Meanwhile existing programs and studies continued. In 1986 several of these initiatives bore fruit.

A new edition of FM 100-5 was published in 1986. The new "how to fight" guidelines refined but essentially reaffirmed ALB, while increasing stress on jointness and adding emphasis to the operational level of warfare. In addition, the Joint Warfare Center was established, an inter-service agency charged with developing simulations which could be integrated into training and exercises. Meanwhile a confrontation with Libya that year demonstrated how far the Armed Forces had gone in improving cooperation, as contingents from all the services took part in several well-coordinated limited operations.

Undoubtedly the most important development of the 1980s was the Goldwater-Nichols Department of Defense Reorganization Act of 1986. This was the product of nearly four years of study, deliberation, and effort by Congress in close communication with representatives of the Executive Branch and the Armed Forces. It was a difficult piece of legislation, touching as it did on the independence of the several branches of the Armed Forces, and the many different proposals examined and rejected. As passed, the act established that the Chairman of the Joint Chiefs of Staff is the senior military commander under the President. Goldwater-Nichols clarified the authority of senior commanders in joint operations, regardless of service, and gave the authority and responsibilty for developing joint warfare doctrine to the Chairman of the Joint Chiefs. It also established specific joint commands, so that these did not have to be improvised in times of emergency. To ensure closer integration with and responsiveness to the nation's political objectives, Goldwater-Nichols improved the role of civilian agencies (including, but not necessarily limited to the President's staff and the State Department) in contingency planning.

Hard on the heels of Goldwater-Nichols came the Nunn-Warner Act of 1987.

This created the U.S. Special Operations Command (SOC). All special warfare forces were subordinated to the SOC, regardless of service. The mission of SOC was to develop special warfare doctrine, tactics, and technologies, to conduct joint special operations training, and to develop plans for the employment of special operations forces. By integrating the special warfare forces of all three services, the intention was to develop a virtually instantaneous response capability.

"Operation Just Cause" in 1989 provided the first field test of the new command structure of the Armed Forces. Relations with Panama had been deteriorating for some time. Evidence that the head of the Panama Defense Forces, General Manuel Noriega, was intimately involved in drug trafficking and other criminal activities led to an attempt by the President of Panama to remove him in February 1988. Noriega staged a coup. This led to U.S. economic and diplomatic sanctions. Noriega's candidate for the presidency in May 1989 was defeated, so he annulled the results. His response to further diplomatic and economic pressure was to send Panamanian troops and militiamen to terrorize domestic opponents and molest American personnel and their families stationed in the country. In December 1989 Noriega declared war on the United States. President Bush immediately ordered SOUTHCOM, the joint services headquarters responsible for South and Central America and the Caribbean, into action. Operation Just Cause began on 20 December. Using troops already in Panama strengthened by additional forces brought in by air and sea, SOUTHCOM quickly secured control of all the principal objectives. Resistance by the PDF was sporadic, that by Noriega's militia, recruited largely from the criminal classes, was often stubborn, if disorganized. Panamanian civilians were largely supportive of the American effort and aided in tracking down Noriegista fugitives. During these operations American women became directly engaged in combat operations for the first time. A complex series of 27 objectives were secured or neutralized on the first day. Organized resistance was broken within 24 hours, and the operation was essentially over in three days. Casualties were low, including (despite attempts to argue the contrary by some politically-motivated individuals) those inflicted on Panamanian forces and civilians. Within a week U.S. troops pulled out. Operation Just Cause provided an excellent demonstration of how far the Armed Forces had come in terms of improving training, readiness, and cooperation. To be sure there were still some problems with interservice communications and turf wars, but these were subject to intensive review, and corrective measures undertaken.

As the decade of military reform closed in the late-1980s, relations with the Soviet Union underwent a marked improvement. The last years of the Brezhnev regime had brought a chilling revival of Cold War tensions, during which the Soviet Union undertook a massive build-up of military power, an invasion of Afghanistan, and a series of interventions in several wars in the Third World, frequently through the use of Cuban, East German, or Yemenite proxies. Mikhail Gorbachev's rise to primacy in the U.S.S.R. in the mid-80s brought about major domestic reforms, and a strong push for rapprochement with the United States. A number of confidence building and disarmament agreements were made, and in 1989 the Cold War came to an end, with the Soviet withdrawal from Eastern Europe.

It was against this background of unprecedented reform and reorganization of American Armed Forces and the end of the Cold War that the Gulf War of 1990-1991 erupted.

The Gulf War

On 2 August 1990 Saddam Hussein, dictator of Iraq, launched an invasion of Kuwait, major oil producing state at the head of the Persian Gulf. Including reserves he had an army of about 1.5 million men, heavily equipped (c. 5,500 tanks, 7,000 other AFV, 3,500 artillery pieces and MLRSs). Two years earlier, the army had emerged from a long and difficult war with Iran (1980-1988) with considerable combat experience, and appeared to be a hardened, battle ready force. During the war with Iran the U.S. had generally supported Iraq with intelligence information, fearing that a disastrous Iraqi defeat would destabilize the Middle East. Other powers, notably several Communist states, some neutrals, and a few Western nations, had provided substantially greater material support, selling Iraq enormous quantities of arms and equipment, paid for through loans made by various oil producing Arab states. Iraq's invasion of Kuwait did not come as a complete surprise, at least on the political level. Although Kuwaiti forces were on alert, they were greatly outnumbered (c. 24,000 to 130,000). The Kuwaitis resisted, often with some success, but with numbers against them, had little chance of repelling the invasion. Surviving Kuwaiti forces soon retreated into Saudi Arabia, and within about three days Iraq was in complete control of the tiny country (c. 18,000 square miles).

The causes of the invasion were complex. While a feeble case could be made that Kuwait was historically a part of what is now known as Iraq, there were other issues of greater importance. Acquiring Kuwait would greatly improve Iraq's access to the sea. In addition, Kuwait was Iraq's principal creditor, having lent enormous sums during the Iran-Iraq War. Iraq had emerged from that war with at least a paper victory, but now found itself unable to repay its debts, $17 billion due to Kuwait, and another $25 billion to Saudi Arabia and the other Gulf states. Annexing Kuwait would cancel that debt, and suggest to the Saudis and Gulf Arabs that they not press for repayment of their loans. Saddam also believed that the end of the Cold War bode ill for Arab interests, of which the Soviet Union had heretofore been a supporter, leaving Israel stronger than ever vis-a-vis the Arabs. A quick move to

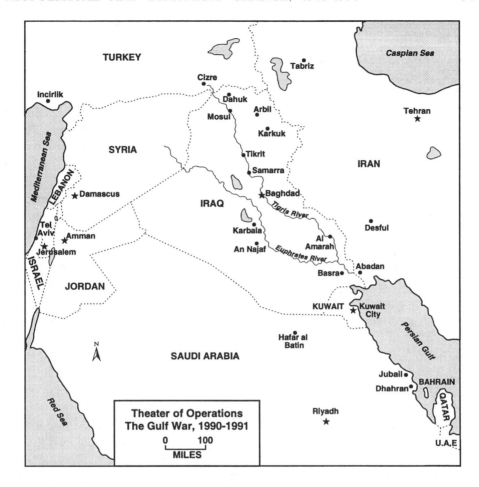

**Theater of Operations
The Gulf War, 1990-1991**

0   100

MILES

secure control of Kuwait would help turn Iraq into a major player on the international scene, with control of over a fifth of the world's petroleum production, more than a billion barrels a year, while placing Iraqi military force in a position to swoop down on the Saudi Arabian and Gulf fields, which provided another quarter of the world production. Several factors encouraged Saddam in the belief that he would be able to effect the annexation of Kuwait without serious interference.

Saddam considered the United Nations a cipher. It might make some feeble protests, but, given the domination of the organization by Third World nations—largely hostile to the U.S. and its allies—hardly likely to do anything more. The only country sufficiently strong militarily to interfere was the United States. However Saddam had made what he believed was a close study of the Vietnam War, and considered himself an expert on the subject. In his view, the U.S. was a paper tiger, riven by internal discord and fearful of war. The U.S. would bluster and make threatening moves, but was most likely to back off from a confrontation in which American blood might be shed. The chances of the U.S. forming a coalition of powers against him seemed unlikely, if only because Arab and Islamic states would not support a war against a brother nation, particularly one by a close ally of Israel. He also had his large army that had seen extensive combat in the war with Iran. And he had what he believed were some aces up his sleeve, including chemical and biological munitions, SCUD missiles, and a nuclear weapons program.

Saddam miscalculated badly. Even before his troops had completed their conquest of Kuwait, the United Nations Security Council overwhelmingly passed an American sponsored resolution condemning the invasion. This was the first in a series of thirteen Security Council resolutions which were passed, mostly unanimously or with no dissenting votes, declaring Iraqi actions in Kuwait void, imposing an economic blockade, and requesting U.N. members' assistance in enforcing various resolutions. The surprising unanimity in the Security Council was matched in the General Assembly: Third World nations may have harbored hostility towards the U.S., but they also considered international boundaries sacrosanct, albeit that those frontiers very likely had been established by imperialist powers. Arab states viewed the attack on brother Arabs as a gross violation of Arab solidarity.

Even as the various resolutions were making their way through the Security Council, President George Bush put together what just a few days earlier would have been considered "an impossible coalition," a loose alliance that brought together industrial democracies, former Soviet Bloc nations, virtually all the Arab nations from conservative monarchies to outright dictatorships, and many other Islamic states as well, all willing to commit troops. Maintaining a shadowy tie to the coalition was Israel, while many other nations, including Japan and the industrializing states of the Pacific Rim, lent moral and financial support, and in some cases provided special services. Perhaps most importantly, the Soviet Union supported American efforts to get Iraq out of Kuwait, and China remained substantially neutral.

Meanwhile, mindful of how the lack of a national consensus had created serious problems during the Vietnam War, the Administration carefully built domestic support for military operations in support of the liberation of Kuwait. The President, the Secretary of State, Secretary of Defense Richard Cheney, and other senior government officials made themselves readily accessible, as did Chairman of the Joint Chiefs of Staff General Colin Powell and General H. Norman Schwarzkopf, commander of CENTCOM, responsible for the Gulf theater of operations. As a result, there was a great deal of open discussion on the matter. The unanimous support in the international community was an additional factor in strengthening domestic support for military action. The effort to build a domestic consensus on the subject of Kuwait found an unexpected ally in Saddam Hussein's attempt to hold Western civilians hostage, his constant threats, and his spurning of repeated efforts by the United Nations, the Soviet Union, and others to convince him that a peaceful solution was in his best interests. The culmination of the effort to ensure popular support for military action came on 12 January 1991 when Congress enacted a joint resolution providing "Authorization for Use of Military Force Against Iraq" (HJR77/SJR2). With even those voting against the resolution pledging to support the troops, a firm domestic base for operations was established.

Operation Desert Shield

In a sense planning for the Gulf War began in 1974. As a result of an oil embargo imposed by OPEC in the wake of the 1973 Arab-Israeli War, the Armed Forces began studying possible operations in the event of a threat to oil supplies created by Iranian or Iraqi intervention in the smaller oil producing Gulf states, or of internal upheaval in those countries. This was at best tentative contingency planning, but it did suggest some of the problems which might have to be faced in the Gulf Theater. Serious planning began under the Carter Administration, with the creation of the Rapid Deployment Force, a task force earmarked for operations in the Middle East. Then came the Israeli-Egyptian peace accords, which helped focus the Army's attention more clearly on the problems of operating in a desert environment, since U.S. troops formed a major element in the multinational force that served as peacekeepers in the Sinai. At the same time, U.S. forces began a series of exercises in cooperation with the Egyptian Armed Forces. The "Bright Star" exercises proved enormously educational for the Armed Forces. There were problems in the suitability and maintenance of equipment, in tactical doctrine, even in rations, with the realization that pork, an accustomed routine part of the American soldier's diet, was wholly unsuitable for Moslem troops. Then in 1983 CENTCOM (Central Command) was created. One of a series of joint regional commands, CENTCOM was responsible for the Middle East. The CENTCOM staff, several hundred officers and enlisted people drawn from all the services, developed systematic plans for the speedy movement of U.S. ground, naval, and air forces to the Middle East in the event of an emergency, integrating the activities of all services, including logistics planning, organization, and operations. A great deal of attention was paid to historical precedents, such as the disastrous British campaign in Iraq in 1915, which gave insights into the difficulties of operating in the area. Some important recommendations resulted, such as changes in training, provision for special desert-proof equipment, and the need for more Arabic speaking personnel. By 1987 CENTCOM was actually conducting operations in the Gulf in support of the reflagging of Kuwaiti tankers to permit American forces to offer them protection during the Iran-Iraq War. By 1989 CENTCOM had developed and extensively wargamed a contingency plan—OPLAN 1002—to counter possible Iraqi attack on Kuwait and other Gulf states.

As a result of the work of CENTCOM, preliminary movement of U.S. forces began on the very day that Iraq invaded Kuwait. Within 48 hours, the commander of CENTCOM, General Schwarzkopf, was briefing the President on military options, even as several U.S. Navy carrier task forces neared the region. Meanwhile elements of the Air Force and Special Forces were en route, as were elements of the 82nd Airborne Division and a brigade of Marines. By then Air Force Col. John A. Warden III, of the Department of Defense staff, had begun outlining plans for an air offensive, designed to combine all U.S. and Coalition air assets into an integrated onslaught that would simultaneously strike at critical targets in Iraq's military forces, infrastructure, economy, and political apparatus. In addition, Department of Defense personnel conducted wargames in conjunction with civilian specialists to examine alternative operational possibilities. Meanwhile, Iraqi forces completed the occupation of Kuwait.

The next few days were the most critical of the war. While U.S. forces were concentrating and moving into the theater, there was some concern that the Iraqis might press on, driving down the Gulf coast to seize Dhahran and the critically important ports in its vicinity, a move which would have greatly impaired American ability to bring heavy equipment into the theater. U.S. ground troops arrived on 5 August, but these were small contingents, serving as advanced parties. On 8 August, a brigade of the 82nd Airborne Division landed. Lightly equipped, the relatively small contingent would have been hard pressed to cope with a major Iraqi offensive, even if supported by the increasing numbers of combat aircraft that were reaching the theater (three carrier air wings plus an F-15 squadron and two fighter squadrons from the RAF) and forces available from Saudi Arabia and the other Gulf states. However, by 20 August the entire 82nd Airborne Division (c. 12,000 troops) was in Saudi Arabia, as was the 7th Marine Expeditionary Brigade, a large (c. 17,000) force equipped for heavy combat, as well as others, including French and Egyptians, plus strong contingents of joint service special operations forces, while air strength had expanded enormously (four carrier air wings, including one French, a Marine air wing, over 200 Air Force combat aircraft, plus those of various Coalition air forces). At the same time, some 70,000 Turkish troops deployed to southeastern Turkey, where, supported by U.S. special warfare forces, and Turkish and Coalition air forces, they threatened northern Iraq.

By this time—less than three weeks into the war—it had become clear that Saddam's forces were digging in along the Kuwaiti-Saudi frontier. In fact, the movement into Kuwait had severely strained Iraqi logistical capacity. While they were probably capable of moving into the northeastern part of Saudi Arabia, seizing Khafji and other small towns along the coast, this would have been of little military significance. To have seriously discomfited the Coalition build-up would have required the seizure of Dhahran and the Gulf ports, nearly 500 kilometers further south. Such an advance was beyond Iraqi capacity to sustain, even in the days when Coalition resources were very thin on the ground. This, of course, was by no means clear at the time, and troops in Saudi Arabia prepared for the possibility of serious defensive fighting. In fact, as was later realized, from late August the build-up in Saudi Arabia and adjacent areas actually provided the muscle needed to back up United Nations demands that Iraq withdraw from Kuwait, and if necessary to effect that withdrawal by force of arms.

From the first days of the build-up, General Schwarzkopf and his staff considered operational plans in the event that military action was required. By 25 August the broad outline of an operational plan had been developed. It called for a massive air offensive to weaken the enemy's political, economic, and military resources, followed by the encirclement and annihilation of enemy forces in Kuwait and southern Iraq. By Schwarzkopf's calculations the earliest a ground offensive could occur would be in December. Reviewed by General Powell and then the President, the plan was approved. Meanwhile the build-up continued. As additional U.S. forces reached the theater of operations, the Armed Forces called up large numbers of reservists and National Guardsmen, eventually totaling nearly 200,000, who generally proved well-trained and effective.

The build-up for Operation Desert Shield demonstrated that the Armed Forces had learned a great deal about contingency planning, jointness, and cooperation since the Vietnam War. However, it also demonstrated that there was still room for improvement. Although on the whole inter-service friction was surprisingly limited, there were some notable lapses in what was a generally harmonious relationship, most obvious when personnel from one service were assigned or attached to elements of another. More significant were oversights in planning, particularly considering that CENTCOM had been preparing for operations in the Gulf for nearly a decade. For example, the sand in northeastern Saudi Arabia caused maintenance problems because it was considerably finer than that with which most equipment was designed to cope, leading to some maintenance problems. The Army also experienced a severe shortage of desert boots and uniforms. Appropriate gear was quickly ordered, but many troops served throughout the war in forest pattern uniforms, and no desert boots were issued before the end of hostilities.

However, a lot had been learned about maintaining troops in a desert environment. With temperatures reaching 140 degrees (60 Celsius), the danger of dehydration was enormous. Since it was clear that local water supplies would be insufficient for the numbers of troops entering the theater of operations, bottled water from commercial sources were procured and distributed until wells could be drilled and desalination plants established. In addition, the troops were subjected to rigid water discipline, including "forcible hydration," mandatory drinking of large amounts of water.

An enormous logistical and operational infrastructure was created. Airfields were improvised often out of portions of highways, defensive positions established, large camps and supply dumps laid out, repair facilities created, and, of course, extensive medical facilities were established. This build-up was helped by the fact that in the years before the Iraqi invasion of Kuwait, Saudi Arabia had established a series of military bases, most notably King Khalid Military City at Hafer al Batin, about 75 kilometers south of the Saudi-Iraqi frontier.

An extraordinary amount of materiel was brought into the theater, about 5.6 million tons, the movement and management of which was effectively controlled by Lieutenant General William G. Pagonis. While some came by air, particularly in the first days of the war, most equipment and cargo (about 95%) arrived by ship. Saudi Arabia and the other Gulf states had extensive port facilities. The "pre-positioning" of heavy equipment at Diego Garcia proved a sound policy, as did the Navy's procurement of a number of high speed transports, capable of making the voyage from the East Coast to Saudi Arabia in 18 days. These measures permitted the rapid movement of troops to the theater by air, where they could then "marry up" with heavy equipment arriving by sea. However, the build-up also revealed that the nation was short of sealift, there being not only insufficient ships but also a shortage of mariners, a problem partially alleviated by chartering foreign flag vessels. Despite the relative shortage of shipping, at the peak of the logistical build-up there was a daily average of about 30,000 tons of supplies and equipment being landed in Saudi Arabia.

Once the danger of an Iraqi offensive had passed, the troops in Saudi Arabia were subject to intensive training. The purpose was not merely to hone their skills, but also to acclimate them to the severe environment and to familiarize them with the problems of operating in the desert. Most exercises involved joint training among the U.S. services and combined training between the forces of different countries. Combined training was a matter of enormous importance. Although some contingents were quite small, altogether 35 countries contributed troops, ships, and aircraft to the Coalition. Several contingents were quite large. In addition to large forces from the U.S. and the Gulf states, Britain, France, Syria, and Egypt each contributed a division or more. Some of the exercises in air-ground cooperation, involved hundreds of airplanes and helicopters, as well as thousands of troops on the ground, and occasionally ships at sea. However, the most important exercises undertaken during this period were a series of practice amphibious landings intended not only to hone the skills of the Navy and Marine Corps, which conducted them, but also as a complex deception, perhaps the most extensive since the Normandy Invasion in 1944. While the build-up proceeded in the Gulf region, even as President Bush built international and domestic support for a military operation to eject Iraq from Kuwait, the psychological and special operations continued.

The first U.S. troops to reach Saudi Arabia were an advanced party of the 5th Special Forces Group, which arrived on 5 August. Special Forces personnel were also the first U.S. troops to deploy to the Iraqi-Saudi frontier, reinforcing Saudi National Guard patrols along the border by mid-August. Over the following weeks and months, U.S. Army Special Forces personnel, as well as U.S. Navy SEALS and British Special Air Service (S.A.S.), undertook dozens of forays into Kuwait and Iraq by air, land, and sea. Often penetrating hundreds of kilometers into enemy territory, they performed a variety of missions. Several Special Forces missions involved determining the "trafficability" of the sand in areas of southern Iraq. On one mission the S.A.S. raided an Iraqi anti-aircraft missile position. After destroying the site, they returned to Saudi Arabia with several prisoners as well as selected electronic components and documents likely to be of interest to intelligence analysts.

Coalition intelligence proved good. A loyalist underground sprang up quickly and maintained a steady stream of information to the Kuwaiti government-in-exile. This enormously valuable source of intelligence was supplemented by satellite and aerial reconnaissance, as well as special operations patrols into the country. The Iraqis had instituted a reign of terror. A program of looting was organized, Kuwaitis who refused to swear allegiance to Iraq were jailed, the mobilization of Palestinian residents was undertaken, and many Kuwaitis were expelled, all part of a program to incorporate Kuwait into Iraq. In addition, many foreign residents, including diplomatic personnel, were taken hostage and released later only after intense international pressure.

It appeared that there were about 500,000 Iraqi troops in Kuwait and adjacent areas, including a substantial contingent of the Republican Guard, Saddam Hussein's personal bodyguard and security force. Troops on the Saudi frontier and along the Persian Gulf coast dug in, using classic Soviet defensive arrangements: earthwork defenses in depth, liberally seasoned with minefields, barbed wire, and anti-tank trenches, covered by interlocking fields of fire from machine guns and anti-tank guns, with mobile reserves held somewhat to the rear. In addition to substantial mechanized forces, the Iraqis had a very large artillery park. Indeed, at least in the initial phase of the war, Iraqi artillery was technically superior, including as it did highly sophisticated Soviet M-46FG, South African G-5, and Austrian GHN-45 field pieces, in calibers of 120-130mm, with unusually long ranges, up to 41 kilometers in the case of the G-5.

The effectiveness of the Iraqi Army was the subject of some controversy. It had acquired a reputation in the popular literature and press of being a seasoned, battle tested force. This impression derived from several sources. The Iraqis had, after all, defeated repeated Iranian offensives during the long war between the two countries. This was an image which Saddam Hussein deliberately promoted in an elaborate series of deceptions for Western journalists and guests: Visitors were often given a tour of a false front line, many kilometers removed from the actual one, where an impressive show was put on by elements of the Republican Guard. A number of notable Western journalists and military experts were taken in by this ruse, and churned out a stream of reports, articles, and interviews stressing the skill and effectiveness of the Iraqi Army.

In fact, the war with Iran had essentially been one of fixed defenses—a virtual reprise of the Western Front in World War I—fought in the swampy region which characterizes much of the southern reaches of their mutual frontier. The Iraqis had developed an impressive system of trench lines. Even when manned by over-aged reservists, these could be successfully defended against repeated offensives by ill-trained, ill-armed, ill-supplied, and ill-led Iranian forces. There had been no serious mobile operations after the initial Iraqi invasion of the disputed territory, and even that operation had been only partially successful. In reality, the Iraqi Army was largely a "leg" infantry force, despite its impressive inventory of mechanized equipment, with little experience of operating in the desert. Historically such an army is at a serious disadvantage when confronted with a mobile force. Much of this was known to military professionals and historians in the West, but the popular impression as to the effectiveness of the Iraqis was of serious importance in planning diplomatic and military strategy.

By November it was clear that neither international pressure nor the economic embargo were going to liberate Kuwait. It was at that point the decision for a major ground offensive was made. The U.S. decided to commit the VII Corps from Germany, and other Coalition partners increased their contingents as well. By mid-January there were more than 500,000 American military personnel in Saudi Arabia and adjacent countries and seas, along with some 270,000 Coalition troops, and almost 100 U.S. and nearly 80 Coalition warships, as well as over 1,100 U.S. combat airplanes and nearly 500 Coalition planes, including forces in Turkey. On 29 November 1990 the United Nations Security Council passed Security Council Resolution Number 678. By a vote of 12 in favor, with two opposed (Cuba and Yemen) and one abstaining (China), the resolution authorized members of the U.N. to "use all means necessary" to implement previous Council resolutions if Iraq did not evacuate Kuwait by 15 January 1991. After two months of intense diplomatic efforts and a tightening economic blockade proved fruitless, the President secured Congressional approval for offensive operations on 12 January. Three days later President Bush authorized the use of force to eject Iraq from Kuwait, giving the

Secretary of Defense, the Chairman of the Joint Chiefs, and the commander of CENTCOM a "window" of several days in which to commence operations.

Operation Desert Storm

At approximately 0200 hours on 17 January a combined arms task force, comprising aircraft from the Air Force and helicopters and troops from the 101st Air Assault Division ("Task Force Normandy") began a deep raid behind enemy lines to destroy two anti-aircraft command centers. In an attack lasting only about four minutes, they created a 10 kilometer gap in the Iraqi anti-aircraft umbrella, giving an almost textbook demonstration of AirLand Battle. As Tomahawk cruise missiles launched from U.S. Navy vessels in the Gulf began to hit targets in Baghdad, literally hundreds of aircraft attacked critical targets in Kuwait and Iraq. Special Operations forces, including U.S. Green Berets and SEALS and British S.A.S. personnel, many already "pre-positioned" as much as 250 kilometers behind Iraqi lines, supported the attacks with laser designators to "paint" targets for precision guided munitions, blew up communications facilities and bridges, and conducted reconnaissance, including searches for SCUD missile launchers, while occasionally engaging Iraqi forces. Iraqi resistance proved negligible. Although anti-aircraft fire was heavy—as the world could see via live satellite broadcast—it was poorly directed and virtually ineffective, while the Iraqi Air Force failed to put in an appearance. Although the intensity of air operations did not again reach that of the first day, a high rate of sorties—an average of 2000 a day—was maintained over the next five weeks, limited only by problems with weather in an unusually bad year. Despite talk of "parallel war," in which all of the enemy's critical systems are attacked simultaneously, the air campaign actually unfolded in a series of overlapping phases, during each of which a particular system was targeted:

Period	Target System	Percent of Sorties*
17 Jan- 1 Feb	Air defense systems and air power	9
18 Jan-26 Feb	SCUD sites and NBC resources	5
19 Jan-15 Feb	Government, command, control, and communications	4
26 Jan-28 Feb	Infrastructure and logistical systems	22
26 Jan- 2 Mar	Forces in the field	20

* *USAF figures for Coalition air sorties, including Navy and Marine fixed wing sorties but not Army, Navy, or Marine helicopter missions.*

Of course, all systems were targeted to some extent throughout the air campaign, and air forces also conducted reconnaissance and logistical support missions (for example tanker aircraft alone accounted for about 20% of all sorties) throughout the period, and cooperated closely with ground forces as well.

The intensity of the air campaign may be gauged by the fact that the volume of munitions dropped on Iraq, about 80,000 tons in nearly six weeks of operations, exceeded the 47,000 ton monthly average dropped during World War II over a much larger area. Moreover, since the Iraqi air defenses and Air Force proved highly ineffective, Coalition losses were low: On the first day only three aircraft were lost, a Navy F-18 Hornet, an RAF Tornado, and one Kuwaiti A-4. Total Coalition losses due to enemy action were only 35 fixed wing aircraft, a rate of 38 per 100,000 sorties, a little more than 2.7 times the U.S. peacetime loss rate from accidents.

Although by far the largest proportion of the munitions used were relatively low tech "iron bombs," the air campaign was characterized by extensive use of precision guided munitions for high value targets and those in urban areas where the risk of death or injury of civilians and of collateral damage to non-military installations was greatest. Considerable care was taken to minimize the risk to civilians and sites of high civic, historical, and religious significance. Some legitimate targets were not attacked due to the difficulty of avoiding civilian casualties or the possibility of damaging important civic or cultural sites. As it became aware of this policy, the Iraqi government responded by shifting military equipment close to such sites as a way of providing protection for them. Despite the effort to minimize civilian losses, there were some, notably when a military communications center in Baghdad was also being used as a civilian bomb shelter. This caused considerable furor in some circles, as did a deliberate attack on a biological warfare site disguised as a "baby milk factory." Nevertheless, by the Iraqi government's own statements, civilian deaths were minimal, apparently only about 1,500. Nor was the Iraqi infrastructure targeted directly: For example, power transmission lines were attacked, but not electrical generating plants; telephone cable systems, but not central switching facilities. The effectiveness of the air campaign sparked some controversy, as the Armed Forces did not effectively communicate the difficulties of bomb damage assessment (BDA) under wartime conditions, a matter partially tied up with service pride and the skepticism of many in the media towards any information emanating from the military.

With elements of his Air Force deserting to Iran, Saddam Hussein found himself unable to cope with the Coalition air onslaught, and resorted to the use of SCUD missiles. The SCUD is essentially a Soviet version of the German V-2 ballistic missile of World War II. Designed in the 1950s, the SCUD has a poor guidance system (50% of missiles land within a mile of target) and can carry a warhead of only about one ton. Barring the use of a nuclear or chemical warhead, it is relatively ineffective as a weapon, except against populated areas. Saddam's use of the SCUD had two objectives, both political. By firing SCUDs at Arab—primary Saudi Arabian—targets he hoped to create political instability through terror, and by firing at Tel Aviv he hoped to provoke Israeli retaliation, which would almost certainly have caused the Coalition to collapse. The SCUD proved a singular failure. The first SCUDs were launched on 18 January, seven against Israel and one against Saudi Arabia. The SCUD fired at Saudi Arabia was intercepted by a Patriot missile, an anti-aircraft system which had been reconfigured to cope with ballistic missiles. The downing of the SCUD was broadcast live worldwide and turned the Patriot into an instant media success. Of the SCUDs fired at Israel, one fell on Tel Aviv, causing several casualties and a media panic over the reported use of chemical weapons and Israeli retaliation, which spread around the world before it was proven false. At the urging of the U.S., which quickly provided Patriot batteries for the defense of Tel Aviv and other cities, the Israeli government refrained from retaliating, a matter of enormous political importance.

Altogether Iraq fired 91 SCUD missiles during the war, 48 at targets in Saudi Arabia, 40 at Israel, and three at Bahrain. Only 13 hit the targets at which they appear to have been aimed. Casualties were few, however. Patriot missiles intercepted 44 of the SCUDS and 34 fell into the sea or landed in unpopulated areas. Fragments from 14 of the SCUDs hit by Patriots caused casualties or damage on the ground, in one case killing 28 and wounding more than 90 American soldiers of the 14th Quartermaster Detachment while they were asleep in a barracks in Dhahran, the greatest American loss in a single incident during the war, and the highest number inflicted by a SCUD. This led to charges that the Patriot was ineffective. To some extent this reaction was attributable to ignorance of elementary physics (since fragments had to fall somewhere) and media skepticism about the military. However, it was also a reflection of failure on the part of the Armed Forces to provide precise information about the abilities and effectiveness of the Patriot and other weapons, and of the nature of war itself.

The Iraqi use of SCUDs set off a desperate "SCUD hunt" by American air and special warfare forces. Known SCUD launching sites had already been targeted in the first days of the air campaign with considerable effectiveness. But the Iraqis had a number of secret sites and, moreover, had improvised mobile SCUD launchers from commercial heavy lift tractor-trailer assemblies. The SCUD hunters were very effective in targeting the fixed sites. During the first week of the fighting the Iraqis managed to fire 38 SCUDs, while in the second week they fired only 18. By then all the fixed sites had been hit, often repeatedly, and CENTCOM communiques on the subject were extremely optimistic. However the mobile launchers remained. During the third week the Iraqis fired only four SCUDs, five during the fourth week, then six in the fifth and four in the sixth week. The perceived failure of the Armed Forces to ferret out all of the SCUD launchers marred an otherwise effective campaign to eliminate the most serious threat to the political existence of the Coalition.

During the air campaign General Schwarzkopf and his staff completed their plans for a massive single envelopment of enemy forces in Kuwait and southern Iraq, what would become known as the "Hail Mary" Operation. When asked what the Coalition plan for coping with the Iraqi army was, General Powell replied, "First, we're going to cut it off, and then we're going to kill it." As part of the operational plan, an elaborate series of deceptions was undertaken. Coalition ground forces continued their intensive training exercises. Particularly well-publicized were several large scale amphibious rehearsals and exercises in breaching fixed defenses, the intention being to convince the Iraqis that Coalition offensive plans envisioned landings on the coast of Kuwait in conjunction with a frontal assault from the south. Much of the training masked the beginning of the redeployment of Coalition forces to the positions they would have to occupy to begin the execution of the envelopment. The introduction of the SCUDs provided a useful mask for some of the movements, as CENTCOM reported that units were being shifted from place to place to prevent the Iraqis from targeting their cantonments. Meanwhile clashes between Coalition and Iraqi ground forces occurred.

Special operations personnel, of course, had been in action behind Iraqi lines for some time, primarily for the purpose of collecting information and supporting the air campaign. These forces several times were engaged by Iraqi troops, each time managing to escape after protracted firefights. Small scale clashes with Iraqi ground forces became more common in late January as Coalition ground forces conducted reconnaissance and probes of enemy positions. For example, on 22 January a patrol from the 3rd Armored Cavalry engaged an Iraqi outpost, killing two and capturing six, at a cost of two men wounded, while the very next day a battalion of the 11th Marines, an artillery unit, bombarded an Iraqi outpost in southern Kuwait. These operations had various objectives. Gathering information, denying it to the enemy, and disrupting enemy preparations were obvious reasons for many of the raids and shellings. However, some of them were undertaken as part of an elaborate cover plan designed to convince the Iraqis that the weight of a Coalition offensive would fall frontally against their forces in Kuwait. Early on 29 January a joint U.S.-Soviet communique was issued calling for an end to the war through diplomacy. Perhaps as a response to that message, the Iraqis made their first—and only—offensive move since overrunning Kuwait, leading to the Battle for Khafji.

A small city, Khafji lies about 20 kilometers south of the Saudi-Kuwaiti frontier, just inland from the coast. On several occasions since the beginning of the air campaign Iraqi artillery had engaged in leisurely shellings of the place, to which

U.S. Marine and Gulf states' gunners had made reply. Late on 29 January an Iraqi armored division undertook a probe near the Gulf coast south from Kuwait into Saudi Arabia. The immediate objective was apparently to feel out Coalition defenses in the vicinity of Khafji. Five widely separated forces advanced on a front of some 50 kilometers. Four of these were apparently intended as diversions to assist the main probe, which would be supported by several small landings along the coast. One of the subsidiary columns was halted by air attacks before it left its assembly area; the other three were beaten off by Marines, Saudi National Guardsmen, and Coalition air power in skirmishes at Umm Hujul (where eleven Marines were killed: seven when an Air Force Maverick missile struck their LAV), Wafra, and in the desert between Wafra and Khafji. The small convoys which were to support the attack by effecting several amphibious landings along the coast were largely destroyed by Royal Navy helicopters and frigates. The main attack was made by a tank brigade (c. 80-100 tanks), supported by other elements of the division. It easily brushed aside a Saudi National Guard patrol—some dozen men in Land Rovers—at the frontier, and advanced southwards. They approached the Saudi defenses in front of Khafji with their guns trained to the rear, as if in response to Coalition leaflets urging surrender, which caused the defenders to let down their guard. As they neared the Saudi lines, the tanks suddenly swung their turrets around and opened fire. Before the Saudis could respond, their position had been penetrated and they fell back. By the early hours of 30 January the Iraqis held the town, which had been evacuated weeks earlier. Saddam Hussein touted the capture of Khafji as a great "victory" over the United States. Although the town had no intrinsic military value, its recapture was of importance, if only to deny Saddam his "victory."

Although Iraqi forces controlled Khafji, small numbers of Saudi troops and an eleven-man Marine Corps forward observer team eluded capture and maintained contact with higher headquarters. These troops were of considerable assistance when the Coalition counterattacked shortly before noon. Supported by Marine artillery and Coalition aircraft, a brigade of the Saudi National Guard and a battalion of Qatari tanks retook Khafji within about 24 hours in sometimes heavy house-to-house fighting, as well as tank-to-tank engagements. Although Iraqi artillery attempted to support the defenders it was repeatedly silenced by rapid and accurate counterbattery fire. Despite the often heavy fighting in Khafji, casualties were surprisingly light: Coalition forces suffered fewer than ten casualties, while the Iraqis lost at least 33 killed, with 430 men captured along with a good deal of equipment. Losses among Iraqi units supporting their attack on and subsequent defense of Khafji could not be determined. The fight for Khafji was a clear demonstration of Coalition superiority. Moreover, it provided the Saudi and Qatari troops an important morale boost, a matter of some importance given that Gulf

Arabs were traditionally not reputed to be great warriors.

Shortly before the attack on Khafji began, Saddam had ordered that oilfields in Kuwait be put to the torch and began pumping crude oil into the Gulf, initiating what some called "ecological warfare." Saddam attempted to blame Coalition air attacks, a propaganda effort in which he was singularly unsuccessful. In fact, like the attack on Khafji, the acts seem to have been intended to shake support for the war in the U.S. and other nations by suggesting the potential disasters that might result if the Coalition undertook a full scale offensive. As a result of his ecological sabotage, CENTCOM was forced to divert resources to impede the flow of crude into the Gulf and support containment and clean-up of the spill.

After the battle for Khafji ground actions became increasingly common. Aggressive patrols were undertaken by Coalition forces. Motorized patrols penetrated inside Iraq, making hit and run raids on Iraqi forces. On 13 February the 1st Cavalry Division, heavily supported by artillery and air power, began a serious probe up the Wadi al Batin, a dry river bed running from Saudi Arabia through the Iraqi lines, which had been the subject of public speculation as a possible line of advance. Over the next several days the division made a series of attacks on Iraqi defenses in and near the wadi. Further to the east, Marine units started a similar series of probes, while off the coast Navy and Marine teams effected landings on numerous small islands and oil installations, as if clearing the way for an amphibious landing. Meanwhile Coalition artillery units registered on Iraqi front lines, keeping rear area positions under fire as well, and Coalition air forces began a systematic program of attacking Iraqi ground units, part of a deliberate attempt to deceive the Iraqis about Coalition plans, and also Coalition tactics, since all attacks were made frontally, with no effort at maneuver. The Iraqi response was as expected, and reserves were moved closer to the Wadi al Batin and the coast. Surprisingly, although none of the attacks were seriously pressed, considerable losses were inflicted on the Iraqis, and over a thousand prisoners were taken; in fact, the number of Iraqi prisoners in Coalition hands was increasing rapidly, as literally thousands of deserters made their way south. Nor were Coalition casualties in this series of probes and reconnaissances serious: U.S. losses were a dozen men killed, several unfortunately by fire from American aircraft or ground forces.

The Iraqis were not the only people fooled by the measures to convince them that the Coalition would undertake a frontal assault against their defenses. Throughout the world journalists, scholars, former military officers, and politicians were convinced that CENTCOM was headed for a bloodbath. Thus one well-regarded military scholar wrote "The Army's armored and mechanized forces can play no offensive role against the vast defensive strength of the Iraqi army," while one senator said, "An effort to oust Iraqi forces from Kuwait would... cost the lives of 20,000 Americans," and another claimed, "We stand on the brink of a catastrophe."

When challenged, Coalition political and military leaders deliberately did not address these concerns in more than vague terms, feeding the impression that they were dodging the issue. However, more careful observers, including many scholars, politicians, former military personnel, journalists, and even ordinary citizens with wargaming experience, proved far more accurate in their assessment of CENTCOM's intentions to undertake a vast encircling movement west of Kuwait. In fact a close study of AirLand Battle and the whole thrust of the reform movement in the Armed Forces, particularly in the Army, made such a conclusion inevitable. That these analysts received little attention in the media was perhaps beneficial to the ultimate success of the cover plan.

As the last week of February drew near, final preparations for a ground offensive were made. West of the Wadi al Batin, two large forces concentrated without the enemy's knowledge. The VII Corps, a heavy force comprising several armored and mechanized divisions, including the British 1st Armoured Division, was situated in the area northwest of King Khalid Military City, while further west was the XVIII Airborne Corps, composed of two airborne divisions and a mechanized infantry division, with the French 6th Light Armored Division covering its exposed left flank, some 300 kilometers west of the Wadi al Batin. Supply dumps capable of sustaining these forces for 60 days had been established in their rear. The enormous mass of troops, equipment, and supplies had been shifted westwards with virtually no inkling of the movement reaching the Iraqis. East of the Wadi al Batin were equally strong forces, two divisions of Egyptians, one of Syrians, two of Marines, and several divisions of Saudi and Gulf states forces, while in the Gulf itself the equivalent of another Marine division formed part of the largest amphibious task force since the Inchon landings in 1950.

The state of the enemy forces in Kuwait and southern Iraqi was not clear. Estimates of the effectiveness of the air campaign and artillery bombardments on the strength and efficiency of Iraqi forces concluded that about a third of the 42 divisions in the theater had been reduced to less than 50% of their full strength. Eleven others were estimated at being between 50% and 75% full strength, while the balance were believed to be at better than 75% of strength, including much of the Republican Guard. Morale was believed to be poor, but it was also believed that many Iraqi units still had a lot of fight in them, particularly the Republican Guard.

The Soviets made a last attempt to convince Saddam Hussein to withdraw from Kuwait peacefully. Facing a deadline of noon on 23 February, a Soviet envoy tried to convince Saddam Hussein to comply with U.N. resolutions regarding Kuwait. Very early on 23 February the Iraqi government informed the Soviets that they would withdraw from Kuwait. However, they attached so many qualifications and conditions—including "linkage" with the Arab-Israel question—that the offer was rejected. By then Coalition ground forces were already on the move.

"The Hundred Hour War"

The offensive plan, against Iraqi forces in Kuwait and southern Iraq, adopted by CENTCOM was to execute a massive encirclement from the south making a wide sweep to the left, swinging around to strike them in the left flank, cutting off their line of retreat to Iraq proper. Coalition ground forces undertook preliminary offensive moves on 22 February, as elements of the 3rd Cavalry Regiment (attached to the XVIII Airborne Corps) and the I Marine Expeditionary Force closed up to and began to breach the sand berm and minefields the Iraqis had constructed along their front lines facing Saudi Arabia. On the 23rd elements of the Marines and the Tiger Brigade (2nd Armored Division) began crossing these obstacles. At the same time, the XVIII Airborne Corps far to the west began moving as the 101st Air Assault Division undertook deep penetration helicopter patrols.

At 0400 on 24 February the offensive officially began, when the 1st and 2nd Marine Divisions attacked the Iraqi defenses on a broad front. Moving deliberately, the Marines systematically breached the Iraqi defenses supported by heavy artillery fire and air attacks. Although the Iraqis attempted to respond with artillery, their positions were rapidly put out of action by counterbattery fire and close air support attacks. At noon the Tiger Brigade of the 2nd Armored Division went into action to begin exploiting the breach, driving a wedge between the Iraqi *III* and *IV Corps*. Although a frontal attack, the calculated pace of the Marine advance and the enormous volume of firepower which supported it kept losses low. Fewer than 50 Marines became casualties. The deliberate Marine advance was intended not only to minimize casualties but to further draw Iraqi attention to the areas of southwestern Kuwait. As the Marines were working their way through the Iraqi lines, far to the west the XVIII Airborne Corps began moving. At 0800 on 24 February 700 helicopters from the 101st Air Assault advanced about 120 kilometers into Iraq in the largest wartime helicopter operation ever. The troops and supplies that were lifted into Iraq established a forward refueling and supply base— called "Cobra Zone"—which sustained the division as it advanced further into Iraq to cut off enemy forces to the south and east. Meanwhile, on the corps' left, the French 6th Light Armored Division, a light, fast moving formation with a brigade of the 82nd Airborne Division attached, advanced north and west to overrun the Iraqi airbase at As Salman and to protect the main forces against a possible enemy advance from the Baghdad area. At 1200 hours the balance of the XVIII Airborne Corps advanced, led by the 3rd Armored Cavalry Regiment, which attacked on a front of ten kilometers, followed by the 24th Mechanized Infantry Division. Against insignificant resistance, the regiment made 125 kilometers in 24 hours. In the afternoon Egyptian and Syrian forces to the west of the Marines launched an attack into Kuwait, while Saudi, Kuwaiti, and Gulf Arab forces struck northwards

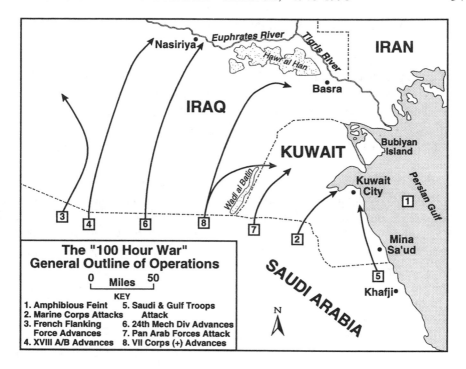

The "100 Hour War"
General Outline of Operations

0 ___ Miles ___ 50

KEY
1. Amphibious Feint   5. Saudi & Gulf Troops
2. Marine Corps Attacks   Attack
3. French Flanking   6. 24th Mech Div Advances
   Force Advances   7. Pan Arab Forces Attack
4. XVIII A/B Advances   8. VII Corps (+) Advances

into Kuwait along the coast east of the Marines, supported by battleship gunfire.

By late afternoon it was clear that the movement into Kuwait had succeeded in attracting Iraqi attention. In response, the enemy shifted elements of the Republican Guard and reserves southwards, exposing them to heavy air attack. At this time, on the afternoon of 24 February, what Napoleon would have called the "mass de maneouvre" advanced.

With the heavily reinforced 1st Mechanized Infantry Division in the lead, VII Corps drove north on a broad front west of the Saudi-Kuwait frontier. Supported by the British 1st Armoured Division, the 1st Mechanized Infantry Division breached the Iraqi defenses and pressed on, while the 1st and 3rd Armored Divisions attacked further to the west, and the 2nd Armored Cavalry Regiment on the corps left swung around the exposed Iraqi flank and began advancing as well. So rapid was the movement of these forces that whole divisions attacking in a broad wedge passed a single point within a half hour.

Almost from the moment the first troops jumped off, Iraqi forces at the front began surrendering in large numbers. By noon the 2nd Marine Division alone had already taken upwards of 800 prisoners, and the numbers swelled as the day wore on. Many of the surrendering Iraqi troops proved to be overage reservists who had been under severe air attack for weeks, living on short rations, and, in many cases, abandoned by their officers. By nightfall hundreds of Iraqis had been killed and there were more than 10,000 Iraqi prisoners, while losses among Coalition forces were small, U.S. troops incurred only four deaths in action.

On 25 February the advance continued. Having overrun As Salman, the French 6th Light Armored Division and the attached brigade from the 82nd Airborne Division set up a defensive screen to cover the left of the Coalition forces. Further east, the 24th Mechanized Infantry Division linked up with the 101st Air Assault Division, elements of which were moving by helicopter from Cobra Zone to establish road blocks and capture airfields over a wide area. In the center, undetected by the enemy, the VII Corps pressed northwards, making better than 100 kilometers, to position itself just west of the Republican Guard. To its east the Egyptian and Saudi forces advanced, while the Marines and the Tiger Brigade clashed with Iraqi forces in several short, sometimes sharp actions as they pressed to the northeast. Meanwhile, along the coast Saudi, Kuwaiti, and other Gulf Arab forces began liberating towns in southern Kuwait, while inside Kuwait the resistance and Coalition special warfare forces attacked Iraqi troops and installations, while Iraqi troops engaged in massive looting and brutal attacks on civilians. By evening several Iraqi divisions had been shattered, and hundreds more Iraqi troops killed, while the prisoner bag rose to some 25,000.

By 26 February a vast area of southern Iraq was firmly in Coalition hands, shielded on the west by the French 6th Light Armored Division and U.S. paratroopers, while the 101st Air Assault Division and the 3rd Armored Cavalry Regiment mopped up Iraqi stragglers, established additional supply bases, and pressed on towards the Euphrates. At the eastern end of the front, Saudi, Kuwaiti, and Gulf Arab forces reached the outskirts of Kuwait City, while the Marines advanced west of the city. At Kuwait International Airport, the 1st Marine Division and Tiger Brigade had a major battle with Iraqi tank brigade forces when U.S. tanks hit Iraqi tanks at ranges of 3,000 meters. The British 1st Armoured Division peeled off from the right flank of VII Corps to attack eastwards in support of the Syrians and Egyptians, a move joined by the 1st Cavalry Division hitherto held in CENTCOM reserve. Meanwhile, the 24th Mechanized Infantry Division—which made some 240 kilometers in 24 hours—aligned itself on the left of VII Corps and began driving to the northwest, smashing through several Iraqi formations as it made for the Euphrates. In the center, the VII Corps executed a right wheel and prepared to attack the Republican Guard just northwest of Kuwait. Screening the corps' front was the 2nd Armored Cavalry. As G Troop approached a ridge line east of the 73rd Meridian it encountered well dug-in Iraqi forces. Having finally realized the danger to their rear, the Iraqis were attempting to make a stand. As G Troop pressed on, it engaged against a brigade of the Republican Guard *Tawakalna Mechanized Infantry Division*. In a six-hour firefight, G Troop beat off repeated

Iraqi attacks. Reinforced with the balance of the regiment's 2nd Squadron and supported by artillery, the cavalrymen gave a devastating demonstration of American firepower, virtually destroying the enemy division with moderate loss to themselves. The "Battle of 73 Easting" was characterized by one of the few offensive moves undertaken by the Iraqis. Despite the often heroic if unskilled courage displayed by the troops of the *Tawakalna Division*, most Iraqi units simply dissolved. Nevertheless, had more Iraqi units offered as much resistance, the cost in blood to Coalition forces would have been far greater. As it was, the Iraqi Army in Kuwait was in a state of collapse. By nightfall over 20 Iraqi divisions had been shattered and the prisoner count was nearing 40,000.

Dawn on 27 February found the French 6th Light Armored Divison and the 2nd Brigade of the 82nd Airborne Division only 130 kilometers southwest of Baghdad. Meanwhile the 24th Mechanized Infantry Division had reached the Euphrates and wheeled to the right to begin a drive on Basra, in the hope of sealing all Iraqi forces into a huge pocket south of that city. During its advance the division shattered elements of two or three Republican Guard divisions in sharp actions at Tal'l and Jalaba desert airfields, and pressed on. During four days of operations this division advanced 368 kilometers, for an average daily rate of 92 kilometers, the most impressive advance against resistance in history. To the 24th Mechanized Division's right was the VII Corps, which plowed its way through a half dozen Iraqi divisions as it moved towards Basra. In the center the British, Syrians, Egyptians, and 1st Cavalry Division had shattered the Iraqi *VII Corps* and were pressing eastwards to link up with the Marines. With the Marines blocking their escape to the west, and Kuwaiti, Saudi, and Gulf Arab forces entering Kuwait City from the south, an enormous stream of Iraqi troops—perhaps 40,000—attempted to flee northwards in thousands of loot-ladened vehicles. Subjected to heavy air and artillery attack, the column was cut off when the Tiger Brigade advanced in a combined arms attack that met fierce resistance. Hundreds of dead and thousands of destroyed vehicles were counted on what the media quickly labeled the "Highway of Death." By the evening of the 27th over 33 Iraqi divisions had been destroyed, and the prisoner bag was over 50,000. At this point, with Coalition forces seemingly successful, President Bush announced that a cease-fire would commence at 0800 on the 28th. In the hours between the announcement and the cease-fire, Coalition forces pressed forward. The Iraq regular army *10th Saladin Armored Division*, considered by many the finest in the Iraqi Armed Forces, fought a desperate rearguard action against Coalition forces from the south and southwest (the British, Syrians, Egyptians, Marines, and Gulf Arab forces) only to be overwhelmed. Meanwhile VII Corps moved eastwards in an attempt to seal off the Basra escape route, the 1st Armored Division severely injuring the *Medina* and *Hammurabi Armored Divisions*, two of the last effective Republican Guard units.

By the time the cease-fire took effect at 0800 on 28 February, 42 Iraqi divisions had been shattered or seriously injured, some 25,000 Iraqi troops had been killed and another 85,000 taken prisoner, while more than 100,000 had simply deserted. Coalition losses were relatively light. About 250 Coalition troops had been killed in combat since the air campaign began, of whom 148 were Americans, including several women. Including non-combat losses, Coalition deaths totaled less than 500, 331 of them Americans. Losses in equipment were small as well. In the days following the cease-fire there were several fights between Coalition forces and enemy units trying to escape northwards, in which two more Iraqi brigades were destroyed. Only six Iraqi divisions, all Republican Guard units, managed to escape the debacle more or less intact, slipping away across a pontoon bridge above Basra in the final hours of the war, in a development that marred an otherwise smashing Coalition victory. The decision to end the ground war was dictated by a variety of factors. There was rising concern over the enormous slaughter which appeared to have been inflicted on the Iraqis; figures approaching 100,000 were widely circulated with "Highway of Death" photographs. In addition, as Coalition forces closed up on each other, the danger of casualties from "friendly fire" increased, a matter already controversial since about a quarter of U.S. losses were so attributable. Then too there was the nature of the political constraints under which the war was waged. The U.N. had authorized the use of force to eject the Iraqis from Kuwait, and by the end of 27 February that mission had been accomplished. To try to go beyond that, to advance further into Iraq in an attempt to unseat Saddam Hussein, would create difficulties in the U.N. and with the nation's Arab partners in the Coalition. In addition, even assuming these constraints were not operable, pressing on might easily have led to the complete collapse of Iraq, creating a power vacuum in the region, with no country sufficiently strong to balance Iran.

The army which the United States committed to the Gulf War was the finest that the nation had ever sent into combat. Its extraordinary effectiveness and efficiency was the result of more than a dozen years of hard work. The war confirmed that training, morale, doctrine, and equipment were essentially sound. The war was a classic demonstration of the AirLand Battle. The integration of all the services had worked, as had the tactics of combining fire with maneuver and "over the horizon warfare." Special operations, psychological warfare and deception had been employed as never before with enormous success. Overall the performance of National Guard and Reserve forces—nearly 200,000 of whom were activated—proved excellent, vindicating the confidence placed in the Reserve Components by a number of the principal military reformers reaching all the way back to Creighton Abrams. An enormous number of new technologies were proven effective, including J-Stars, the F-117 "Stealth" fighter-bomber, the use of satellite reconnaissance in a tactical role, and particularly the use of so-called "smart bombs." However, the war also revealed that there was still work to be done.

There were some command problems during the war. In retrospect, several commanders appear to have been excessively cautious, and CENTCOM did not deal with them as effectively as it might. There also were some intelligence breakdowns. Several proved to be quite important. Although CENTCOM concluded from the location of the Replublican Guard divisions that they were acting as a reserve for the Iraqi forces deployed further south, in retrospect it appears that they were actually positioned to prevent Iraqi regular army forces from abandoning their forward positions. As a result, the Republican Guard did not advance as far forward as was expected when the Marines attacked northwards, which played an important role in permitting a major portion of the Republican Guard to escape the Iraqi debacle. Other notable problems in intelligence gathering included the failure to discover that the Iraqis had improvised numerous mobile SCUD launchers, a reminder that even the most inept foe can come up with some surprising improvisations. Also, the overestimate of the number of Iraqi troops actually in the theater and the failure to realize the extent of demoralization and desertion in the Iraqi ranks. Although logistical planning was generally extremely good, there were problems as well. Despite years of planning there were shortages of desert pattern uniforms and boots, also of such things as batteries for electronic equipment. In addition, the nation's ability to move supplies and equipment was severely strained. Shortages of airlift and sealift developed, which were only partially met by chartering foreign flag ships and aircraft. There were also some unanticipated health problems resulting from diseases and parasites endemic to the region which seem to have been minor, but the full consequences have yet to be determined. The war also demonstrated that there were still some problems in jointness, as interservice rivalry still occasionally reared its head. Civil Affairs personnel sometimes found that there was a distinct lack of interest in the role and mission, a matter which could have created problems in a protracted war. Although overall personnel —both men and women— performed their duties very well, there were a number of unanticipated problems. The most widely publicized was that of the 17,000 "two soldier families," where both parents in a family were on active duty or in Reserve Components.

Although relations between the media and military were better than during the war in Vietnam, there were still some tensions which were not effectively resolved. Military public information personnel did not effectively communicate some of the complexities of issues over which the media—and the public—expressed concerns, such as casualties from friendly fire (35 Americans killed and 72 wounded in 26 incidents), the difficulties of bomb damage assessment, the problem of maritime mines in the Gulf, and "secret weapons" such as fuel air explosives, and fire trenches, which the Iraqis were alleged to have. There was also a tendency for press releases and briefings to be too optimistic, which led to occasional embarrassment, as during the so-called "SCUD hunt."

There was also a strong tendency to underestimate the enemy. To be sure, this was fueled by an increasingly obvious display of ineptitude on the part of the Iraqi armed forces. However, it is never a good idea to underestimate the enemy. The Iraqis were quick to discover ways to more effectively camouflage tanks and other vehicles in the desert, so that far more of them survived the air attack than what was believed to have been the case from bomb damage assessment. Saddam Hussein's torching of the Kuwaiti oil fields and dumping of crude into the Gulf were unanticipated moves which could have created serious problems for Coalition forces.

One of the most serious failings in the war came right at the end: framing the details of the cease-fire. In effect, the nation's political leadership and the Armed Forces failed to plan in detail for the peace. As a result, the terms of the cease-fire left a number of loopholes. One consequence was that Saddam Hussein was able to survive a widespread uprising intent on his overthrow. Although U.S. forces intervened in Northern Iraq to establish a safety zone for the Kurds, who were subjected to a genocidal campaign by Saddam, American forces otherwise did not interfere in Iraqi internal affairs.

The very success of the Armed Forces in the Gulf War is likely to create some problems, both internally and in terms of public perception. For example, the very critical role of the Navy and the Marine amphibious forces afloat were largely unnoticed and unacknowledged. It is also important to realize that the war may not be a useful guide to the future of warfare. The experience gained in the war will be of some help in refining doctrine and training, and in designing new equipment. However, the struggle has also created a popular impression that wars can be fought with few casualties. The low casualty rate in the Gulf War was one consequence of the unique nature of the conflict. It is highly unlikely that a future enemy will be so accommodating as to allow the U.S. more than six months to build up its forces. Nor is it likely that a future foe will replicate what one historian called the "wish chess" character of the war, in which the enemy made exactly the moves we would have wished him to make. In addition, the war occurred at a time when a major portion of the nation's troops in Europe could safely be withdrawn. U.S. action was made easier by the surprising unity displayed by most of the world's nations in the face of Iraqi aggression: Several nations had the ability to severely impede the Coalition merely by passing satellite intelligence information to Iraq. Of particular concern is the overselling of the effectiveness of the air campaign, to the point that the claim was advanced that the ground war was superfluous. The long term effect of the Gulf War on the Armed Forces in general and the Army remains to be seen.

Confronting the Future

The Army came out of the Gulf War with its prestige at a higher level than at any time since the end of World War II in 1945. It also went right into a major reduction in force, a consequence of the end of the Cold War which had been delayed by the war in the Gulf. This touched off an ongoing debate about the role and form that the Army—and the Armed Forces in general—should have in an age when the nation faced only a modest, though real, threat of major war, but numerous potential problems of a lesser nature. Indeed, the end of the Cold War saw the Armed Forces engaging in more, rather than fewer, operations. The end of the Cold War resulted not only in the collapse of the Soviet Union, but also the dissolution of Yugoslavia and the fall of many dictatorial regimes in the Third World. Many of these developments have lead to complex internal struggles, with calls for international support to establish peace and orderly government, and bring relief to peoples suffering from starvation, massacre, and torture. And when peace does occur, as in the resolution of the long standing Arab-Israel conflict, the need for an American military role in monitoring the terms of the settlement has often arisen.

During the 1990s, U.S. troops have become involved in peacekeeping and peacemaking missions—so-called "Operations Other Than War"—in places literally halfway across the globe. Some of these missions have proven highly successful, at least in the short term, such as the protection of the Kurds in Northern Iraq and the restoration of a popularly elected government in Haiti. On the other hand, the 1992-1993 mission to feed the starving millions in Somalia turned out badly, and the consequences of still other missions in Macedonia, Bosnia, and, perhaps, the Middle East, cannot yet be determined. One result of the multiplication of such missions is that the Army and the Armed Forces in general have been urged to develop special organizations and equipment tailored to permit the more effective performance of such missions, including the introduction of what have been termed "non-lethal weapons," to minimize possible casualties in operations other than war. In addition, the Armed Forces have been called upon to take an increasing role in the prevention of drug smuggling and securing the nation's frontiers against illegal immigrants. A considerable debate has developed about the ability of the Army to perform such missions without weakening its ability to perform its primary mission, the waging of war.

The post-Gulf War period has seen other debates in the Armed Forces as well. The idea of "information warfare" has been championed by some. Suggesting a radical breakthrough in the nature of war, information warfare postulates that information is a weapon, and that, for example, by manipulating stock exchanges, computer records, and communications, a force could attack and bring an enemy to his knees with minimal bloodshed, although it is difficult to understand how Iraq could have been defeated by this method. Similarly, the idea of "parallel war" has received considerable attention, particularly in view of the attempt to depict the air campaign during the Gulf War as a demonstration of parallel war. Put simply, parallel war is a revival of the historic Douhetian theories that wars can be won entirely through air power, which now has the capability of simultaneously targeting all of an enemy's critical systems, once again minimizing bloodshed. Despite the fact that the weight of historical evidence does not support such notions, they draw support from a broad spectrum of people both in and out of the Armed Forces, because they appear neat, logical, and "scientific." They also feed calls for greater reduction in conventional forces, which in the mid-90s stand at 1.5 million men and women, about 60% of their strength during the Gulf War, and about half their peak strength during the Cold War.

The debate over the future shape of America's military forces is complex. Merely engaging in "bean counting" is not a reliable guide, yet a common one. The issue of how much money is being spent, or what percentage of the GNP, or how its being spent, can rapidly degenerate into comparing apples and oranges. Some factions in the debate are undoubtedly driven by an excessive "defense mentality," yet others are equally motivated by excessive optimism about the imminence of global peace. The reconciliation of these diverse views will be long in coming. Meanwhile, the Army will change, and yet will remain the same.

Suggested Readings

by

Brig. Gen. William A. Stofft

Editors' note. In place of the lengthy general bibliography found in earlier editions of this volume, the editors are substituting a personal essay by the Chief of Military History on the subject of reading history. Bibliographic information on the volumes mentioned in this essay, along with that for other general works recommended by the editors, is appended below.

These remarks are addressed to this volume's principal audience—future officers of the United States Army. Taking advantage of your goodwill and general interest in a new subject, I want to suggest that developing a habit of reading military history is both useful and rewarding. Many of our great captains of war read military history in their spare time. I believe that, like them, you will discover that a familiarity with histories that carefully and clearly analyze our country's military past will provide you with a new and special perspective on your profession.

Some of the books I'm going to mention are classics and appear elsewhere in this volume's formal bibliography. Others do not, but they all rate a place on my personal suggested reading list. Not only are they among my own favorites, they also serve a major intention of the Army: to stimulate a lasting interest in military history among Army officers. As the Army's leaders have frequently put it, an understanding of military history is essential in our future military leaders.

Before I give you my personal reading list, let me urge you to take advantage of the many fine military journals available to Army officers to keep themselves abreast of the latest trends in our profession. Begin with the fine periodicals published by the various branch schools. For generations, officers have gained valuable insights from studying the pages of *Infantry, Armor, Field Artillery,* and the rest. For a broader view of military matters, I recommend that you pick up the Command and General Staff College's *Military Review,* which specializes in articles about combined arms war, and the Army War College's *Parameters,* which will provide you with a useful survey of current thinking on military strategy and theory.

My personal recommendations begin with three volumes that introduce the student to the battlefield, the epicenter of the soldier's profession. *The Face of Battle, Company Commander,* and *Seven Firefights in Vietnam,* all superb books, approach the battlefield from different perspectives, but each analyzes the performance of the individual soldier under fire and convincingly demonstrates both the reality of fear and the overriding influence of military discipline and leadership on the outcome of battle. I promise they will linger long in your memory.

Every officer needs some notion of how the art of war has evolved throughout western history. I'd suggest that you start by sampling the work of four modern masters of our craft. Sir John Winthrop Hackett distilled a lifetime study into the brilliant chapters of his brief survey, *Profession of Arms*. Bernard Brodie is especially recommended for his examination of the philosophical dimensions of warfare in his masterful *War and Politics*. J. F. C. Fuller focuses on the evolution of military operations in his *The Decisive Battles of the Western World;* while the authors in Peter Paret's collection, *Makers of Modern Strategy: Military Thought From Machiavelli to the Nuclear Age,* concentrate on the strategy of war in the West. Taken together, these insightful and beautifully written analyses create the essential context in which American military history must be placed.

Knowledge of our own military past has benefited greatly from the work of gifted historians who have specialized in interpreting the American approach to war. Four of the best in terms of originality and clarity of thought are Walter Millis, who in his *Arms and Men* describes the evolution of American military institutions in the context of the nation's social and economic forces; T. Harry Williams, who examines the effects of military organization on strategy in his short but provocative *Americans at War: The Development of the American Military System;* Samuel P. Huntington, who presents a classic interpretation of the role of the professional soldier in a free society in *The Soldier and the State;* and Russell Weigley, who demonstrates the grand sweep of America's military past in *The American Way of War: A History of United States Military Strategy and Policy* and *History of the United States Army.*

Military historians have always and with good reason depended on the biographer's craft to help define the role of great commanders. Here are six of the best: Flexner's *George Washington,* Freeman's *Lee's Lieutenants,* Henderson's *Stonewall Jackson,* Pogue's *George C. Marshall,* Blumenson's *The Patton Papers,* and the articles in Roger Spiller's concise and informative *Dictionary of Military Biography.* The student often finds biography a particularly human introduction to the complexities of our military past. These authors reveal in fascinating detail the personalities of these great captains, the times in which they lived, and the changing face of war.

I've discovered not only that novelists and poets can illuminate the essential truths of our profession in memorable ways, but that fictionalized accounts of warfare can often provide a unique and broad perspective on the nature of conflict. Remarque's *All Quiet on the Western Front* and Forester's *The General,* masterworks of fiction, cut through the confusion of the Great War with unequaled precision and poignancy. Shaara's *Killer Angels* puts you with great immediacy into the mind of the Civil War commander, providing thereby an impressive lesson in military leadership. *Once an Eagle,* Myrer's realistic portrait of the modern Army officer, makes the point well that his training in peacetime is the key to a soldier's success in war. Finally, let me press on you the *Book of War Poetry* compiled by the Oxford University Press. Here we see in distilled form and beautiful language the inner convictions, along with the doubts and fears, that have possessed the warrior over time.

It's a source of pride to me and, I hope, of inspiration to those of you who plan to make the study of military history a part of your Army career that some important books in our field are the work of serving Army officers. General Dave Palmer's insights into military strategy shine through his study of the Vietnam War, *Summons of the Trumpet,* and of the American Revolution, *The Way of the Fox,* while General John Galvin shares his special knowledge of modern tactics in *Air Assault: The Development of Airmobile Warfare.* Although Col. Robert Doughty's *The Seeds of Disaster: The Development of French Army Doctrine, 1919–1939,* Col. Harold Nelson's *Leon Trotsky and the Art of Insurrection,* and Lt. Col. Harold Winton's *To Change an Army* focus on other armies in other times, they address issues that have broad implications for our own Army today. Nelson has joined with the distinguished military history professor Jay Luvaas to produce several books that I am convinced will stand the test of time. The Army War College guides to the battles of Gettysburg, Antietam, and Chancellorsville are proving invaluable to those of us who, by means of staff rides, use the experience of great commanders of the past to prepare us for future tests. Finally, the novelist's skills have enabled Lt. Col. Jim McDonough in his *Platoon Leader* and Maj. H. W. Coyle in his *Team Yankee: A Novel of World War III* to add new perspectives to issues that you will be encountering as serving officers.

Let me conclude by urging you to dip into three books that newspaper critics were once prone to call "good reads": William Prescott's *The Conquest of Mexico,* Cecil Woodham-Smith's *The Reason Why: The Charge of the Light Brigade,* and Matthew Brennan's *Brennan's War.* Good reads they certainly are, but beware: they are also solid and serious examples of the historian's craft, and they just might hook you for life on reading military history.

GENERAL WORKS

The Battlefield

Cash, John A., Albright, John N., and Sandstrum, Allan W. *Seven Firefights in Vietnam.* Washington: Government Printing Office, 1970.

Esposito, Vincent, ed. *The West Point Atlas of American Wars.* 2 vols. New York: Frederick A.
      Praeger, 1959.
Keegan, John. *The Face of Battle.* New York: Viking Press, 1976.
MacDonald, Charles B. *Company Commander.* New York: Ballantine Books, 1966.

Western Military History

Brodie, Bernard. *War and Politics.* New York: Macmillan, 1973.
Doughty, Robert A. *The Seeds of Disaster: The Development of French Army Doctrine, 1919–1939.*
      Hamden, Conn.: Anchor Books, 1985.
Fuller, J. F. C. *The Decisive Battles of the Western World, and Their Influence Upon History.*
      London: Eyre and Spottiswoode, 1954.
————. *A Military History of the Western World.* 3 vols. New York: Funk and Wagnalls, 1954–56.
Hackett, Sir John Winthrop. *Profession of Arms.* Washington: Government Printing Office, 1988.
Nef, John U. *War and Human Progress: An Essay on the Rise of Industrial Civilization.* New York:
      Norton, 1968.
Nelson, Harold W. *Leon Trotsky and the Art of Insurrection, 1905–1917.* London: Frank Cass, 1988.
Paret, Peter, Craig, Gordon A., and Gilbert, Felix, eds. *Makers of Modern Strategy: Military
      Thought From Machiavelli to the Nuclear Age.* Princeton: Princeton University Press, 1986.
Preston, Richard A., Wise, Sydney F., and Werner, Hermon O. *Men in Arms: A History of
      Warfare and Its Relationships With Western Society.* New York: Frederick A. Praeger, 1962.
Ropp, Theodore. *War in the Modern World.* Durham: Duke University Press, 1959.
Winton, Harold R. *To Change an Army: General Sir John Burnett-Stuart and British Armored
      Doctrine, 1927–1938.* Lawrence: University Press of Kansas, 1988.

American Military Thought

Hagen, Kenneth J., and Roberts, William R., eds. *Against All Enemies: Interpretations of American
      Military History From Colonial Times to the Present.* New York: Greenwood Press, 1986.
Hammond, Paul. *Organizing for Defense: The American Military Establishment in the Twentieth
      Century.* Princeton: Princeton University Press, 1961.
Heller, Charles E., and Stofft, William A., eds. *America's First Battles, 1776–1965.* Lawrence:
      University Press of Kansas, 1986.
Huntington, Samuel P. *The Soldier and the State: The Theory and Politics of Civil-Military
      Relations.* Cambridge: Belknap Press, 1959.
Millett, Allan R., and Maslowski, Peter. *For the Common Defense: A Military History of the United
      States of America.* New York: The Free Press, 1984.
Millis, Walter. *Arms and Men: A Study in American Military History.* New York: Putnam, 1956.
Nelson, Otto L., Jr. *National Security and the General Staff.* Washington: Combat Forces Press,
      1946.
Weigley, Russell F. *The American Way of War: A History of United States Military Strategy and
      Policy.* Bloomington: Indiana University Press, 1977.
————. *History of the United States Army.* 2d ed. Bloomington: Indiana University Press, 1984.
Williams, T. Harry. *Americans at War: The Development of the American Military System.* Baton
      Rouge: Louisiana State University Press, 1960.

Specialized Studies in American Military History

Ambrose, Stephen. *Duty, Honor, Country: A History of West Point.* Baltimore: Johns Hopkins
      University Press, 1966.
Ball, Harry P. *Of Reasonable Command: A History of the U.S. Army War College.* Carlisle Barracks,
      Pa.: Alumni Association of the U.S. Army War College, 1983.
Coffman, Edward. *The Old Army: A Portrait of the American Army in Peacetime, 1784–1898.* New
      York: Oxford University Press, 1986.

Galvin, John R. *Air Assault: The Development of Airmobile Warfare*. New York: Hawthorne Books, 1969.

Huston, James A. *The Sinews of War: Army Logistics, 1775–1953*. Washington: Government Printing Office, 1966.

Janowitz, Morris. *The Professional Soldier: A Social and Professional Portrait*. Glencoe, Ill.: The Free Press, 1960.

Nalty, Bernard. *Strength for the Fight: A History of Black Americans in the Military*. New York: The Free Press, 1986.

Nelson, Harold W., and Luvaas, Jay. *The U.S. Army War College Guide to the Battle of Gettysburg*. Carlisle, Pa.: South Mountain Press, 1986.

———. *The U.S. Army War College Guide to the Battle of Antietam*. Carlisle, Pa.: South Mountain Press, 1987.

———. *The U.S. Army War College Guide to the Battle of Chancellorsville*. Carlisle, Pa.: South Mountain Press, 1988.

Nenninger, Timothy K. *The Leavenworth Schools and the Old Army: Education, Professionalism, and the Officer Corps of the United States Army, 1881–1918*. Westport, Conn.: Greenwood Press, 1978.

Palmer, Dave R. *Summons of the Trumpet: U.S.-Vietnam in Perspective*. Novato, Calif.: Presidio Press, 1978.

———. *The Way of the Fox: American Strategy in the War for America, 1775–1783*. Westport, Conn.: Greenwood Press, 1975.

Military Biography

Blumenson, Martin. *The Patton Papers*. 2 vols. Boston: Houghton Mifflin, 1974.

Flexner, James. *George Washington*. 4 vols. Boston: Little, Brown, 1965–72.

Freeman, Douglas Southall. *Lee's Lieutenants: A Study in Command*. 3 vols. New York: Scribners, 1942–44.

Henderson, George F. R. *Stonewall Jackson and the American Civil War*. New York: Longmans, Green, 1900.

Pogue, Forrest C. *George C. Marshall*. 4 vols. New York: Viking, 1987.

Spiller, Roger J., et al., eds. *Dictionary of American Military Biography*. 3 vols. Westport, Conn.: Greenwood Press, 1984.

Bibliography

Higham, Robin, and Mrozek, Donald, eds. *A Guide to the Sources of United States Military History*. Hamden, Conn.: Archon Books, 1975 (with Supplements I, 1981, and II, 1984).

Jessup, John E., Jr., and Coakley, Robert W., eds. *A Guide to the Study and Use of Military History*. Washington: Government Printing Office, 1970.

Further Readings

Brennan, Matthew. *Brennan's War*. Novato, Calif.: Presidio Press, 1985.

Coyle, H.W. *Team Yankee: A Novel of World War III*. Novato, Calif.: Presidio Press, 1987.

Forester, C. S. *The General*. Baltimore: Nautical and Aviation, 1987 .

McDonough, James R. *Platoon Leader*. Novato, Calif.: Presidio Press, 1985.

Myrer, Anton. *Once an Eagle*. New York: Dell, 1970.

Prescott, William H. *The Conquest of Mexico*. New York: Modern Library, 1931.

Remarque, Erich M. *All Quiet on the Western Front*. New York: Fawcett, 1987.

Shaara, Michael. *Killer Angels: A Novel About the Four Days at Gettysburg*. New York: McKay, 1974.

Stallworthy, Jon, ed. *Oxford Book of War Poetry*. New York: Oxford University Press, 1984.

Woodham-Smith, Cecil. *The Reason Why: The Charge of the Light Brigade*. New York: Dutton, 1960.

Chapter 16: Transition and Change, 1902–1917

Recommended Readings

Abrahamson, James L. *America Arms for a New Century: The Making of a Great Military Power.* New York: The Free Press, 1981.
Ball, Harry P. *Of Responsible Command: A History of the U.S. Army War College.* Carlisle Barracks: Alumni Association of the U.S. Army War College, 1983. Chapters 1–7.
Challener, Richard D. *Admirals, Generals, and American Foreign Policy, 1898–1914.* Princeton: Princeton University Press, 1973.
Finnegan, John R. *Against the Specter of a Dragon: The Campaign for American Military Preparedness, 1914–1917.* Westport: Greenwood Press, 1974.
Hagen, Kenneth J., and Roberts, William R., eds. *Against All Enemies: Interpretations of American Military History From Colonial Times to the Present.* Westport: Greenwood Press, 1986. Chapter 11, "The Army Enters the Twentieth Century, 1904–1917" by Timothy K. Nenninger.
Hewes, James E., Jr. *From Root to McNamara: Army Organization and Administration, 1900–1963.* Washington: Government Printing Office, 1975. Pp. 1–21.
Lane, Jack C. *Armed Progressive: A Study of the Military and Public Career of Leonard Wood.* San Rafael: Presidio Press, 1978.
Leopold, Richard W. *Elihu Root and the Conservative Tradition.* Boston: Little, Brown, 1954.
Morison, Elting E. *Turmoil and Tradition: A Study of the Life and Times of Henry L. Stimson.* Boston: Houghton Mifflin, 1960. Chapters 9–15.
Nenninger, Timothy K. *The Leavenworth Schools and the Old Army: Education, Professionalism, and the Officer Corps of the United States Army, 1881–1918.* Westport: Greenwood Press, 1977.
Smythe, David. *Guerrilla Warrior: The Early Life of John J. Pershing.* New York: Scribner's, 1973.

Other Readings

Beale, Howard K. *Theodore Roosevelt and the Rise of America to World Power.* Baltimore: Johns Hopkins Press, 1956.
Clendenen, Clarence C. *Blood on the Border: The United States Army and the Mexican Irregulars.* New York: Macmillan, 1969.
Detrick, Martha. *The National Guard in Politics.* Cambridge: Harvard University Press, 1965.
Deutrich, Mabel E. *Struggle for Supremacy: The Career of General Fred C. Ainsworth.* Washington: Public Affairs Press, 1962.
Langley, Lester D. *The Banana Wars: United States Intervention in the Caribbean, 1898–1934.* 2d ed. Lexington: University Press of Kentucky, 1985.
McCullough, David. *The Path Between the Seas: The Creation of the Panama Canal, 1870–1914.* New York: Simon & Schuster, 1977.
Millett, Allan R. *The Politics of Intervention: The Military Occupation of Cuba, 1906–1909.* Columbus: Ohio State University Press, 1968.
Skowronek, Stephen. *Building a New American State: The Expansion of National Administrative Capacities, 1877–1920.* Cambridge: Cambridge University Press, 1982. Chapters 1, 2, 4, 7, and Epilogue.
Twitchell, Heath, Jr. *Allen: The Biography of an Army Officer, 1859–1930.* New Brunswick: Rutgers University Press, 1974. Chapters 5–7.

Chapter 17: World War I: The First Three Years

Recommended Readings

Falls, Cyril B. *The Great War.* New York: Putnam, 1959.
DeWeerd, Harvey A. *President Wilson Fights His War: World War I and the American Intervention.* New York: Macmillan, 1968.

SUGGESTED READINGS 387

Hewes, James E., Jr. *From Root to McNamara: Army Organization and Administration, 1900–1963.* Washington: Government Printing Office, 1973. Pp. 21–31.
Kreidberg, Marvin A., and Henry, Merton G. *History of Military Mobilization in the United States Army, 1775–1945.* Department of the Army Pamphlet 20–212. Washington: Government Printing Office, 1955. Pp. 189–376.
Lafore, Laurence P. *The Long Fuse: An Interpretation of the Origins of World War I.* 2d ed. Philadelphia: Lippincott, 1971.

Other Readings

Ropp, Theodore. *War in the Modern World.* Durham: Duke University Press, 1959. Pp. 204–47.
Smythe, Donald. *Pershing: General of the Armies.* Bloomington: Indiana University Press, 1986.
Twitchell, Heath, Jr. *Allen: The Biography of an Army Officer, 1859–1930.* New Brunswick: Rutgers University Press, 1974. Chapter 8.

Chapter 18: World War I: The U.S. Army Overseas

Recommended Readings

Barbeau, Arthur E. *The Unknown Soldiers: Black American Troops in World War I.* Philadelphia: Temple University Press, 1974.
Beaver, Daniel. *Newton D. Baker and the American War Effort, 1917–1919.* Lincoln: University of Nebraska Press, 1966.
Brain, Paul F. *The Test of Battle: The American Expeditionary Forces in the Meuse-Argonne Campaign.* Newark: University of Delaware Press, 1987.
Chambers, John W. II. *To Raise an Army: The Draft Comes to Modern America.* New York: The Free Press, 1987.
Coffman, Edward M. *The Hilt of the Sword: The Career of Peyton C. March.* Madison: University of Wisconsin Press, 1966.
———. *The War to End All Wars: The American Military Experience in World War I.* Madison: University of Wisconsin Press, 1986.
Kennedy, David M. *Over Here: The First World War and American Society.* New York: Oxford University Press, 1980.
Millett, Allan R. *The General: Robert L. Bullard and Officership in the United States Army, 1881–1925.* Westport: Greenwood Press, 1975. Chapters 14–16.
Pogue, Forrest C. *George C. Marshall: Education of a General, 1880–1939.* New York: Viking, 1963. Chapters 9–12.
Ropp, Theodore. *War in the Modern World.* Durham: Duke University Press, 1959. Pp. 247–55.
Smythe, Donald. *Pershing: General of the Armies.* Bloomington: Indiana University Press, 1986.
Stokesbury, James L. *A Short History of World War I.* New York: William Morrow, 1981.
Twitchell, Heath, Jr. *Allen: The Biography of an Army Officer, 1859–1930.* New Brunswick: Rutgers University Press, 1974. Chapter 9.

Other Readings

Asprey, Robert B. *At Belleau Wood.* New York: Putnam, 1965.
Hagen, Kenneth J., and Roberts, William R., eds. *Against All Enemies: Interpretations of American Military History From Colonial Times to the Present.* Westport: Greenwood Press, 1986. Chapter 12, "Over Where? The AEF and the American Strategy for Victory, 1917–1918" by Allan Millett.
Harbord, James G. *The American Army in France.* Boston: Little, Brown, 1936.
Holley, I. B., Jr. *Ideas and Weapons: Exploitation of the Aerial Weapon by the United States During World War I.* New Haven: Yale University Press, 1953.
Huston, James A. *The Sinews of War: Army Logistics, 1775–1953.* Washington: Government Printing Office, 1966. Pp. 308–87.
Lane, Jack C. *Armed Progressive: A Study of the Military and Public Career of Leonard Wood.* San Rafael: Presidio Press, 1978.

Marshall, George C. *Memoirs of My Services in the World War, 1917–1918*. Boston: Houghton Mifflin, 1976.

Pershing, John J. *My Experiences in the World War.* 2 vols. New York: Stokes, 1931.

Pitt, Barrie. *1918—The Last Act.* New York: Norton, 1963.

Snow, William J. *Signposts of Experience: World War Memoirs of Major General William J. Snow.* Washington: U.S. Field Artillery Association, 1941.

Stallings, Laurence. *The Doughboys: The Story of the AEF, 1917–1918.* New York: Harper, 1963.

Chapter 19: Between World Wars

Recommended Readings

Cline, Ray S. *Washington Command Post: The Operations Division.* U.S. Army in World War II. Washington: Government Printing Office, 1951. Chapters 1–4.

Griffith, Robert K. *Men Wanted for the U.S. Army: America's Experience With an All-Volunteer Army Between the World Wars.* Westport: Greenwood Press, 1982.

Huntington, Samuel P. *The Soldier and the State: The Theory and Politics of Civil Military Relations.* Cambridge: Harvard University Press, 1957. Chapter 11.

Hurley, Alfred E. *Billy Mitchell: Crusader for Air Power.* Rev. ed. Bloomington: Indiana University Press, 1975.

Killigrew, John W. *The Impact of the Great Depression on the Army.* New York: Garland, 1979.

Koistinen, Paul A. C. *The Military-Industrial Complex: A Historical Perspective.* New York: Praeger, 1980. Chapter 3.

Kreidberg, Marvin G., and Henry, Merton G. *History of Military Mobilization in the United States Army, 1775–1945.* Washington: Government Printing Office, 1955. Chapters 12–15.

Lisio, Donald J. *The President and Protest: Hoover, Conspiracy, and the Bonus Riot.* Columbia: University of Missouri Press, 1974.

Lee, Ulysses. *The Employment of Negro Troops.* U.S. Army in World War II. Washington: Government Printing Office, 1966. Chapters 1–3.

Matloff, Maurice, and Snell, Edwin M. *Strategic Planning for Coalition Warfare, 1941–1942.* U.S. Army in World War II. Washington: Government Printing Office, 1953. Chapters 1–4.

Millett, Allan R. *The General: Robert L. Bullard and Officership in the United States Army, 1881–1925.* Westport: Greenwood Press, 1975. Chapters 22–23.

Weigley, Russell F. *The American Way of War: A History of United States Military Strategy and Policy.* Bloomington: Indiana University Press, 1977. Pp. 223–41.

Chapter 20: World War II: The Defensive Phase

Recommended Readings

Cline, Ray S. *Washington Command Post: The Operations Division.* U.S. Army in World War II. Washington: Government Printing Office, 1951. Chapters 5–7.

Conn, Stetson, and Fairchild, Byron. *The Framework of Hemisphere Defense.* U.S. Army in World War II. Washington: Government Printing Office, 1960. Chapter 7.

Greenfield, Kent Roberts, ed. *Command Decisions.* Washington: Government Printing Office, 1960. Chapters 6 and 7.

Leighton, Richard M., and Coakley, Robert W. *Global Logistics and Strategy, 1940–1943.* U.S. Army in World War II. Washington: Government Printing Office, 1956. Chapters 6–7 and 14–15.

Matloff, Maurice, and Snell, Edwin M. *Strategic Planning for Coalition Warfare, 1941–1942.* U.S. Army in World War II. Washington: Government Printing Office, 1953. Chapters 8, 12, and 16–17.

Millett, John D. *The Organization and Role of the Army Service Forces.* U.S. Army in World War II. Washington: Government Printing Office, 1954. Chapter 2.

Prange, Gordon. *At Dawn We Slept: The Untold Story of Pearl Harbor.* New York: McGraw-Hill, 1981.

Watson, Mark S. *Chief of Staff: Prewar Plans and Preparations.* U.S. Army in World War II. Washington: Government Printing Office, 1950. Chapter 15.

Other Readings

Churchill, Winston S. *The Grand Alliance*. The Second World War, vol. 3. Boston: Houghton
    Mifflin, 1950.
————. *The Hinge of Fate*. The Second World War, vol. 4. Boston: Houghton Mifflin, 1950.
Conn, Stetson, Engelman, Rose C., and Fairchild, Byron. *Guarding the United States and Its
    Outposts*. U.S. Army in World War II. Washington: Government Printing Office, 1964.
Craven, Wesley F., and Cate, James L., eds. *Plans and Early Operations*. The Army Air Forces in
    World War II, vol. 1. Chicago: University of Chicago Press, 1948.
Green, Constance M., Thomson, Harry C., and Roots, Peter C. *The Ordnance Department:
    Planning Munitions for War*. U.S. Army in World War II. Washington: Government Print-
    ing Office, 1955.
Gwyer, J. M. A., and Butler, J. R. M. *Grand Strategy*. History of the Second World War, United
    Kingdom Military Series, edited by J. R. M. Butler, vol. 3. London: Her Majesty's Station-
    ery Office, 1964.
Lord, Walter H. *Day of Infamy*. New York: Henry Holt, 1957.
Morison, Samuel E. *The Battle of the Atlantic, September 1939–May 1943. The Rising Sun in the
    Pacific, 1931–April 1942. Coral Sea, Midway and Submarine Actions, May 1942–August 1942.*
    All in History of U.S. Naval Operations in World War II. 15 vols. Boston: Little, Brown,
    1947–62.
Morton, Louis. *The Fall of the Philippines*. U.S. Army in World War II. Washington: Govern-
    ment Printing Office, 1952.
Pogue, Forrest C. *George C. Marshall: Ordeal and Hope, 1939–1942*. New York: Viking, 1966.
Romanus, Charles F., and Sunderland, Riley. *Stilwell's Mission to China*. U.S. Army in World War
    II. Washington: Government Printing Office, 1953.

Chapter 21: Grand Strategy and the Washington High Command

Recommended Readings

Cline, Ray S. *Washington Command Post: The Operations Division*. U.S. Army in World War II.
    Washington: Government Printing Office, 1951. Chapters 12–13 and 15–16.
Coakley, Robert W., and Leighton, Richard M. *Global Logistics and Strategy, 1943–1945*. U.S.
    Army in World War II. Washington: Government Printing Office, 1968. Chapters 11, 22, 25,
    and 32.
Greenfield, Kent Roberts, ed. *Command Decisions*. Washington: Government Printing Office,
    1960. Chapters 10, 15, 16, and 22.
Huston, James A. *The Sinews of War: Army Logistics, 1775–1953*. Washington: Government
    Printing Office, 1966. Chapter 26.
Leighton, Richard M., and Coakley, Robert W. *Global Logistics and Strategy, 1940–1943*. U.S.
    Army in World War II. Washington: Government Printing Office, 1956. Chapters 25–27.
Matloff, Maurice. *Strategic Planning for Coalition Warfare, 1943–1944*. U.S. Army in World War
    II. Washington: Government Printing Office, 1959. Chapters 1, 16, 22, and 23.
————. *Mr. Roosevelt's Three Wars: FDR as War Leader*. The Harmon Memorial Lectures in
    Military History, no. 6. Colorado Springs: U.S. Air Force Academy, 1964.
————. "The American Approach to War, 1919–1945." In *The Theory and Practice of War*.
    Edited by Michael Howard. New York: Frederick A. Praeger, 1966.
Millett, John D. *The Organization and Role of the Army Service Forces*. U.S. Army in World War
    II. Washington: Government Printing Office, 1954. Chapters 3–5.
Pogue, Forrest C. *George C. Marshall: Organizer of Victory 1943–1945*. New York: Viking, 1973.

Other Readings

Churchill, Winston S. *The Second World War*. 6 vols. Boston: Houghton Mifflin, 1948–53. See
    particularly *The Hinge of Fate* (1950), *Closing the Ring* (1951), and *Triumph and Tragedy*
    (1953).

Ehrman, John. *Grand Strategy.* History of the Second World War, United Kingdom Military Series, edited by J. R. M. Butler, vols. 5 and 6. London: Her Majesty's Stationery Office, 1956.

Feis, Herbert. *Churchill, Roosevelt, Stalin: The War They Waged and the Peace They Sought.* Princeton: Princeton University Press, 1957.

Greenfield, Kent Roberts. *American Strategy in World War II: A Reconsideration.* Baltimore: Johns Hopkins Press, 1963.

————, Palmer, Robert P., and Wiley, Bell I. *The Organization of Ground Combat Troops.* U.S. Army in World War II. Washington: Government Printing Office, 1947.

Lee, Ulysses. *The Employment of Negro Troops.* U.S. Army in World War II. Washington: Government Printing Office, 1966.

Morison, Elting E. *Turmoil and Tradition: A Study of the Life and Times of Henry L. Stimson.* Boston: Houghton Mifflin, 1960.

Morison, Samuel E. *Strategy and Compromise.* Boston: Little, Brown, 1958.

Sherwood, Robert. *Roosevelt and Hopkins: An Intimate History.* Rev. ed. New York: Harper, 1950.

Stimson, Henry L., and Bundy, McGeorge. *On Active Service in Peace and War.* New York: Harper, 1948.

Chapter 22: World War II: The War Against Germany and Italy

Recommended Readings

Bennett, Ralph. *ULTRA in the West: The Normandy Campaign, 1944–45.* New York: Scribner's, 1979.

Blumenson, Martin. *Anzio: The Gamble That Failed.* Philadelphia: Lippincott, 1963.

————. *The Patton Papers.* 2 vols. Boston: Houghton Mifflin, 1972–74.

Bradley, Omar N., and Blair, Clay. *A General's Life: An Autobiography.* New York: Simon & Schuster, 1983.

Collins, Joseph Lawton. *Lightning Joe: An Autobiography.* Baton Rouge: Louisiana State University Press, 1979.

Eisenhower, John S. D. *The Bitter Woods.* New York: Putnam, 1969.

Ellis, John. *The Sharp End: The Fighting Man in World War II.* New York: Scribner's, 1980.

Greenfield, Kent Roberts, ed. *Command Decisions.* Washington: Government Printing Office, 1960.

Hastings, Max. *Overlord: D-Day and the Battle for Normandy.* New York: Simon & Schuster, 1984.

Heckler, Ken. *The Bridge at Remagen.* New York: Ballantine Books, 1957.

Kennett, Lee B. *G.I.: The American Soldier in World War II.* New York: Scribner's, 1987.

Lewin, Ronald. *ULTRA Goes to War.* New York: McGraw-Hill, 1978.

MacDonald, Charles B. *Company Commander.* New York: Ballantine Books, 1966.

————. *A Time for Trumpets: The Untold Story of the Battle of the Bulge.* New York: William Morrow, 1985.

Pogue, Forrest C. *George C. Marshall: Organizer of Victory, 1943–1945.* New York: Viking, 1973.

Ryan, Cornelius. *A Bridge Too Far.* New York: Pocket Books, 1984.

Toland, John. *The Last 100 Days.* New York: Random House, 1965.

Other Readings

Blumenson, Martin. *Breakout and Pursuit.* U.S. Army in World War II. Washington: Government Printing Office, 1961. Chapters 4, 11, 12, and 13.

Cole, Hugh M. *The Ardennes: Battle of the Bulge.* U.S. Army in World War II. Washington: Government Printing Office, 1964. Chapters 1, 5, 19, and 25.

————. *The Lorraine Campaign.* U.S. Army in World War II. Washington: Government Printing Office, 1950.

Garland, Albert N., and Smyth, Howard McGaw. *Sicily and the Surrender of Italy.* U.S. Army in World War II. Washington: Government Printing Office, 1965. Chapters 6, 7, and 9.

Greenfield, Kent Roberts, ed. *Command Decisions.* Washington: Government Printing Office, 1969.

Harrison, Gordon. *Cross-Channel Attack*. U.S. Army in World War II. Washington: Government
    Printing Office, 1951. Chapters 6 and 8.
Howe, George G. *Northwest Africa: Seizing the Initiative in the West*. U.S. Army in World War II.
    Washington: Government Printing Office, 1957. Chapters 14, 23, and 24.
Huston, James A. *The Sinews of War: Army Logistics, 1775–1953*. Washington: Government
    Printing Office, 1966. Chapter 30.
MacDonald, Charles B. *The Siegfried Line Campaign*. U.S. Army in World War II. Washington:
    Government Printing Office, 1963. Chapters 14 and 15.
———, and Mathews, Sidney T. *Three Battles: Arnaville, Altuzzo, and Schmidt*. U.S. Army in
    World War II. Washington: Government Printing Office, 1954.
Pogue, Forrest C. *The Supreme Command*. U.S. Army in World War II. Washington: Govern-
    ment Printing Office, 1954.
Ruppenthal, Roland P. *Logistical Support of the Armies*. 2 vols. U.S. Army in World War II.
    Washington: Government Printing Office, 1953–59.
Weigley, Russell F. *Eisenhower's Lieutenants: The Campaign of France and Germany, 1944–1945*.
    Bloomington: Indiana University Press, 1981.

Chapter 23: World War II: The War Against Japan

Recommended Readings

James, D. Clayton. *The Years of MacArthur, 1941–1945*. Boston: Houghton Mifflin, 1975.
Lewin, Ronald. *The American Magic: Codes, Ciphers, and the Defeat of Japan*. New York: Farrar,
    Straus & Giroux, 1982.
Morison, Samuel Eliot. *New Guinea and the Marianas*. History of U.S. Naval Operations in
    World War II, vol. 8. Boston: Little, Brown, 1953. Chapters 14–16.
Pogue, Forrest C. *George C. Marshall: Organizer of Victory 1943–1945*. New York: Viking, 1973.
Prange, Gordon. *At Dawn We Slept*. New York: McGraw-Hill, 1981.
Schoenberger, Walter S. *Decision of Destiny*. Athens: Ohio University Press, 1970.
Smith, Robert Ross. *The Approach to the Philippines*. U.S. Army in World War II. Washington:
    Government Printing Office, 1953. Chapters 12–14.
Spector, Ronald H. *Eagle Against the Sun: The American War With Japan*. New York: The Free
    Press, 1985.
Toland, John. *The Rising Sun: The Decline and Fall of the Japanese Empire, 1936–1945*. New York:
    Random House, 1970.
Tuchman, Barbara. *Stilwell and the American Experience in China, 1911–1945*. New York: Mac-
    millan, 1971.

Other Readings

Craven, Wesley F. and Cate, James L., eds. *Matterhorn to Nagasaki*. The Army Air Forces in
    World War II, vol. 5. Chicago: University of Chicago Press, 1953.
Crowl, Philip A. *Campaign in the Marianas*. U.S. Army in World War II. Washington: Govern-
    ment Printing Office, 1959.
———, and Iseley, Jeter A. *The U.S. Marines and Amphibious War*. Princeton: Princeton Univer-
    sity Press, 1951.
Falk, Stanley. *Decision at Leyte*. New York: Norton, 1966.
Miller, John, jr. *Guadalcanal: The First Offensive*. U.S. Army in World War II. Washington:
    Government Printing Office, 1949.
Morison, Samuel Eliot. *Aleutians, Gilberts and Marshalls* and *Victory in the Pacific*. History of U.S.
    Naval Operations in World War II, vols. 7 and 14. Boston: Little, Brown, 1951–60.
Romanus, Charles F., and Sunderland, Riley. *Stilwell's Command Problems*. U.S. Army in World
    War II. Washington: Government Printing Office, 1956.
Smith, Robert Ross. *Triumph in the Philippines*. U.S. Army in World War II. Washington:

Chapter 24: Peace Becomes Cold War, 1945–1950

Recommended Readings

Backer, John H. *Winds of History: The German Years of Lucius DuBignon Clay*. New York: Van Nostrand Reinhold, 1983.

Bradley, Omar, and Blair, Clay. *A General's Life: An Autobiography*. New York: Simon & Schuster, 1983.

Clay, Lucius D. *Decision in Germany*. New York: Doubleday, 1950.

Gaddis, John L. *Strategies of Containment: A Critical Appraisal of Postwar American National Security Policy*. New York: Oxford Universty Press, 1982.

James, D. Clayton. *The Years of MacArthur: Triumph and Disaster, 1945–1964*. Boston: Houghton Mifflin, 1985.

MacGregor, Morris J., Jr. *The Integration of the Armed Forces, 1940–1965*. Washington: Government Printing Office, 1981.

Millis, Walter. *Arms and the State*. New York: The Twentieth Century Fund, 1958. Chapters 4, 5, and 6.

Perry, John Curtis. *Beneath the Eagle's Wings: Americans in Occupied Japan*. New York: Dodd, Mead, 1980.

Pogue, Forrest C. *George C. Marshall: Statesman, 1945–1959*. New York: Viking, 1987.

Weigley, Russell F. *The American Way of War: A History of American Military Policy and Strategy*. Bloomington: Indiana University Press, 1977. Chapter 15.

Other Readings

Bernardo, Maj. C. Joseph, and Bacon, Eugene H. *American Military Policy, Its Development Since 1775*. Harrisburg: Military Service, 1955. Chapters 20 and 21.

Gimbel, John. *The American Occupation of Germany: Politics and the Military, 1945–1949*. Stanford: Stanford University Press, 1968.

Nelson, Daniel J. *A History of U.S. Military Forces in Germany*. Boulder: Westview Press, 1987. Chapter 1.

Reid, Escott. *Time of Fear and Hope: The Making of the North Atlantic Treaty, 1947–1949*. Toronto: McClelland and Stewart, 1977.

Schnabel, James F., Condit, Kenneth W., and Watson, Robert J. *The History of the Joint Chiefs of Staff: The Joint Chiefs of Staff and National Policy*. 4 vols. Wilmington: Michael Glazer, 1979. Vols. 1, 2, and 4.

Schaller, Michael. *The American Occupation of Japan: The Origins of the Cold War*. New York: Oxford University Press, 1985.

Ziemke, Earl F. *The U.S. Army in the Occupation of Germany, 1944–1946*. Washington: Government Printing Office, 1975. Chapters 17–24.

Chapter 25: The Korean War, 1950–1953

Recommended Readings

Alexander, Bevin. *Korea, The First War We Lost*. New York: Hippocrene, 1986.

Appleman, Roy E. *East of Chosin: Entrapment and Breakout in Korea, 1950*. College Station: Texas A&M University Press, 1987.

Blair, Clay. *The Forgotten War: America in Korea*. New York: Times Books, 1988.

Fehrenbach, T. R. *This Kind of War: A Study in Unpreparedness*. New York: Macmillan, 1963.

Goulden, Joseph C. *Korea, The Untold Story of the War*. New York: Times Books, 1982.

James, D. Clayton. *Years of MacArthur: Triumph and Disaster, 1945–1964*. New York: Houghton Mifflin, 1985.

MacDonald, C. A. *Korea: The War Before Vietnam.* New York: The Free Press, 1987.
Marshall, S. L. A. *Pork Chop Hill: The American Fighting Man in Action—Korea, Spring 1953.* New York: Jove, 1986.
Millis, Walter. *Arms and the State.* New York: The Twentieth Century Fund, 1958. Chapter 7.
Pogue, Forrest C. *George C. Marshall: Statesman.* New York: Viking, 1987.
Whiting, Allen S. *China Crosses the Yalu.* New York: Macmillan, 1960. Chapters 3–7.

Other Readings

Appleman, Roy E. *South to the Naktong, North to the Yalu.* U.S. Army in the Korean War. Washington: Government Printing Office, 1961.
Clarke, Mark W. *From the Danube to the Yalu.* New York: Harper, 1954.
Collins, J. Lawton. *War in Peacetime: The History and Lessons of Korea.* Boston: Houghton Mifflin, 1969.
Cowdrey, Albert E. *The Medics' War.* U.S. Army in the Korean War. Washington: Government Printing Office, 1987.
Gugeler, Russell A. *Combat Actions in Korea.* Washington: Government Printing Office, 1970.
Heller, Charles E., and Stofft, William A., eds. *America's First Battles, 1776–1965.* Lawrence: University Press of Kansas, 1986. Chapter 9, "Task Force Smith and the 24th Division: Delay and Withdrawal, 5–19 July 1950" by Roy K. Flint.
Hermes, Walter G. *Truce Tent and Fighting Front.* U.S. Army in the Korean War. Washington: Government Printing Office, 1966.
MacArthur, Douglas. *Reminiscences.* New York: McGraw-Hill, 1964.
Ridgway, Matthew B. *The Korean War.* New York: Doubleday, 1967.
Schnabel, James F. *Policy and Direction: The First Year.* U.S. Army in the Korean War. Washington: Government Printing Office, 1972.

Chapter 26: The Army and the New Look

Recommended Readings

Gavin, James M. *War and Peace in the Space Age.* New York: Harper, 1958. Chapters 5J, 5K, and 7.
Kaufmann, William W., ed. *Military Policy and National Security.* Princeton: Princeton University Press, 1956. Chapters 1, 4, and 8.
Kissinger, Henry A. *Nuclear Weapons and Foreign Policy.* New York: Harper, 1957. Chapters 2 and 12.
O'Connor, Raymond G., ed. *American Defense Policy in Perspective: From Colonial Times to the Present.* New York: John Wiley, 1965. Chapter 20.
Osgood, Robert E. *Limited War: The Challenge to American Strategy.* Chicago: University of Chicago Press, 1957. Chapters 1, 9, and 10.
Ridgway, Matthew B. *Soldier: The Memoirs of Matthew B. Ridgway.* New York: Harper, 1956. Chapters 30–38.
Taylor, Maxwell D. *The Uncertain Trumpet.* New York: Harper, 1959. Chapters 3, 4, and 8.

Other Readings

Acheson, Dean. *Power and Diplomacy.* Cambridge: Harvard University Press, 1958.
Finletter, Thomas K. *Foreign Policy: The Next Phase.* New York: Harper, 1958.
Garthoff, Raymond L. *Soviet Strategy in the Nuclear Age.* New York: Praeger, 1958.
Kahn, Herman. *On Thermonuclear War.* Princeton: Princeton University Press, 1960.
Knorr, Klaus, ed. *NATO and American Security.* Princeton: Princeton University Press, 1959.
Millis, Walter. *Arms and Men: A Study in American Military History.* New York: Putnam, 1956. Chapter 7.

Stanley, Timothy W. *American Defense and National Security.* Washington: Public Affairs Press, 1956.

Chapter 27: Global Pressures and the Flexible Response

Recommended Readings

Eliot, George Fielding. *Reserve Forces and the Kennedy Strategy.* Harrisburg: Stackpole, 1962.
Greenberg, Lawrence M. *United States Army Unilateral and Coalition Operations in the 1965 Dominican Republic Intervention.* Washington: Center of Military History, 1987.
Halle, Louis J. *The Cold War as History.* New York: Harper & Row, 1967. Chapters 37 and 38.
Hewes, James E., Jr. *From Root to McNamara: Army Organization and Administration, 1900–1963.* Washington: Government Printing Office, 1975. Chapters 8–10.
Kaufman, William W. *The McNamara Strategy.* New York: Harper & Row, 1964. Chapters 1, 2, and 5.
Kissinger, Henry A. *The Troubled Partnership: A Re-appraisal of the Atlantic Alliance.* New York: McGraw-Hill, 1965. Chapters 1–3.
O'Connor, Raymond G., ed. *American Defense Policy in Perspective: From Colonial Times to the Present.* New York: John Wiley, 1965. Chapter 21.
Schlesinger, Arthur W., Jr. *A Thousand Days: John F. Kennedy in the White House.* Boston: Houghton Mifflin, 1965. Chapters 10, 15, and 30.
Taylor, Maxwell D. *Responsibility and Response.* New York: Harper & Row, 1967. Chapters 1–4.
Trewhitt, Henry L. *McNamara.* New York: Harper & Row, 1971.

Other Readings

Deitchman, Seymour J. *Limited War and American Defense Policy.* Cambridge: M.I.T. Press, 1964.
Donnelly, Charles H. *U.S. Defense Policies in 1961.* 87th Congress, 2d Session, House Document no. 502. Washington: Government Printing Office, 1962.
———. *U.S. Defense Policies in 1962.* 88th Congress, 1st Session, House Document no. 155. Washington: Government Printing Office, 1963.
———. *U.S. Defense Policies in 1963.* 88th Congress, 2d Session, House Document no. 335. Washington: Government Printing Office, 1964.
———. *U.S. Defense Policies in 1964.* 89th Congress, 1st Session, House Document no. 285. Washington: Government Printing Office, 1965.
———. *U.S. Defense Policies in 1965.* 89th Congress, 2d Session, House Document no. 344. Washington: Government Printing Office, 1966.
Heaps, Willard A. *Riots, U.S.A.: 1765–1965.* New York: The Seeburg Press, 1966.
Heller, Deane, and Heller, David. *The Berlin Wall.* New York: Walker, 1962.
Sorensen, Theodore C. *Kennedy.* New York: Harper & Row, 1965.

Chapter 28: The U.S. Army in Vietnam

Recommended Readings

Bergen, John D. *Military Communications: A Test for Technology.* U.S. Army in Vietnam. Washington: Government Printing Office, 1986.
Clarke, Jeffrey J. *Advice and Support: The Final Years, 1965–1973.* U.S. Army in Vietnam. Washington: Government Printing Office, 1988.
Hammond, William M. *Public Affairs: The Military and the Media, 1962–1968.* U.S. Army in Vietnam. Washington: Government Printing Office, 1988.
Herring, George C. *America's Longest War: The United States and Vietnam, 1950–1975.* New York: John Wiley & Sons, 1979.

Krepinevich, Andrew F. *The Army and Vietnam*. Baltimore: Johns Hopkins University Press, 1986.

Lewy, Guenter. *America in Vietnam*. New York: Oxford University Press, 1978.

Meyerson, Joel D. *Images of a Lengthy War*. U.S. Army in Vietnam. Washington: Government Printing Office, 1986.

Palmer, Bruce. *The 25-Year War: America's Military Role in Vietnam*. Lexington: University Press of Kentucky, 1984.

Race, Jeffrey. *War Comes to Long An: Revolutionary Conflict in a Vietnamese Province*. Berkeley: University of California Press, 1972.

Spector, Ronald H. *Advice and Support: The Early Years, 1941–1960*. U.S. Army in Vietnam. Washington: Government Printing Office, 1983.

Stanton, Shelby L. *The Rise and Fall of an American Army: U.S. Ground Forces in Vietnam, 1965–1973*. Novato, Calif.: Presidio Press, 1985.

Summers, Harry G. *On Strategy*. San Rafael: Presidio Press, 1986.

Westmoreland, William C. *A Soldier Reports*. Garden City: Doubleday, 1976.

Other Readings

Cash, John A., Albright, John N., and Sandstrum, Allan W. *Seven Firefights in Vietnam*. Washington: Government Printing Office, 1970.

Donovan, David. *Once a Warrior King: Memories of an Officer in Vietnam*. New York: McGraw-Hill, 1985.

Downs, Fred. *The Killing Zone*. New York: W. W. Norton, 1978.

Fall, Bernard B. *The Two Vietnams: A Political and Military Analysis*. 2d rev. ed. New York: Praeger, 1967.

Herrington, Stuart A. *Silence Was a Weapon*. Novato, Calif.: Presidio Press, 1982.

Oberdorfer, Don. *Tet!* Garden City: Doubleday, 1971.

The Pentagon Papers: The Defense Department History of United States Decisionmaking on Vietnam. Senator Gravel edition, 4 vols. Boston: Beacon Press, 1971.

Pike, Douglas. *Viet Cong: The Organization and Techniques of the National Liberation Front of South Vietnam*. Cambridge: M.I.T. Press, 1966.

Santoli, Al. *To Bear Any Burden*. New York: E. P. Dutton, 1985.

Tolson, Lieutenant General John J. *Airmobility, 1961–1971*. Vietnam Studies. Washington: Government Printing Office, 1974.

Chapter 29: The U.S. Army in An Era of Geopolitical and Strategic Change

Recommended Readings

Cochrane, Alexander S., *Planning the Gulf War Air Campaign*. Washington: Office of the Secretary of the Air Force, 1993.

Dunnigan, James F., and Bay, Austin, *From Shield to Storm: High-Tech Weapons, Military Strategy, & Coalition Warfare in the Persian Gulf*. New York: William Morrow, 1992.

Dunnigan, James F., and Macedonica, Raymond M., *Getting it Right: American Military Reforms After Vietnam to the Gulf War and Beyond*. New York: William Morrow, 1993.

Friedman, Lawrence, and Karsh, Efraim, *The Gulf Conflict, 1990-1991: Diplomacy and War in the New World Order*. Princeton: Princeton University Press, 1993.

Friedman, Norman, *Desert Victory: The War for Kuwait*. Annapolis: Naval Institute Press, 1991.

Gordon, Michael R., and Trainor, Bernard, *The Generals' War: The Inside Story of the Conflict in the Gulf*. Boston: Little, Brown, 1995.

Kirkpatrick, Charles E., *Building the Army for Desert Storm* (Land Warfare Papers, No. 9). Washington: Institute for Land Warfare, 1991.

Scales, Robert H., Jr., *Certain Victory: The U.S. Army in the Gulf War.* Washington: The U.S. Army
    Desert Storm Study Project, 1993.
Summers, Harry G., *On Strategy II: A Critical Analysis of the Gulf War.* New York: Dell, 1992.
Wright, Robert K., *Battle for Panama: Inside Operation JUST CAUSE.* McLean, VA.: Brassey's
    (US), 1993.

Other Readings

Conduct of the Persian Gulf War. Washington: The Department of Defense, 1992.
de la Billiere, Peter, *Storm Command: A Personal Account of the Gulf War.* London: Harper Collins,
    1992.
DeLong, Kent, *Mogadishu! Heroism and Tragedy.* Westport, CT: Praeger, 1995
DiNardo, Richard L., and Hughes, Daniel J., "Some Cautionary Thoughts on Information Warfare,"
    Air Power Journal, Winter 1995, pp. 69-79.
The Media and the Gulf War, edited by Robert E. Denton, Jr. Westport, Ct: Greenwood Press, 1993.
Gulf War Air Power Survey. Washington: The U.S. Air Force, 1993.
Hutchison, Kevin Don, *Operation Desert Storm/Desert Shield: Chronology and Fact Book.*
    Wesptort, CT: Greenwood Press, 1995.
Powell, Colin, *My American Journey.* New York: xyz, 1995.
Perusse, Roland I., *Haitian Democracy Restored.* Lanham, MD: University Press of America, 1995.
Schwarzkopf, H. Norman, with Peter Petre, *It Doesn't Take a Hero.* New York: Bantam, 1992.

Index

Asia mainland, 115, 250-251. *See also by name of country.*
Assam, 180
Assistant Chief of Staff, Force Development, 266
Atlantic Charter, 79
Atlantic Coast regions, 4, 93, 133
Atlantic theater, 76-80, 86, 94-95, 97-98, 100-101, 142, 234, 253
Atlas missile, 234
Atomic bomb, 115-116, 122, 184, 197-198, 201-202. *See also* Nuclear weapons.
Atrocities, 29, 59-60
ATTLEBORO, 305, 306
Attu, 97, 160, 164
Australia, 89-91, 96-97, 160, 236, 296
Australian Air Force, 208
Australian Army, 54, 162-163, 167, 178-179, 208, 299
Australian Navy, 89, 208
Austria, 17, 26, 29, 60, 75, 154, 254
Aviation Section, Signal Corps, 8
Avranches, 146-147
Azores Islands, 79, 97

B-29 bomber, 165, 171-173, 179, 182, 183
B-52 bomber, 299, 309, 313-314, 322, 325, 338-339, 342
Baghdad Pact, 237-238
Bahia Honda, 10
Baker, Newton D., 37, 41
Balikpapan, 179
Balkans region, 17, 82-83, 108, 110-112, 138-141, 155
Balloons, 8
Baltic Sea region, 75
Baltimore, Md., 260
Ban Me Thuot, 310-312
Barricourt, 57, 60
Bases, development of, 96-97, 104, 160, 163-164, 169, 179-180, 185, 235-236
Bastogne, 151-153. *See also* Ardennes counteroffensive.
Bataan, 91-93, 177
Battle Command Training Program (BCTP), 351
Bau Bang, 302, 306-307

Bay of Pigs, 251-252
Bayonet, 3
Bear Cat, 308
Beirut, 238
Belgium, 21, 23, 46, 55, 58, 60, 147, 151, 196, 208, 255
Belleau Wood, 48
Ben Het, 335
Ben Suc, 306
Berlin, 108, 113, 154-155, 191, 200-201, 251-252, 254-255, 262, 270, 272, 285
Biak Island, 171-172
Bicol peninsula, 177
Bien Hoa Air Base, 295, 307-308
Bien Hoa Province, 307-308
Binh Dinh, 319, 321
Binh Dinh Pacification Campaign, 317, 319-320
Binh Dinh Province, 317-318, 320, 326
Binh Duong Province, 305
Binh Gia, 293
Binh Xuyen, 278
Bir Hacheim, 100
Bismarck, Otto von, 17
Bismarck Archipelago, 161-162
Bismarck Sea, 164
Bizerte, 135
Blanc Mont, 59
Bliss, General Tasker H., 41
Blockades, 21-24
Bloody Ridge, 223
Boatner, Brig. Gen. Haydon L., 225
Bohol Island, 178
Boi Loi woods, 301
BOLERO, 100, 125
Bomber aircraft, 233-234, 262. *See also by name or number.*
Bomber offensives, 83, 105-107, 141-142, 171-174, 180, 182-186, 292-293, 331, 338-339, 344
Bong Son plain, 317-318, 319-320
Bonin Islands, 174
"Bonus March," 70-71
Bosnia, 379
Bougainville, 167
Bouresches, 48
Bradley, Lt. Gen. Omar N., 137, 144-147, 156